"WE ARE ALL ATHENIANS . . .
for the ideas of ancient Greece
have permeated our whole culture."

"A knowledge of classical mythology is indispensable
in understanding and appreciating much of the great
literature, sculpture, and painting of both the ancients
and the moderns. Unless we know the marvelous
stories of the deities and heroes of the ancients, their
great literature and art as well as much later work
down to the present day will remain unintelligible.
Through the centuries from Chaucer, Spenser, Shakespeare, and Milton on, not only the major writers but
also hundreds of lesser writers have retold the old tales
or used them as a point of departure for new interpretations in terms of contemporary problems and
psychology."

From the author's Introduction

Professor J. E. Zimmerman received his A.B. and A.M.
from Baylor University, and has taught at the University of Texas, the University of Southern California,
and Washington University in St. Louis. Professor Zimmerman has had teaching and administrative experience
at many educational levels. He has been, for example,
both an instructor and principal in elementary and
secondary schools, and is presently an Associate Professor of English at Arizona State University.

Dictionary
of
Classical
Mythology

by J. E. Zimmerman

BANTAM BOOKS
TORONTO · NEW YORK · LONDON · SYDNEY

*This low-priced Bantam Book was printed
from new plates. It contains the complete
text of the original hard-cover edition.*
NOT ONE WORD HAS BEEN OMITTED.

DICTIONARY OF CLASSICAL MYTHOLOGY

*A Bantam Book / published by arrangement with
Harper & Row, Publishers*

PRINTING HISTORY

Harper & Row edition published April 1964

2nd printing ...... January 1965	3rd printing ..... February 1965
4th printing .... October 1965	
Bantam Matrix edition / March 1966	
2nd printing .... November 1967	4th printing .... October 1965
3rd printing .... June 1968	5th printing .... August 1969
6th printing .... May 1970	
Bantam edition / November 1971	
8th printing .... May 1972	11th printing .... November 1975
9th printing .... July 1973	12th printing .... April 1977
10th printing .... July 1974	13th printing .... December 1978
14th printing .... September 1980	

On the cover, Oedipus and the Sphinx
from an Attic cup in the Vatican Museum, Rome.

ISBN 0-553-14483-9

Published simultaneously in the United States and Canada

Bantam Books are published by Bantam Books, Inc. Its trademark, consisting of the words "Bantam Books" and the por-
trayal of a bantam, is Registered in U.S. Patent and Trademark
Office and in other countries. Marca Registrada. Bantam
Books, Inc., 666 Fifth Avenue, New York, New York 10103.

PRINTED IN THE UNITED STATES OF AMERICA

22 21 20 19 18 17 16

To my WIFE
and to the Boys
CARL, DOYLE, JOHN, RICHARD, TOM

ACKNOWLEDGMENTS

The author's indebtedness to many people and to many books is very great. He owes much to other handbooks and to the classical authors. Acknowledgment and gratitude are especially due to the many good books, both classical and modern, that are recommended in Suggestions for Further Reading at the back of the book. There are many others. Dr. Collice Portnoff, illustrious classical scholar at Arizona State University, gave much valuable advice and encouragement. And without my wonderful students, the book would never have been written.

CENTURIES OF OLD STORIES · AN EVER-NEW DELIGHT

𲀀𲀀𲀀𲀀𲀀𲀀𲀀𲀀𲀀𲀀𲀀𲀀𲀀𲀀𲀀𲀀𲀀𲀀𲀀𲀀𲀀𲀀𲀀

The Importance of Mythology

We are all Athenians in a sense, for the ideas of ancient Greece have permeated our whole culture.

Not only has Greek and Roman mythology furnished inspiration, exerted influence, and provided subject matter for many masterpieces of poetry, prose, sculpture, and painting, but its stories are interesting and entertaining in themselves, to say nothing of having provided the source of classical allusions which appear continually in editorials, addresses, lectures, advertisements, and conversations. Scientists have found mythology a treasure chest in providing names for animals, plants, constellations, planets, and— more recently in our space age—for missiles and space vehicles like Gemini, Apollo, Mercury, and Zeus. The old myths have also been a source of inspiration for designers, engravers, and other craftsmen.

A knowledge of classical mythology is indispensable in understanding and appreciating much of the great literature, sculpture, and painting of both the ancients and the moderns. Unless we know the marvelous stories of the deities and heroes of the ancients, their great literature and art as well as much later work down to the present day will remain unintelligible. Through the centuries from Chaucer, Spenser, Shakespeare, and Milton on, not only the major writers but also hundreds of lesser writers have retold the old tales or used them as a point of departure for new interpretations in terms of contemporary problems and psychology. Often modern writers use the old myths as symbols, though they may change the original story so much that it is not recognizable except to the really perceptive reader. An intelligent reader of much English, American, and continental poetry and prose, or an attentive observer of Renaissance or modern sculpture and painting needs to be acquainted almost as much with mythology as with the world of nature and of human nature.

The Greeks based their literature, as well as their sculpture and painting, more on mythology than on any other one source, and the Romans, having little mythology of their own, used the material from Greece and changed the names to a Roman form, such as Zeus to Jupiter, Hera to Juno, Athena to Minerva, Aphrodite to Venus, etc.

An English scholar H. A. Guerber has written, "The importance of classical mythology from an educational standpoint has never been more generally recognized than it is today." Whitman said, "Great are the myths." John Keats knew mythology almost by heart and after reading Chapman's translation of Homer, wrote: "Much have I traveled in the realms of gold, and many goodly states and kingdoms seen."

For the twentieth-century reader, there is still a great deal of gold in these stories. Like Odysseus and his dramatic encounters with gods and men as he sailed home from Troy to Ithaca, we too can learn much from the stories of the ancient gods and the Greek and Roman heroes, much that is applicable to our life today.

Two Chief Sources of Our Knowledge of Mythology

Two imperishable treasures of our cultural heritage, ancient literature and ancient art, are the chief sources of our knowledge of mythology. The subject matter of greatest importance to the ancients was from myth, and their masterpieces of literature and achievements of sculpture were inspired by their religious beliefs, the family of the gods and goddesses, and the adventures of their heroes. To understand the spirit of the ancient myths and of the ancient Greeks as revealed in their masterworks of literature and art—in the epics, in didactic poetry, tragedy, comedy, lyric poetry, elegiac poetry, in the great prose: history, biography, geography, philosophy—and to appreciate the strength and beauty of these ancient works, a knowledge of mythology is indispensable.

Between 1200 B.C. and 850 B.C. two epics by Homer, *The Iliad* and *The Odyssey,* and two didactic poems by Hesiod, *Works and Days* and the *Theogony,* provide us with early and very important sources of our knowledge of mythology. Between 600 B.C. and 400 B.C., among the Greeks, Aeschylus, Sophocles, Euripides, Aristophanes, Herodotus, Pindar, Alcaeus, Anacreon, Arion, Ibycus, Sappho, Simonides of Ceos, and Stesichorus flourished and contributed in comedies, tragedies, history, and lyric poetry an abundance of mythological riches. The tragedies of Aeschylus, Sophocles, and Euripides, with their thrilling accounts of Agamemnon, the Seven against Thebes, Prometheus, Oedipus, Antigone, Ajax, Philoctetes, Alcestis, Medea, Hippolytus, Heracles, Helen, Andromache, Orestes, and Electra, to name only sixteen of the thirty-two subjects—and thirty-two of the thirty-three extant tragedies are based on mythology—make enjoyable reading. The comedies of Aristophanes and the history of Herodotus are rich in mythological story, and the lyric poems contribute much information. In the first century B.C., the Greek historian Diodorus Siculus, and, among the Romans, Horace, Ovid, Vergil, Catullus, Propertius, and Tibullus, increased our knowledge of myth. The greatest things of this century were *The Odes and Epodes* of Horace; the *Metamorphoses, Fasti,* and *The Heroides* of Ovid; and the incomparable *Aeneid* of Vergil. In the first century A.D., we have Seneca, Statius, and Strabo; in the second century A.D., Apollodorus, Apollonius Rhodius, and

Pausanias. The *Bibliotheca* or *Library* of Apollodorus; the *Argonautica* of Apollonius Rhodius; the *Periegesis of Greece,* or *Description of Greece* by Pausanias are probably the most important contributions of these two centuries. Lesser writers, too, whose works are not listed here, have all added much to our knowledge of mythology.

The second chief source of our knowledge of the mythology of the ancients, besides their literature, is their works of art, both sculptural and pictorial, with incomparable masterpieces of sculpture in gold and ivory, bronze, marble, and clay; engraved coins and gems; frescoes, and paintings on cups, plates, and vases.

The greatest of the ten famous sculptors among the ancient Greeks was Phidias, renowned for his colossal figures in gold and ivory of Zeus at Olympia and of Athena Parthenos at Athens, and his famous Amazon at Ephesus and Aphrodite at Elis.

Praxiteles, most famous for his "Aphrodite of Cnidos" and his "Hermes and the Infant Dionysus," also created remarkable figures of Apollo, Artemis, Leto, Eros and the Satyr, and of Marsyas and the Muses playing the flutes. Almost all of our knowledge about the Greek sculptors, since most of their masterpieces have been lost, is derived from ancient writers like Pausanias and others, and from later copies of the works, but the original of "Hermes and the Infant Dionysus" was discovered at Olympia in 1877.

Other famous Greek sculptors, also using mythological subjects, were Lysippus with figures of Apollo, Heracles, Poseidon, and Zeus; Myron and his famous Discobolus; Polyclitus and his Hera at Argos and a great Amazon. The five other great Greek sculptors, Bryaxis, Calamis, Leochares, Scopas, and Timotheus created statues of Aphrodite, Apollo, Ganymede, Hermes, Heracles, and Poseidon. The favorite deity of the ancients for sculpture was Apollo, for seven of the ten great Greeks fashioned statues of him, the most famous one the Apollo Belvedere in the Vatican.

In addition to the colossal individual figures, the temples

dedicated to the gods were graced with sculptures of mythological figures. Particularly famous sculptural works decorated the temples of Zeus at Olympia and the Parthenon. Some of the famous friezes of the Parthenon were taken to England in 1803 by Lord Elgin, and are now known as the Elgin Marbles in the British Museum. They show such mythological figures as Zeus, Athena, Aphrodite, Artemis, Hephaestus, Helios, Heracles, Dionysus, Dione, Poseidon, Hermes, Iris, Demeter, and Persephone, among others. Many of the friezes had been destroyed before Lord Elgin conveyed his collection to England and occasioned Lord Byron's famous poem, "The Curse of Minerva," a satire in which vehement resentment is expressed against Lord Elgin as the despoiler of Greece.

These statues revealed the ancient devotion to the gods, and the figures were considered sacred and were directly associated with religious worship. In sculpture not connected with worship, the emphasis was on vast strength, in the figures of Heracles and Poseidon; on charm, grace, and beauty in the case of Aphrodite; on earnestness and solemnity in the presentation of Athena.

The popularity of mythological subjects for frescoes is mentioned by Pausanias and others. Among ancient paintings on cups, plates, and vases were such subjects of the Trojan War as Helen, Menelaus, Agamemnon, the Amazons, Achilles, Hector, Ajax, Patroclus, Odysseus, Diomedes, and the Judgment of Paris; other subjects to appear frequently were Theseus slaying the Minotaur, Ariadne on Naxos, Medea and the Golden Fleece, Orpheus and Eurydice, the Labors of Hercules, Cerberus, Oedipus, Artemis, Demeter, Athena, and Poseidon.

The appeal of mythological subjects for sculptors and painters of the Renaissance and later was not diminished. Among the favorite subjects used by Correggio, Michelangelo, Millais, Millet, Raphael, Rembrandt, Reni, Rubens, Tintoretto, Titian, Turner, Van Dyck, and Da Vinci—and there were scores of others—were Achilles, Aeneas, Aphrodite, Apollo, Athena, Eros and Psyche, Daphne, Ganymede, Heracles, Medusa, Niobe, Orpheus, Persephone, Perseus, Prometheus, Theseus, and scenes from the Trojan War.

Mythology in Later Literature

Following the use of mythological subject matter by the ancients, there has been no diminishing interest in myth by the many great poets, lesser poets, and prose writers of England, Scotland, America, France, Italy, and Spain. Matthew Arnold's "Palladium," "Philomela," "Dejaneira," "Urania," and "Euphrosyne"; Robert Bridges' "Eros and Psyche," "Prometheus the Firegiver," "Achilles in Scyros," "Demeter," "Isle of Achilles," "Return of Ulysses," and "Feast of Bacchus"; Chaucer's "The Legend of Good Women," *Troilus and Criseyde, The House of Fame,* "The Knight's Tale," "The Monk's Tale," and *The Parlement of Fowls;* John Keats' "Hymn to Apollo," "Endymion," "Hyperion," "On a Picture of Leander," "Ode to Maia," "Ode to Psyche," "Ode on a Grecian Urn"; W. S. Landor's "Dirce," "Dryope," "Europa," "Iphigenia and Agamemnon," "Niobe," "Hippomenes and Atalanta," Orpheus and Eurydice," "Hercules," "Pluto," "Alcestis," "Penelope"; Marlowe's *Tragedy of Dido, Queen of Carthage;* Milton's "Comus," "Lycidas," and *Paradise Lost;* William Morris' *The Earthly Paradise* and "The Life and Death of Jason"; Shelley's "Arethusa," "Hymn to Apollo," "Hymn to Mercury," *Prometheus Unbound, Oedipus Tyrannus;* Swinburne's *Atalanta in Calydon,* "Tiresias," "Erechtheus," "The Garden of Proserpine," "Eurydice," and "Phaedra"; Tennyson's "Amphion," "The Death of Oenone," "Demeter and Persephone," "Hero to Leander," "Tiresias," "Ulysses," "Oenone," "The Lotos Eaters," "The Hesperides," and "To Vergil"; and Wordsworth's "Laodamia" are just a few examples of mythological subject matter, inspiration, and influence in verse and prose.

Mythology in Twentieth-Century Literature

Continued interest in our century is evident in hundreds of general books, essays, criticisms, studies, dramas, novels, and poems. Among authors drawing heavily on mythology are: Jean Anouilh (*Antigone; Eurydice; Medée*); Berthold Brecht (*Antigone*); Jean Cocteau (*Antigone; Mythologie; Oedipe Roi; Orphée*); T. S. Eliot (mythological themes in several poems); E. M. Forster ("The Story of a Panic" and "The Road from Colonus"); Andre Gide (*Oedipe; Philoctetes; Prométhée; Theseus*); Jean Giraudoux (*Amphitryon 38; Electre; The Trojan War Shall Not Take Place*); Robert Graves (*Myths of Ancient Greece; Hercules, My Shipmate; The Anger of Achilles; The Greek Myths; The Siege and Fall of Troy*); Hugo von Hofmannsthal (*Ariadne auf Naxos; Elektra; Ödipus und die Sphinx*); Aldous Huxley ("Leda"); Robinson Jeffers (*Tower beyond Tragedy; Solstice*); James Joyce (*Ulysses*); Nikos Kazantzakis (*Odyssey*); Archibald MacLeish (*The Trojan Horse*); John Masefield (*Tale of Troy*); Eugene O'Neill (*Mourning Becomes Electra*); Stephen Phillips (*Ulysses*); Mary Renault (*The King Must Die; The Bull from the Sea*); Rainer Maria Rilke (*Sonnets to Orpheus; Orpheus; Eurydice; Hermes*); Jean-Paul Sartre (*Les Mouches*); W. B. Stanford (*The Ulysses Theme*); Michael Tippett (*King Priam*); John Updike (*The Centaur*); Thornton Wilder (*Alcestiade*); W. B. Yeats ("To Dorothy Wellesley," "Delphic Oracle upon Plotinus," "Byzantium," and "Leda and the Swan").

Greatest Stories from Mythology

According to Hesiod, mythology begins with Chaos, the name of the shapeless mass whose appearance could not be described as there was no light by which it could be seen. Chaos has been called the oldest of the gods. The offspring of Chaos and his wife Nyx or Nox were Erebus (Darkness), and then Aether (Light) and Hemera (Day). From Aether and Hemera sprang Gaea (Earth) who created Uranus (Heaven). Uranus and Gaea became the parents of twelve gigantic children called Titans, known as the first race, whose brothers were the Cyclopes and Hecatoncheires. Hesiod says there were twenty Titans, Apollodorus thirteen, Hyginus six, but the accepted number is twelve. The Titans are sometimes confused with the Giants until we recall that the Titans fought against Cronus and the Giants against Zeus. Two of these Titans, Cronus and Rhea, were the parents of six of the twelve great Olympians (Hades, Poseidon, Zeus, Demeter, Hera, and Hestia), the next great group in mythology. Some sources name thirteen Olympians; the other seven were all children of Zeus, Athena springing out of his head, Apollo and Artemis his offspring by Leto, Hephaestus and Ares by Hera, Aphrodite by Dione or born from the foam of the sea, and Hermes by Maia.

From Uranus and Gaea through the twelve great Olympians we have most of the deities of the highest order, or greater deities, but others of high repute were Amphitrite, Dionysus, Persephone, and Themis. Three Olympian brothers divided the government of the world between them: Zeus, the heavens; Poseidon, the sea; Hades (Pluto), the Underworld. The earth was left for general government.

The Greeks had many other deities called inferior or lesser deities, including groups such as the Charites, Fates, Furies, Harpies, Hesperides, Horae, Muses, Nymphs, River Gods, Sirens, and Wind Gods, and individual figures like Asclepius, Eos, Eris, Eros, Faunus, Hebe, Hymen, Iris, Nike, Pan, Tyche, and a host of others, all of whom came after the Titans and Olympians. Then came the great heroes or demigods, whose origin was partly divine. These were divided into three classes: the demigods, such as Prometheus; the earlier heroes, such as the Argonauts, Bellerophon, Chiron, Daedalus, Heracles, Meleager, Oedipus, Perseus, and Theseus; and the later heroes of Thebes and Troy. Among the demigods, the earlier heroes, and the later heroes, come the contributors to mankind like Prometheus, and the many figures of great strength, fine form, and noble courage. They were adventurers, servants of civilization, founders of great families, and destroyers of monsters. After long struggle and final victory, they were translated after death into gods and entitled to sacrifice and worship. They have been called the "knights of history."

Among the greatest and most interesting *adventure* stories are those of Aeneas, Apollo, Bellerophon, Daedalus, Heracles, Jason, Meleager, Oedipus, Odysseus, Perseus, Theseus, and the earlier war between the Titans and Olympians. The greatest *destroyers of monsters* were Apollo, Bellerophon, Heracles, Odysseus, Oedipus, Perseus, and Theseus. Among the great *expeditions* are Greek mythology's four main rallying points: the journey of the Argonauts, the Calydonian boar hunt, the campaign against Thebes, and the Trojan War. Others were the journeys of Odysseus home to Ithaca and of Aeneas to Italy.

Famous families included the Titans and the Olympians, Achilles and his son Peleus, the house of Atreus (Agamemnon, Clytemnestra, Orestes, and Electra), Odysseus and Penelope, Perseus and Andromeda, and the house of Troy (Priam and Hecuba and their children). Among the greatest individual *heroes* are Achilles, Aeneas, Bellerophon, Hector, Jason, Oedipus, Odysseus, Perseus, Prometheus, and Theseus. Some of the most terrible *monsters* were the Calydonian boar, Cerberus, the Chimera, the Cyclopes, the Harpies, the Hecatoncheires, the Lernean hydra, Medusa, the Minotaur, the Nemean lion, Polyphemus, Python, and the Sphinx. Mythology is replete with great *love stories*, such as the tales of Artemis and Endymion, Baucis and Philemon, Ceyx and Alcyone, Cupid and Psyche, Orpheus and Eurydice, Perseus and Andromeda, Pygmalion and Galatea, Pyramus and Thisbe, Theseus and Hippolyta, and the numerous affairs of Zeus and some of the other Olympians.

Recurring Themes in Mythology

Through the myths we become acquainted with the earliest civilization, history, ideas, imagination, philosophy, religion, society, and science of the Greeks. Mythology was considered history, it explained the mysteries of nature, and it was closely allied to religion. One theory (Euhemerism) maintained that the gods and goddesses had once been actual kings, queens, and warriors who destroyed the oppressors of society. Another theory held that the gods and goddesses were the earth, heavens, sun, moon, stars, sea, winds, and fire, and explained the phenomena of nature. Earthquakes resulted when a giant rolled over in his grave, and volcanoes erupted when he breathed fire.

In religion, myths were stories about the acts of the gods, superhuman beings who brought about the flood, took sides in the Trojan War, and punished the sins of heroes and lesser folk. The famous families reflect the social life of ancient times, and famous heroes its ideals. Progress came through struggle—Zeus overthrowing the Titans, the Lapiths conquering the Centaurs, Heracles in his twelve labors overcoming malevolent elements in nature for the good of society, Prometheus giving fire to mankind at great sacrifice to himself. Mythology answered the important questions of the ancient Greeks about a dangerous and mysterious world. What are the heavens, sun, moon, stars, thunder, lightning, fire, life, death, the afterworld?

The two themes recurring most often are love in all of its phases and personal suffering and struggle. *Lovers* anxious for the safety of their husbands (Alcestis, Laodamia,

Penelope); bestial (Pasiphae); betrayed (Ariadne, Deianira, Dido, Hypsipyle, Medea, Oenone, Phyllis); dying for love (Alcyone, Hero and Leander, Laodamia); illicit (Aegisthus, Clytemnestra, Helen, Paris, Myrrha); invisible (Cupid and Psyche); joyful (Perseus and Andromeda, the reunited Odysseus and Penelope, Philemon and Baucis, the old couple who wanted to die at the same time and were changed into an oak and a linden tree); loyal (Penelope, Perseus, Hypermnestra); punished for love (Canace, Hypermnestra); sorrowful(Hector and Andromache, Pyramus and Thisbe); victims of unlawful passion (Canace, Myrrha, Phaedra); vengeful (Medea);—these are some of the most celebrated lovers.

Personal suffering and struggle against loneliness, oppression, tyranny, and violence are depicted in the accounts of Achilles, Aeneas, Apollo, Prometheus, Hector, Oedipus, Antigone, Perseus, Theseus, Philoctetes, and many others, as the intellectual, persuasive, and spiritual oppose the animal, brute, and violent.

Other universal themes which appear again and again are the consciousness of a supreme being, man as the most important creation in the universe, pleasure in the world of nature, the survival of the fittest, heroism, human choice, jealousy, hate, and revenge.

Ineradicably associated with mythology are the three cardinal principles that have actuated humanity through the ages: man's effort to account for his existence, his endeavor to explain the world in which he lives, and his belief in a place of reward and a place of punishment.

Mythology and Etymology

Our language has become richer and more flexible because of the many terms which have come into English from mythology. Only a few examples will suffice: Achilles,

Achillean; Aurora, auroral; Bacchus, bacchic; Chaos, chaotic; Flora, floral; Hypnos, hypnotic; Lethe, lethal; Luna, lunacy; Mars, martial; Mercury, mercurial; Tantalus, tantalize.

Useful Features of This Book

There are nearly 2,100 entries in the *Dictionary of Classical Mythology*. Each entry is followed by its pronunciation, using a simple scheme which indicates long vowels and accents, as in Athena (a thē′ na). If the character has other names or variant spellings for the same name, these are shown; e.g., the entry for *Gaea* shows also Ge, Gaia. For characters with both Greek and Roman names, both are given, as under *Heracles,* Hercules (Roman); *Athena,* Minerva (Roman); *Ceres,* Demeter (Greek). A brief account of the entry subject is presented, with remarks where the stories vary. Sometimes the story has been told by only one ancient writer; on the other hand, several ancient writers may have given different versions. There are individual identifications of the characters who share the same name. Note, for example, the entry for *Eurydice*.

In the case of the more important entries, as well as for some minor ones, examples of use in both ancient and later literature are cited. Often the section of the ancient source work is indicated by a Roman numeral: *Iliad* ii. Suggestions for Further Reading, at the back of the book, gives an account of the ancient sources most frequently used and referred to in the book.

A great number of cross references should increase the usefulness of the book. Where additional information on a character may be found in another entry, it is also cross referenced. When the first member of a group is listed, as *Calliope* for the first of the nine Muses, the names of the other eight are given also. And under each individual name of the Muses will be found a reference back to the complete list. The same method is followed for the three Furies, the three Fates, and other groups.

It is the author's hope that readers will find the book a handy and convenient reference work, one that will provide information, pleasure, and profit in understanding the allusions to mythology which add so much beauty, power, truth, and vitality to ancient and modern literature and to so many other aspects of our daily life.

J. E. Z.

Arizona State University
1964

Key to Old Sources Given in Abbreviated Form

Aeneid—Vergil
Apollodorus—*Bibliotheca* or *Library*
Apollonius Rhodius—*Argonautica*
Argonautica—Apollonius Rhodius
Dares Phrygius—*De Excidio Trojae Historia*
Dictys Cretensis—*Ephemeris Belli Troiani*
Diodorus Siculus—*Library of History*
Eclogues, The—Vergil
Fasti—Ovid
Georgics, The—Vergil
Herodotus—*History*
Heroides—Ovid
Hyginus—*Fables*
Iliad—Homer
Met.—*Metamorphoses*, by Ovid
Odes and Epodes—Horace
Odyssey—Homer
Pausanias—*Description of Greece* or *Periegesis of Greece*
Pindar—*Odes*
Strabo—*Geography*
Theogony—Hesiod
Works and Days—Hesiod

·DICTIONARY·
OF·CLASSICAL
·MYTHOLOGY·

A

Abas (a′ bas). 1. A son of Celeus and Metanira of Eleusis. Changed into a lizard by Demeter for mocking her. *Met.* v. 7. 2. A famous centaur, skilled in hunting. *Met.* xii. 3. A Greek killed by Aeneas during the Trojan War. *Aeneid* iii. 4. A companion of Aeneas, killed in Italy. *Aeneid* x. 5. A son of Poseidon.

Abderus (ab der′ us). Armor bearer for Heracles, torn to pieces by the mares of Diomedes. Apollodorus ii.

Absyrtus (ab sur′ tus). Son of Aeetes, king of Colchis, and Idya. Killed by his sister Medea after she and Jason had seized the Golden Fleece. Apollodorus i.

Abydos (a bī′ dos). City in Asia Minor. The home of Leander, the lover of Hero, who lived in Sestos (Sestus) across the Hellespont. *Heroides* xviii, xix; Marlowe, *Hero* *and Leander;* Byron, *The Bride of Abydos;* Tennyson, "Hero to Leander."

Academe (ak a dēm'). Also Academia. The grove near ancient Athens where Plato (427–347 B.C.) taught.

Acamas (ak' a mas). **1.** A son of Antenor. *Iliad* xi. **2.** A captain of the Thracians, allies of the Trojans in the Trojan War, killed by Telamonian Ajax. *Iliad* xi. **3.** A son of Theseus and Phaedra. With Diomedes, he went to Troy to demand that Helen be returned to her husband, Menelaus of Sparta, after her elopement with Paris. In Troy, Acamas fell in love with Laodice, a daughter of King Priam. Pausanias x.

Acantha (a kan' tha). A nymph loved by Apollo. Changed into a flower (Acanthus).

Acarnan (a kar' nan). Son of Alcmaeon and Callirrhoe. Zeus answered his mother's prayer that he grow to manhood in a single day to avenge the murder of his father.

Acastus (a kas' tus). Argonaut, son of Pelias, brother of Alcestis; killed by Peleus.

Acca Laurentia (ak' a lo ren' shi a). Wife of Faustulus, the shepherd of King Numitor's flocks; nurse of Romulus and Remus.

Acerbas (a sur' bas). Also called SICHAEUS, q.v. Priest of Heracles at Tyre. Married Dido before she founded Carthage. *Aeneid* i.

Acersecomes (a sur' se com ēz). A surname of Apollo. The word "Acersecomes" means unshorn.

Acesius (a ses' i us). Used as surname of Apollo in Elis and Attica as god of medicine. The word "Acesius" means healer. Pausanias xi.

Acestes (a ses' tēz). Son of a Sicilian river god. Assisted Priam in the Trojan War, after which he settled near Mount Eryx in Sicily, where he entertained Aeneas during his voyage to Italy. Helped bury Aeneas' father Anchises on Mount Eryz. Won archery contest at the funeral games in honor of Anchises. *Aeneid* v.

Acestium (a ses' ti um). A woman whose children were torchbearers in the festivals of Demeter. *Pausanias* i.

Acetes (a sē' tēz). Also **Acoetes** (a kō' e tēz). 1. A Lydian sailor, pilot of a ship whose crew found Dionysus asleep, kidnaped him and carried him away. All except Acetes were changed into sea creatures. *Met.* iii. 2. An attendant of Evander. *Aeneid* xi.

Achaea (a kē' a). 1. An ancient province in the Peloponnesus. 2. A name of Pallas.

Achaeans (a kē' anz). With the Aeolians, Dorians, and Ionians, the principal peoples of ancient Greece. Since the Trojan War probably took place during the period of their greatest power, Homer often called all the Greeks Achaeans.

Achaeus (a kē' us). Son of Xuthus and Creusa of Thessaly. Another Achaeus, a king of Lydia, was hanged for extortion.

Acharnians, The (a kar' ni anz). A comedy by Aristophanes.

Achates (a kā' tēz). A faithful companion and friend who accompanied Aeneas from Troy to Italy. *Aeneid* i.

Acheloides (ak e lō' i dēz). A patronymic of the Sirens, daughters of Achelous, a river god. *Met.* v.

Achelous (ak e lō' us). The oldest of the three thousand sons of Oceanus and Tethys. Worshiped as a river god throughout Greece. According to some legends he was the son of Sol by Terra. He was the father of the three Sirens (Leucosia, Ligeia, Parthenope); some legends say Calliope was their mother, others that they were the daughters of Terpsichore. Famous for his contests with Heracles for the hand of Deianira. *Apollodorus* i, ii; *Met.* viii.

Achemenides (ak e men' i dēz). A Greek who fought at Troy, sailed for home with Odysseus, and was marooned at the cave of Polyphemus. When Aeneas stopped at the island of Polyphemus in Sicily, Achemenides warned him of many giants and begged Aeneas to take him away. *Aeneid* iii; *Odyssey* ix.

Acheron (ak' e ron). One of the five rivers in Hades, the river of woe across which Charon ferried the dead. (The other four: Cocytus, wailing; Lethe, forgetfulness; Phlegethon, fire; Styx, by which the gods sealed their oaths.) *Aeneid* ii; *Paradise Lost* ii.

Achilleis (ak i lē' is). Also *Achilleid*. Epic poem about Achilles by Statius. The poem is unfinished; only the first book and 167 lines of the second still exist.

Achilles (a kil' ēz). Son of Peleus and the sea goddess THETIS, q.v. Educated by the centaur Chiron. Father of NEOPTOLEMUS (Pyrrhus), q.v. Greatest Greek warrior of the Trojan War. Killed Hector, the greatest Trojan warrior. Slain by Paris. Central figure in Homer's *Iliad*. Many stories about Achilles in *Aeneid;* Apollodorus; Dares; Dictys; *Met.; Odyssey;* Statius' *Achilleid;* and others.

Acidalia (a si dā' li a). A surname of Aphrodite, from a fountain in Boeotia, sacred to her, in which she bathed with the three GRACES, q.v. *Aeneid* i; *Fasti* v.

Acis (ā' sis). Son of Faunus. Passionately loved Galatea. His rival, Polyphemus, crushed him to death with a rock. The gods changed him into a stream which rises from Mount Aetna. *Met.* xiii.

Acmon (ak' mon). A Greek follower of Diomedes. Wounded Aphrodite in the Trojan War; she changed him into a bird.

Acmonides (ak mon' i dēz). A cyclops.

Acoetes (a kō e tēz). See ACETES.

Acontius (a kon' shi us). A youth of the island of Ceos. He went to Delos, where he fell in love with Cydippe, whose parents forbade their marriage on account of his obscure origin. He wrote verses on an apple (some legends say an orange) which he threw to Cydippe—"I swear by Artemis to marry no one but Acontius." When her parents desired to marry her to other men, Cydippe fell ill. The parents consulted an oracle, learned her oath was binding, and permitted her to marry Acontius. *Heroides* xx, xxi; William Morris, *The Earthly Paradise.*

Acrias (ak' ri as). One of the many suitors of Hippodamia. Pausanias vi.

Acrisius (a kris' i us). Great-grandson of Danaus, son of Abas and Aglaia. Father of DANAE, q.v. Grandfather of Perseus by whom, years later, he was accidentally killed. Apollodorus i, ii; *Met.* iv; Pausanias ii.

Acrocorinth (ak' rō kor inth). Hill above the city of Corinth, site of a famous temple to Aphrodite. Poseidon, Helios, Briareus, and Aphrodite are associated with Acrocorinth. Celebrated today for its ruins.

Acron (ak' ron). 1. A friend of Aeneas, killed by Mezentius. *Aeneid* x. 2. A king killed by Romulus in single combat after the rape of the Sabines.

Acropolis (a krop' o lis). 1. The citadel of any ancient Greek city. 2. The citadel of Athens, once the site of ancient Athens. A huge rock which rises about 300 feet above the modern city, is 512 feet above sea level, about 1,000 feet long from east to west, and 400 feet wide. Here Athena and Poseidon contended for control of Athens, and here, the famous palaces of Cecrops and Erechtheus were built. The Propylea (the east gate of any temple), the Temple of Athena Nike, the Erechtheum, the Portico of the Caryatids, the museum (built in 1878, severely damaged in World War II, not reopened until 1955), and the Parthenon, the most perfect product of Athenian art, dedicated to Athena Parthenos ("parthenos" means virgin), remain the great attractions for modern visitors. The Parthenon was begun by Pericles in 447 B.C. and by 438 B.C. was ready to contain the great gold-and-ivory statue of Athena by Phidias; all traces of the statue have vanished.

Actaeon (ak tē' on). The hunter who made Artemis angry when he saw her naked at the river's edge and stayed to watch her bathe. She changed him into a stag, and he was devoured by his own hounds. *Met.* iii; Pausanias ix.

Actaeus (ak tē′ us). Earliest king of Attica. His daughter Aglauros married Cecrops, who is often called the founder and first king of Athens.

Actis (ak′ tis). A son of Rhode and Helios. Banished from Rhodes, he went to Egypt and founded the city of Heliopolis. The Colossus of Rhodes was built in his honor.

Actium (ak′ shi um; ak′ ti um). A promontory on the western coast of ancient Greece (Epirus), made famous by the naval victory of Augustus over Antony and Cleopatra, September 2, 31 B.C.

Actor (ak′ ter). 1. A companion of Heracles in his expedition against the Amazons. 2. Father of Menetius by Aegina. 3. A friend of Aeneas. *Aeneid* ix. 4. A son of Poseidon. 5. Brother of Augeas, the father of Eurytus. Apollodorus ii. 6. One of the Argonauts.

Adamanthaea (ad a man thē′ a). The Cretan nurse of Zeus who suspended his cradle from a tree that he might be found neither on the earth, in the sea, or in heaven.

Ades (ā′ dēz). Same as Aides, HADES, ORCUS, PLUTO, UNDERWORLD, DIS. Greek god of hell. Orcus and Dis are Latin names for Hades and Pluto. Ancient poets used the word *hades* or *ades* to mean hell itself.

Adherbas (ad her′ bas). According to some legends, the same as SICHAEUS q.v., SYCHAEUS, SICHARBAS, ACERBAS; husband of Dido. *Aeneid* i.

Admeta, Admete (ad mē′ ta; ad mē′ tē). Daughter of Eurystheus, who appointed the Twelve Labors of Heracles. Obtaining the golden girdle of Hippolyta, queen of the Amazons, was one of the labors because Admeta coveted it. Apollodorus i.

Admetus (ad mē′ tus). Husband of Alcestis, who volunteered to die for him. He participated in the Calydonian boar hunt and was one of the Argonauts. Euripides, *Alcestis*.

Adonia (a dō′ ni a). Festivals in honor of Adonis held in Phoenicia, Greece, and Egypt.

Adonis (a don′ is; a dō′ nis). Son of CINYRAS, q.v., by his daughter Myrrha. Famous for his great beauty; favorite of Aphrodite, who bore him a son and a daughter. He was torn to pieces by a wild boar and from his blood sprang the flower called *anemone*. Apollodorus i, ii; *Met.* x; Vergil, *Eclogue* x.

Adraste (a dras' tē). Attendant of Helen at the court of Menelaus.

Adrastea, Adrastia (ad ras tē' a; ad ras tī' a). A nymph of Crete to whose care Rhea entrusted the infant Zeus. Apollodorus i.

Adrastus (a dras' tus). King of Argos and leader of the Seven against Thebes. All were killed except Adrastus. *Aeneid* vi; *Iliad* v; Euripides, *The Suppliant Women*.

Aea (ē' a). City in Colchis, home of King Aeetes, where Jason and the Argonauts sought the Golden Fleece.

Aeacides (ē as' i dēz). Sons or descendants of Aeacus; applied to Achilles, Ajax, Peleus, and Telamon.

Aeacus (ē' a kus). Son of Zeus and Aegina. Father of Peleus and Telamon; a man of such high integrity that after his death Zeus made him one of the three judges of Hades (Minos and Rhadamanthus were the other two). Apollodorus iii; *Met.* vii; Pausanias i.

Aeaea (ē ē' a). 1. Circe's island, where Odysseus remained with her for one year. 2. Another name for Circe. *Aeneid* iii; *Odyssey* x.

Aedon (ā ē' don). Wife of Zethus, king of Thebes. She planned to murder Niobe's oldest son, but by mistake killed her own. When she attempted to kill herself, she was changed into a nightingale. *Odyssey* xix.

Aeetes (ē ē' tēz). King of Colchis; brother of Circe, Pasiphae, and Perses; father of Medea. The Golden Fleece sought by Jason and the Argonauts was in a sacred grove in Colchis. Apollodorus i; *Met.* vii; Pausanias ii.

Aegaeon (ē jē' on). One of the three Hecatoncheires, the hundred-handed giants (CENTIMANI, q.v.), children of Uranus and Gaea. The other two giants were Cottus and Gyges. Another name for Aegaeon is Briareus, a name the gods used; mortals used the name Aegaeon. *Aeneid* x; *Iliad* x; *Met.* ii; *Theogony.*

Aegeus (ē′ jus; ē′ jē us). Son of Pandion; brother of Pallas, Nisus, and Lycus; husband of Aethra; father of Theseus. Aegeus killed himself when he thought Theseus had lost his life on the mission to kill the Minotaur. Apollodorus i; Pausanias i.

Aegiale (ē jī′ a lē). One of the HELIADES, q.v., so named for Helios; sister to Phaethon. At the death of Phaethon, she and her sisters were so grieved that the gods changed them into poplar trees and their tears into amber. Apollodorus i; *Iliad.*

Aegialeus (ē jī′ a lus). Son of Adrastus; the only one of the EPIGONI, q.v., to be killed in the war against Thebes. Apollodorus i; Pausanias i.

Aegina (ē jī′ na). Daughter of Asopus (a river god) and Metope. Mother of Aeacus by Zeus. Changed into a flame of fire; one legend says she was changed into the island that bears her name. Apollodorus i; Pausanias ii.

Aegis (ē′ jis). The goatskin shield or breastplate of Zeus. In the center of the shield was the head of Medusa, the Gorgon. It is said that the goatskin was that of Amalthea, the goat that nursed the infant Zeus. The word "aegis" means goatskin. *Aeneid* viii.

Aegisthus (ē jis′ thus). Son of Thyestes by Pelopia, his own daughter. Lover of Clytemnestra; he helped her kill her husband Agamemnon on his return home from the Trojan War. After reigning seven years, Aegisthus and Clytemnestra were murdered by Orestes, Pylades, and Electra. The story of Aegisthus is found in Aeschylus, *Agamemnon;* Euripides, *Orestes, Electra; Odyssey* iii and xi; Seneca, *Agamemnon;* Sophocles, *Electra.*

Aegle (ēg′ ēl). 1. One of the three Hesperides who guarded the Golden Apples. 2. One of the three Graces. 3. One of the HELIADES, q.v. 4. Youngest daughter of Asclepius, god of medicine.

Aegyptus (ē jip′ tus). Son of Belus, a king of Egypt;

brother of Danaus. Gave his fifty sons in marriage to his brother's fifty daughters. *Heroides* xiv.

Aella (ă el′ a). An Amazon slain by Heracles. The name "Aella" means whirlwind; she was very swift.

Aello (ă el′ ō). One of the three Harpies. (The other two: Celeno and Ocypete.) *Theogony; Met.* xiii.

Aemonides (ē mon′ i dēz). A priest of Apollo in Italy; killed by Aeneas. *Aeneid* x.

Aeneadae (ē nē′ a dē). A name used by Vergil for the companions and friends of Aeneas. *Aeneid* i.

Aeneades (ē nē′ a dēz). The descendants of Aeneas.

Aeneas (ē nē′ as). The son of the Trojan prince Anchises and the goddess Aphrodite. Cared for by a nymph of Mount Ida and educated by Chiron the centaur. Husband of Creusa, the mother of Ascanius (or Iulus). Fought with great valor in the Trojan War. On his way to Italy he was received kindly by Dido; in Italy he became the founder of the Roman race. Married Lavinia, daughter of Latinus. His adventures parallel those of Odysseus. Most of Aeneas' life is recounted in Vergil's *Aeneid*. Other stories of Aeneas are in the *Odyssey* xiii, xx; Apollodorus iii; *Met.* xiv; Pausanias ii; Chaucer, *House of Fame* and *The Legend of Good Women;* Purcell's opera, *Dido and Aeneas.*

Aeneas Silvia (sil′ vi a). Son of Aeneas; founder of Alba Longa, where his descendants reigned many years, and where the Vestal Virgin Rhea Silvia gave birth to Romulus and Remus, founders of Rome 753 B.C.

Aeneid, The (ē nē′ id). An epic in twelve books, by Vergil.

Aeolia (ē ō′ li a). The island of the winds; home of Aeolus, god of the winds.

Aeolides (ē ō′ li dēz). Descendants of Aeolus.

Aeolus (ē′ ō lus). Also Hippotades. God of the winds. *Aeneid* i; *Met.* xi; *Odyssey* x.

Aepytus (ē′ pi tus). **1.** A king of Messenia; son of Cresphontes and Merope. To recover his kingdom, he killed

Polyphontes, who had married Merope against her will and usurped the crown. 2. A son of Elatus, who reared Evadne. 3. A king of Arcadia; a descendant of Stymphalus.

Aerope (a er' ō pē). Mother of Agamemnon, Menelaus, and Anaxibia by Atreus; some legends say by Plisthenes. She committed adultery with her brother-in-law Thyestes and bore him twins. In revenge Atreus killed the twins, cut up their bodies, cooked them, and set them before Thyestes as food.

Aesacus (ē' sa kus). One of Priam's fifty sons.

Aeschylus (es' ki lus). 525–456 B.C. One of the three great Greek tragedians. Wrote approximately ninety plays; only seven have survived; six of the seven, *Agamemnon, Choephoroe, Eumenides, Prometheus Bound, Seven against Thebes, The Suppliant Maidens* are based on mythology. *The Persians* is based on history.

Aesculapius (es kū lā' pi us). Asclepius (Greek). God of healing and medicine. Son of Apollo by Coronis. Physician to the Argonauts, he restored many to life. Married Epione, by whom he had two sons, Machaon and Podalirius (famous in medicine), and one daughter, Hygeia, the Greek goddess of health. See also PAEAN. Apollodorus iii; *Iliad* iv; *Met.* ii; Pausanias ii; *Homeric Hymns.*

Aeson (ē' son). King of Thessaly and father of Jason. He entrusted Jason's education to Chiron the centaur. Aeson was restored to youth by Medea. *Met.* vii.

Aesyetes (ē si ē' tēz). Father of Antenor. *Iliad* ii.

Aether (ē' ther). Greek god of light.

Aetheria (ē ther' i a). One of the HELIADES, q.v.; sister to Phaethon. After Phaethon's death, she was changed into a poplar tree that wept tears of amber.

Aethiopia. See PENTHESILEA.

Aethra (ēth' ra). 1. Daughter of Pittheus, king of Troezen. Wife of Aegeus; mother of Theseus. *Heroides* x; *Iliad* iii; Ovid. 2. One of the seven Oceanids, sisters of Hyas; they died of grief over the death of their brother and were changed into stars called the Hyades. Some legends say Aethra was the mother of the Hyades by Atlas.

Aetna (et′ na). A Sicilian nymph after whom Mount Aetna (Etna) was named. Zeus imprisoned the giants under this mountain; Vulcan had his forge there; Enceladus is buried there. *Aeneid* iii; *Met.* v; *Theogony.*

Aetolia (ē tō′ li a). A section of central Greece named for Aetolus, the son of Endymion.

Aetolus (ē′ tō lus). Son of Endymion.

Afer (ā′ fer). Africus (Latin). The southwest wind.

Afterthought. An epithet for EPIMETHEUS, q.v., the brother of Prometheus.

Agacles (ag′ a klēz). In the *Iliad,* a king of the Myrmidons.

Agamede (ag a mē′ dē). Daughter of Augeas, the owner of famous stables. Agamede used herbs for healing.

Agamemnon (ag a mem′ non). Son of Atreus and Aerope; brother of Menelaus and Anaxibia. King of Mycenae and Argos; commander-in-chief of the Greek forces in the Trojan War. Husband of Clytemnestra; father of Orestes, Electra, and Iphigenia. Upon his victorious return home from Troy, he was murdered by CLYTEMNESTRA, q.v., and her paramour Aegisthus. *Aeneid* vi; *Iliad* ii; *Met.* xii; *Odyssey* iv; Aeschylus, *Agamemnon* and *Choephoroe;* Euripides, *Electra, Iphigenia in Aulis, Iphigenia in Tauris, Orestes;* Sophocles, *Electra* and *Ajax;* Seneca, *Agamemnon.* Chaucer, Crébillon, T. S. Eliot, Giraudoux, Gluck, Jeffers, Meredith, O'Neill (*Mourning Becomes Electra*), Hofmannsthal, Racine, Sartre, Shakespeare, and Tennyson have also used the story.

Agamemnon. 1. A tragedy by Aeschylus. 2. A play by Seneca.

Aganippe (ag a nip′ ē). 1. Wife of Acrisius and mother of Danae. (Some name Eurydice as the mother of Danae.) 2. A celebrated fountain at the foot of Mount Helicon in Boeotia that flows into the Parnassus; sacred to the Muses. *Met.* v.

Agapenor (ag a pē′ nor). King and leader of the Arcadians who went with the Greeks to the Trojan War; Commander of Agamemnon's fleet. *Iliad* ii.

Agasthenes (a gas′ thē nēz). 1. One of the many suitors of Helen; engaged in the Trojan War. 2. A son of Augeas, king of Elis. Apollodorus iii; *Iliad* ii; Pausanias v.

Agathon (ag′ a thon). 1. One of the fifty sons of Priam. *Iliad* xxiv. 2. Greek tragedian, friend of Plato.

Agave (a gā′ vē). Daughter of Cadmus and Hermione (Harmonia); mother of Pentheus. Agave denied the godhead of Dionysus and in punishment was driven mad. At a festival in honor of Dionysus in which only women participated, her son Pentheus was found spying on the rites; Agave and other Bacchanals were so frenzied that they thought he was a wild animal and tore him to pieces. Apollodorus iii; *Met.* iii.

Agavus (a gā′ vus). A son of Priam. *Iliad* xxiv.

Agelaos, Agelaus (aj e lā′ os). 1. Ancestor of Croesus, king of Lydia. Some legends say he was the son of Hercules and Omphale. Apollodorus ii. 2. Chief herdsman for Priam. Instructed to kill the infant Paris, Agelaos saved him and reared him as his own son. 3. A Trojan slain by Diomedes. *Iliad.* 4. One of Penelope's suitors. *Odyssey* xx. 5. A son of Ixion who became a king of Corinth.

Agenor (a jē′ nor). 1. Son of Poseidon and Libya; brother of Belus; king of Phoenicia; husband of Telephassa; father of Cadmus, Cilix, Europa, and Phoenix. Apollodorus ii. 2. Son of the Trojan Antenor, and one of the bravest of the Trojans.

Ages of Mankind. Golden, Silver, Bronze (Brass, Brazen), and Iron. In *Works and Days,* Hesiod mentions five ages, a Heroic Age after the Bronze. *Met.* i lists four. Vergil, Milton, and Shelley describe the Golden Age.

Aglaia (a glā′ ya). 1. Daughter of Zeus and Eurynome; wife of Hephaestus, according to some legends; youngest of the three Graces (see CHARITES). 2. Wife of Abas; mother of Acrisius and Proetus.

Aglauros (a glo′ ros). 1. Daughter of Actaeus, first king of Athens. 2. Daughter of Cecrops, she was changed into a stone by Hermes. *Met.* ii.

Aglaus (a glā′ us). 1. The poorest man in Arcadia, he was pronounced by an oracle happier than Gyges, king of Lydia. 2. A son of Thyestes by Aerope, naiad wife of Atreus. As punishment for the father's adultery, Atreus had the child killed, cooked, and served to Thyestes as food.

Agno (ag′ nō). A nymph who nursed the infant Zeus. Pausanias viii.

Agora (ag′ ōr a). The Greek word for market place.

Agraulos (a gro′ lus). See AGLAUROS.

Agriope (ag rī′ ō pē). See EURYDICE.

Agrius (ā′ gri us). 1. Son of Gaea; one of the Giants. Apollodorus i. 2. A centaur that attacked Heracles. Apollodorus ii. 3. Son of Circe by Odysseus; there were two other sons of these parents, Latinus and Telegonus. *Theogony.* 4. Father of Thersites, who had the foulest tongue and ugliest appearance of all the Greeks at Troy. *Iliad.* 5. Brother of Oeneus, whose throne he usurped; Agrius killed himself when he was driven from the throne by Diomedes, Oeneus' grandson. Apollodorus i. *Iliad* xiv.

Aias (ā′ yas; ā′ as). Ajax (Roman). Son of Telamon of Salamis and Periboea (Eriboea). He is called Telamonian Aias or Greater Aias; next to Achilles, he was the bravest of the Greeks in the Trojan War. He contended with Odysseus for the armor of the dead Achilles and was enraged when Odysseus won. Stories about him vary. Later poets say his defeat by Odysseus caused him to go mad and kill himself. Some legends say he was so enraged that he slaughtered a whole flock of sheep, supposing them to be the sons of Atreus, who had given preference to Odysseus; after that Aias stabbed himself. Other legends say he was killed by Paris or that Odysseus murdered him. Apollodorus iii; *Iliad* i; *Met.* xiii; *Odyssey* xi; Pausanias i.

Aias. Called Lesser Aias, Locrian Aias, and the Runner. Son of Oileus and leader of the Locrians in the Trojan War, he was insolent and conceited. *Aeneid* i; *Iliad* ii, xxiii; Pausanias x; Seneca, *Agamemnon*. *Odyssey* iv has an account of his self-destruction, told by Proteus to Menelaus.

Aides (ā′ i dēz; ī′ dēz). See ADES.

Aidoneus (ā i dō′ nus; –ne us). A poetic term for ADES, q.v.

Aidos (ī′ dos). The Greek personification of Conscience.

Aigialeus (a jī′ a lūs; ē jī′ a lūs). See AEGIALEUS.

Ajax (ā′ jaks). See AIAS.

Ajax. A play by Sophocles.

Alalcomenae (al al kō mē′ nē). A village in Boeotia, where Alalcomeneus reared Athena and where he built a temple to her.

Alalcomenean Athena (al al kō mē′ nē an a thē′ na). A Boeotian name for the goddess of wisdom.

Alalcomeneus (al al kō mē′ nūs). According to some legends, the first man.

Alastor (a las′ ter). 1. The name of one of the horses used by Pluto when he abducted Persephone. 2. Armor bearer to Sarpedon, the Lycian king; killed by Odysseus in the Trojan War. *Iliad* v; *Met.* xxiii.

Alba Longa (al′ ba long′ ga). A town in Italy (now Rome) founded by AENEAS SILVIA, q.v., son of Aeneas, and ruled by his descendants.

Albion (al′ bi on). Son of Poseidon and Amphitrite. Came to Britain and introduced the arts of ship building and astrology. Some early writers say the word *Albion* (another name for Great Britain) was invented by Edmund Spenser.

Albuna, Albunea (al bū′ na; al bū nē′ a). A Roman nymph with the gift of prophecy.

Alcaeus (al sē′ us). 1. Son of Perseus and Andromeda; father of Amphitryon and Anaxo; grandfather of Hera-

cles. From Alcaeus, Heracles has been called Alcides. **2.**
A son of Androgeus; grandson of Minos; accompanied
Heracles to fetch the girdle of Amazonian queen Hip-
polyta. **3.** A son of Heracles by Omphale. **4.** A celebrated
lyric poet (610–580 B.C.) of Mytilene, Lesbos, Greece.
Apollodorus ii.

Alcander (al kan' der). An attendant of Sarpedon, killed
by Odysseus. *Met.* xiii.

Alcandre (al kan' drē). Wife of Polybus, king of Egyptian
Thebes during the Trojan War, who entertained Menelaus and Helen on their way home from Troy. *Odyssey*
iv.

Alcathous (al kath' ō us). **1.** Son of Pelops and Hippodamia. King of Megara, who with Apollo rebuilt the
walls of the city. Pausanias i. **2.** Husband of Hippodamia,
the daughter of Anchises. Some legends say he was slain
by Idomeneus, others that he was the last Trojan slain
by Achilles. *Iliad* xii. **3.** A friend of Aeneas killed in the
Rutulian War. *Aeneid* x.

Alcenor (al sē' nor). Also Alcanor. An Argive who was the
only man, except another Argive (Chromius) and one
Spartan (Othryadas), to survive a battle between three
hundred Argives and three hundred Spartans. Herodotus
i.

Alcestis (al ses' tis). Daughter of Pelias and Anaxibia, and
wife of Admetus. She volunteered to die for her husband
on the promise of Apollo that Admetus should never die
if someone were found to die in his stead. Some legends
say Heracles brought Alcestis back from Hades. Apollodorus i; Pausanias v; Euripides, *Alcestis;* Chaucer, *Legend of Good Women;* Milton's twenty-third sonnet.

Alcestis. A play by Euripides.

Alceus (al sē' us). See ALCAEUS.

Alcides (al sī' dēz). Name for Heracles, from Alcaeus.

Alcidice (al sid' i sē). Wife of Salmoneus; she died when
her daughter Tyro was born. Apollodorus i.

Alcimede (al sim' ē dē). Mother of Jason by Aeson. She

tried to persuade Jason not to go to Colchis. (Apollodorus says Ploymede was the mother of Jason.)

Alcimedon (al sim' ē don). **1.** His daughter Phillo was ravished by Heracles. Pausanias viii. **2.** A captain of the Myrmidons under Patroclus. *Iliad.*

Alcimenes (al si mē' nēz). Also Alcimedes (al si mē' dēz). A son of Jason and Medea. Alcimenes and Thessalus, the two oldest children, were twins. Diodorus Siculus iv. Some authorities believe Thessaly may have been named for Thessalus. Apollodorus and Pausanias also wrote of Medea's children.

Alcinous (al sin' ō us). King of the Phaeacians; husband of Arete; father of Nausicaa. Befriended Odysseus and listened to the recital of his adventures. Apollodorus i, iii; *Odyssey* vi, vii, viii.

Alcippe (al sip' pē). **1.** Daughter of Ares and Aglauros, ravished by Halirrhothius (son of Poseidon), who was killed by Ares. For this murder, Ares was tried at a place called the Areopagus (Hill of Ares; Mars' Hill) and was acquitted by the Olympian gods who sat as judges in what has been called the first murder trial. Apollodorus iii. **2.** Wife of Euenus and mother of Marpessa. **3.** A woman who gave birth to an elephant. **4.** Mother of Daedalus. **5.** An attendant of Helen and Menelaus in Sparta. *Odyssey* iv.

Alcmaeon (alk mē' on). Son of Amphiaraus and Eriphyle; one of the EPIGONI, q.v. Apollodorus iii; *Met.* ix; Pausanias v.

Alcmaon (alk' mā on). Son of Thestor; slain by Sarpedon for having wounded Glaucus, a beloved companion of Sarpedon. *Iliad.*

Alcmena, Alcmene (alk mē' nē). Daughter of King Electryon of Argos by Anaxo. Wife of Amphitryon. She became the paramour of Zeus (the last mortal woman Zeus embraced) and the mother of Heracles. Iphicles was Heracles' twin, but Amphitryon was his father. After Amphitryon's death, Alcmena married Rhadamanthus. Apollodorus ii; *Odyssey* xi; Pausanias i.

Alcon (al′ kon). Skilled archer who helped Heracles get the cattle of Geryon and participated in the Calydonian boar hunt.

Alcyone (al sī′ ō nē). Same as Halcyone. 1. Daughter of Aeolus; wife of Ceyx, king of Thessaly; was changed into a kingfisher after death. *Met.* xi; Chaucer, *The Book of the Duchess*. 2. Daughter of Atlas; one of the Pleiades; mother of Arethusa by Poseidon. Apollodorus iii; Pausanias ii. 3. Sister of Eurystheus, the king who commanded the Twelve Labors of Heracles. 4. Wife of Meleager. 5. Name sometimes given to Cleopatra. *Iliad* ix.

Alcyoneus (al sī′ ō nus). 1. Son of Uranus and Gaea; one of the Giants; brother of Porphyrion. Apollodorus i. 2. A herdsman who stole the cattle of Helios and was killed by Heracles.

Alecto (a lek′ tō). One of the three Furies. Other names for the Furies are Dirae, Erinyes, Eumenides, Furiae, Semnae. *Aeneid* vii.

Alector (a lek′ tor). King of Argos; father of Iphis and Capaneus. Apollodorus iii; Pausanias ii.

Alectryon (a lek′ tri on). The youth Ares (Mars), during his dalliance with Aphrodite (Venus), stationed at the door to watch against the approach of the sun. Alectryon fell asleep and Apollo came and discovered the lovers ("When the net was unwound Venus was found ravelled with Mars"). They were exposed by Hephaestus (Venus' husband), in each other's arms, before all the gods. Ares was so enraged that he changed the unfortunate youth into a rooster, who must forever announce the approach of the sun. Lucian.

Aletes (a lē′ tēz). 1. Son of Hippotes; first of the Heraclidae; for many years king of Corinth. Pausanias ii. 2. An aged gentleman and faithful companion of Aeneas. *Aeneid* i. 3. A son of Clytemnestra by her paramour Aegisthus; he became ruler of Mycenae after Orestes murdered Clytemnestra and Aegisthus. Later Orestes also murdered Aletes and became king of Mycenae. Hyginus.

Alethia (al ē thī′ a). Veritas (Roman). Daughter of Zeus; one of Apollo's nurses; Greek goddess of truth.

Alexander (al eg zan′ der). PARIS, q.v. Homer calls Paris *Alexandros,* which means champion. *Iliad* xxiv.

Alexandra (al eg zan′ dra). Another name for CASSANDRA, q.v.

Alirrothius (al lir rō′ thi us). Son of Poseidon. He tried to cut down the olive tree which had sprung from the ground and given the victory to Athena in her contest with Poseidon. Alirrothius missed his mark and cut his legs so severely that he died immediately.

Alitherses (a li ther′ sēs). Also Halitherses, Halithersus. The soothsayer who told Penelope that Odysseus would return and wreak great vengeance upon her suitors. *Odyssey* ii.

Alkmene (alk mē′ nē). See ALCMENA.

Aloeus (a lō′ us). Son of Uranus and Gaea; father of the twins Otus and Ephialtes, two of the Giants, who grew nine inches every month and were only nine years old when they made war against the gods and were killed by Apollo and his twin sister Artemis. *Aeneid* vi; *Iliad* v; *Odyssey* xi; Pausanias ix.

Aloidae (a lō ī′ dē). Giants descended from Aloeus.

Alpheus (al fē′ us). A river god who pursued the wood nymph Arethusa until she was changed into a stream by Artemis. Heracles made use of the waters of the river Alpheus in Elis to help cleanse the Augean stables. *Aeneid* iii; *Met.* v; Pausanias v.

Althaea (al thē′ a). Mother of Meleager, the hero of the Calydonian boar hunt. Apollodorus i. *Iliad* ix; *Met.* viii; Pausanias viii.

Altis (al′ tis). The sacred grove around the Temple of Zeus at Olympia in which the statues of the Olympic conquerors were placed. Pausanias v.

Amalthea (am al thē′ a). 1. The goat that nursed the infant Zeus in a Cretan cave. One of the goat's horns was called *cornucopia,* the horn of plenty, because (having been broken off) it would be filled with whatever its owner desired. Pausanias vii. 2. Daughter of King Melissus of Crete; according to some mythologists, she fed the infant Zeus goat's milk. 3. The Roman Sibyl who sold the three Sibylline books to Tarquin, king of Rome.

Amasenus (am a sē′ nus). The river over which Metabus threw his daughter Camilla. *Aeneid* vii.

Amata (a mā′ ta). Wife of King Latinus; mother of Lavinia, the wife of Aeneas in Latium. *Aeneid* vii.

Amazons (am′ a zonz), **Amazones.** Tribe of female warriors who lived east of the Greek regions of Asia Minor. They cut off their right breasts in order to use the bow more easily—*Amazon* means breastless. They had no dealings with men except for breeding and as opponents in war; they reared only their female young. Bellerophon, Heracles, Perseus, Theseus all fought against them. Theseus abducted their queen Hippolyta (also called Antiope). Penthesilea, another queen, aided the Trojans in the Trojan War; she was killed by Achilles. Lampeto and Marpesia were two other famous queens. *Aeneid* v; Apollodorus ii; Herodotus iv; Pausanias vii.

Ambrosia (am brō′ zhi a). The food of the gods; nectar was their drink. *Ambrosia* means immortal. *Aeneid* i; *Iliad* i, xiv, xvi, xxiv; *Met.* ii.

Ammon (am′ on). Egyptian god the Greeks identified with Zeus and the Romans with Jupiter. *Met.* xv; Pausanias iii.

Amor (ā′ mor). Also Eros. Cupid (Roman). The son of Aphrodite (Venus), and the god of love.

Amphiaraus (am fi a rā′ us). Also called Amphiorax. One of the Seven against Thebes, participated in the Calydonian boar hunt, and was an Argonaut. He has been called one of the seven soothsayers. Apollodorus i, ix; *Met.* ix; *Odyssey* xv.

Amphictyon (am fik′ ti on). Son of Deucalion and Pyrrha.

The first man to draw omens, interpret dreams, mix water with wine. Pausanias i, x.

Amphilochus (am fil' ō kus). Son of Amphiaraus and Eriphyle; brother of Alcmaeon. A soothsayer; one of the EPIGONI, q.v. Took part in the Trojan War. Pausanias.

Amphimachus (am fim' a kus). A suitor of Helen; took part in the Trojan War; was slain by Hector. *Iliad*.

Amphimedon (am fim' ē don). A suitor of Penelope. *Odyssey*.

Amphinomus (am fin' ō mus). Among her suitors, the most pleasing to Penelope; killed by Telemachus. *Odyssey*.

Amphion (am fi' on; am' fi on). Son of Zeus and Antiope; Twin of Zethus. Musician and builder of the walls of Thebes. Husband of Niobe. Apollodorus iii; *Odyssey* xi; Pausanias vi.

Amphiorax (am fi' o raks). See AMPHIARAUS.

Amphitea (am fit' tē a). 1. Wife of Adrastus, king of Argos; mother of Aegialeus, Aegialea, Argia, and Deipyle. Apollodorus i. 2. Wife of Autolycus; mother of Anticlea, the wife of Laertes. *Odyssey* xix.

Amphitrite (am fi trī' tē). Goddess of the sea; wife of Poseidon; mother of Triton. Daughter of Oceanus and Tethys. Sometimes her name is taken for the sea itself. Apollodorus iii; *Met.* i; *Theogony*.

Amphitryon (am fit' ri on). Husband of ALCMENA, q.v., who was the mother of Heracles by Zeus. *Aeneid* viii; Apollodorus ii; Pausanias viii.

Amulius (a mū' li us). Usurped the crown of Alba Longa from his brother Numitor. Later killed by Romulus and Remus, the grandchildren of Numitor, who restored the crown to their grandfather.

Amycus (am' i kus). 1. Son of Poseidon; a famous boxer who challenged all travelers to fight him. Those who refused were thrown into the sea; those who accepted were killed in the match. Finally killed by Polydeuces in a match after he had refused the Argonauts food and water. *Argonautica* ii. **2.** The name of two companions of Aeneas killed by Turnus. *Aeneid* i, xii. **3.** A son of Ixion and the cloud. *Met*. xii.

Amymone (a mi mō' nē). One of the fifty daughters of Danaus; her mother was Europa. She married Enceladus, son of Aegyptus, and murdered him on their wedding night. Apollodorus ii; Pausanias ii.

Amyntor (am' in tor). **1.** The father of Phoenix and tutor of Achilles. *Iliad* ix. **2.** Father of Astydamia, carried away by Heracles.

Amythaon (a mi thā' on). **1.** The son of Cretheus, king of Iolchos, by Tyro. Father of Bias and Melampus. With his brother Neleus, he re-established the Olympic games. *Odyssey* xi. **2.** Another brother was Aeson, the father of Jason. Apollodorus i.

Anacreon (a nak' rē on). 570–478 B.C. Greek lyric poet.

Anadyomene (an a di om' ē nē). APHRODITE, q.v. This is also the name of a valuable painting (by Apelles) of Aphrodite represented as rising from the sea; it was brought to the temple of Julius Caesar in Rome. The lower part of the painting was defaced, and no painters in Rome were able to repair it.

Anax (a' naks). Giant; son of Uranus and Gaea. Pausanias i.

Anaxarete (an ak sar' ē tē). A Greek princess who was loved by Iphis, a man of humble birth. She mocked his love, and in despair Iphis hanged himself on the door of her house. She was completely unmoved at his death, and Aphrodite turned her to stone. *Met*. xiv.

Anaxibia (an ak si' bi a). **1.** Daughter of Atreus and Aerope, and sister of Agamemnon and Menelaus. She became the mother of seven sons and two daughters by Nestor. Pausanias ii. **2.** Daughter of Bias, brother of Melampus (the first man with power to foretell the future). By Pelias, king of Iolchos, she became the mother of Alcestis, Hippothoe, Pelopea, and Pisidice. Apollodorus i.

Anaxo (a nak' so). Mother of Alcmena.

Ancaeus (an sē' us). Son of Poseidon and an Argonaut. A skillful navigator, after the death of Tiphys he became helmsman of the *Argo*. Some legends say he was the strongest of the Argonauts except Heracles.

Anchialos (an kī' a los). One of the Phaeacians; father of Mentes; a great warrior. *Odyssey*.

Anchises (an kī' sēz). Son of Capys and Themis. He had such a beautiful complexion that Aphrodite became interested, came down from heaven to investigate and became pregnant. Their famous son was AENEAS, q.v. Aeneas was educated by Chiron the centaur. He saved his father's life after the battle of Troy, and Anchises accompanied his son on the voyage to Italy. Anchises died in the west-coast town of Drepanum, in Sicily, at the age of eighty, and was buried on nearby Mount Eryx. *Aeneid* i, ii; Apollodorus iii; *Iliad* xx; Pausanias viii; *Theogony* v.

Anchisia (an kī' si a). Mountain named for Anchises.

Ancile (an sī' lē). The sacred shield of Ares (Mars) guarded by the Salii (Roman priests) in Rome.

Andraemon (an drē' mon). 1. A captain of the Aetolians in the Trojan War; father of Thoas. *Iliad*. 2. Husband of Dryope, after she was ravished by Apollo and had a son by the god.

Androgeus (an droj' ē us). Son of Minos and Pasiphae. A skillful wrestler; killed by the Marathonian bull. Minos declared war on Athens and King Aegeus (father of Theseus) to avenge his son. Peace was re-established on the condition that Aegeus send annually seven boys and seven girls from Athens to Crete to be devoured by the Minotaur. *Aeneid* vi; Apollodorus ii; Pausanias i.

Andromache (an drom' a kē). Devoted and faithful wife of Hector; mother of their son Astyanax. Warned Hector against engaging in battle during the Trojan War. After the war, she became a concubine of Neoptolemus and later married Helenus. Aeneas found her at Epirus on his way to Italy. *Iliad* vi; *Aeneid* iii; Apollodorus iii; Pausanias i.

Andromache. 1. A play by Euripides. **2.** A play by Racine.

Andromeda (an drom' e da). Daughter of Cepheus, king of Joppa in Ethiopia, and Cassiopeia. To appease Poseidon, Andromeda was chained to a rocky cliff to be devoured by a monster. Perseus saw her and fell in love with her; he rescued and married her and was always faithful; they had six sons and a daughter. After her death, Andromeda was made a constellation by Athena. Apollodorus ii.

Anna (an' a). Sister of Dido. *Aeneid* ii.

Antaeus (an tē' us). **1.** Son of Poseidon and Gaea. A Giant and wrestler of Libya; invincible while he touched the earth (his mother Gaea). Heracles strangled him while holding him off the ground. **2.** A friend of Turnus, killed by Aeneas. *Aeneid* x.

Anteia (an tī' a). Wife of Proteus; loved Bellerophon.

Antenor (an tē' nor). A counselor of Priam, he kept up a secret correspondence with the Greeks (chiefly with Menelaus and Odysseus) during the Trojan War; he advised the Trojans to return Helen and conclude the war. It is said he advised stealing the Palladium and making the Trojan horse. Spared at the sack of Troy, he founded the city in Italy that is now Padua. *Aeneid* i; *Iliad* iii, vii, viii, xi; *Met.* xiii.

Anteros (an' te ros). Greek god of passion; son of Ares and Aphrodite, brother of Eros (Amor, Cupid). Also called the god of mutual love and tenderness. Pausanias i.

Anticlea (an ti klē' a). Also Anticleia, Anticlia. Daughter of the notorious robber Autolycus. She enjoyed the favors of Sisyphus, and some legends say that Sisyphus was really the father of Odysseus, although Laertes is usually given the credit. *Odyssey* xi, xix. In *Met.* xiii Odysseus was accused by Ajax of being the son of Sisyphus.

Antigone (an tig' o nē). Daughter of Oedipus, king of Thebes, by his mother Jocasta. Sister of Eteocles, Polynices, and Ismene. Antigone was with her father when he died at Colonus, and according to some accounts, Theseus helped her bury him near Athens. Pausanias says that the grave of Oedipus, between the Acropolis and the Areopagus, was pointed out in later times. Sophocles says that the manner of Oedipus' death was known only to Theseus, and that a being from heaven came to bear him away, or that, according to most accounts, the earth opened, and Oedipus disappeared into its depths. Antigone returned to Thebes, where both her brothers were killed. They met in single combat and slew each other in the expedition of the Seven against Thebes. Against the wishes of her uncle Creon, who became king of Thebes, she performed funeral rites for Polynices, and was ordered by Creon to be buried alive. Some legends say she killed herself before the sentence was carried out; others that Haemon, her lover and Creon's son, secretly married her and carried her away. Apollodorus iii; Sophocles, *Antigone*.

Antigone. A play by Sophocles.

Antilochus (an til' o kus). Eldest son of Nestor. Went to the Trojan War with his father. Became great friend of Achilles, whom he told of the death of Patroclus. The three friends were buried in the same grave. *Odyssey* iv.

Antinous (an tin' o us). The most brutal, cruel, insolent suitor of Penelope. Among the first killed by Odysseus and Telemachus. *Odyssey* i, xvi, xvii, xxii.

Antiope (an tī' o pē). 1. Daughter of Nycteus, a king of Thebes. Mother of the twins Amphion and Zethus by Zeus. She was persecuted by Dirce, who was put to death by the twins. Apollodorus iii; *Met.* vi; *Odyssey* xi; Pausanias ii. 2. A queen of the Amazons (see HIPPOLYTA). Some legends say Antiope was a sister of Hippolyta. Antiope was given in marriage by Heracles to Theseus. She was the mother of Hippolytus by Theseus. Some legends say Theseus killed her when she interfered with his marriage to Phaedra.

Antiphas (an' ti fas). One of the twin sons of Laocoon,

killed by a huge sea serpent because Laocoon had defamed the temple of Apollo. The Trojans believed Laocoon was punished because he doubted the divinity of the Wooden Horse.

Antiphates (an tif′ a tēz). **1.** Son of the soothsayer Melampus; killed in the Trojan War. *Iliad* xii. **2.** A king of the Laestrygones, the man-eating Giants of Italy, whose followers devoured one of Odysseus' men, and with stones sank all the ships except the ship in which Odysseus traveled. *Met.* xiv.

Antiphonus (an tif′ o nus). A son of Priam who went with his father to Achilles' tent to redeem the body of Hector. *Iliad* xxiv.

Antiphos, Antiphus (an′ ti fus). **1.** Son of Priam, killed by Agamemnon in the Trojan War. *Iliad* ii. **2.** Grandson of Heracles; went to Trojan War with thirty ships. *Iliad* ii. **3.** Intimate friend of Odysseus who was devoured by Polyphemus. *Odyssey* xvii.

Anubis (a nū′ bis). In Egyptian mythology the same as Hermes.

Apeliotes (a pel′ i o tēz). Lips; southeast wind.

Aphareus (af′ ar yus). King of Messina; grandson of Perseus. *Pausanias* iii.

Aphrodite (af ro dī′ tē). Venus (Roman). The goddess of love, one of the twelve Olympians. Some legends say she was brought forth from ocean foam near Cyprus or Cythera; others that she was the daughter of Zeus and Dione. One of the most celebrated deities of the ancients, she was known as the goddess of beauty, mother of love, queen of laughter, mistress of the graces and of pleasures, patroness of courtesans. Zeus was refused by her and for her obstinacy gave her in marriage to his ugly and deformed son Hephaestus (Vulcan). She was notoriously unfaithful; her intrigue with Ares (exposed by Apollo) is famous. The mother of many—Deimos, Eros, Anteros, Hermione, Phobus by Ares; Hermaphroditus by Hermes; Priapus by Dionysus; Eryx by Poseidon (according to Apollodorus); Aeneas by Anchises. Paris gave her the

APPLE OF DISCORD, q.v., and she helped him win Helen. She abandoned Olympus because she was partial to Adonis. Her mysterious girdle CESTUS, q.v., gave beauty, grace, and elegance to the most deformed, excited love, and rekindled extinguished ardors. Not an exciting figure in Homer, she is even wounded by Diomedes in the battle at Troy. *The Homeric Hymns,* Hesiod, Homer, Ovid, Vergil, Pausanias, Euripides—many others—tell her story. Shakespeare, *Venus and Adonis;* Spenser, *The Faerie Queene, Epithalamion, Prothalamion,* "An Hymne in Honour of Beautie"; John Peele Bishop, "When the Net Was Unwound Venus Was Found Ravelled with Mars"; many allusions in Byron, Donne, Milton, Pope, Rossetti, and so on.

Apollo (a pol' ō). Sol (Roman). Also called Helios, Helius, Hyperion, Phoebus. One of the twelve Olympians. Son of Zeus and Leto; born on the island of Delos, which was raised by Poseidon to escape the wrath of Hera. His famous twin sister was Artemis (Diana). The sun god, and god of fine arts, medicine, music, poetry, and eloquence. Had many amours: Leucothoe, Daphne, Issa, Bolina, Coronis, Clymene, Cyrene, Chione, Calliope, and others. Destroyer of monsters—Python, Cyclops. Famous oracles at Delphi, Delos, Tenedos. His Colossus was one of the Seven Wonders of the ancient world. Many references among the ancients: Apollodorus, *The Homeric Hymns,* Homer, Ovid, Pausanias, Vergil. In English literature: Keats, "Hyperion"; Shelley, "Hymn to Apollo"; Francis Thompson, "Daphne"; and scores of allusions in Arnold, Cowley, Marvell, Milton, Shakespeare, Spenser. See also HELIOS.

Apollodorus (a pol o dō' rus). *ca.* 140–115 B.C. Famous Athenian mythologist, grammarian, and historian. His *Bibliotheca (Library),* a valuable work in three books, is a history of the gods and an important source of mythology.

Apollonius Rhodius (ap o lō' ni us rō' di us). A Greek epic poet of the second century B.C. His *Argonautica,* an epic poem in four books, tells the story of Jason and the Argonauts in search of the Golden Fleece. Vergil's conception of Dido in the *Aeneid* owes much to the *Medea* of Apollonius.

Appiades (ap pī′ a dēz). Name applied to five deities: Concordia, Minerva, Pax, Venus, and Vesta, because a temple was erected to them near the Appian Way.

Apple of Discord. Into the assembly of the gods at the marriage of Peleus and Thetis, the goddess of discord, Eris (who had not been invited), rolled a golden apple inscribed *For the Fairest*. Three goddesses—Aphrodite, Athena, Hera—claimed it. At the Judgment of Paris, it was awarded to Aphrodite. The award was an indirect cause of the Trojan War, and of Hera's determination to destroy Troy. Tennyson, "Oenone."

Apples of the Hesperides (hes per′ i dēz). They grew on a tree given Hera as a wedding gift when she married Zeus, guarded by the Hesperides, daughters of Atlas, and by a dragon, Ladon, who never slept. Atlas was tricked into giving three of these apples to Heracles (his eleventh labor). Heracles gave them to Athena, who returned them to the garden of the Hesperides. *Met*. iv; *Theogony;* Tennyson, "The Hesperides."

Apsyrtus (ap ser′ tus). Same as ABSYRTUS, q.v.

Apuleius (ap u lē′ us). Roman philosopher of the second century A.D. His *Metamorphoses or The Golden Ass,* the only Latin novel extant, tells the story of Cupid and Psyche, and many other unusual adventures. In English literature, Fielding, Smollett, and Robert Graves have made use of this material.

Aquarius (a kwā′ ri us). The water bearer; the eleventh sign of the zodiac, which the sun enters January 21. Also the name of a constellation.

Aquilo (ak′ wi lō). Roman name for Boreas, the north wind.

Arachne (a rak′ nē). Daughter of Idmon, a dyer. She was so skillful in weaving that she challenged Athena to a weaving contest. When Athena ripped the cloth, Arachne hanged herself in despair and was changed into a spider. *Met.* vi.

Arae (ā' rē). Rocks in the Mediterranean, between Africa and Sardinia, where Aeneas lost most of his fleet and where the Africans and Romans ratified a treaty. *Aeneid* i.

Arcadia (ar kā' di a). Also Arcady (ar' ka de). A mountainous and sparsely populated country in the middle of the Peloponnesus, much celebrated by poets of antiquity. PAN, q.v., lived there; Callisto, Coronis, and Lycaon are associated with the district; Hermes was born in a cave on Mount Cyllene. Arcadia was adopted by the poets as a symbol of quiet rustic life. The pastoral tradition in literature began with Theocritus, continues in Vergil, and is found in many English poets, among them Spenser; Sidney, *Arcadia* (a prose romance); Lodge; Fletcher; Shakespeare; Milton; Pope, *Pastorals;* Crabbe; Cowper; Goldsmith; Wordsworth.

Arcas (ar' kas). Son of Zeus and Callisto; king of Arcadia (which was named for him); he taught the Arcadians agriculture and the art of spinning wool. His mother was changed by Zeus into the constellation Great Bear; Arcas was translated into Little Bear (Arcturus), located in the heavens behind his mother as her guardian. Apollodorus iii; *Fasti;* Pausanias viii.

Ardea (ar' de a). Son of Odysseus and Circe, changed into a heron. *Aeneid* vii; *Met.* xiv.

Areopagitae (ar e op' a ji tē). Judges of the criminal court of Athens. The site of the court was the Areopagus, a hill below the Acropolis. Ares was first to be tried in the court—for the murder of Halirrhothius, who had ravished his daughter Alcippe.

Areopagus (ar e op' a gus). The Hill of Ares, where the Areopagitae convened.

Ares (a' rēs). Mars (Roman). God of war; one of the twelve Olympians. Son of Zeus and Hera. Illicit lover of Aphrodite. His sons are Deimos and Phobos (gods of terror and tumult), Fear, Panic, and Trembling. Enyo, goddess of battle, and Eris, goddess of discord, are variously described as sister, mother, wife, and daughter of Ares. The vulture and the dog, as scavengers of the battlefield, are his favorite bird and animal. He favored the Trojans during the Trojan War. *Aeneid* viii; Apollodorus i; *Iliad* v; *Odyssey* i; Pausanias i; *Theogony; Homeric Hymns.*

Arete (a rē′ tē). 1. Wife of Alcinous, king of the Phaeacians; mother of Nausicaa. Daughter of Rhexenor. 2. A name for the goddess of virtue. 3. A daughter of Dionysus. Apollodorus i; *Odyssey* vii, viii.

Arethusa (ar e thū′ sa). 1. A wood nymph, daughter of Oceanus. She was very beautiful and liked hunting, was an attendant of Artemis. Pursued by the river god Alpheus, offering his love, she fled from him and prayed to Artemis to save her; Artemis changed her into a stream. *Met.* x. 2. The name of one of the Hesperides. Shelley, "Arethusa."

Aretos, Aretus (a rē′ tos; –tus). 1. A son of Nestor and Anaxibia. *Odyssey* iii. 2. A son of Priam slain by Automedon, the charioteer of Achilles. *Iliad* xvii. 3. A famous warrior whose only weapon was an iron club. Killed by Lycurgus, king of Arcadia. Pausanias viii.

Arge (ar′ jē). 1. A beautiful huntress, changed into a stag by Apollo. 2. One of the Cyclops. Hesiod. 3. A daughter of Thespius; by Heracles she had two sons. Apollodorus ii. 4. A nymph, daughter of Zeus and Hera. Apollodorus i.

Argeia, Argia (ar jē′ a; –jī′ a). 1. Daughter of Adrastus; wife of Polynices. She was killed by Creon for burying Polynices, and Theseus avenged her death by killing Creon. 2. Argia was the mother of Argos, who built the *Argo* for Jason.

Arges (ar′ jēz). Also Arge. Son of Uranus and Gaea; a Cyclops with only one eye in his forehead.

Argestes (ar jes′ tēz). The east wind. Hesiod.

Argiope (ar jī′ o pē). Another name for Telephassa, wife of Agenor and mother of Cadmus, Cilix, Phoenix, and Europa. Apollodorus ii.

Argiphontes, Argeiphontes (ar ji fon' tēz). The name applied to HERMES, q.v., after he killed Argus, the hundred-eyed giant who had been guarding Io. *Argiphontes* means slayer of Argus.

Argives (ar' jīvs; ar' gīvs). The Greeks of Argos and Argolis, but used for all of the inhabitants of Greece by Homer and other poets. In the *Iliad* Homer calls all the people Argives or Achaeans or Danaans. The term "Greek" was not used by Homer.

Argo (ar' go). The name of the ship built by Argos (Argus), on which Jason sailed to find the Golden Fleece at Colchis. Some ancients maintained that this ship was the first that ever sailed on the sea. *Argonautica* i; Seneca, *Medea*. See also JASON.

Argolis (ar' go lis). An ancient district of the eastern Peloponnesus, between Arcadia and the Aegean Sea. Argos was the chief town.

Argonautae (ar go no' tē), **Argonauts.** The name given Jason and his fifty-five companions who sailed on the *Argo* about seventy-nine years before the Trojan War, in search of the Golden Fleece. Apollonius Rhodius names all fifty-six in his *Argonautica;* other writers give about a dozen names not listed in Rhodius' book. The story of the Argonauts has been told many times—by Euripides, Flaccus, Pindar, Seneca, Chaucer, Corneille, William Morris, Robert Graves, and Anouilh, to name only a few.

Argonautica, The (ar gō no' ti ka). Epic poem by Apollonius Rhodius.

Argos, Argus (ar' gos). 1. The name of the principal town in Argolis, Greece. 2. The builder of the ship *Argo* for Jason. 3. The name of Odysseus' dog. *Odyssey* xvii. 4. The hundred-eyed giant who guarded Io. *Met.* i. 5. A king of Argos who reigned seventy years. 6. A son of Agenor. 7. A son of Zeus and Niobe, Zeus' first child by a mortal. 8. The name of one of the dogs of Actaeon.

9. A son of Jason and Medea. 10. A grandson of Aeetes, king of Colchis, who tried to persuade his grandfather to give Jason the Golden Fleece. See also TROEZEN.

Argyripa (ar ji rip′ a). A town built at Apulia by Diomedes after the Trojan War. *Aeneid* xi.

Ariadne (ar i ad′ nē). A daughter of King Minos of Crete, and of Pasiphae. With a ball of thread, she helped Theseus find his way out of the labyrinth where he had been confined to be devoured by the Minotaur. Ariadne fell in love with Theseus, married him, but was soon deserted on the island of Naxos (Dia). The god of the island, Bacchus, found the forlorn Ariadne, married her, and had many children by her. Stories vary concerning both her life and her death. Apollodorus iii; *Heroides* x; *Met.* viii; *Odyssey* xi.

Aries (ā′ ri ēz). The Ram, the first sign of the zodiac, into which the sun enters March 21.

Arimaspi (ar i mas′ pī). Also Arimaspians. People conquered by Alexander the Great. In myth, the one-eyed horsemen living near a stream which flows with gold; the stream was guarded by griffins.

Arion (a rī′ on). 1. Fabulous wingèd horse sprung from Demeter and Poseidon. Possessed marvelous powers of speech; its right feet were those of a man. Adrastus, in the expedition against Thebes, took Arion with him; the horse savèd his life. Apollodorus iii; Pausanias viii. 2. Famous lyric poet and musician who obtained immense wealth by his profession.

Arisbe (a ris′ bē). 1. Daughter of the seer Merops; first wife of Priam. 2. A wife of Dardanus, daughter of Teucer.

Aristaeus (ar is tē′ us). Son of Apollo and Cyrene. Traveled over much of the world; finally settled in Greece, where he married Autonoe, daughter of Cadmus. Later fell in love with Eurydice and pursued her, indirectly caused her death. He was a keeper of bees, learned to raise olives, and was the inventor of bookkeeping. See also

EURYDICE, ORPHEUS. Apollodorus iii; *Georgics;* Herodotus; Pausanias x.

Aristomachus (ar is tom' a kus). 1. Father of Hippomedon, one of the Seven against Thebes. 2. A man who raised bees for fifty-eight years.

Aristophanes (ar is tof' a nēz). 448–388 B.C. Writer of Greek comedies. Only eleven of his forty comedies are extant; certain authorities believe he wrote at least fifty-four. He has been called the greatest comic dramatist in world literature—"by his side Molière seems dull and Shakespeare clownish," as Lemprière said. *The Acharnians, The Birds, The Clouds, The Ecclesiazusae, The Frogs, The Knights, Lysistrata, Peace, Plutus, The Thesmophoriazusae, The Wasps* all contain much mythological material.

Arnaeus, Arnaios (ar' nē us). See IRUS. A beggar in the palace of Odysseus and the errand boy of the suitors of Penelope. *Odyssey.*

Arne (ar' nē). Daughter of Aeolus. To be with her, Poseidon changed himself into a bull. *Met.* vi; Pausanias ix.

Arsinoe (ar sin' ō ē). 1. Mother of Asclepius by Apollo, according to some mythologists, although Coronis is usually accepted as the mother of Asclepius. 2. Wife of Alcmaeon, one of the Epigoni. Apollodorus iii. 3. Nurse of Orestes; she put her own son in the bed of Orestes, where he was killed by Aegisthus, and Orestes was saved.

Artacia (ar tā' shi a). A spring in the land of the Laestrygones at which the companions of Odysseus met the daughter of King Antiphates.

Artemis (ar' te mis). Diana (Roman). Other names: Cynthia, Delia, Hecate, Luna, Phoebe, Selene. Daughter of Zeus by Leto (Latona); twin sister of Apollo. The moon goddess and goddess of hunting. Also goddess of childbirth, as Lucina (Roman). Patroness of unmarried girls and of chastity. She fell in love with ENDYMION, q.v. Changed Actaeon into a stag. Stories of her used by many English poets: Byron, Drayton, T. S. Eliot, Keats, Lyly, Milton, Spenser; scores of allusions to her in

Shakespeare. *Aeneid* i; Apollodorus i; *Met.* iii; *Odyssey* v; Pausanias viii; *Homeric Hymns*. See also TRIVIA.

Aruns (ar′ unz; a′ runz). A soldier who slew Camilla and was killed by a dart of Artemis. *Aeneid* xi.

Aryans (ar′ yanz). A tribe of ancients from whom the Indians, Persians, Phrygians, Greeks, Romans, Germans, Norsemen, Russians, and Celts are descended, and who probably developed the myth, or germ theory, concerning the development of leaves and fruits, varying according to soil and climate.

Arybas (ar i′ bas). A native of Sidon, whose daughter was carried away by pirates. *Odyssey* xv.

Ascalaphus (as kal′ a fus). 1. Son of Acheron, the river god. In Hades, Ascalaphus saw Persephone eat pomegranate seeds. When he learned that Persephone could leave the lower world provided she had eaten no food, he informed Pluto and she was required to divide her year between the earth and the lower world. Demeter, the mother of Persephone, changed Ascalaphus into an owl for his tattling. Apollodorus i; *Met.* v; Chaucer, *Troilus and Crisyede*. 2. A son of Ares, who became one of the Argonauts, and also participated in the Trojan War. *Iliad* ii.

Ascanius (as kā′ ni us). Son of Aeneas and Creusa. He was saved from Troy by his father and accompanied him to Italy. There he was called Iulus or Ilus; he succeeded his father in Latium and moved the kingdom from Lavinium to Alba Longa, where he and his descendants reigned 420 years, until the time of Numitor. *Aeneid* i.

Asclepius (as klē pi us). See AESCULAPIUS.

Ashtoreth (ash′ to reth). The Phoenician goddess Astarte, goddess of fertility and sexual love; identified by the Greeks with APHRODITE, q.v. Also a moon goddess, identified by the Greeks with ARTEMIS (Selene), q.v.

Asius (ā′ si us). 1. A brother of Hecuba. 2. A Trojan killed by Idomeneus. *Iliad*. 3. A companion of Aeneas in Italy. *Aeneid* x.

Asklepios. See AESCULAPIUS.

Asopus (a sō′ pus). A river god; son of Poseidon. His wife, Metope, the daughter of Ladon, was the mother of two famous sons, Pelasgus and Ismenus, and many daughters including the celebrated Aegina, Ismene, and Salamis. Apollodorus i; Pausanias ii.

Asphodel (as′ fo del). The flower that grows in Hades. The asphodel of the early English and French poets was the daffodil.

Asphodel Fields. The meadow of the dead, where Odysseus found such heroes as Achilles, Patroclus, Agamemnon, and many others. *Odyssey* xxiv.

Assaracus, Assarakos (a sar′ a kus). Father of Capys, who was the father of Anchises. *Aeneid* i; *Iliad* xx.

Astarte (as tar′ tē). See ASHTORETH.

Asteria (as tē′ ri a). 1. Daughter of the titans Coeus and Phoebe; sister of Leto; by Perses the mother of Hecate. Changed into a quail. *Met.* vi. 2. One of the fifty daughters of Danaus. 3. A daughter of Atlas. Apollodorus ii. 4. A town in Greece. *Iliad* ii.

Asterion (as tē′ ri on). Also Asterius (–us). 1. Son of Cometes, one of the Argonauts. 2. A king of Crete, son of Minos II and Pasiphae. Europa was brought by Zeus to Crete; there she bore their three sons, Minos, Rhadamanthus, and Sarpedon. When Zeus left Europa, Asterion married her and reared the three sons. Apollodorus ii; *Met.* ii. 3. Some legends say Asterion was the name given to the Minotaur, for he was the strongest being of his age. Apollodorus iii. 4. The name of a river in the Peloponnesus.

Asterope (as ter′ o pē). Another name for Sterope, one of the Pleiades greatly beloved by the gods.

Astraea, Astrea (as trē′ a). Roman goddess of justice. Lived on earth during the Golden Age, but the wickedness and impiety of mankind during the Brazen and Iron ages drove her to heaven, where she was placed among the constellations of the zodiac under the name

Virgo. In English poetry she is the symbol of innocence and purity. *Met.* i; *Theogony;* Spenser, *Faerie Queene;* Dryden, "Astraea Redux"; Wordsworth, *Memorials of a Tour on the Continent.*

Astraeus (as trē′ us). A titan who warred against Zeus; son of Crius and Eurybia; brother of Pallas and Perses; father of the winds and the stars by Eos, the goddess of dawn.

Astyanax (as tī′ a naks). Son of Hector and Andromache. He was very young when the Greeks besieged Troy; his mother saved him from the flames of the city. Because Odysseus feared Astyanax would inherit the virtues of Hector, the boy was hurled to death from Troy's walls. *Aeneid* ii; *Iliad* vi; *Met.* xiii; Euripides says he was killed by Menelaus; Seneca says the son of Achilles, Pyrrhus (Neoptolemus) killed the boy.

Astydamia (as ti da mī′ a). Wife of Acastus, the son of Pelias. Some say she was a daughter of Pelops and Hippodamia and the mother of Amphitryon. Others say she was a daughter of Amyntor, carried away by Heracles, to whom she bore a son named Tlepolemus (or Ctesippus). Apollodorus iii; *Heroides* ix.

Atalanta, Atalante (at a lan′ ta). **1.** Atalanta of Arcadia, heroine of the Calydonian boar hunt. **2.** Atalanta of Boeotia, daughter of Schoeneus, king of Scyros. Some legends say there was just one Atalanta. She desired perpetual virginity, but her great beauty gained her many admirers; in proposed races, she killed those she conquered; she was finally defeated and married by Hippomenes (Melanion). Apollodorus i; *Met.* viii, x; Pausanias i; Morris, *The Earthly Paradise;* Swinburne, "Atalanta in Calydon."

Ate (ā′ tē). Also Eris; Discordia (Roman). A daughter of Zeus. Goddess of all evil, infatuation, and mischief. Not invited to the marriage of Peleus and Thetis, she rolled the Golden Apple that led to the Judgment of Paris, a main cause of the Trojan War. *Iliad* xix. Hesiod says she was a daughter of Eris. See also DISCORDIA.

Athamas (ath′ a mas). Son of Aeolus; king of Thebes; husband of Nephele, by whom he had two children, Phryxus and Helle. The children fled to Colchis on a golden ram (Helle drowned en route; the Hellespont is named for her). Later, Athamas married Ino, daughter of Cadmus, by whom he had two sons, Learchus and Melicertes; Ino and Melicertes were changed into minor sea deities and given the names Leucothea and Palaemon.

Athena (a thē′ na). Also Athene, Pallas Athena, and a score of other familiar names; Minerva (Roman). One of the twelve Olympians; born out of the head of Zeus. (Milton uses this myth to describe the birth of sin from the head of Satan; *Paradise Lost* ii. 752–758.) Goddess of wisdom, skills, warfare. Many famous stories about her in *Aeneid, Iliad, Homeric Hymns, Odyssey,* Pausanias, Aeschylus' *Eumenides,* Sophocles' *Oedipus,* and many other ancients. Famous in English literature are Byron's *The Curse of Minerva;* Tennyson's "Oenone."

Athena Nike (nī′ kē). Famous temple on the Acropolis, dedicated to Athena as goddess of victory.

Athena Parthenos (par′ the nos). The virgin goddess; the term "Parthenos" means virgin. The name of the ivory-and-gold statue by Phidias, once in the Parthenon. Pausanias gives a wonderful description of the statue. A fine Roman copy is in the National Museum at Athens.

Athens (ath′ enz). Also Athenai, Athinai; Athenae (Roman). The city of Athena; capital of modern Greece. The center of ancient Greek culture, but not so important a place as Thebes, Mycenae, and other cities. Athenian mythology begins with Cecrops; Erichthonius was his successor; other important names associated with Athenian mythology include Theseus (greatest of all Athenian heroes), Aegeus, Pandion, Erechtheus, Philomela, Procne.

Atlantiades (at lan tī′ a dēz). Offspring of Atlas. A patronymic of Hermes, the Pleiades, and the Hesperides as offspring of Atlas.

Atlantides (at lan′ ti dēz). The seven daughters of Atlas by Pleione, daughter of Oceanus. Also called Pleiades or Pleiads. Their names were Alcyone, Celaeno, Electra, Maia, Merope, Sterope (Asterope), and Taygete.

Atlas (at′ las). A Titan; son of Iapetus and Clymene; brother of Prometheus, Epimetheus, and Menoetius. Held the heavens on his shoulders. He was tricked into giving Heracles three of the golden apples of the Hesperides. Turned to stone by Perseus. *Aeneid* iv; Apollodorus i; *Met.* iv; *Theogony.*

Atreus (ā′ trūs; ā′ trē us). Son of Pelops and Hippodamia; brother of Thyestes, Chrysippus, Troezen, and Pittheus. Father of Agamemnon and Menelaus by Aerope. Shocked the gods by feeding Thyestes his own child. Tantalus, the son of Zeus, was the founder of this foredoomed family, followed by Pelops, Atreus and Thyestes, Agamemnon and Menelaus, Clytemnestra, Helen, Pelopia, Aegisthus, Orestes, Electra, and Iphigenia. The tragic story of the house of Atreus has been a poetic gold mine for thousands of years. Eight of thirty-three surviving Greek tragedies deal with this family: Aeschylus, *Agamemnon, Choephoroe,* and *Eumenides;* Euripides, *Electra, Iphigenia at Aulis, Iphigenia among the Tauri, Orestes;* Sophocles, *Electra.* Seneca, *Agamemnon, Thyestes;* Alfieri, *Agamemnon, Orestes;* Goethe, *Iphigenie auf Tauris;* Milton, "Pelop's Line"; O'Neill, *Mourning Becomes Electra;* Chaucer, Shakespeare, Rossetti, T. S. Eliot, Jeffers, Crébillon, Giraudoux, Gluck, Hofmannsthal, Racine, Sartre, Voltaire, and many others have made use of this story.

Atridae (a trī′ dē). Also Atrides (a trī′ dēz). A patronymic given by Homer to Agamemnon and Menelaus as sons of Atreus.

Atropos (at′ ro pos). Also Morae; Fatae (Latin); Parcae (Roman). One of the three Fates; the other two are Clotho and Lachesis; daughters of Erebus and Nyx. Atropos carries the shears and cuts the thread of life; Clotho carries the spindle and spins the thread of life; Lachesis carries the globe or scroll and determines the length of the thread of life. The Fates appear in the work of many English poets: Chaucer, Spenser, Shakespeare, Donne, Herbert, Shelley, Byron, Browning, Marlowe, Tennyson, Hardy, Henley.

Attica (at′ i ka). The region of the Greek peninsula that includes Athens and Eleusis. The name came from Atthis, daughter of Cranaus.

Auge (o′ jē). Also Augea, Auga. 1. An Arcadian princess, priestess of Athena; violated by Heracles, she became the mother of Telephus. 2. Auge was originally a name of Artemis, worshiped in Arcadia as goddess of childbirth. Apollodorus ii, iii; Pausanias viii. 3. The heroine of a lost play by Euripides.

Augean Stables (o jē′ an). Cleaning these stables in a single day was the sixth labor of Heracles. The stables contained three thousand cattle, and had not been cleaned for thirty years. Heracles diverted the rivers Alpheus and Peneus to wash away the dirt. The term "Augean stable" is now applied to anything filthy.

Augeas (o′ jē as). King of Elis, owner of the Augean stables. Did not keep his promise to give Heracles one tenth of his herds for cleaning the stables. Joined the expedition of the Argonauts. Apollodorus ii.

Aulis (o′ lis). The port in Boeotia from which twenty-seven groups of Greeks (Boeotians, Locrians, Athenians, Lacedaemonians, Mycenaeans, Spartans, etc.) with a total of 1,116 ships sailed for Troy and the start of the Trojan War. *Aeneid* iv; *Iliad* ii; *Met.* xii.

Aura (o′ ra). Daughter of Eos (Aurora); goddess of the breeze.

Aurora (o rō′ ra); **Eos** (Greek). Daughter of Hyperion and Thia (Thea); some legends say she was the daughter of Uranus and Gaea. Goddess of the dawn. Her love affair with TITHONUS, q.v., is famous. *Aeneid* vi; Apollodorus i; *Iliad* viii; *Met.* iii; *Odyssey* x; *Theogony*.

Ausonia (o sō′ ni a). One of the ancient names of Italy, from Auson, a son of Odysseus. Aeneas speaks of Ausonia in *Aeneid* iii.

Auster (os′ ter); **Notus** (Greek). The south (strictly speaking, southwest) wind.

Autolycus (o tol′ i kus). 1. Son of Hermes by Chione, a daughter of Deucalion. He was a famous thief—stole the cattle of Sisyphus, and changed their identifying marks. 2. One of the Argonauts. Apollodorus i; *Met.* i; *Odyssey* xiv.

Automedon (o tom′ e don). Went to the Trojan War with ten ships. Charioteer of Achilles and later of Pyrrhus. *Aeneid* ii; *Iliad* ix.

Autonoe (o ton′ o ē). Daughter of Cadmus; sister of Agave. Wife of Aristaeus; mother of Actaeon and Macris. *Met.* iii.

Aventine (av′ en tīn). **Aventinus** (Latin). **Aventino** (Italian). One of the seven hills of Rome. The others are: Caelian, Capitoline, Esquiline, Palatine, Quirinal, and Viminal.

Avernus (a ver′ nus). Also Averno. A lake the ancients considered to be the entrance to hell. From a cave in this lake Aeneas entered Hades. *Aeneid* iv.

Axine (ak′ sīn; ak′ sin). Also Euxine. The friendly sea, now called the Black Sea. This sea was first called Axeinus, which means unfriendly, because the inhabitants of its coasts were very savage. After the arrival of foreigners had made the natives friendlier, the sea was called Euxenus, which means hospitable.

B

Baalbek (bal′ bek). Modern name for HELIOPOLIS, q.v. A town in ancient Syria, thirty-four miles from Damascus. A center of the worship of the sun god Baal, and today notable for its ruins of the temples of Aphrodite, Dionysus, and Zeus.

Babylon (bab′ i lon). 1. A son of Belus who founded the city that bears his name. 2. Home of Queen SEMIRAMIS, q.v. 3. Home of Pyramus and Thisbe. 4. Ancient city of Mesopotamia, capital of Babylonia, on the Euphrates River (possibly the biblical Babel), famous for its Hanging Gardens. 5. The city of Babylon is historically associated with Nebuchadnezzar, Cyrus, Xerxes, Darius the Great, and Alexander the Great.

Bacchae (bak' ē). Also Bacchantes. Priestesses (followers) of Dionysus, the god of wine.

Bacchae, The. A play by Euripides.

Bacchanalia (bak a nā' li a). Festivals in honor of Dionysus.

Bacchus (bak' us). The Roman name for Dionysus (Greek), god of wine. Son of Zeus and Semele, a daughter of Cadmus. His amours were not numerous. He married Ariadne after she had been forsaken on Naxos by Theseus, and they had many children. Many of the ancients have written stories about Bacchus—Apollodorus, Euripides, Herodotus, Homer, Ovid, Pausanias, Seneca, Vergil, and others.

Balius (bā' li us). One of the immortal horses that belonged to Achilles. The name of its mate was Xanthus. Offspring of Podarge (a harpy) and Zephyrus (the west wind). *Iliad* xvi.

Bassarides (bas' a ri dēz). Also Bassarids (bas' ar idz). Names for followers of Dionysus (Bacchus).

Batia (ba tī' a). 1. Daughter of Teucer; wife of Dardanus. 2. Wife of Oebalus; mother of Hippocoon.

Baton (bā' ton). Charioteer of Amphiaraus, whom he accompanied in the war of the Seven against Thebes.

Battus (bat' us). 1. A shepherd of Pylos who saw Hermes steal the cattle of Apollo; he promised not to tell, but broke his promise and was changed into a stone. *Met.* ii. 2. A Lacedaemonian advised by the oracle at Delphi to build the town of Cyrene. Herodotus; Pausanias.

Baucis and Philemon (bo' sis; fi lē' mon). Entertained the gods Zeus and Hermes most hospitably in their humble cottage in Phrygia. As a reward for this kindness their cottage was changed into a beautiful golden-roofed marble temple. Baucis and Philemon desired to die at the same time, and their bodies were changed into trees, an oak and a linden. *Met.* viii.

Bear, Great. Also Ursa Major (ur′ sa). The Big Dipper. See ARCAS.

Bear, Little. Also Ursa Minor. The Little Dipper. See ARCAS.

Bebryces (beb rī′ sēz). A country in Asia where Amycus, son of Poseidon and a famous boxer, was king. The Argonauts, on their way to Colchis, visited these people, where Amycus challenged all comers to a boxing match and was killed by Polydeuces. Apollodorus i; *Argonautica* ii.

Bellerophon (be ler′ o fon). Grandson of Sisyphus; son of Glaucus and Eurymede. One of the seven great destroyers of monsters; slayer of the Chimera; conqueror of the Solymi and the Amazons. Tried to fly to heaven on the winged horse Pegasus and perished. Apollodorus ii; *Iliad* vi; Pausanias ix; *Theogony;* William Morris, *The Earthly Paradise.*

Bellona (be lō′ na). Also Enyo (Greek). Roman goddess of war. Some legends say she was the wife of Ares (Mars); others that she was his sister. *Aeneid* viii; Pausanias iv; *Theogony.*

Belus, Belos (bē′ lus). 1. A king of ancient Babylon. 2. A king of Egypt; son of Poseidon and Libya; twin of Agenor; father of the famous twins Aegyptus and Danaus; some legends say he was the father of Dido and of Agenor. 3. A son of Phoenix.

Berenice (ber e nī′ se). 1. A woman very famous for her beauty. 2. A woman who married her own brother. 3. The word "Berenice" means bringer of victory.

Beroe (ber′ o ē). 1. An old woman of Epidaurus; nurse of Semele, the beautiful daughter of Cadmus and Harmonia, and mother of Dionysus by Zeus. *Met.* iii. 2. A woman whose form was assumed by Iris when she advised the Trojans to burn their ships while Aeneas and his followers were celebrating the funeral games of Anchises. *Aeneid* v.

Bia (bī′ a). A daughter of Pallas and Styx, who was ordered by Hephaestus to bind Prometheus to a rock in the Caucasus as punishment for his theft of fire from heaven for mankind. Apollodorus i.

Bias (bī′ as). 1. A king of Argos; son of Amythaon and Idomene; brother of the soothsayer Melampus. Bias fell in love with Pero, daughter of King Neleus of Pylos, and married her after he delivered some stolen cattle to Neleus. Apollodorus i; *Odyssey* xi; Pausanias ii. 2. One of the seven wise men (sages) of Greece. The other six were Chilon, Cleobulus, Periander, Pittacus, Solon, and Thales.

Bibliotheca (bib li o thē′ ka). Also *Library*. A work by Apollodorus; three books, it contains a history of the gods and is an important source of mythology.

Biblis (bib′ lis). Also Byblis, Byblos, Byblus. 1. A woman who fell in love with her twin brother Caunus. She was changed into a fountain. *Met.* ix. 2. An ancient city in Phoenicia which, some accounts say, is the oldest city in the world. Ruins of a large temple of Adonis are there.

Bifrons (bī′ fronz). JANUS, q.v., acquainted with both the past and the future. The word "bifrons" means two fronts or faces. *Aeneid* vii.

Birds, The. A comedy by Aristophanes; probably his masterpiece. Contains much mythological material.

Biton and **Cleobis** (bī′ ton; klē′ o bis). Herodotus tells the story of these two sons of Cydippe, who pulled their mother's chariot to the acclamations of the multitude when no oxen were available. The mother requested of Hera, whose priestess she was at Argos, the greatest gift that could be granted a mortal, and the sons slept and awoke no more. "Call no man happy until he is dead," Sophocles.

Blessed Isles. Also ELYSIAN FIELDS, q.v., Elysium. Heaven, paradise.

Boeotia (bē ō' sha). Greek province, whose capital was Thebes. In Boeotia were Mount Helicon, frequented by the Muses, and the port of Aulis, from which the Greeks sailed for Troy. Famous natives of this province are Hesiod, Pindar, and Plutarch.

Bona Dea (bō' na dē' a). Also Cybele, Ops, Rhea, Vesta; Fauna, Fatua (Roman). Goddess of fecundity and fertility worshiped only by women. Female counterpart of PAN (*Faunus,* Roman), q.v., the god of fertility. Bona Dea was so chaste that no man but her husband saw her after her marriage. Ovid, *Ars Amoris.*

Boreas (bō' re as). Also Aquilo. The north wind. Apollodorus iii; Herodotus; *Iliad* xx; *Met.* vi; *Theogony.*

Bosphorus (bos' fo rus). Also Bosporus (bos' po rus). The strait that connects the Euxine (Black) Sea and the Propontis Sea (Sea of Marmara) and separates Asia from Europe. The Argonauts passed through this strait.

Briareus (brī ar' e us). Also Aegaeon. One of the three Hecatoncheires, the hundred-handed Giants; son of Uranus and Gaea; brother of Cottus and Gyges. The gods called him Briareus, mortals used the name Aegaeon. Some legends say the Giants had one hundred hands and fifty heads. *Aeneid* vi; Apollodorus i; *Iliad* i; *Theogony.*

Briseis (brī sē' is). A Trojan girl captured by the Greeks and given to Achilles. When Agamemnon demanded her from him, Achilles refused to take further part in the Trojan War. *Iliad* i; *Heroides* iii.

Briseus (brī' sūs). Father of Briseis.

Britomartis (brit o mar' tis). Daughter of Zeus and Charme. Cretan nymph who served Artemis, goddess of hunters, fishers, and sailors. Loved and pursued by Minos, she threw herself into the sea to avoid him. Pausanias ii.

Brize (brī' zē). The gadfly sent by Hera to torture Io.

Bromius (brō' mi us). A surname of Bacchus. *Met.* iv.

Brontes (bron′ tēz). One of the three Cyclops (Cyclopes); had one eye in the middle of the forehead. Son of Uranus and Gaea; brother of Arges and Steropes. *Aeneid* viii.

Bronze (Brass, Brazen) Age. The third of four ages of mankind. Hesiod says there were five ages—he includes a heroic age. In the bronze age men ate flesh and fought one another all the time. The other ages were gold, silver, iron.

Broteas (brot′ e as). 1. Son of Tantalus and brother of Pelops. 2. A man famous for his skill with boxing gloves. He and his brother Ammon, also a skillful boxer, remained undefeated.

Brutus (broō′ tus). In medieval, not classical, legend, a great-grandson of Aeneas and first king of Britain.

Bubona (bū bō′ na). See EPONA.

Bucephalus (bū sef′ a lus). The favorite war horse of Alexander the Great. The horse's head resembled that of a bull; the horse always knelt for his master to mount. At the age of thirty the horse died, and Alexander built a city which was named for it—Bucephalia (now Jhelum) in India.

Busiris (bū sī′ ris). An Egyptian king and despot who sacrificed strangers entering his realm. Heracles killed him. Apollodorus; Herodotus; Ovid.

Butes (bū′ tēz). 1. Son of Pandion; brother of Erechtheus, Philomela, and Procne. 2. An Argonaut. Apollodorus iii. 3. A son of Boreas.

Buto (bū′ tō). Egyptian goddess, mother of the sun and moon. Considered by the Greeks to be the same as Latona (Leto).

Byblis (bib′ lis). See BIBLIS.

C

Cabiri (ka bī′ rī). Ancient secret mystery rites, second only to the Eleusinian, held in high veneration in parts of

Greece, Samothrace, Lemnos, Thebes, Macedonia, and Phrygia. Some accounts say only two deities, Zeus and Dionysus, were worshiped; others mention three and four deities. Herodotus; Pausanias; Strabo.

Caca (kā′ ka). Ancient Roman goddess of the hearth, later supplanted by Vesta.

Cacus (kā′ kus). Son of Hephaestus and Medusa, a Giant represented as three-headed, half-human, vomiting flames. A famous thief, he stole some of the cattle of Geryon from Heracles. Heracles went to the cave of Cacus, found his stolen cattle, and slew the Giant. *Aeneid* viii.

Cadmea (kad mē′ a). Also Cadmeia. The name of the citadel or acropolis of Thebes, named after Cadmus, the founder of Thebes. Sometimes the name is used for Thebes itself, and the Thebans are then called Cadmeans. Statius, *Thebiad;* Chaucer, *Troilus and Criseyde.*

Cadmus (kad′ mus). Son of Agenor, king of Phoenicia, and Telephassa (Argiope). Brother of Europa, Cilix, and Phoenix. Famous for the search for his sister Europa whom Zeus had carried away. Overcame a dragon at Thebes with the assistance of Athena; sowed the dragon's teeth on the plain. Immediately a company of armed men, "Spartae," sprang up, ready for attack. Cadmus cast a stone into their midst; in the resulting confusion all but five of the warriors slew each other. The survivors became allies of Cadmus and helped him build Thebes. He married Harmonia, daughter of Aphrodite, and had a son, Polydorus, and four daughters: Agavis, Autonoe, Ino, and Semele. Cadmus was the first to introduce the use of letters into Greece. In Illyria, Cadmus and Harmonia were changed into beautiful spotted snakes. Herodotus; *Met.* iii; *Theogony.*

Caduceus (ka dū′ se us; ka dū′ shus). The messenger's golden staff, rod, or wand, with serpents intertwined on top. The staff was given to Hermes (Mercury) by Apollo in return for the lyre. *Aeneid* iv.

Caelian Hill (sē′ li an). One of the seven hills of Rome. See AVENTINE.

Caeneus (sē′ nūs). **1.** A Thessalian woman, daughter of Poseidon and Elatus; she obtained from Poseidon the power to change her sex, and she became an invulnerable warrior among the Lapithae; she changed her name from Caenis to Caeneus. In the battle of the Lapithae against the Centaurs, she offended Zeus, and in punishment she was buried under a huge pile of pine trees and changed into a bird. *Aeneid* vi; *Met.* xii. **2.** One of the Argonauts. **3.** A Trojan killed by Turnus. *Aeneid*.

Caenis (sē′ nis). See CAENEUS.

Caesar (sē′ zar). Twelve Roman emperors had the surname Caesar. In *Aeneid* vi, Anchises sees the unborn soul of the Roman hero Augustus Caesar.

Caieta (kā yē′ ta). Aeneas' old nurse. *Aeneid* vii. A town built at the place where she died received its name from her.

Calais (kal′ a is). The son of Boreas and Orithyia; with his twin brother Zetes (Zethes) he accompanied the Argonauts to Colchis. In Bithynia they were presented with wings for delivering Phineus from the perpetual persecution of the Harpies. They were both killed during the Argonautic expedition and changed into birds. *Met.* viii.

Calchas (kal′ kas). A celebrated soothsayer, son of Thestor, an Argonaut. Went with the Greeks to Troy. Homer called Calchas the wisest of all the soothsayers or seers, "most excellent of augurs, who knew of things that were and that should be and that had been before." *Iliad* i. Calchas foretold: (1) Troy could not be taken without the aid of Achilles. (2) The Greek fleet could not sail from Aulis to Troy unless Iphigenia was sacrificed by Agamemnon to Artemis. (Some accounts, however, say Artemis substituted a ram, and Iphigenia was saved.) (3) The plague in the Greek army could not be stopped until Chryseis was restored to her father. (4) Troy could not be taken without a siege of ten years. Calchas was informed that as soon as he found a man more skilled than himself in divination he must perish, and this happened near Colophon, after the Trojan War. He was unable to tell how many figs were in the branches of a certain fig tree, and when Mopsus mentioned the exact number, Calchas died of grief. Aeschylus, *Agamemnon;* Euripides, *Iphigenia in Aulis.*

Caletor (ka lē′ tor). A cousin of Hector. He was descended from famous names: Dardanus, Ilus, Tros. In the Trojan War he tried to set fire to the ship of Protesilaus, but was killed by Telamonian (Greater) Ajax. *Iliad* xv.

Callidice (ka lid′ i sē). Some legends say that after the Trojan War, on his return to Ithaca, Odysseus married the queen of Thesprotia, Callidice. He became king of Thesprotia and had a son, Polypoetes, by Callidice. After her death Odysseus gave the throne to Polypoetes and returned to Ithaca.

Calliope (ka lī′ o pē). Daughter of Zeus and Mnemosyne. The Muse of epic or heroic poetry. Mother of Orpheus by Apollo. Horace says she could play any musical instrument. (The other eight Muses are Clio, Erato, Euterpe, Melpomene, Polyhymnia or Polymnia, Terpsichore, Thalia, Urania.)

Callirrhoe (ka lir′ o ē). 1. A daughter of Scamander; married Tros, by whom she had Assarcus, Ganymede, and Ilus. She was an ancestor of Aeneas. 2. The name of the fountain in Attica where Callirrhoe killed herself. Pausanias vii. 3. A daughter of Oceanus and Tethys; mother of Echidna, Orthus, and Cerberus by Chrysaor. Hesiod. 4. A daughter of Lycus, tyrant of Libya, who received Diomedes warmly after his return from Troy. When Diomedes abandoned her, Callirrhoe took her own life. 5. A daughter of Achelous; married Alcmaeon, one of the Epigoni; mother of ACARNAN, q.v. Pausanias viii. 6. A daughter of Niobe.

Callisto (ka lis′ tō). See ARCAS.

Calpe (kal′ pē). A mountain in Spain, opposite Mount Abyla on the coast of Africa. The two mountains, Calpe and Abyla, were called the Pillars of Heracles; Heracles had erected these pillars while on his journey to fetch the cattle of Geryon. Calpe is now called Gibraltar.

Calyce (kal' i sē). A daughter of Aeolus; mother of Endymion. Apollodorus i; Pausanias v.

Calydon (kal' i don). 1. The grandson of Endymion. 2. The town in Greece where the Calydonian boar was hunted.

Calydonian Boar Hunt (kal' i dō' ni an). Calydonia was ruled by Oeneus and his wife Althea; their son was Meleager. When Oeneus neglected to recognize the divinity of Artemis, she sent a wild boar to ravage the country. The princes of the age assembled to hunt this boar. Meleager killed the animal with his own hands and gave its head to Atalanta, with whom he was in love. This action caused a quarrel over the spoils, and as a result Meleager killed his uncles Plexippus and Toxeus, the brothers of Althea. Among the heroes of the age present for the hunt were Castor and Polydeuces; Jason; Theseus and his friend Pirithous; Peleus, father of Achilles; Telamon, father of Ajax; Amphiaraus of the Seven against Thebes; Admetus; the huntress Atalanta; and the two brothers of Althea, Plexippus and Toxeus, uncles of Meleager. Some accounts say this story of the hunt is fourth in importance of the great incidents and heroic rallying points of Greek myth; the other three stories, in the order of their importance, are: (1) The Fall of Troy, (2) The Seven against Thebes, (3) The Argonauts, or the Search for the Golden Fleece. Apollodorus; Homer; Hyginus; Ovid; Pausanias; Strabo; Swinburne, "Atalanta in Calydon."

Calypso (ka lip' sō). A daughter of Atlas. Some legends say she was a daughter of Oceanus and Thetis. She lived on the island of Ogygia, where Odysseus was shipwrecked. She received him hospitably and offered him immortality if he would remain with her. Odysseus refused, but stayed seven years and had two sons by her. At his departure she was inconsolable. *Odyssey* vii, xv; *Theogony*.

Camenae (ka mē' nē). Latin name for the Muses. The Camenae were fountain nymphs, goddesses of prophecy and of healing; they were later identified fully with the Muses.

Camilla (ka mil' a). A daughter of Metabus. When she was young, her father dedicated her to the service of Artemis. She became a virgin warrior and queen of the Volsci (Volscians). She assisted Turnus against Aeneas. She fought with one breast bared to give freedom to her bow arm. She was a swift runner, comparable to Atalanta. She was killed by the spear of Aruns. *Aeneid* vii, xi.

Campus Martius (kam' pus mar' shi us; mar' shus). The Field of Mars in Rome—dedicated to Mars (Ares). Roman youths performed exercises on the field—wrestled, boxed, hurled the javelin, threw the discus, rode horses, drove chariots. The place was adorned with arches, columns, porticos, and statues.

Canace (kan' a sē). Also Canache (kan' a kē). One of the six daughters of Aeolus and Enaretta (Enarete). She had a child by her brother Macareus. At the command of her father she killed herself. Apollodorus i; *Heroides* xi.

Cancer (kan' ser). 1. The Crab, the fourth sign of the zodiac, into which the sun enters June 22. 2. A crab which battled Heracles as he attacked the Lernean Hydra, his second labor.

Canens (kan' enz). Daughter of Janus; wife of Picus. Picus was changed by Circe into a purple woodpecker because he spurned her love. Canens grieved for him so much in seeking him six days and nights that she literally dissolved in tears. *Met.* xiv.

Capaneus (kap' a nūs; ka pā' ne us). One of the Seven against Thebes. When he boasted that even Zeus could not stop him from entering Thebes, Zeus killed him with a thunderbolt. (The six others in the Seven against Thebes are Adrastus, Amphiaraus, Hippomedon, Parthenopaeus, Polynices, and Tydeus.) Aeschylus, *Seven against Thebes;* Euripides, *The Suppliant Women; Met.* ix.

Capitol (kap′ i tol). A temple of incredible magnificence and riches, dedicated to Jupiter (Zeus) in Rome. *Aeneid* vi.

Capitoline (kap′ i to līn). 1. A chief museum of antiquities in Rome. 2. Smallest of the seven hills of Rome, associated with Zeus and other gods. See AVENTINE.

Capricorn (kap′ ri korn). Also Capricornus. The Goat, the tenth sign of the zodiac, which the sun enters December 22.

Capys (ka′ pis). 1. Son of Assaracus; father of Anchises; grandfather of Aeneas. 2. One of the Trojans who mistrusted the Wooden Horse. Later he went with Aeneas to Italy and founded the city of Capua.

Caria (kā′ ri a). A section of Asia Minor that contained the cities of Miletus, Halicarnassus, Cnidus, the river Maeander, and Mount Latmos. On Mount Latmos ENDYMION, q.v., sleeps immortally.

Carme (kar′ mē). Also Charmel. A nymph and attendant of Artemis; mother of Britomartis by Zeus.

Carmenta (kar men′ ta). Also Postverta, NICOSTRATA, q.v. A fountain nymph; goddess of healing and of the future; one of the Camenae. *Aeneid* viii.

Carpo (kar′ pō). One of the goddesses of the Seasons. See HORAE.

Carthage (kar′ thij). One of the most famous cities of the ancient world, situated on the north coast of Africa. The Carthaginians were formidable rivals of the Romans, with whom they fought the three Punic Wars. The first began in 264 B.C., the second in 218 B.C., the third in 149 B.C., when Carthage was destroyed and captured. Mythology relates that Carthage was established by Queen Dido, who welcomed Aeneas, fell in love with him, and committed suicide when he deserted her after little more than one year. *Aeneid* i.

Carya (kar′ i a). A city in Laconia named after Carya, a girl with whom Dionysus was in love. When she died, she was changed into a walnut tree.

Caryatis (kar i at′ is). Also Caryatids (kar i at′ idz). Caryatis was the name given Artemis when she reported the death of the Laconian girl Carya. The literal meaning of the word "Caryatis" is "of the walnut tree." Female statues which served as columns of temples, most notably those of the Erechtheum on the Acropolis in Athens, were called Caryatids.

Cassandra (ka san′ dra). Also Alexandra. One of the twelve daughters of Priam and Hecuba of Troy. The twin of Helenus, she had fifty brothers. She was the most beautiful of Priam's daughters and was courted by many princes. Apollo loved her and promised to give her what she desired if she would gratify his passion. She asked for the power of prophecy, but as soon as she obtained the gift, refused to fulfill the bargain. Apollo could not withdraw the gift of prophecy he had granted her, but he wet her lips with his tongue, thus effecting a curse that no reliance would ever be placed upon her predictions. She would indeed be able to foretell the future, but no credence would ever be given to her prophecy. Her name has become synonymous with prophets of doom whose warnings are heeded too late. The Trojans thought she was insane, and among her predictions that were disregarded were: (1) If Paris went to Sparta, Troy would be destroyed. (Paris abducted Helen from Sparta.) (2) The Trojan War would end in disaster for Troy. (3) There were armed Greeks in the Wooden Horse. (4) Hecuba would be changed into a female dog. (5) She herself would be carried away into slavery. (6) Agamemnon had lost what he loved most—his wife and children. (7) The death of Agamemnon. (8) ORESTES, q.v., would avenge the death of his father. *Iliad* vi, xiii; *Aeneid* ii; *Odyssey* iv; Pausanias i; Chaucer, *Troilus and Crisyede;* Shakespeare, *Troilus and Cressida;* Meredith, "Cassandra"; Byron, *Don Juan;* Tennyson, "Oenone"; Robinson Jeffers, "Cassandra."

Cassiopeia (kas i o pē′ a). Also Cassiepea, Cassiope, Cassi-
opea. Mother of Andromeda by Cepheus, king of Joppa
in Ethiopia. She angered Poseidon when she boasted that
she was more beautiful than the Nereids, and he sent a
huge sea monster to ravage Ethiopia. Cassiopeia was
made a northern constellation, containing the thirteen
stars called Cassiopeia; the five brightest stars in the
constellation resemble a chair, hence Cassiopeia's Chair.
Met. iv.

Castalia (kas tā′ li a; –tāl ya). A nymph, daughter of
Achelous, pursued by Apollo. She was turned into a
spring on Mount Parnassus; the spring thereafter was
called Castalia and became sacred to Apollo and the
Muses.

Castalides (kas tal′ i dēz). A name for the nine Muses, derived from the spring Castalia.

Castor and **Pollux** (kas′ ter; pol′ uks). Twin brothers, sons
of Leda, wife of King Tyndareus of Sparta. To entice
Leda, Zeus had changed himself into a beautiful swan.
The twins had two sisters, Helen and Clytemnestra. Pollux (Polydeuces) and Helen were the offspring of Zeus;
Castor and Clytemnestra were the offspring of Tyndareus. All four children were destined for fame. Castor
became an excellent horseman; Pollux became an expert
boxer. Both brothers joined the Argonauts and were in
the Calydonian boar hunt. When the twins died they
were placed in heaven as Gemini (Twins), a constellation which became the third sign of the zodiac, which
the sun enters May 21. *Aeneid* vi; *Met.* vi; Euripides,
Helen; The Homeric Hymns; Spenser, "Prothalamion."

Castores (kas tor′ ēz). Roman name for CASTOR, q.v.

Cattle of Geryon (jē′ ri on). Also Geryones. Captured by
Heracles as his tenth labor. Geryon was a celebrated
monster, son of Chrysaor and Callirrhoe; he had three
bodies and three heads; he was the owner of large flocks
which were guarded by a two-headed dog named Orthos
and by a shepherd named Eurythion. By order of Eurystheus, Heracles went to Gades, the home of Geryon,

destroyed him, Orthos, and Eurythion, and carried away all the flocks. *Aeneid* vii; *Theogony*.

Cattle of the Sun. The cattle, sacred to Apollo, lived on the island of Thrinacia, where the men of Odysseus, in spite of his warning, killed and ate some. When the men of Odysseus put out to sea, a storm destroyed the ship, and all were drowned except Odysseus. *Odyssey* xii.

Catullus (ka tul' us). 87–54 B.C. Roman lyric poet who wrote much about mythology. Gayley, "The Wedding of Peleus and Thetis" (translation of Catullus).

Caucasus (ko' ka sus). Also called Caucasus Mountains. Here Zeus chained Prometheus, whose liver was continually devoured by vultures. It is said that Mount Caucasus burned when Phaethon's chariot came too close to the earth. *Aeneid* iv; Herodotus iv.

Caunus (ko' nus) and **Biblis.** Biblis fell passionately in love with her brother Caunus, who resisted her advances and fled to Caria. *Met.* ix.

Caurus (ko' rus). Another name for Zephyrus, the west wind.

Cebren (sē' bren). Father of Asterope. Apollodorus iii.

Cebriones (seb rī' o nēz). Brother and charioteer of Hector.

Cecropia (sē krō' pī a). Original name for Athens, in honor of Cecrops, its founder. The ancients often used the word for Attica, and the Athenians were called Cecropidae. *Aeneid* vi; *Met.* vii.

Cecropians. Same as Cecropidae. See CECROPIA.

Cecrops (sē' krops). Son of Gaea. The upper half of his body was man, the lower half serpent. The first king of Attica, Cecropia was named in his honor. He had three daughters—Aglauros, Herse, and Pandrosos. He ruled for fifty years. The contest between Athena and Poseidon for the possession of Athens took place during his reign. Poseidon brought a salt-water well as his offering (some legends say a horse). Athena produced the olive tree, and Cecrops instructed his subjects to cultivate the olive and to look upon Athena as the patroness who would watch over their city. Apollodorus iii; Herodotus; *Met.* xi; Pausanias i.

Cedalion (se dā′ li on). A man sent by Hephaestus to carry the blind Orion from Lemnos to the abode of the sun; there Orion's sight was restored by the brilliance of Apollo's light.

Celaeno (se lē′ nō). 1. One of the seven daughters of Atlas and Pleione. From Pleione, the daughters derived the name PLEIADES, q.v. 2. One of the Danaides. 3. One of the Harpies. 4. A daughter of Poseidon and Ergea.

Celeus (sē′ le us; sel′ e us). King of Eleusis who befriended Demeter when she was searching for Persephone. He taught his son agriculture and invented several agricultural instruments. Father of Triptolemus and Demophoon by Meganira. Apollodorus; Ovid; Pausanias; Vergil.

Celmus (sel′ mus). A man who was a playfellow of the child Zeus. He was changed into a magnetic stone for saying Zeus was mortal. *Met.* iv.

Centaurs (sen′ torz). People of Thessaly, half-man, half-horse. CHIRON, q.v., was the most famous of the Centaurs. Their battle with the Lapithae (Lapiths) is famous. *Aeneid* vi; Apollodorus; *Iliad*; *Met.* xii; *Odyssey*; Pausanias.

Centaurus (sen to′ rus). 1. Son of Ixion and Nephele; by various mares he sired the centaurs. 2. A southern constellation between Argo and Scorpio. 3. A ship in the fleet of Aeneas which had as decoration the figure of a centaur. *Aeneid* v.

Centimani (sen tim′ a nī; sen ti mā′ nī). Same as Hecatoncheires. The hundred-handed giants born to Uranus and Gaea. Their names are Briareus, Cottus, Gyges.

Ceos (sē′ os). An island of the Cyclades in the Aegean Sea, birthplace of Simonides, Greek lyric and elegiac poet, and author of the famous lines: "Go, stranger, and to Lacedaemon tell/That here, obeying her behests, we fell," the epitaph for the Spartans who fell at Thermopylae.

Cephallenia (sef a lē′ ni a). Largest of the Ionian islands west of the Greek mainland. In Homer, this island was the center of Ithaca, where Odysseus ruled.

Cephalus and Procris (sef′ a lus; prō′ kris, prok′ ris). Cephalus, son of King Deioneus of Thessaly, married Procris, daughter of King Erechtheus of Athens. Eos (Aurora), goddess of dawn, saw Cephalus, fell in love with him, and spirited him away, only to be spurned. Enraged at his rejection, Eos sent him back to Procris as a stranger and he seduced her. When Cephalus was changed back into his own form, Procris, ashamed that she had yielded, fled and became one of Diana's huntresses. Later the couple were reconciled but Procris was jealous. One morning, as she spied on her husband in the woods, he heard a noise, thought it was a wild animal, and threw a javelin which killed her. *Met*. vii.

Cepheus (sē′ fūs; sē′ fe us). 1. A son of King Belus; brother of Danaus and Aegyptus; father of Andromeda, and one of the Argonauts changed into a constellation after death. *Met*. iv. 2. A son of Aleus who was also an Argonaut and who participated in the Calydonian boar hunt. Apollodorus. 3. The father of Asterope.

Cephissus (se fis′ us). 1. A man who was changed into a sea monster by Apollo. *Met*. vii. 2. The father of Narcissus. 3. Three famous rivers in Greece: in Attica near Eleusis; in Attica near Athens; in Boeotia and in Phocis near the sacred shrine of Delphi and Mount Parnassus. The three Graces were particularly fond of the river near the sacred shrine. *Iliad* ii; *Met*. i; Pausanias ix.

Cer (sēr). Also Ker (kēr). The Greek goddess of violent death. Daughter of Nyx and sister of the Moerae (Parcae, Fates).

Cerambus (se ram′ bus). A man changed into a beetle by nymphs. He flew to Mount Parnassus to escape Zeus' deluge. *Met*. vii.

Ceras (sē′ ras). People of Cyprus changed into bulls.

Cerberus (ser′ ber us). The three-headed dog (Hesiod says he had fifty heads) that guards the entrance to Hades.

He kept the living from entering the infernal regions, but Aeneas, Odysseus, and Orpheus passed him when they visited there. This dog was an offspring of Typhon and Echidna. To bring Cerberus from the underworld was the twelfth labor of Heracles. *Aeneid* v; *Odyssey* xi; Pausanias ii; *Theogony*.

Cercopes (ser kō′ pēz). Men of Lydia, thievish gnomes, who were changed into monkeys by Heracles when they stole his weapons. *Met.* xiv.

Cercyon (sur′ si on). A king of Eleusis who required all strangers to wrestle with him; he defeated all but Theseus and put them to death. Theseus conquered and killed him. *Met.* vii; Apollodorus iii.

Cerealia (sē ri ā′ li a). Festivals at Rome in honor of Ceres.

Ceres (sē′ rēz). Demeter (Greek). Daughter of Cronus and Rhea. One of the twelve great Olympians, and one of the six who were offspring of Cronus and Rhea; the others were three sons—Zeus, Poseidon, Hades—and two other daughters, Hera and Hestia. Ceres was the goddess of agriculture—grain, harvest, fruits, flowers, fertility of the earth. She was greatly grieved when her daughter Persephone (Proserpina) was abducted by Pluto. The marvelous horse Arion was born of her union with Poseidon. The celebration of the Eleusinian Mysteries was held in her honor; her beneficence made her highly respected. Apollodorus, Hesiod, Ovid, Pausanias, and many others.

Cermalus (sur′ ma lus). One of the seven hills of earliest Rome. The others were called Cispius, Fagutal, Oppius, Palatium, Sucusa, and Velia.

Cerynea (sur i nē′ a). A town in Achaea and a mountain in Arcadia.

Cerynean Hind (Stag) (sur i nē′ an). The wonderful stag with golden antlers and brazen hoofs, sacred to Artemis, that roamed in the hills of Cerynea, between Arcadia and Achaea. The capture of this fabled animal was the third (some legends say the fourth) labor of Heracles.

Cerynitia (sur i nish′ a). A forest in Cerynea where Heracles found the Cerynean hind.

Cerynitis (ser i nī′ tis). A sacred hind or stag.

Cestus (ses′ tus). Aphrodite's magic, love-inspiring, beauty-enhancing girdle. Aphrodite (Venus) is represented either entirely naked or with some scanty drapery called a *cestus*. The cestus has played a part in many myths; Hera once borrowed it from Aphrodite to charm Zeus during the Trojan War; this would take his mind off helping the Trojans and give the Greeks a chance to win.

Ceto and **Phorcys** (sē′ tō; for′ sis). A daughter and son of Oceanus (Pontus) and Gaea. By her brother Phorcys, Ceto had many strange offspring: the three Graeae, the three Gorgons, the three Sirens, Scylla, the three Hesperides, Ladon who guarded the Golden Apples, and Echidna. According to Hesiod's *Theogony*, Echidna was the daughter of Callirrhoe.

Ceus (sē′ us). 1. The father of Troezen. *Iliad* ii. 2. A son of Uranus and Gaea, who married Phoebe (Artemis), by whom he had Leto (Latona) and Asteria. *Aeneid* iv; *Theogony*.

Ceyx (sē′ iks) and **Halcyone** (Alcyone). Ceyx is celebrated for his tender love for his wife Alcyone. He was drowned at sea; a dream informed Alcyone of his death. His body was washed ashore, and her grief for him was so great that both Ceyx and she were changed into kingfishers. *Met.* xi. In English poetry, Chaucer, Dryden, Keats, and Milton have used this myth.

Chalciope (kal sī′ o pē). Daughter of Aeetes, king of Colchis; sister of Medea. She married Phryxus (Phrixus) when he arrived in Colchis on the golden-fleeced ram. Chalciope persuaded her sister Medea to help Jason obtain the Golden Fleece, because her four sons, shipwrecked on their way from Colchis to Hellas, had been rescued by Jason and the Argonauts, who were on their way to Colchis in search of the Golden Fleece. *Heroides* xvii.

Chalcis (kal′ sis). **1.** A daughter of Asopus. **2.** Chief city of Euboea, where Aristotle died.

Chaos (kā′ os). The rude and shapeless mass whose appearance could not be described, for there was no light by which it could be seen. It existed before the formation of the universe; and from it a Supreme Power created the world. Hesiod was the first poet to write about Chaos, and succeeding poets have used his conception as the basis for their own interpretations. *Aeneid* iv and *Met.* i present Chaos as one of the oldest of the gods and as one of the deities of the infernal regions. His wife was Nyx or Nox; his son was Erebus (Darkness), who dethroned and supplanted Chaos. Erebus married his mother Nyx, by whom he had two beautiful children, Aether (Light), and Hemera (Day), whose child was Eros (Amor, or Love). Then was created Pontus (the sea). Gaea (Ge, Tellus, Terra) followed, and then came Uranus (Coelus), the overhanging heavens, born of Gaea (the earth; Mother Earth). Gaea united with her son Uranus and produced the first race, the twelve Titans.

Chariclo (ka rik′ lō; kar′ i klō). **1.** A nymph highly favored by Athena. She was the mother of Teiresias the seer. Apollodorus i. **2.** A daughter of Apollo, who married the centaur Chiron. *Met.* ii.

Charis (kā′ ris). A goddess of the Greeks surrounded by delight, graces, and pleasures, who married Haphaestus. Some legends say she was one of the Graces. *Iliad* xviii.

Charites (kar′ i tēz). Also Charities, Graces, Gratiae. Another name for the three Graces (Aglaia, Euphrosyne, and Thalia), daughters of Zeus and Eurynome; other legends say they were the daughters of Helius and Aegle; Zeus and Aphrodite; Dionysus and Aphrodite. They were constant attendants of Aphrodite. Young, beautiful, modest, personifications of gracefulness. Homer speaks of only two Graces. Spenser; Matthew Arnold, "Euphrosyne."

Charme (kar′ mē). Same as CARME, q.v.

Charon (kā′ ron; kar′ on). A god of hell; son of Erebus

and Nyx. For a fee (a coin) placed in the mouth of the dead at the time of burial, he would ferry the souls over the rivers Acheron and Styx to the infernal regions. Those not honored with a funeral, however, were condemned to wander on the shore for a hundred years before they were permitted to enter the boat. Few passed **Charon** without proper burial. Exceptions were Orpheus who charmed him with his lyre; Heracles who terrified him; Aeneas who bribed him with the Golden Bough; and Odysseus who descended into hell to discourse with the ghosts of deceased heroes. Some mythologists write of several back entrances to the infernal regions where Charon and his fee could be avoided. *Aeneid* vi; Seneca, *Hercules.*

Charybdis (ka rib′ dis). A monster, the daughter of Poseidon and Gaea. Zeus threw her into the sea where she gulps waters eternally and spews them out again. She stole the oxen of Heracles. Later, Charybdis was identified with a dangerous whirlpool off the coast of Italy, opposite the rocky cave where the monster Scylla lived. This place proved fatal to a part of the fleet of Odysseus. "Between Scylla and Charybdis" has come to mean "to avoid one evil, we fall into a greater." *Aeneid* iii; *Odyssey* xii.

Cheiron. See CHIRON.

Chelone (ke lō′ nē). A nymph changed into a tortoise for refusing to attend the nuptials of Zeus and Hera. She was condemned to perpetual silence for ridiculing these deities.

Children of Heracles. See HERACLIDAE.

Chilon (ki′ lon). Also Chilo (ki′ lo). One of the seven sages (wise men) of Greece.

Chimaera (kī mē′ ra). Also Chimera. A fire-breathing monster with the head of a lion, the body of a goat, and the tail of a serpent. Slain by Bellerophon. The Sphinx and the Nemean Lion were offspring of the Chimaera and Orthos. According to Hesiod, the Chimaera was the daughter of Hydra, but others name the Chimaera as the daughter of Typhon and Echidna. Apollodorus i; *Aeneid* vi; *Iliad* vi; *Met.* iv; *Theogony.*

Chione (kī′ o nē). 1. A daughter of Daedalion, loved and visited by Apollo and Hermes on the same night. She gave birth to twin sons: Autolycus (notorious for his robberies) by Hermes, and Philammon (famous musician) by Apollo. Chione was proud of her association with the gods and preferred her beauty to that of Artemis. She was killed by the goddess and changed into a hawk. *Met.* xi. 2. A daughter of Boreas and Orithyia, and mother of Eumolpus by Poseidon. When she threw her son into the sea, Poseidon saved him. Apollodorus iii; Pausanias i.

Chios (kī′ os). Greek island in the Aegean Sea named for Chione. Chios is famous for its harbor that can accommodate eighty ships. It has always been famous for its wine and fruit. According to ancient writers (Pausanias, Strabo) no adultery was committed on this island for seven hundred years.

Chiron (kī′ ron). Also Cheiron. Stories of parentage vary: Cronus and Philyra; Zeus was the father; Ixion and Nephele. Chiron was the one gentle, learned, wise member of the centaurs, half-man, half-horse. Famous for his knowledge of medicine, music, shooting; taught mankind the use of plants and medicinal herbs; instructed the greatest heroes of the age in many polite arts: Achilles, Aeneas, Asclepius, Heracles, Jason, Peleus. Chiron had nothing in common with his fellow centaurs except his appearance. *Aeneid* vi; Apollodorus ii; *Iliad* xi; *Met.* ii; Pausanias iii; Arnold, "Empedocles on Etna."

Chloris (klō′ ris). Flora (Roman). Goddess of flowers. Daughter of Amphion and Niobe, married Zephyrus. Some legends say she married Neleus, king of Pylos, was the mother of Nestor, eleven other sons, and one daughter. All her sons except Nestor were killed by Heracles. *Odyssey* xi; Pausanias ii; Herrick, "Corinna's Going A-Maying."

Choephoroe, The (ko ef' o rē). Also called *The Libation Bearers*. A tragedy by Aeschylus.

Chromios (krō' mi os). Also Chromius. An Argive who with Alcenor and one other, survived a battle between three hundred Argives and three hundred Spartans. Herodotus i. See also ALCENOR.

Chronos (krō' nos). Also Chronus; Saturn (Roman). God of time.

Chrysaor (krī sā' or; kris' a or). Son of Medusa and Poseidon; he sprang full-grown from the body of Medusa when Perseus cut off her head. According to Hesiod, Chrysaor was the father of Echidna and Geryon by Callirrhoe, and—according to other mythologists—he was also the father of the Chimera. *Theogony*.

Chryse (krī' sē). Same as Comana. A city of Cappadocia, notorious for its temple full of thousands of prostitutes.

Chryseis (krī sē' is). A daughter of Chryses, a priest of Apollo. She was captured by Achilles but awarded to Agamemnon. Apollo sent a plague to avenge her capture, and the Greeks were compelled to return Chryseis to her father. Then Agamemnon took Briseis, another captive of Achilles, and the famous quarrel resulted. Achilles, angry because he had lost both Briseis and Chryseis, withdrew from the Trojan War. *Iliad* i; Graves, *The Anger of Achilles*. See also PATROCLUS.

Chryses (krī' sēz). Father of Chryseis.

Chrysippus (krī sip' pus). A natural son of Pelops, highly favored by his father, was carried away to Thebes by Laius, whereupon Hera sent the Sphinx to punish Thebes. Hippodamia, wife of Pelops, killed Chrysippus because she was afraid the kingdom would go to him instead of to her own sons, Atreus and Thyestes. Apollodorus iii; Pausanias vi.

Chrysothemis (kri soth' e mis). 1. Homer's name for IPHIGENIA, q.v., daughter of Agamemnon and Clytemnestra; sister of Electra and Orestes. *Iliad* ix. 2. Pausanias gives this name to a Cretan who won the first poetical or musical prize in the Pythian games. Pausanias x.

Chthonius (tho' ni us). One of the SPARTAE, q.v.

Cicones (sik' o nēz). Also Ciconians (si kō' ni anz). Inhabitants of Thrace encountered by Odysseus on his way home from Troy. He plundered Ismarus, their chief city, and in revenge the Cicones killed six men from each of Odysseus' ships. Odysseus was angry because the Cicones had aided the Trojans. *Met.* x; *Odyssey* ix.

Cilicia (si lish' i a). A province in Asia Minor between Aeolia and Troas, named after Cilix. He and his brothers Cadmus and Phoenix, accompanied by their mother Telephassa, set out to find his sister Europa who had been kidnapped by Zeus. They were unsuccessful until Cadmus consulted the oracle at Delphi which said, "Follow the cow, and settle where she rests." Apollodorus iii; Herodotus ii.

Cilissa (sī lis' a). 1. The nurse of Orestes, who placed her own son in Orestes' bed to be murdered by Aegisthus. 2. A town in Phrygia.

Cilix (sil' iks; sī' liks). A son of Agenor and Telephassa (some legends say of Phoenix); brother of Cadmus, Phoenix, Phineus, Thasus, and Europa. See also CILICIA.

Cimmeria (si mir' i a). A land of perpetual darkness, visited by Odysseus on his way home from Troy.

Cimmerians (si mer' i anz). A people who live in perpetual darkness beyond the great river Oceanus on the western coast of Italy. Homer drew his images of hell and Pluto from this dark, gloomy country, and Vergil and Ovid placed the rivers of the infernal regions in Cimmeria. *Aeneid* vi; *Met.* xi; *Odyssey* xiii.

Cimon (sī' mon). 1. A ruler of Athens who brought from Skyros a gigantic skeleton, believed to be that of Theseus, which was laid with great solemnity in a specially built shrine called the Theseum. This Cimon, a historical figure, was the son of Miltiades, who won the battle of Marathon. 2. The father of Miltiades. Herodotus and

Thucydides tell the story of Cimon, Miltiades, and Marathon.

Cinyras (sin' i ras). King of Cyprus, son of Paphus, descendant of Pygmalion and Galatea. His daughter Myrrha, whose mother had boasted that she was more beautiful than Aphrodite herself, was cursed by the vengeful goddess with an uncontrollable passion for her father. Through a trick of her nurse, Myrrha shared her father's bed night after night, although Cinyras did not realize who she was. When he discovered the truth, he threatened to kill Myrrha, and when she fled he killed himself. As a result of this incest, Myrrha became pregnant; she was changed into a myrrha tree, the trunk of which was split by the goddess of childbirth, and her son Adonis emerged. *Met.* x.

Circe (sur' se). Daughter of the sun god Helius (Hyperion) and Perseis; sister of Aeetes and Pasiphae; married a prince of Colchis whom she murdered in order to obtain his kingdom, and was expelled by her subjects and carried by her father to the island of Aeaea. Circe was an enchantress celebrated for her knowledge of magic and venomous herbs. She used her skill for evil purposes and was noted for her cruelty. Odysseus, returning from the Trojan War, visited her on Aeaea, and all his companions (except Eurylochus, who did not taste the potions of Circe) were changed into swine. Odysseus, fortified by a herb called *moly,* demanded the restoration of his men, and Circe complied. Odysseus remained with Circe one year and had by her a son, Telegonus (two sons, according to Hesiod). *Aeneid* iii; Apollodorus i; Apollonius Rhodius; *Met.* xiv; *Odyssey* x; *Theogony.*

Cispius (sis' pi us). One of the seven hills of earliest Rome. See CERMALUS.

Cisseus (sis' ūs). 1. The father of Hecuba. *Aeneid* vii. 2. The son of Melampus, companion of Heracles, brother of Gyas, ally of Turnus, killed by Aeneas. *Aeneid* x. 3. A son of Aegyptus. Apollodorus ii.

Cithaeron (si thē' ron). 1. A mountain in Boeotia where Oedipus as a child was exposed to die; where Actaeon was torn to pieces by his own dogs; where Heracles killed an immense lion. The mountain was sacred to Zeus and Dionysus, and a home of the Furies. *Aeneid* iv; Apollodorus ii; Pausanias ix. 2. A very cruel king, brother of Helicon, who murdered his father. The gods changed him into the mountain which bears his name.

Claros (klā′ ros). Location of an oracle of Apollo in Iona which Ceyx had planned to consult, but he was drowned before he could do so. *Met.* i.

Cleite. See CLITE.

Cleobis (klē′ o bis). Brother of BITON, q.v.

Cleobulus (klē o bū′ lus; kle ob′ ū lus). One of the seven sages of Greece. See BIAS.

Cleodora (klē o dō′ ra). 1. A nymph, the mother of Parnassus. 2. One of the Danaides.

Cleodoxa (klē o doks′ a). One of the daughters of Amphion and Niobe, changed into stone as punishment for her mother's pride. Apollodorus iii.

Cleone (kle ō′ nē). Daughter of the river god Asopus, for whom Cleonae, a town between Argos and Corinth, was named.

Cleopatra (kle ō pā′ tra). 1. The daughter of Boreas and Orithyia, sister of Calais and Zetes, wife of Phineus. Apollodorus iii. 2. Daughter of Idas and Marpessa; wife of Meleager. *Iliad* ix. 3. One of the Danaides. 4. Daughter of Tros and Callirrhoe. Apollodorus iii. 5. The name of seven queens of Egypt.

Clio (klī′ ō). One of the nine daughters of Zeus and Mnemosyne; one of the nine Muses. Muse of history, her symbol is the wreath of laurel and the scroll. For names of all the Muses, see CALLIOPE. *Theogony.*

Clite (klī′ tē). Also Cleite. The wife of King Cyzicus of the Doliones, a people who received the Argonauts hospitably and gave them sheep and wine. A day after the Argonauts sailed away, a violent storm drove them back. The Doliones did not recognize the Argonauts in the night; they thought their ancient enemies, the Pelasgians, had come to raid them, and a furious battle ensued in which Cyzicus and many of his men were killed. Jason gave the king a costly burial and erected a monument over his grave. Clite in her grief hanged herself. Apollodorus i; *Argonautica* i. See also CYZICUS.

Cloanthus (klō an' thus). The winner of the boat race at the funeral games for Anchises. *Aeneid* v.

Clotho (klō' thō). The youngest of the three Fates (Fatae, Morae, Parcae). She carries the spindle and spins the thread of life. See ATROPOS.

Clouds, The. A comedy by Aristophanes.

Clymene (klim' e nē). There are about ten mythological characters by this name, including: **1.** Daughter of Oceanus and Tethys; wife of Iapetus; mother of Epimetheus, Menoetius, and Prometheus. **2.** Mother of Phaethon and the Heliades by Apollo. **3.** A daughter of Crateus, a king of Crete; sister of Aerope, who became the mother of Agamemnon and Menelaus. Apollodorus ii. **4.** One of the Nereides, who became the mother of Mnemosyne by Zeus. **5.** Mother of Atalanta by Iasus. **6.** A female servant of Helen, who accompanied her mistress when Paris abducted her. *Iliad* iii. **7.** Some legends say the mother of Homer was named Clymene.

Clymenus (klī' me nus). **1.** A man of Arcadia who fell in love with his own daughter, Harpolyce, and ravished her. After her marriage to Alastor, the father continued his incestuous relationship and she bore a son, Harpalyce, whom she killed, cut up, cooked, and served to her father. The son was changed into an owl, and Clymenus hanged himself. Hyginus. **2.** A king of Orchomenus in Boeotia, accidentally killed by a Theban. His son Erginus avenged his death by making war against Thebes and winning. Pausanias ix. **3.** A descendant of Heracles. Pausanias vi. **4.** A son of Aeneus, king of Calydon. Pausanias vi.

Clytemnestra (klī tem nes' tra). Also Clytaemnestra. Daughter of Tyndareus, king of Sparta, by Leda (who was also the mother of Castor). By Zeus, Leda was the mother of Helen and Pollux. Clytemnestra became the wife of Agamemnon and the mother of Orestes, Electra (Laodice), Iphigenia, and Chrysothemis (according to some mythologists, Iphigenia and Chrysothemis are the same). When Agamemnon went to the Trojan War, Clytemnestra became the paramour of Aegisthus (some sources say she publicly married him). When Agamemnon returned from the Trojan War, Aegisthus and Clytemnestra murdered him. Orestes later killed the murderers of his father. *Aeneid;* Apollodorus; *Iliad; Met.; Odyssey;* Pausanias; Aeschylus, *Agamemnon, Choephoroe, Eumenides;* Euripides, *Electra, Iphigenia at Aulis, Iphigenia among the Tauri, Orestes;* Seneca, *Agamemnon;* Sophocles, *Electra;* Chaucer; Shakespeare; Milton; Byron; Eliot; Rossetti; O'Neill.

Clytie (klī′ tē; klī′ ti ē; klish′ i ē). Also Clytia. Daughter of Oceanus and Tethys, passionately loved by Apollo. Her heart was broken when Apollo deserted her. She was changed into a sunflower (heliotrope, marigold, or any plant that turns toward the sun), the symbol of faithfulness, unwavering devotion, and love. *Met.* iv.

Clytius (klish′ i us). 1. A son of Uranus and Gaea, one of the Giants who waged war against the gods; he was killed by Hephaestus (some legends say by Heracles). Apollodorus i. 2. A son of Laomedon, brother of Priam; the only one of Laomedon's sons not killed when Heracles sacked Troy. *Iliad* x. 3. A youth in the army of Turnus. *Aeneid* x. 4. A son of Aeolus, follower of Aeneas in Italy, killed by Turnus. *Aeneid* ix. 5. A son of Eurytus of Oechalia; participated in the Calydonian boar hunt and went with Jason to Colchis. *Argonautica.*

Clytus (klī′ tus). Some legends say he is the same as Clytius (Klytios), son of Dolops, killed by Hector. *Iliad* xi.

Cnidus (nī′ dus). Ancient city of Caria in Asia Minor; site of a shrine to Aphrodite and of a famous statue of her by Praxiteles, the first sculpture of the goddess in the nude. Praxiteles made two statues of her, one draped which the Athenians chose, the other a nude, refused by

the Athenians but purchased by the Cnidians. Pausanias
i, ii, v, viii, x.

Cnossus (nos′ us). Also Cnosus, Gnossus, Gnosus, Knossos.
Capital of Crete; site of Minoan palaces discovered by
Heinrich Schliemann in 1886. Many ancient ruins of
interest. Arthur Evans visited Cnossus in 1894, began
excavations in 1900, and made discoveries comparable to
those of Schliemann at Mycenae (Mykene). King Minos,
Pasiphae, the Minotaur, the labyrinth of Daedalus, Theseus, Ariadne are associated with Cnossus. Pausanias i,
iii, v, viii, ix.

Cocalus (kok′ a lus). A king of Sicily who was hospitable
to Daedalus when he arrived in Sicily after his flight
from Minos in Crete. When Minos arrived in Sicily in
pursuit of Daedalus, the daughters of Cocalus killed him.
Met. viii.

Cocytus (ko sī′ tus). The river of wailing in Hades. One of
the five rivers of Hades. See ACHERON for names of the
other four.

Coelus (sē′ lus). Also Uranos, Uranus, Ouranus. Also called
"overhanging heavens." Son of Gaea (Earth) whom she
afterwards married. Gaea bore Uranus as a personification of heaven which covered the earth (Gaea). This
marriage produced the first race, the twelve TITANS, q.v.
Some legends say there were forty-five children. Apollodorus i; Aeschylus, *Prometheus; Theogony.*

Coeus (sē′ us). Son of Uranus and Gaea; one of the twelve
Titans; husband of Phoebe, the moon; father of Leto
and Asteria. *Theogony.* According to Vergil and the
Romans, Enceladus was his brother, and his sister was
Fama (goddess of fame, some say of rumor); his daugh-
ter was Latona (Leto).

Colchis (kol′ kis). An Asian country, famous for the expedition of the Argonauts and as the birthplace of
Medea.

Colonus (ko lō′ nus; ko lōn′ us). An eminence near Athens,
where Oedipus retired during his banishment, the events

of which Sophocles dramatized in *Oedipus at Colonus,*
one of his great tragedies. Colonus was the birthplace of
Sophocles. The place was sacred to the Furies in their
later role of gentle and kind goddesses. Antigone was
here with Oedipus when he died.

Colossus of Rhodes (ko los' us; rōdz). Celebrated bronze
statue of Apollo on the island of Rhodes. In ancient
times it was known as one of the Seven Wonders of the
World. It fell into ruins, and in A.D. 672 the ruins were
sold by the Saracens to a Jew, who loaded nine hundred
camels with brass. The value has been estimated at
thirty-six thousand pounds in English money.

Comana (ko mā' na). Same as CHRYSE, q.v.

Comatas (ko mā' tas). A goatherd on the slopes of Mount
Helicon; servant of the nine Muses, who saved his life
after his master had confined him for many months in a
chest for sacrificing a goat to the Muses. The Muses
treated Comatas with utmost kindness.

Cometes (kom ē' tēz). Son of Sthenelus. Aegialia, wife of
Diomedes, a close friend of Sthenelus, became the mistress of Cometes.

Comus (kō' mus). Roman god of revelry, feasting, drinking, mirth, and nocturnal entertainments. Milton, *Comus.*

Concordia (kon kor' di a). Pax (Roman). Goddess of harmony, peace, and domestic concord.

Consentes (kon sen' tēz). Also Consentes Dii (di' i). The
Roman name for the twelve great Greek Olympians,
hence the Roman names Jupiter, Juno, Athena, Apollo,
Mars, and the like.

Consivius (kon siv' i us). Janus as the god of civilization;
also called the Sower.

Consus (kon' sus). Roman god of councils and counsel.

Copia (kō' pi a). Roman goddess of plenty, represented
bearing a horn filled with grapes and other fruits.

Copreus (ko' pre us; kop' rūs). Son of Pelops and Hippodamia who carried the orders of Eurystheus to Heracles. Once owner of the famous horse, Arion. Heracles

killed him by throwing him from the wall of Tiryns. Apollodorus ii.

Cora (kō′ ra). Also Core, Kora, Kore; Libera (Roman). The word "Cora" means maiden and was another name for PERSEPHONE, q.v., daughter of Demeter (Ceres), and wife of Pluto (Hades). She was the queen of Hades. *Aeneid* iv; *Met.* v; *Theogony;* Swinburne, "The Garden of Proserpine"; Shelley, "Song of Proserpine"; Woodberry, "Proserpine."

Corcyra (kor′ sĭ ra). 1. Largest of the seven islands in the Ionian Sea; famous for the shipwreck of Odysseus, and the gardens of Alcinous, in *Odyssey* vii, where it is called Scheria and Phaeacia. Modern Corfu. 2. A daughter of Asopus and Metope, carried away by Poseidon to this island named after her. 3. Some mythologists say the island was formed when Cronus threw the sickle with which he had mutilated Uranus into the sea. Some accounts say Jason and Medea were married in a cave on this island and that Demeter once visited here. Another legend makes Alcinous a descendant of Poseidon and Corcyra.

Corcyraean Bull (kor sĭ rē′ an). A bull of Corcyra that bellowed at the sea and kept fishermen from catching fish—until he was sacrificed to Poseidon.

Corfu (kor′ fōō; kor′ fū). Formerly CORCYRA, q.v.

Corinth (kor′ inth). Also Korinthos. Ancient city of Greece in Argos in the Peloponnesus on the Isthmus and Gulf of Corinth; founded by Sisyphus, son of Aeolus; received its name from Corinthus, son of Pelops. In 146 B.C. the Romans found immense riches here and totally destroyed the city by fire. A famous temple of Aphrodite was here; many names of mythology—Apollo, Poseidon, Briareus, Melicertes, Isthmian games, Sisyphus, Neleus, Theseus, Jason, Medea, Aeetes, Asopus, Pirene Spring, Athena putting the bridle on Pegasus for Bellerophon, Glauce and her father Creon—are associated with this famous place. Julius Caesar established a colony here; Augustus made it the capital of Achaea; Hadrian built public works; the New Testament of the Holy Bible, Pausanias, and Strabo refer to its prosperity and riches; there are references in *Iliad* xv and *Met.* ii. In 1858 Old Corinth was destroyed by an earthquake and New Corinth almost totally destroyed by another earthquake in 1928. Many excavations by the American School of Classical Studies in Athens. These are still in progress; and many things have come to light. There is a fine new museum in Corinth.

Corinth Canal. Connects Ionian Sea with Aegean Sea. Caligula sent an engineer to survey the site; Nero began the work in A.D. 67, and was sent six thousand Jewish prisoners from Judea by Vespasian; a French company began the digging of the present canal in 1882; a Greek company completed the work in 1893. Length 6,939 yards; width 76 feet, 6 inches, exactly as at Suez; depth of water 26 feet, 3 inches.

Corinthus (kor in' thus). Son of Zeus.

Cornucopia (kor nū kō' pi a). Also called the horn of plenty; named after the horn of the goat AMALTHEA, q.v., that suckled the infant Zeus. The horn is always full of food and drink.

Coroebus (ko rē' bus). 1. An ally of the Trojans because he desired Cassandra; killed by Diomedes. 2. A man of Argolis who killed the monster serpent named Poene sent by Apollo to ravage the country. A plague also afflicted Argolis and Coroebus went to consult the oracle at Delphi, where he was instructed to build a temple to Apollo on Mount Geranis. Pausanias i.

Corona (ko rō' na). 1. The constellation known as Ariadne's crown. 2. A town in Messenia where Ino came ashore transformed as the sea goddess Leucothea.

Coronis (ko rō' nis). 1. Mother of Asclepius by Apollo. Pausanias ii. 2. Daughter of Coronaeus of Phocis; changed into a crow by Athena. *Met.* ii. 3. Daughter of Ares, attacked by Apollo. 4. Daughter of Atlas and Pleione.

Coronus (ko rō′ nus). 1. Son of Caeneus, king of the Lapithae; accompanied Jason in search of the Golden Fleece, and later became king of the Lapithae. He was killed by Heracles. *Argonautica*. 2. A son of Apollo.

Corus (kō′ rus). Another name for the north or northwest wind.

Corybantes (kor i ban′ tēz). Also Curetes. Priests of Cybele (Rhea) in Phrygia. Stories of their parentage vary: Ovid says they were a people of Crete produced from rain. *Met*. iv. Some legends say the parents were Apollo and Thalia, Apollo and Athena, Helios and Athena, Zeus and Calliope, Cronus and Rhea. Some accounts say they moved from Mount Ida to Crete, where they reared and educated Zeus. Their knowledge of all the arts was extensive.

Corydon (kor′ i don). A young rustic swain or young country fellow. In the *Eclogues* of Vergil and the *Idyls* of Theocritus, Corydon is the name of a shepherd.

Coryphaeus (kor i fē′ us). The chorus leader in Greek tragedy.

Corythus (kor′ i thus). 1. A king of Corinth. 2. A king of Laconia whose shepherds found Telephus, son of Heracles and Auge, abandoned on a mountain. Corythus reared him as his own son. The same shepherds also found Parthenopaeus, son of Meleager and Atalanta, abandoned on the same mountain, and took him to be cared for by Corythus. Apollodorus i. 3. The son of Paris and Oenone. Oenone, furious when Paris deserted her for Helen, sent Corythus to guide the Greeks to Troy—where Paris killed him when he too fell in love with Helen.

Cos (kōs). Also Kos. An island in the Aegean Sea where Hera sent a storm to shipwreck Heracles.

Cothurnus (ko thur′ nus). Buskin—a high, thick-soled boot, once worn by actors in tragic drama and often used as symbol of tragedy. Milton, "Il Penseroso," ll. 97–102.

Cottus (kot′ us). One of the Hecatoncheires; brother of BRIAREUS, q.v., and Gyges.

Cotytto (kō tit′ ō). Same as Cotys (ko′ tis; kot′ is). **1.** Greek goddess of debauchery. At her festivals, nothing but carousing and wantonness prevailed; death was the punishment for revealing what was seen or done at these sacred festivals; they were riotous and licentious. **2.** A name for the father of Asia. **3.** A son of Manes by Callirrhoe. **4.** A king of Thrace. **5.** A person who imagined that he should marry Athena, and who murdered some of his servants who wished to dissuade him from expectations so frivolous and inconsistent.

Cratais (kra tā′ is; kra tē′ is). Also Crataeis. Same as Hecate. The mother of the sea monster, Scylla. *Odyssey* xii.

Cratus (krā′ tus). A son of Uranus and Gaea, persuaded by Hephaestus into blinding Prometheus. Aeschylus. *Prometheus Bound*.

Creon (krē′ on). **1.** A king of Corinth. Son of Sisyphus. Creon promised his daughter Glauce (sometimes Creusa) to Jason, who had repudiated his wife Medea. Medea sent a gown covered with poison to Glauce. The poison caused a fire which consumed Glauce, the palace, and Creon and his family. Apollodorus i; Euripides, *Medea*. **2.** A king of Thebes, the father of Megara, who became the first wife of Heracles. **3.** Another king of Thebes, the son of Menoeceus and the brother of Jocasta, who became the mother and later the wife of Oedipus, to whom Creon gave his throne when Oedipus solved the riddle of the Sphinx. Apollodorus iii; Pausanias i; Sophocles, *Antigone*.

Cresphontes (kres fon′ tēz). Husband of Merope; father of Aegyptus, whose fifty sons married the fifty daughters of his brother Danaus.

Cressida (kres′ i da). Also Cressid (kres′ sid); in Chaucer Criseyde. Belongs to medieval, not ancient, myth. She was the mistress of Troilus. The name is derived from

CHRYSEIS, q.v. Boccaccio, *Filostrato;* Chaucer, *Troilus and Criseyde;* Shakespeare, *Troilus and Cressida;* Henryson, *The Testament of Cresseid.*

Creta (krē′ ta). Also Crete (krē′ te). Mother of Pasiphae.

Cretan Bull. The seventh labor of Heracles was to overthrow this awful but beautiful brute, at once a gift and a curse bestowed by Poseidon upon Minos of Crete. This bull became the father of the Minotaur by Pasiphae. See also MARATHONIAN BULL.

Crete (krēt). Largest of the Aegean islands, the place of origin and center of Minoan civilization; a most important island, not only in Greek civilization and in many archeological discoveries by Sir Arthur Evans, but also for many mythological associations, among them: (1) Zeus, in the form of a gentle snow-white bull, abducted Europa, swam away through the sea to Crete, and had by Europa a son, Minos, later king of Crete. (2) King Minos figures as a minor character in many stories. (3) Pasiphae, wife of King Minos, gave birth to the Minotaur in Crete. (4) Theseus killed the Minotaur in the labyrinth built in Crete by Daedalus for King Minos. (5) The Corybantes (Curetes) reared and educated Zeus in Crete. (6) During the Golden Age, the Titans were associated with Crete. (7) According to one account, Athena was born in Crete, from the head of Zeus. (8) Zeus and Hera married in Crete. (9) Teucer, ancestor of the Trojans, came from Crete. (10) Ariadne fled from Crete with Theseus. (11) Crete sent soldiers to Troy; Idomeneus and Meriones were the Cretan leaders. *Iliad.* Some mythologists suggest that the palace of Alcinous mentioned in the *Odyssey* may have been modeled after the palaces of Crete.

Cretheis (krē′ the is). In Pindar, the wife of Acastus. She accused Peleus falsely of attempted adultery and told his wife that he was going to desert her and marry Sterope, the daughter of Cretheis. Later, Peleus killed both Acastus and Cretheis. Some mythologists say Cretheis is the same as Hippolyta or Astyadamia.

Cretheus (krē′ the us; krē′ thūs). 1. Son of Aeolus by Enarete. Married Tyro, the daughter of his brother Salmoneus; adopted her twins Pelias and Neleus; had by her Aeson, Pheres, and Amythaon. Apollodorus i. 2. A companion of Aeneas. He loved the Muses, the lyre, and song. Unprepared for war, he was killed by Turnus. *Aeneid*.

Creus (krē′ us). Also Crius (krī′ us). One of the Titans; husband of Eurybea (Eurybia).

Creusa (kre ū′ sa). 1. A daughter of CREON, q.v., king of Corinth; Creusa was also called Glauce. 2. A daughter of Priam and Hecuba; wife of Aeneas. 3. Mother of Telamon. 4. One of the Nereides. 5. One of the Danaides. 6. A daughter of Erechtheus, king of Athens, and mother of Janus by Apollo. Some accounts say she was the mother of Ion by Apollo. She deserted her son Ion, but when she later married Xuthus, she was reunited with Ion. 7. Apollodorus and Pausanias say Ion was the son of Xuthus by Creusa.

Crius (krī′ us). Same as Creus. He became the father of Astraeus, Pallas, and Perses by Eurybia.

Crocale (krok′ a lē). A nymph, an attendant of Diana. Crocale was the hairdresser who arranged Diana's hair at the time Actaeon spied her bathing and was changed into a stag. *Met.* iii.

Crocus (krō′ kus). A beautiful youth in love with the nymph Smilax; he was changed into a flower because of his impatience, and Smilax was changed into the flower bearing her name or into a yew tree. *Met.* iv.

Croesus (krē′ sus). The richest of mankind. Aesop, the noted fable writer, lived under his patronage in Lydia where Croesus was king. In a conversation with Solon, Croesus wished to be thought the happiest of mankind, but Solon replied: "Call no man happy until he is dead," and gave the preference to poverty and virtue rather than to wealth. Herodotus i.

Crommyonian Sow (krom i ō′ ni an). Also called Phaea. A savage sow that ravaged Crommyon, a section of country in Corinth; killed by Theseus on his journey from Troezen to Athens. *Met.* vii. Some mythologists say that Phaea was a female bandit called a sow; other mythologists maintain that Phaea was a prostitute who murdered and plundered. One legend names Phaea as the mother of the Calydonian boar.

Cronia (krō′ ni a). Festivals in Athens in honor of Cronus.

Cronus (krō′ nus). Also Cronos, Kronos; Saturn (Roman). A Titan; the youngest son of Uranus and Gaea. Cronus and Rhea were the parents of six of the twelve Olympians—Zeus, Hades, Poseidon, Demeter, Hera, Hestia. Apollodorus i; *Iliad; Met.;* Pausanias v, vii, viii, ix, x; *Theogony; Homeric Hymns.*

Crotus (krō′ tus). Son of Eumene. Nurse of the nine Muses. Since he loved hunting and was a skilled archer, he was placed among the constellations as Sagittarius.

Crow. Sacred bird of Apollo. Crows were originally snow-white. Apollo changed the feathers to black for bringing him news of the unfaithfulness of Coronis. In Chaucer's "Manciple's Tale," the white crow becomes black for tattling, has his tongue plucked out, and is thrown to the devil.

Crumissa (kru mis′ sa). Poseidon carried Theophane to this island on which the golden-fleeced ram was born.

Ctesippus (te sip′ us). 1. A son of Heracles by Deianira (or Astydamia). 2. A suitor of Penelope killed by Eumaeus.

Ctimene (tim′ i nē; ti sim′ i nē). The sister of Odysseus. *Odyssey* xv.

Cumae (kū′ mē). An ancient city, about ten miles west of present-day Naples; home of the Sibyl who lived in a cave which had a hundred different openings. She was called the Cumaean Sibyl. This was the place where Aeneas landed in Italy. *Aeneid* iii; *Met.* xv.

Cumaean Sibyl (ku mē′ an sib′ il). The most famous prophetess in mythology. Given power of prophecy and a thousand years of life by Apollo, whose mistress she refused to be, one year of life for each grain of sand she could hold in her hand. Forgot to ask for continuing youth, and this Apollo refused to give because she spurned his love. She lived the thousand years in her cave at Cumae; she was seven hundred years old when she helped Aeneas. *Aeneid* iii; *Met.* xiv.

Cupid (kū′ pid). Also **Amor, Eros** (Greek). Roman god of love. Son of Hermes (Mercury) and Aphrodite (Venus). *Aeneid* i; *Met.* i; *Theogony;* Apuleius, *The Golden Ass;* Keats, "Endymion" and "Ode to Psyche"; Bridges, "Eros and Psyche."

Cupid and Psyche (sī′ kē). A famous love story in *The Golden Ass* by Apuleius.

Curetes (ku rē′ tēz). See CORYBANTES.

Cyane (sī′ a nē). 1. A nymph of Syracuse. Criminally attacked by her drunken father, she avenged herself by dragging him to an altar and offering him as a sacrifice. 2. A nymph of Sicily who tried to prevent Hades from taking Persephone to the underworld. Hades changed her into a fountain. *Met.* v.

Cyanean Rocks (sī′ a nē an). Same as SYMPLEGADES, q.v.

Cyanee (sī an′ ē ē). The mother of CAUNUS and BYBLIS, q.v.

Cybele (sib′ e lē). Also **Ops** (Roman); **Dindymene; Rhea.** The Phrygian name for Rhea, the Titan earth goddess; daughter of Gaea; wife of Cronus. Also called Magna Mater by the Romans. *Aeneid* ix.

Cyclades (sik′ la dēz). Islands in the Aegean Sea.

Cyclopes (sī klō′ pēz). Also **Cyclops** (sī′ klops). Three sons of Uranus and Gaea: Arges, Brontes, Steropes. Each had one eye in the middle of the forehead. In *Odyssey* ix they are the sons of Poseidon, one-eyed cannibals, and shepherds. Odysseus blinded Polyphemus, who had eaten several of Odysseus' men.

Cyclops, The. A play by Euripides.

Cycnus (sik′ nus). Also **Cygnus** (sig′ nus), **Cygnet.** The word "cycnus" means swan; "cygnet" means a young swan.

1. A son of Poseidon and Calyce, abandoned at birth by his mother, but cared for by a swan. As an ally of the Trojans he was invulnerable, and Achilles could not kill him with darts, spear, or sword, but had to smother him. When Achilles went back for the body, it was no longer there. Cycnus had been changed into a swan. *Met.* xii. **2.** A son of Ares and Pelopea, killed by Heracles; Ares changed Cycnus into a swan. **3.** A son of Ares and Pyrene, killed by Heracles; Ares changed this son into a swan. **4.** A son of Apollo and Hyrie, changed into a swan. *Met.* **5.** A son of Sthenelus; Cycnus grieved so much at the death of his friend Phaethon that Apollo changed the son into a swan. *Met.* ii; *Aeneid* x. Many tales of swan transformation in English and continental literature; the best known is *Knight of the Swan,* who is called *Helias.*

Cydippe (si dip′ e). **1.** Mother of Biton and Cleobis, two devoted sons. See BITON. **2.** A girl loved by Acontius. **3.** An attendant of Cyrene who was the mother of Diomedes, the owner of man-eating mares. *Heroides* xx, xxi.

Cyllarus and **Hylonome** (sil′ a rus; hi lon′ o mē). Cyllarus was the most beautiful of the Centaurs, passionately fond of Hylonome. They died at the same time. *Met.* xii.

Cyllene (si lē′ nē). **1.** Mother of Lycaon by Pelasgus. Apollodorus iii. **2.** A nymph on Mount Cyllene in Arcadia who nursed Hermes in the cave where he was born. *Aeneid* viii; *Met.* xiii; Pausanias viii. **3.** The mountain in Arcadia where Hermes was born. **4.** A famous seaport in Elis.

Cylleneius (se lē′ ni us). Hermes.

Cynosura (sīn o sū′ ra). Same as Ursa Minor. A nymph of Ida in Crete; she was one of the nurses of the infant Zeus. She was changed into the star that bears her name.

Cynthia (sin′ thi a). Name (from Mount Cynthus) of Artemis, Delia, Diana, Hecate, Luna, Phoebe, Selene; goddess of the moon, hunting, etc. See ARTEMIS.

Cynthius (sin′ thi us). A name for Apollo, from Mount Cynthus, where Leto gave birth to Apollo and Artemis.

Cynthus (sin' thus). Name of a mountain on the island of Delos in the Aegean Sea; birthplace of Apollo and Artemis which gave the names Cynthius to Apollo, and Cynthia to Artemis. *Met*. vi.

Cyparissus (sip a ris' us). A youth loved by Apollo. The youth killed one of Apollo's favorite stags, and Apollo changed Cyparissus into a cyprus tree. *Aeneid* iii; *Met*. x.

Cypris (sī' pris). Another name for Aphrodite (Venus), taken from the name of the island of Cyprus, near which she is said to have risen from the foam. Many temples on this island are consecrated to Aphrodite.

Cyprus (sī' prus). Large island in the Mediterranean Sea southeast of Greece. Some legends say Aphrodite emerged from the sea near this island.

Cypselus (sip' se lus). 1. A man of Corinth, who killed the Bacchiade. 2. The father of Merope. 3. A son of Aepytus, who became king of Arcadia.

Cyrene (sī rē' nē). A daughter of Hypseus, king of the Lapithae. She loved to hunt and wrestle lions. Apollo saw her wrestle a lion, fell in love with her; and was the father of her two sons Aristaeus and Idmon, the latter a famous seer. Pindar.

Cythera (sith' er a; si thir' a). Famous island in the Ionian Sea which contends with Cyprus for the honor of being the island to which Aphrodite floated when she rose from the foam. *Aeneid* i; *Met*. iv.

Cytherea (sith e rē' a). Name for Aphrodite, taken from the island of Cytherea, a center of her worship.

Cyzicus (siz' i kus). 1. A king of the country of the same name; the Argonauts landed here on their way to Colchis. 2. A peninsula where the Argonauts stopped. Apollodorus i; *Argonautica*. See also CLITE.

D

Dactyls (dak′ tilz). Ten women of Mount Ida in Phrygia, famous for working copper and iron. Pausanias, v, viii, ix.

Daedalion (de dā′ li on). Son of Phosphorus; brother of Ceyx; father of Chione (Philonis), who was loved by Apollo and Hermes. When Chione was slain by Artemis, Daedalion threw himself from the summit of Mount Parnassus, and Apollo changed him into a hawk. *Met.* xi.

Daedalus (dē′ da lus; ded′ a lus). The first aviator. A descendant of Erechtheus, king of Athens, he was the most ingenious artist of the age. He invented the axe, wedge, wimble, level, sails for ships, and many other mechanical instruments. Talos, his nephew, promised to be as ingenious an inventor as his uncle so Daedalus killed him. After this murder Daedalus and his son Icarus fled Athens to Crete; there Daedalus built the famous labyrinth for Minos. When Minos ordered him confined in the labyrinth, Daedalus made wings with feathers and wax for himself and Icarus, but the wax on Icarus' wings melted and he fell into what is now the Icarian Sea. The father landed at Cumae, where he built a temple to Apollo. *Aeneid* vi; *Met.* viii; Apollodorus iii; Chaucer, Shakespeare, Joyce, Auden, and others.

Daemon (dē′ mon). Also Demon. Among the ancients, a spirit presiding over persons, places, private counsels, secret intentions, society. Ancient philosophers held that every man had two daemons—one good, one bad.

Dagan (dä′ gan). Also Dagon (dā′ gon). The fish god; some accounts list him as the god of the earth. Milton, *Paradise Lost.*

Damastes (da mas′ tēz). Also Procrustes and Polypemon. He was called "The Stretcher," because he made people fit his Procrustean bed. If they were too short, he stretched them to fit; if they were too long, he cut off their legs.

He was the father of another notorious outlaw, Sinis, the "Pine Bender." Damastes and Sinis were killed by Theseus. Apollodorus iii.

Damon and **Pythias** (dā' mon; pith' i as). Famous Pythagorean philosophers of Syracuse, noted for their intimate friendship. Some accounts say Damon, others Pythias, was condemned to death for plotting against King Dionysius of Syracuse. The friend of the condemned man offered to die in his place. Dionysius was so impressed with such devotion that he not only freed the suspected traitor but asked to be admitted to their friendship.

Danaans (dan' a anz). A name given to the people of Argos from Danaus, their king, and later applied to all Greeks. Homer did not use the label "Greek"; he calls the people Achaeans, Argives, and Danaans with apparent impartiality. Sometimes Vergil and Ovid use the word "Danai."

Danae (dan' a ē). Daughter of King Acrisius of Argos, and of Aganippe. Mother of Perseus by Zeus, who visited her in the form of a golden shower in her prison tower (some legends say in a bronze underground chamber) where her father had imprisoned her after an oracle told him his daughter's son would cause his death. Many years later, when Acrisius was a spectator at a discus-throwing contest in Larissa where he had fled from Argos, he was accidentally struck and killed by a discus thrown by Perseus. *Aeneid* vii; Apollodorus ii; *Iliad* xiv; *Met.* v.

Danai (dan' a ī). Same as DANAANS, q.v.

Danaidae (da nā' i dē). Also Danaids, Danaides (dan' a idz; da nā' i dēz). The fifty daughters of Danaus who married the fifty sons of Aegyptus, brother of Danaus. Forty-nine killed their bridegrooms on their wedding night, and as punishment for the murders were doomed forever to draw water with a sieve in Hades. Hypermnestra spared Lynceus, and they became progenitors of the rulers of Argos. Apollodorus ii; Hyginus; Pausanias ii; Strabo; Aeschylus, *The Suppliant Maidens;* Chaucer, *Legend of Good Women.*

Danaus (dan' a us). Son of Belus, king of Egypt; twin of Aegyptus; father of the DANAIDAE, q.v.

Daphne (daf' ne). Nymph pursued by Apollo. Her father Peneus came to her rescue by transforming her into a laurel tree. Apollo promptly adopted the laurel as his tree. Pausanias x; Milton.

Daphnis (daf' nis). **1.** A son of Hermes by a Sicilian nymph. The infant was exposed to the elements and left to die, but he was found and reared by shepherds, and educated by nymphs. Pan taught him to play the flute and sing; the Muses inspired him with a love of poetry; and he is said to have invented pastoral song and story. He fell in love with Piplea and tried to win her from her master Lityerses by defeating him in a reaping contest; when he was on the verge of losing, Heracles killed Lityerses. Daphnis was extremely fond of hunting; and when five of his dogs died he refused food and died also. **2.** A shepherd on Mount Ida turned to stone by a jealous nymph. *Met.* iv. **3.** A son of Paris and Oenone.

Daphnis and **Chloe** (klō' e). The famous lovers in an old Greek pastoral romance attributed to Longus (fourth or fifth century A.D.).

Dardanelles (dar da nelz'). Ancient name Hellespont. The strait that joins the Aegean Sea and Sea of Marmara received its name from Helle, sister of Phrixus, who fell from the golden-fleeced ram into this body of water. The strait is also celebrated in the story of Hero and Leander; a famous bridge of boats was built to span it by Xerxes when he invaded Greece. Herodotus ix; *Met.* xiii.

Dardanus (dar' da nus). Son of Zeus and Electra; ancestor of the Trojans. A city he built near the foot of Mount Ida in Phrygia he named Dardania, which became part of Troy. Dardanus taught his subjects to worship Athena and gave them the Palladium. *Aeneid* v; Apollodorus iii; *Iliad* xx; Pausanias vii.

Dardanus, Mares of. Boreas changed himself into a horse, united himself with the mares of Dardanus, and became the father of twelve steeds so swift none could overtake them.

Dares (dar' ēz). A companion of Aeneas in Italy. A famous pugilist, he was killed by Turnus. *Aeneid* v.

Dares Phrygius (dar' ēz; dā' rez; frij' i us). Appears in Homer's *Iliad* as a priest of Hephaestus who perhaps had written an earlier story about Troy. Homer does not mention Dares Phrygius' story of Troy, but some authorities believe he was a Phrygian who during the Trojan War wrote a history of Troy in the Greek language. A Latin prose translation by Cornelius Nepos is extant.

Daulis (do' lis). A nymph who gave her name to the city of Daulis, where Philomela and Procne (Progne) made Tereus eat the flesh of his son; the nightingale into which Philomela was changed is often called *daulias avis*. Daulis is situated in Phocis, twelve miles east of Delphi. Pausanias x.

Daunus (do' nus). A king who was on the throne of Apulia when Diomedes arrived there; Diomedes married one of his daughters. Daunus was the father of Turnus by Venilia. *Aeneid*.

Death. Also Thanatos (than' a tos) (Greek); Mors (morz) (Roman). Born of Nyx without a father; twin brother of Hypnos (Somnus), god of sleep. Not worshiped as a god. Hesiod says he was hated by the other gods, but in many literary allusions he is presented as a healer and remover of pain.

Deianeira (dē ya nī' ra). Also Deianira, Dejanira. The second wife of Heracles (Megara was the first). She unwittingly killed Heracles by sending him a garment steeped in the poisoned blood of the centaur Nessus; this garment, Nessus had said, had power to reclaim a husband from unlawful loves. *Met.* ix; *Heroides* ix; Chaucer, "The Monk's Tale."

Deidamia (dē i da mī' a). Daughter of Lycomedes, king of Scyros, at whose court Achilles, disguised as a girl to avoid going to the Trojan War, seduced Deidamia; she became the mother of Neoptolemus (Pyrrhus). After Achilles' death, Neoptolemus gave his mother to Helenus as his wife. Apollodorus iii.

Deimos (dī′ mos). Also Fear, Terror. A son and attendant of Ares (Mars). Some accounts say Terror (Pallor) is a brother of Deimos.

Deino (dī′ nō). Daughter of Phorcys and Ceto. One of the three Graeae; the other two are Enyo and Pephredo. The three were guardians of the Gorgons; they had one eye and one tooth among them.

Deiphobe (de if′ o bē). Another name for the Cumaean Sibyl. Daughter of Glaucus, who became a sibyl of Cumae and led Aeneas to the infernal regions. *Aeneid* vi.

Deiphobus (de if′ o bus). A son of Priam and Hecuba. After the death of Paris, Deiphobus married Helen by force. He was one of the great heroes of the Trojan War. *Aeneid* vi; *Iliad* xiii.

Deiphyle (de if′ i lē). Also Deipyle (de ip′ i lē). A daughter of Adrastus, king of Argos; wife of Tydeus, by whom she had Diomedes, who became king of Argos and was one of the Epigoni. Apollodorus i.

Dejanira (dē ja nī′ ra). See DEIANEIRA.

Delia (dē′ li a). Another name for Artemis, Cynthia, Diana, Hecate, Luna, Phoebe, or Selene; goddess of the moon. Artemis was called Delia because she was born on the island of Delos. Delia was also the name of a festival, instituted by Theseus in honor of Apollo, celebrated on the island of Delos.

Delight (de līt′). The daughter of Eros and Psyche.

Delius (dē′ li us). Another name for Apollo, because he was born on the island of DELOS, q.v.

Delos (dē′ los). The Aegean island on which Leto (Latona) gave birth to the twins Apollo and Artemis. The island was raised from the sea by Poseidon to afford Leto a place of refuge from the wrath of Hera. The story of Delos and the twins is found in *Aeneid* iii; Apollodorus i; *Argonautica* i; Diodorus Siculus ii; *Homeric Hymns* iii, iv, xxi, xxv, xxvii; Pausanias i; Strabo viii, x; Byron, *Don Juan*.

Delphi (del′ fī). Also Delphoi. Sometimes called Pytho because the serpent Python was killed there. The name Delphi comes from Delphus, a son of Apollo. Delphi was the site of the most famous oracles of Apollo. The ancients believed that Delphi was the middle of the earth. It is located in Phocis, on the slopes of Mount Parnassus. Many characters and stories of mythology are associated with Delphi: Apollo, Gaea, Poseidon, Pytho, Dionysus, Hephaestus, Gyges, Croesus; many consulted the oracle. Apollonius ii; Herodotus; *Met*. x; Pausanias x.

Delphus (del′ fus). Son of Apollo and Celaeno for whom Delphi was named.

Deluge (del′ ūj). The flood sent by Zeus at the end of the Iron Age; Parnassus alone overtopped the waves. Only Deucalion (son of Prometheus) and Pyrrha (daughter of Epimetheus) found refuge on Parnassus and were saved.

Demeter (de mē′ ter). Also CERES (Roman), q.v. One of the twelve great Olympians. Goddess of agriculture, productive soil, fruitfulness of mankind, and guardian of marriage. Mother of Plutus, the god of wealth, by Iasion, mother of Persephone by Zeus. Apollodorus; *Theogony*; Pausanias; *Homeric Hymns*.

Demios (dē′ mi os). Dread is another name for this son and attendant of Ares (Mars). His brothers were Terror, Panic, Fear, Phobos (Alarm), and Trembling; Eris was a sister.

Demodocus (de mod′ o kus). Also Demodochus. A minstrel at the court of Alcinous of Phaeacia. Odysseus visited this court on his way home from Troy. *Odyssey* viii.

Demophon (dē′ mo fon; dem′ o fon). A son of Theseus who went to Troy and fell in love with Laodice, a daughter of Priam. On the way home from Troy, he fell in love with Phyllis, daughter of the king of Thrace; she hanged herself when he did not return from Athens as he had promised. *Heroides* ii; Pausanias x; Chaucer, *Legend of Good Women*.

Demophoon (de mof' o on). Also Demophon. **1.** Some legends say Demophoon was a son of Celeus and Meganira, nursed by Demeter when she stopped in his home while searching for Persephone. Demeter planned to give him eternal youth, but was startled when his mother screamed; Demeter dropped him, and the spell was broken. **2.** A friend of Aeneas. *Aeneid* xi.

Description of Greece. A work by Pausanias.

Destiny (des' ti ni). One of the ancient deities not subject to Zeus. Destiny and the three Fates alone dared to oppose the sovereign will of Zeus, and they continued to issue their irrevocable edicts even after Zeus supplanted his father Cronus and began to rule over all.

Destroyers of Monsters. Among the most famous were Apollo, Bellerophon, Heracles, Odysseus, Oedipus, Perseus, Theseus. See also MONSTERS.

Deucalion (du kā' li on). The Noah of mythology. See DELUGE. Deucalion and Pyrrha were instructed by Themis to replace the loss of mankind by throwing behind them the bones of their mother (the stones of the earth). Those thrown by Deucalion became men; those thrown by Pyrrha became women. Apollodorus i; *Met.* i; Pausanias i.

Dia (dī' a). **1.** A Lapith; wife of Ixion, mother of Pirithous, the close friend of Theseus. **2.** Dia (Naxos) is the name of the Aegean island on which Theseus abandoned Ariadne and where she married Bacchus.

Diana (dī an' a). Another name for the moon goddess. See ARTEMIS, TRIVIA.

Dice (dī' sē). Also Dike (dī' kē). Goddess of justice; one of the three Horae (Hours, Seasons) (the other two were Eirene [Irene], goddess of peace, and Eunomia, goddess of wise legislation and order). As goddesses of the seasons, they produced order in both nature and society. They were the daughters of Zeus and Themis. Apollonius i; *Iliad* v; Pausanias v; *Theogony*.

Dicte (dik' tē). The cave in the mountains of Crete where Zeus was born. *Met.* viii.

Dictynna (dik tin′ a). A nymph loyal to Artemis, she invented fishermen's nets. To avoid Minos, she threw herself into the sea, and was caught in fishermen's nets, hence her name. Pausanias ii.

Dictys (dik′ tis). A fisherman from the island of Seriphus who discovered Danae and Perseus in a chest, befriended them, and was later made king by Perseus. He was the husband of Clymene. Apollodorus i.

Dictys Cretensis (kre ten′ sis). A native of Cnossus who accompanied Idomeneus, leader of the Cretans, to Troy; he is believed to have written a diary of the Trojan War, *Ephemeris Belli Troiani,* discovered after an earthquake during the reign of Nero. The authenticity of the work has been questioned; the work of DARES PHRYGIUS, q.v., with this doubtful work of Dictys, was the chief source of legends for the literature of the Middle Ages, including that written by Boccaccio and Chaucer. A Latin translation was obtainable in the Middle Ages.

Dido (di′ dō). Also Elissa. Daughter of Belus, king of Tyre. Her husband Sichaeus was secretly murdered for his money by her brother Pygmalion. She went to Africa, founded Carthage, and became its queen. When Aeneas came to Carthage, on his way to Italy after the Trojan War, Dido fell in love with him. When he left for Italy she uttered a curse against the Trojans and then stabbed herself with her sword. *Aeneid* i, iv; *Heroides* vii; *Met.* xiv; Marlowe, *Dido, Queen of Carthage;* Tennyson, "To Virgil."

Dii (dī′ ī). Also Di (dī). Roman name for the twelve great gods of the Greeks (Greek name in parentheses). Apollo (Apollo), Ceres (Demeter), Diana (Artemis), Jove or Jupiter (Zeus), Juno (Hera), Mars (Ares), Mercury (Hermes), Minerva (Athena), Neptune (Poseidon), Venus (Aphrodite), Vesta (Hestia), Vulcan (Hephaestus). See also CONSENTES; GODS; OLYMPIANS.

Dike (dī′ kē). See DICE.

Dindymene (din di mē′ nē). Also Rhea, Ops (Roman).

Another name for Cybele. Mother of the gods; the name comes from Mount Dindymus in Phrygia, sacred to her.

Dino (dī′ nō). Also Deino. One of the Graeae.

Diodorus Siculus (dī ō dō′ rus   sik′ ū lus). A Greek historian of the first century B.C. whose history, divided into forty books of which a dozen still exist, is a valuable source of information about history and mythology.

Diomedes (dī o mē′ dēz). 1. Son of Tydeus and Deipyle. King of Aetolia; one of the bravest chieftains in the Trojan War. One of the Epigoni. Loyal supporter of Agamemnon, a favorite of Athena and—next to Achilles—the mightiest hero among the Greeks. When he was wounded by Pandarus, Athena healed him. When Diomedes wounded Aeneas, Aphrodite saved the latter, her son. Diomedes fought many, wounded Ares, killed Dolon, Rhesus, and others. With Odysseus he helped bring Philoctetes from Lemnos, stole the horses of Rhesus, stole the Palladium, entered Troy in the Wooden Horse; with Phoenix, he helped bring Neoptolemus from Scyros. *Aeneid* i; Apollodorus i; *Iliad* ii, v, vi, x, xxiii; *Met.* xiv; Pausanias ii. 2. Son of Ares and Cyrene. King of Thrace, who fed his horses (the Mares of Diomedes) human flesh. The eighth labor of Heracles was to destroy the Mares of Diomedes, but first Diomedes was killed and given to the mares to devour. Some legends say the mares were not destroyed by Heracles, but captured, tamed, and consecrated to Hera who set them free (other legends say they escaped) to roam until they were torn to pieces on Mount Olympus by the wild beasts of Apollo. Apollodorus ii; Pausanias iii.

Dione (dī ō′ nē). Mother of Aphrodite by Zeus. When Aphrodite was wounded by Diomedes, Dione comforted her daughter. Dione foretold the death of Diomedes for daring to wage war against the immortals. Aphrodite is sometimes called Dione. *Aeneid* iii; *Iliad* v.

Dionysia (dī o nish′ i a; dī o nish′ a). Festivals held at Athens in honor of Dionysus (Bacchus). Early Greek drama developed in connection with this festival. Euripides, *The Bacchae; Aeneid* xi; *Met.* iii.

Dionysus (dī o nī′ sus). Also Bromius, Liber, BACCHUS (Roman), q.v. God of wine and revelry. Youngest of the twelve great Olympians. Sometimes incorrectly spelled Dionysius.

Dioscuri (dī os kū′ ri). Castor and Pollux. See CASTOR.

Dirae (dī′ rē). Also Erinyes, Eumenides, Furiae, Semnae. Another name for the three Furies: Alecto, Megaera, and Tisiphone. Daughters of Acheron and Nyx. Some legends maintain they were called Furies in Hell, Harpies on Earth, and Dirae in Heaven. *Aeneid* iv.

Dirce (dur′ sē). Wife of King Lycus of Thebes after he had left Antiope. Antiope had two sons by Zeus, Amphion and ZETHUS, q.v., born on Mount Cithaeron; they put Dirce to death because she had mistreated their mother. They killed Lycus and tied Dirce to the tail of a wild bull that dragged her to death. The gods changed Dirce into a fountain. Pausanias ix.

Dis (dis; dēs). Roman name for Hades or Pluto.

Discordia (dis kor′ di a). Also Discord, Eris (Greek). Goddess of discord and strife. Daughter of Zeus and Hera; twin of Ares. Sister of Fear, Panic, Terror, and Trembling, the four sons of ARES, q.v. Famous for rolling the Apple of Discord across the floor at the wedding of Peleus and Thetis. This apple, marked *For the Fairest,* was claimed by three goddesses—Aphrodite, Athena, and Hera. It led to the Judgment of Paris and indirectly to the Trojan War. *Aeneid* viii; *Theogony;* Tennyson, "Oenone"; Blackie, "Judgment of Paris"; Daniel, "Tethys' Festival"; Landor, "Peleus and Thetis"; Peele, "Arraignment of Paris."

Dithyramb (dith′ i ram; dith′ i ramb). Also Dithyrambus. 1. A wild song sung by the Bacchanals, followers of Bacchus. 2. Dithyrambus is also a name for Bacchus.

Dodona (dō dō′ na). A city in Epirus; site of the most famous oracle of Zeus, probably the oldest of the Greek oracles, built by Deucalion after the deluge. Apollodorus i; Herodotus ii; *Odyssey* xiv; Pausanias vii.

Dodonides (dō dŏ′ ni dēz). See HYADES.

Doliones (do li ŏ′ nēz). The people on the peninsula of Cyzicus ruled by a king of the same name; they were friendly when the Argonauts stopped in their country. *Argonautica* i.

Dolius (dō′ li us). A faithful servant in the house of Odysseus and Penelope. He cared for Laertes during Odysseus' twenty-year absence and helped defeat the relatives of Penelope's suitors. *Odyssey* iv.

Dolon (dō′ lon; dol′ on). A Trojan noted for his swiftness sent by Hector to spy on the Greeks; seized by Diomedes and Odysseus, he revealed the plans of the Trojans, in the hope of saving his life, but was put to death by Diomedes as a traitor. *Aeneid* xii; *Iliad* x.

Dolopes (dol′ o pēz). People of Thessaly, where Peleus reigned; he sent them to the Trojan War under Phoenix; they conquered Scyros. Like many of the Greeks, they were sailors and navigators. *Aeneid* ii.

Dolphin (dol′ fin). Fish sacred to Poseidon; symbol of Poseidon. In early Christian art, the dolphin symbolized diligence, love, and swiftness.

Dorians (dō′ ri anz). One of the great peoples of Greece, descendants of Dorus, a son of Helen.

Dorides (dō′ ri dēz). Another name for the Nereides derived from their mother Doris.

Doris (dor′ is; dō′ ris). Daughter of Oceanus and Tethys. Wife of Nereus; their fifty daughters were called the Nereids. Doris was a goddess of the sea; her name is often used to mean the sea itself. *Theogony; Eclogues.*

Dorus (dō′ rus). 1. Father of the Dorians, in a province called Doris, between Mount Ossa and Mount Olympus. 2. A son of Apollo and Phthia.

Drances (dran′ sēz). A friend of Latinus and enemy of Turnus, who advised peace with Aeneas. *Aeneid* xi.

Drepanum (drep' a num). A town in Sicily near Mount Eryx, where Cronus threw the mutilated genitals of Uranus, and where Aeneas on his way to Italy buried his father Anchises. *Aeneid* iii.

Dryades (drī' a dēz). Also Dryads (drī' adz), Hamadryads (ham a drī' adz). Nymphs who presided over the woods; they lived in trees and each died at the same moment as her tree.

Dryas (drī' as). 1. Father of Lycurgus, king of Thrace, who went with Eteocles to the Theban War and was killed there. 2. Son of Ares; participated in the Calydonian boar hunt. 3. A centaur at the wedding of Pirithous. 4. A son of Lycurgus, driven mad for his disrespect toward Dionysus. 5. One of the fifty sons of Aegyptus; murdered by his wife Eurydice on his wedding night. 6. A daughter of Faunus who so hated the sight of men that she never appeared in public.

Dryope (drī' ō pē). 1. A woman of Lemnos, whose shape Aphrodite assumed to persuade all the females of the island to murder all the men. 2. A nymph of Arcadia, the mother of Pan by Hermes. 3. A nymph ravished by Apollo and changed into a poplar tree. 4. A nymph of a fountain named Pegae; she fell in love with Hylas, pulled him into the fountain to dwell with the nymphs.

Dryopes (drī' o pēz). An ancient people, descended from Dryops, who were carried away by Heracles to Delphi as slaves. Later they moved to the Peloponnesus and to Asia Minor.

Dryops (drī' ops). 1. A son of Apollo. 2. A son of Priam. 3. A friend of Aeneas in Italy. *Aeneid* x.

Dullness (dul' nes). An early, obscure deity who ruled the world until Athena joined Olympus to preside over peace, defensive war, needlework, and wisdom.

Dymas (dī' mas). 1. The father of Hecuba and grandfather of Hector. *Iliad*. 2. A Trojan, disguised in armor taken from a dead Greek, accidentally killed by the Trojans. *Aeneid* ii.

E

Eagle. Bird sacred to Zeus; abducted Ganymede, the most beautiful of mortals, to be Zeus' cupbearer. The eagle was often sent by Zeus as an omen.

Earth Goddesses. *Greek:* Gaea, Ge, Rhea; Demeter, Cora, Core, Kora, Kore, Persephone. *Phrygian:* Cybebe, Cybele. *Roman:* Tellus, Terra, Terra Mater, Ops; Ceres, Libera, Proserpina, Proserpine.

Ecclesiazusae, The (ē kle zi a zo′ sē). A comedy by Aristophanes.

Echidna (e kid′ na). See also CETO. A monster, half-woman, half-serpent. By Typhon she was the mother of such monsters as Cerberus, Geryon, the Lernean Hydra, and Orthos. Some legends say she was the mother (by her son Orthos) of the Sphinx and of the Nemean Lion. Others say she gave birth to the Chimera and to Ladon, to the vultures and to Scylla, and that Heracles had three children by her. Ceto and Phorcys were her parents. Apollodorus ii; *Met.* ix; Herodotus iii; Pausanias viii; *Theogony.*

Echion (e kī′ on). 1. One of the Argonauts. 2. One of the warriors who sprang up from the dragon's teeth sown by Cadmus. See SPARTAE. 3. One of the Greeks in the Trojan Horse.

Echo (ek′ ō). A daughter of Gaea; one of Hera's attendants and confidante of Zeus' many amours; deprived of speech by the jealous Hera; lover of Pan and Narcissus. When Narcissus did not return her love, she pined away and was changed into a stone which still retained the power of speech. *Met.* iii.

Eclogues, The (ek′ logs). Ten short pastoral poems by Vergil; contain many mythological allusions.

Eetion (e ē′ ti on). Father of Andromache, wife of Hector. Eetion and his seven sons were killed by Achilles. *Iliad* xii.

Egeria (e jēr′ i a). A nymph in Italy, courted by Numa Pompilius, whose wife she became. Egeria often acted as adviser to her husband, suggesting many laws for the governing of Rome; and he told the Roman people that he was instituting more laws with her sanction and approval. When Numa died, she was so heartbroken that she melted into tears and was changed into a fountain by Diana. *Aeneid* vii; *Met.* xv.

Eidothea (ī do thē′ a). Also Idothea (ī dŏ′ the a). **1.** A daughter of Proetus, king of Argos; she was restored to her senses by Melampus. *Odyssey* xi. **2.** A daughter of Proteus, king of Egypt; she told Menelaus how he could return safely to Sparta. *Odyssey* iv; Euripides, *Helen*. **3.** A nymph who helped educate Zeus.

Eidyia (ī dī′ ya). Also Idyia. A daughter of Oceanus and Tethys; wife of Aeetes, king of Colchis; mother of Absyrtus (Apsyrtus) and Medea. Apollodorus i.

Eileithyia (ī lī thī′ ya). Also Ilithyia; Lucina (Roman). Goddess of childbirth.

Eioneus (e yŏ′ ne us). **1.** A Greek killed by Hector. *Iliad* viii. **2.** The father of Rhesus. *Iliad* x.

Eirene (ī rē′ ne). Also Irene; Pax (Roman). Goddess of peace and one of the Horae.

Elara (ē lā′ ra). By Zeus the mother of Tityus, a celebrated giant. Apollodorus i.

Elatus (ĕ′ la tus). **1.** The son of Arcas, king of Arcadia, and Erato. **2.** One of Penelope's suitors. *Odyssey* xxii. **3.** An ally of Priam. **4.** Father of Polyphemus. **5.** An Argonaut.

Electra (e lek′ tra). **1.** Daughter of Agamemnon and Clytemnestra; sister of Orestes, Iphigenia, and Chrysothemis; wife of Pylades; mother of Medon and Strophius. Electra incited her brother Orestes to avenge their father's murder by killing their mother and her lover Aegisthus. Aeschylus, *Choephoroe;* Sophocles, *Electra;* Euripides, *Orestes.* **2.** A daughter of Atlas and Pleione. One of the PLEIADES, q.v. She had a love affair with Zeus and became the mother of Dardanus, founder of the royal house of Troy. **3.** Wife of Thaumas; mother of Iris and of the Harpies. **4.** A sister of Cadmus; **5.** One of Helen's female attendants.

Electra. The title of two Greek tragedies, one by Sophocles and one by Euripides.

Electra Complex. The unconscious tendency of a daughter to be attached to her father and hostile toward her mother.

Electryon (e lek' tri on). Son of Perseus and Andromeda; brother of Alcaeus, whose daughter Anaxo he married; became the father of ALCMENA, q.v., the mother of Heracles. Electryon was accidentally killed by Amphitryon. Alcmena had Heracles by Zeus; she was the last mortal woman Zeus embraced. Iphicles was a twin of Heracles, but Amphitryon was his father.

Eleusinian Mysteries (el u sin' i an). The most famous religious mysteries of the ancient world, founded by Eumolpus; consisted of purifications, fasts, rites, and dramas portraying the legend of Demeter and Persephone. The mysteries were believed to insure happiness in the future world, imparted formulas to be used by each soul on its passage to the future world, and forecast resurrection and immortality of men.

Eleusis (e lū' sis). A town fourteen miles west of Athens, site of the Eleusinian Mysteries.

Elgin Marbles (el' jin). Greek sculptures of Theseus, Lapiths, Centaurs, three Fates, Iris, and others from the Parthenon, now in the British Museum.

Elis (ē' lis). A city and country in the Peloponnesus; the city became famous in the days of Demosthenes, though it did not exist in the days of Homer. Olympia, the site of the Olympic Games, is in Elis, and the country was famous for its horses, whose speed was well known and often tried at the Olympic games. Many mythological names are associated with Elis, among them Heracles, Augeas, Endymion, Epeus, and Oxylus.

Elissa (e lis′ a). Also Elisa. Another name for DIDO, q.v. *Aeneid* iv.

Elpenor (el pē′ nor). A companion of Odysseus on his homeward journey from Troy. He was changed into a swine by Circe's potions and afterward restored to his former shape. *Met.* xiv; *Odyssey* x.

Elysian Fields (e lizh′ an). Also Elysium (e lizh′ i um); Isles of the Blest, Blessed Isles, Heaven, Paradise. The home of the blessed in the afterlife. Homer calls it "the Elysian plain and the world's end . . . where life is easiest for men. No snow is there, nor yet great storm, nor any rain. . . ." *Odyssey* iv. Also described in *Aeneid* vi.

Enarete (en a′ rē te). Wife of Aelous and mother of his six sons and six daughters.

Enceladus (en sel′ a dus). A giant killed by the thunderbolts of Zeus in a war against the gods; buried beneath Mount Aetna. When the giant turns over, an earthquake results; when he hisses and thrusts out a fiery tongue, the volcano erupts. One of the several myths of the ancients to explain earthquakes and volcanic eruptions, even as other myths explain other phenomena. *Aeneid* iii.

Endeis (en dē′ is). Daughter of Chiron; wife of Aeacus; mother of Telamon and Peleus. Apollodorus iii; Pausanias ii.

Endymion (en dim′ i on). Son of Zeus and Calyce; king of Elis. The moon goddess Artemis saw Endymion naked as he slept on Mount Latmos and was so enamored of his beauty that she came down from heaven and made love to him in his dreams. Endymion begged Zeus for perpetual youth, sleep, and immortality so he could prolong this pleasant dream forever. Artemis bore him fifty daughters and according to legend she still visits him nightly in his immortal sleep. Pausanias v; Keats, "Endymion," "I Stood on Tiptoe"; Lyly, *Endymion*; Disraeli, *Endymion*.

Enipeus (e nī′ pe us). A river in southern Greece of which Tyro, daughter of Salmoneus, became enamored. Poseidon assumed the shape of the river in order to make love to her, and she bore two sons, Neleus and Pelias.

Enna (en' a). Also Henna (hen' a). A town in Sicily with a beautiful plain, where Persephone was gathering flowers when she was abducted by Hades (Pluto).

Entellus (en tel' us). A famous boxer; won boxing contest at the funeral games for Anchises. *Aeneid* v.

Enyalius and **Enyo** (e ni ā' li us; e nī' ō). A god and goddess, minor war deities, companions of Ares, who is sometimes called Enyalius. Enyo, a sister of Ares, is the Roman Bellona, goddess of war.

Enyo (e nī' ō). 1. Greek goddess of war; Bellona in Rome. 2. One of the GRAEAE, q.v., daughters of Ceto and Phorcys; the other two Graeae were Dino (Deino) and Pephredo.

Eos (ē' os). Also Aurora, Mater Matuta (Roman). Goddess of the dawn. Many English poets have echoed Homer in describing the goddess of dawn as rosy-fingered and saffron-robed: Milton, Herrick, Tennyson, Shakespeare, Spenser. See AURORA.

Epaphus (ep' a fus). Son of Zeus and Io. Founder of Memphis in honor of his wife, a daughter of the Nile. Father of Libya, who became the mother (by Poseidon) of Aegyptus and Danaus. Some accounts say the twins of Libya were Agenor and Belus. Herodotus ii; *Met.* i.

Epeiros (e pī' ros). Also Epirus. A country of northern Greece. Dodona, famous for its oracle of Zeus, was in Epeiros.

Epeus (e pē' us). Also Epeius (ep ē' us). 1. The designer and builder of the Wooden Horse. *Aeneid* ii. 2. A son of Endymion. Pausanias v.

Ephesus (ef' e sus). City in Asia Minor; site of the celebrated sanctuary of Artemis, one of the Seven Wonders of the World—425 feet long, 200 feet wide, 60 feet high, its roof supported by 127 columns. Pausanias vii.

Ephialtes (ef i al' tēz). 1. One of the Giants, brother of

Otus, son of Poseidon. He grew nine inches every month; he was only nine years old when the Giants undertook the war against the gods. Some accounts say he was a son of Uranus and Gaea. **2.** A Greek who betrayed the Spartans at Thermopylae.

Epicaste (ep i kas' te). Another name for JOCASTA, q.v. Homer; Pausanias ix.

Epidaurus (ep i do' rus). A town north of Argolis in the Peloponnesus where Asclepius, god of medicine, had a famous temple. In 1900 the Greeks discovered there a well-preserved theater that seats 14,000 and has perfect acoustics, even though in the open air.

Epigoni (e pig' o nī). Sons of the Seven against Thebes, called "After-born": Aegialeus, son of Adrastus; Thersandros, son of Polynices; Alcmaeon, son of Amphiaraus; Diomedes (Diomed), son of Tydeus; Polydorus, son of Hippomedon; Sthenelos, son of Capaneus; Promachus, son of Parthenopaeus. By a curious irony, the only one of their number killed when they sacked Thebes was the only one whose father had not fallen in the previous siege of Thebes, Aegialeus, son of Adrastus. The siege of the Epigoni followed by ten years the earlier war. Apollodorus i, iii; Pausanias vi.

Epimenides (ep i men' i dēz). The Rip Van Winkle of mythology because of the story of his sleep of fifty-seven years. He was a shepherd of Crete who wrote poetry, taught religion, and worked miracles. One day while looking for lost sheep, he was overcome by slumber and lay down in a cave. Some legends list his name among the seven sages of Greece, and credit him with being the first to build temples in Greece.

Epimetheus (ep i mē' thūs; ep i mē' the us). The word "Epimetheus" means afterthought. Son of Iapetus (one of the twelve Titans) and Clymene; brother of Prometheus, Atlas, and Menoetius; husband of Pandora. He and Pandora were the parents of Pyrrha, wife of Deucalion. Apollodorus i; *Theogony*.

Epione (e pī' o nē). Wife of Aesculapius; mother of two

sons famous in medicine, Machaon and Podalirius, and of Hygeia, goddess of health. Pausanias ii.

Epirus (e pī' rus). See EPEIROS.

Epona (ep' o na). Also Bubona. Roman goddess, protector of horses, cows, and oxen. She was a beautiful girl, the offspring of a man and a mare.

Erato (er' a tō). 1. One of the nine daughters of Zeus and Mnemosyne. The Muse of lyric poetry, love poetry, marriage songs. Her symbol is the lyre. Invoked by lovers, especially in April. *Aeneid* vii; Apollodorus x; Ovid, *Amores*. 2. One of the Nereides. 3. One of the Dryades. 4. One of the Danaides.

Erebus (er' e bus). Also Erebos. Sometimes Hades. 1. Son of Chaos and Darkness, who married Nyx; father of Hemera (Day) and Aether (Light). Some legends say he was a brother of Nyx, Aether, and Hemera. *Aeneid* iv. 2. The place in the underworld through which the souls of the dead must pass to reach Hades.

Erechtheum (e rek' the um; er ek thē' um). A white marble temple on the Acropolis, sacred to Athena. It included a shrine of Athena, the tomb of Erechtheus, the salt spring of Poseidon, and other memorials. In the courtyard stood Athena's sacred olive tree. The temple was built in the fifth century B.C. under Pericles.

Erechtheus (e rek' thūs; –the us). Son of Pandion; sixth king of Athens; father of Cecrops. Butes was his twin, Philomela and Procne his famous sisters. Some accounts say he was the first to introduce the mysteries at Eleusis. Apollodorus iii; *Met.* vi; Pausanias ii.

Eriboea (er i bē' a). Also Periboea. 1. Another name for Aphrodite. *Iliad* v. 2. The mother of Telamonian (Greater) Ajax. Sophocles. 3. The wife of Aeneus, king of Calydon, and mother of Tydeus. 4. The wife of Aloeus and stepmother of Ephialtes and Otus. 5. The wife of Polybus, king of Corinth, who educated Oedipus as her own child. 6. The mother of Penelope.

Erichthonius (er ik thō' ni us). Also Erechtheus. 1. Deformed fourth king of Athens, he had tails of serpents for legs. Invented chariots and the manner of harnessing horses to pull the chariots. *Met.* ii; Apollodorus iii; Pausanias iv. **2.** A son of Dardanus, who ruled Troy.

Eridanus (e rid' a nus). The modern Po; the river into which Phaethon fell from his chariot. Near this river the Heliades, mourning the death of their brother, were changed into poplar trees. *Aeneid* vi; *Met.* ii; Pausanias i.

Erigone (e rig' o nē). **1.** A daughter of Icarius, who hanged herself when she learned that her father had been killed by drunken shepherds. She was changed into the constellation Virgo. Apollodorus iii; *Met.* vi. **2.** A daughter of Aegisthus and Clytemnestra; had a son by Orestes. She brought Orestes to trial for the murder of her mother; hanged herself when Orestes was acquitted before the Areopagus. Pausanias ii.

Erinyes (e rin' i ēz). Also Erinys, Eumenides, Semnae; Dirae, Furiae, Furies (Roman). The three avenging spirits, usually called the three Furies: Alecto (Unresting), Megaera (Jealous), Tisiphone (Avenger). Aeschylus, *The Eumenides;* Sophocles, *Oedipus at Colonus;* Chaucer, *Troilus and Criseyde;* Shakespeare, *Richard III;* Milton, *Paradise Lost,* "Lycidas"; Byron, *Manfred.*

Eriopis (er i ō' pis). **1.** A daughter of Medea. Pausanias ii. **2.** Wife of Oileus and mother of Locrian (Lesser) Ajax. *Iliad* iii.

Eriphyle (er i fī' lē). Wife of Amphiaraus of the Seven against Thebes. Her acceptance of bribes led to the death of her husband and to her murder by her son. *Aeneid* vi; Apollodorus i; *Odyssey* xi; Pausanias v.

Eris (ē' ris; er' is). See DISCORDIA.

Erisichthon (er i sik' thon). Also Erysichthon. A man of Thessaly who derided and offended Demeter by cutting down trees in her sacred grove. In revenge, she cursed him with such insatiable hunger that at last he ate his own legs, and eventually consumed himself completely. *Met.* viii.

Eros (ē′ ros; er′ os; ir′ os). Amor, Cupido, Cupid (Roman). See CUPID. Greek god of love.

Erulus (er′ ū lus). A son of Feronia, goddess of orchards and woods; a king in Italy. At his birth his mother had given him three lives and triple arms. Evander had to kill him three times the same day. *Aeneid* viii.

Erycina (er i sī′ na). A Roman name for Aphrodite.

Erymanthian Boar (er i man′ thi an). The third labor of Heracles was to capture the savage boar that haunted Mount Erymanthus in Arcadia. On this expedition Heracles accidentally wounded his old friend Chiron in the knee.

Erymanthus (er i man′ thus). A mountain in Arcadia, sacred to Artemis; the haunt of a savage boar that so frightened Eurystheus that he hid himself in a brass jar. *Aeneid* vi; *Met.* ii; Pausanias viii.

Erysichthon. See ERISICHTHON.

Erytheis (er i thē′ is). One of the Hesperides who guarded the Golden Apples in the GARDEN OF THE HESPERIDES, q.v. Most mythologists say there were three Hesperides: Aegle, Erytheis, and Arethusa. Apollodorus names four— Aegle, Arethusa, Erytheis, and Vesta. The names and number of the Hesperides vary; Hespera (Hespere) is still another name. The Hesperides were daughters of Atlas and Hesperis.

Erythia (er i thī′ ya; –thē′ a). 1. A daughter of Geryon. 2. Name of the island where Geryon ruled.

Eryx (e′ riks). 1. A son of Butes and Aphrodite, according to Apollonius and Vergil; a son of Poseidon and Aphrodite, according to Apollodorus. Half-brother of Aeneas. A boxer who killed those he defeated; Heracles defeated and killed him. He is buried on the mountain in Sicily that bears his name. 2. The mountain in Sicily, near Drepanum, where Anchises is buried.

Esquiline (es′ kwi līn; –lin). One of the seven hills of Rome. Criminals were executed on this hill, and birds of prey came to devour the dead bodies. Vergil, Horace, and

Propertius had houses there; the churches of Santa Maria Maggiore and San Pietro in Vincoli are on this hill, and the Colosseum stands nearby. See AVENTINE.

Eteocles (e tē′ o klēz). A son of Oedipus and Jocasta; brother of Polynices, Antigone, and Ismene. When Oedipus left Thebes, the two brothers agreed to rule alternately, each a year, but Eteocles refused to surrender the throne and banished Polynices. Polynices resolved to punish the treachery, and raised an army of Argives to attack Thebes. Both brothers were killed in single combat. Apollodorus iii; Pausanias v; Aeschylus, *Seven against Thebes;* Euripides, *The Phoenician Women.*

Ethiopia (ē thi ō′ pi a). Among the ancients, a country south of Greece near the great river Oceanus, visited by Bacchus.

Ethiopians (ē thi ō′ pi anz). Inhabitants of Ethiopia; they were turned black the day Phaethon tried to drive the chariot of the sun.

Etna (et′ na). Also Aetna. Mountain in Sicily; site of the tomb of Enceladus and of the forge of Hephaestus. Zeus confined the Giants under this mountain; the Cyclops, servants of Hephaestus, made the thunderbolts of Zeus there.

Euboea (ū bē′ a). 1. The largest island (after Crete) in the Aegean Sea; the chief city was Chalcis. 2. A nurse of Hera. 3. A mistress of Hermes. 4. A daughter of Thespius. Apollodorus ii; *Met.* xiv; Pausanias ii.

Eubuleus (ū bū′ lē us). A swineherd of Eleusis who saw the earth open and swallow up one of his swine. Then he saw a chariot drawn by black horses, and it, too, disappeared into the earth, bearing a godlike stranger with a girl in his arms; the girl was Persephone, the stranger was Hades (Pluto). Pausanias i, vi.

Eudora (ū dor′ a). 1. One of the Nereides. 2. One of the Atlantides. 3. One of the five Hyades.

Eudorus (ū dor′ us). A son of Hermes and Polymela; commander of the Myrmidons and a close friend of Achilles in the Trojan War. *Iliad* xvi.

Euhemerus (ū hē′ mer us; ū hem′ er us). A Greek writer who lived in the fourth century B.C. He wrote *Sacred History*, a work about Greek mythology in which he maintained that the gods were originally human heroes and the myths distorted historic events.

Eumaeus (ū mē′ us). The faithful and trustworthy swine-herd of Odysseus, who knew his master after an absence of twenty years, and helped him slay the suitors of Penelope. *Odyssey* xiii–xvii, xxi. See also PENELOPE.

Eumedes (ū mē′ dēz). 1. A Trojan, son of Dolon. He went to Italy with Aeneas, killed by Turnus. *Aeneid* xii. 2. The father of Dolon, killed in the Trojan War by Diomedes. *Iliad*.

Eumelus (ū mē′ lus). 1. A son of Admetus and Alcestis. He went to the Trojan War with the fleetest horses in the Greek army. *Iliad* ii, xxiii. 2. A man whose daughter was changed into a bird. *Met.* vii. 3. A follower of Aeneas who informed him that the Trojan women had set the ships on fire. *Aeneid* v. 4. A member of the Bacchiadae who wrote a history of Corinth, and some works about Bacchus, Medea, the Titans, and Hades, all of which have been lost. Pausanias ii.

Eumenides (ū men′ i dēz). Also Dirae, Furiae, Furies, Semnae, ERINYES, q.v.

Eumenides, The. A play by Aeschylus.

Eumolpus (ū mol′ pus). Founder of the Eleusinian Mysteries. His descendants were called Eumolpidae. The priesthood of the Eleusinian Mysteries remained in the family for 1,200 years—a remarkable fact as those appointed to the holy office were obliged to remain in perpetual celibacy. Apollodorus ii.

Eunomia (ū nō′ mi a). A daughter of Zeus and Themis. Goddess of order and wise legislation; one of the Horae. Her sisters were Dice (Justice) and Eirene (Peace).

Eupeithes (ū pī′ thēz). A prince of Ithaca; the father of

Antinous, one of the chief suitors of Penelope. *Odyssey* xvi.

Euphorbus (ū for' bus). A Trojan; according to some legends he killed Protesilaus, the first Greek ashore and the first Greek killed at Troy. *Met.* xv; *Iliad* xvi, xvii. (Some legends say Hector killed Protesilaus.)

Euphrosyne (ū fros' i nē). Also Joy. A daughter of Zeus and Eurynome; one of the three Graces (Charites). The other two Graces were Aglaia (Brilliance) and Thalia (Bloom of Life). The name "Euphrosyne" means joy.

Euripides (ū rip' i dēz). 480–406 B.C. One of the three great Greek tragedians. Of his ninety plays, all based on mythology, only nineteen are extant: *Alcestis, Andromache, The Bacchae, The Cyclops, Electra, Hecuba, Helen, Heracles, The Heraclidae, Hippolytus, Ion, Iphigenia in Aulis, Iphigenia in Tauris, Medea, Orestes, The Phoenissae, Rhesus, The Suppliants,* and *The Trojan Women.* (*Rhesus* is generally attributed to Euripides, and is therefore included above.)

Europa (ū rō' pa). The daughter of Agenor, king of Phoenicia, and of Telephassa; sister of Cadmus, Cilix, and Phoenix. Zeus transformed himself into a white bull with whom Europa was charmed; she climbed on his back, and Zeus carried her away to Crete. She had three sons by Zeus: Minos, Sarpedon, and Rhadamanthus. Apollodorus ii; *Met.* ii.

Eurus (ū' rus). Also Volturnus (Roman). The east wind. *Met.* xi.

Euryale (ū rī' a lē). **1.** One of the immortal Gorgons, daughter of Ceto and Phorcys. The other two Gorgons were Stheno (immortal) and Medusa (mortal), who was killed by Perseus. **2.** A queen of the Amazons. **3.** A daughter of Minos. **4.** A daughter of Proetus. *Theogony.*

Euryalus (ū rī' a lus). **1.** One of the Argonauts; fought against Thebes; was a follower of Diomedes; went to the Trojan War. Defeated by Epeios in a boxing match at the funeral games of Patroclus. *Iliad* ii, xxiii. **2.** A Trojan who came to Italy with Aeneas, he became famous for his immortal friendship with Nisus. On a night raid against the Rutulians, Euryalus was attacked and killed, and Nisus, going to the rescue of his friend, perished with him. Their great friendship, like that of Theseus and Pirithous, Orestes and Pylades, and others, has become proverbial. *Aeneid* ix.

Eurybates (ū rib′ a tēz). 1. Agamemnon sent Talthybios and Eurybates to the tent of Achilles to fetch Briseis. *Iliad* i. 2. Odysseus, disguised as a beggar, speaks to Penelope about Eurybates' accompanying Odysseus to Troy in order to assure her that Odysseus was still alive after an absence of twenty years. *Odyssey* xix. 3. An Argive warrior who often won at the Nemean Games. Pausanias i. 4. One of the Argonauts. *Argonautica*.

Eurybea (ū ri bē′ a; ū rib′ i a). Also Eurybia. 1. A daughter of Pontus and Gaea; wife of Crius, one of the twelve Titans; mother of Astraeus, Pallas, and Perses. 2. Mother of Lucifer and of all the stars. Hesiod. 3. A daughter of Thespius. Apollodorus.

Eurycleia (ū ri klē′ a; ū ri klē′ ya; ū ri klī′ a). Also Euryclea. Odysseus' aged nurse. When, after twenty years away, Odysseus returned home disguised as a beggar, she recognized him by the scar of a wound given him by a wild boar. *Odyssey* xix.

Eurydamas (ū rid′ a mas). 1. An interpreter of dreams. *Iliad* v. 2. One of Penelope's suitors. *Odyssey* xxii.

Eurydice (ū rid′ i sē). There are at least a dozen women in mythology named Eurydice. 1. The wife of Orpheus is the best-known. She perished from the bite of a snake as she fled from the pursuit of Aristaeus. Orpheus, heartbroken at the loss of his wife, journeyed to Hades to try to bring her back. He was given permission on condition that he would not look behind him before reaching the earth. He had almost fulfilled the condition when he looked back to be sure Eurydice was following and thus lost her forever. *Met.* x; Apollodorus i; Landor, *Orpheus and Eurydice;* Milton, "L'Allegro," Vergil, *Georgics* iv (the oldest account of Eurydice); and many others. **2.** Wife of Creon, king of Thebes; mother of Haemon, the lover of Antigone who killed himself in grief over Antigone's death. **3.** Mother of Danae. **4.** A daughter of Adrastus. **5.** Mother of Alcmena. **6.** A wife of Aeneas. **7.** A daughter of Lacedaemon. **8.** One of the Danaides. **9.** Wife of Lycurgus. **10.** A daughter of Actor. **11.** A daughter of Amphiaraus. **12.** Wife of Nestor. Apollodorus and Pausanias tell about many of these women.

Eurylochus (ū ril′ o kus). The only companion of Odysseus who did not taste of Circe's potions. He was less wise in Sicily when he carried away the sacred cattle of Apollo, for which all except Odysseus were shipwrecked and drowned. *Met.* xiv; *Odyssey* x.

Eurymachus (ū rim′ a kus). The best of Penelope's suitors. *Odyssey* xvi, xxii.

Eurymede (ū rim′ i dē). Wife of Glaucus and mother of Bellerophon. Apollodorus i.

Eurynome (ū rin′ o mē). **1.** According to Hesiod, the mother of the three Graces (Charites) by Zeus. **2.** An attendant of Penelope. *Odyssey* xvii. **3.** The mother of Leucothea by Orchamus. *Met.* **4.** The mother of Asopus by Zeus. Some mythologists list Poseidon as the father of Asopus. Apollodorus i.

Eurypylus (ū rip′ i lus). **1.** A Trojan lover of Cassandra, killed by Pyrrhus. *Iliad* xi. **2.** A soothsayer. *Aeneid* ii. **3.** A son of Poseidon, killed by Heracles. Apollodorus ii.

Eurystheus (ū ris′ thē us; ū ris′ thūs). The taskmaster of Heracles, he commanded the Twelve Labors; finally killed by Hyllus, a son of Heracles. *Aeneid* viii; Apollodorus ii; *Met.* iv; Pausanias i.

Eurytion (ū rit′ i on). Also Eurythion. **1.** The centaur who caused the quarrel at the wedding of Pirithous and Hippodamia. **2.** A centaur killed in the fight between the centaurs and Lapithae. **3.** A herdsman of Geryon. **4.** One of the Argonauts. **5.** A king of Sparta. **6.** A centaur killed by Heracles. **7.** A son of Actor. **8.** A famous archer and friend of Aeneas. *Aeneid* v; Apollodorus; Pausanias.

Eurytus (ū′ ri tus). **1.** One of the Argonauts. **2.** A member of the Calydonian boar hunt. **3.** Several of this name killed by Heracles. **4.** A king, the father of Iole, killed by Heracles when Iole was not allowed to marry him. **5.** One of the Giants killed in the war against the gods. **6.** A son of Augeas.

Euterpe (ū ter′ pē). The Muse of music and lyric poetry; her symbol was the flute. Some legends say she invented the flute and all the wind instruments. She loved wild melodies and associated more with Bacchus than with Apollo.

Euxine (ūk′ sĭn). Same as AXINE, q.v. The body of water now called the Black Sea. Associated with Heracles, the Argonauts, and the Trojan War. The word "Euxine" means hospitable, friendly.

Evadne (ē vad′ nē). Daughter of Iphis (Iphicles). Wife of Capaneus. When her husband was struck by one of Zeus' thunderbolts in the war of the Seven against Thebes, she threw herself on his funeral pyre and perished in the flames. Her fidelity is a marked contrast to the weakness of ERIPHYLE, q.v., who was dishonest, treacherous, and deceitful. *Aeneid* vi.

Evander (e van′ der). Son of the nymph Carmenta by Hermes. Before the Trojan War, he settled in Italy in the area where Rome was later founded. He entertained Heracles when he returned from the conquest of Geryon and was the first to raise altars to Heracles. Before Evander left Troy, he had met Anchises, and when Aeneas arrived in Italy, Evander was most hospitable and assisted him in the conquest of the Rutulians. Evander had a beloved son Pallas, and named the town he built on the Palatine Hill (the future site of Rome) Pallanteum after his son. Pallas was killed in the war. Evander introduced the Greek alphabet and the worship of Greek deities into Italy. After his death he was honored as a god by his subjects, and an altar was built to him on Mount Aventine. *Aeneid* viii.

Evenus (ē vē′ nus). Son of Ares and Alcippe; father of Marpessa. Marpessa was loved by Apollo, but she chose the mortal Idas as her husband; she became the mother of Cleopatra, Meleager's wife, of whom Homer wrote "fair Kleopatra, daughter of Marpessa, fair-ankled daughter of Euenos (Evenus)." *Iliad* ix.

Everes (ēv′ er ēz; ē vē′ rēz). Father of Teiresias by Chariclo.

F

Fagutal (fa′ gū tal). One of the seven hills of earliest Rome. See CERMALUS.

Fama (fā′ ma). Also Pheme (Greek). Goddess of fame.

Fasti (fas′ tī). In poetical Roman calendar form, Ovid writes of the origins and ceremonies of Roman festivals.

Fatae (fa′ tē). See ATROPOS.

Fauna (fo′ na). Also BONA DEA, q.v. Sometimes called Bona Mater. Wife (some accounts say daughter) of Faunus. Goddess of fertility, nature, farming, animals. She never saw a man after her marriage with Faunus. Her uncommon chastity brought her rank among the gods after her death. Her followers are called Fauni. *Aeneid* vii.

Faunus (fo′ nus). Also Pan. God of agriculture, crops, prophecy, fertility, and country life. *Aeneid* vii.

Faustulus (fos′ tu lus). The shepherd who found Romulus and Remus in the forest where they had been fed by a she-wolf. He defied the orders of the authorities, concealed the twin boys, and reared them as his own sons.

Favonius (fa vō′ ni us). Roman name for Zephyrus, the west wind.

Fear. A son of Ares (Mars).

Februus (feb′ ru us). Also Februa. Roman god of purification, to whom the month of February was sacred.

Feronia (fe rō′ ni a). Roman goddess of orchards, groves, and woods. The mother of ERULUS, q.v. *Aeneid* viii.

Fides (fī′ dēz). Roman goddess of faith, oaths, and honesty; first paid divine honors by Numa Pompilius.

Fields of Mourning. Also Vale of Mourning, Wailing Fields. That part of the lower world inhabited by the souls of unhappy lovers who had committed suicide, among them Dido, Evadne, Laodamia, and Phaedra. *Aeneid* vi.

Flood. See DELUGE.

Flora (flō′ ra). Also CHLORIS, q.v. Goddess of flowers, gardens, and love. She married Zephyrus and received from him the gifts of presiding over flowers and of enjoying perpetual youth.

Floralia (flō rā′ li a). Festivals at Rome in honor of Flora; instituted during the age of Romulus.

Fons (fōnz). Son of Janus and Juturna; Roman god of springs.

Forethought. A name for PROMETHEUS, q.v.

Fornax (for′ naks). Roman goddess who presided over the baking of bread; her first festivals were instituted by Numa Pompilius.

Fortuna (for tū′ na). Also Tyche (Greek). **1.** Goddess of fortune; sometimes called the goddess of chance, whose symbol is a wheel indicating her fickleness. **2.** One of the Parcae. Pindar. **3.** A daughter of Oceanus. Homer.

Forty of the Greatest Stories from Mythology. Aeneas, Ages of Mankind, Alcestis, Aphrodite, Apollo, Arcadia, Ares, Argonauts, Artemis, Athena, Atreus, Bellerophon, Calydonian boar hunt, Centaurs, Cronus, Daedalus, Deucalion and Pyrrha, Dionysus, Eros, Fate, Hades, Hera, Heracles, Hermes, Hero and Leander, Hestia, Odysseus, Orpheus, Pan, Pandora, Perseus, Philoctetes, Philomela, Prometheus, Pygmalion, Pyramus and Thisbe, Thebes, Theseus, Teiresias, Trojan War, Zeus. Some writers point out that the four greatest events and heroic rallying points of Greek mythology are: Troy, Thebes, the Argonauts, and the Calydonian boar hunt. Many of the heroes of the age were present at these events.

Four Ages of Mankind. Gold, silver, bronze, iron. See AGES OF MANKIND.

Fraus (frā' us). Daughter of Orcus (Dis, Hades, Pluto) and Night (Nox, Nyx); Roman goddess of treachery.

Frogs, The. A comedy by Aristophanes.

Fulgora (ful gō' ra). Roman goddess of lightning; she gave protection from the effects of violent thunderstorms.

Furies. Also Dirae, Eumenides, Furiae, Semnae. See ERINYES.

Furina (fu rī' na). Roman goddess of robbers. Some accounts say she is one of the Furies.

G

Gaea (jē' a). Also Ge, Gaia; Tellus, Terra (Roman). Mother Earth; after Chaos, the most ancient divinity. Earth as a goddess. After Chaos, Gaea appeared and bore Uranus, the personification of Heaven that covered the Earth. Gaea united with her son Uranus to produce the first race, the twelve Titans, six males and six females. Uranus and Gaea were also the parents of the Cyclops, the Centimani, and the Giants. Other offspring are attributed to Gaea, among them Antaeus, Cecrops, Ceto, Charybdis, the Erinyes, Erechtheus, Ladon, Nereus, Oceanus, Phorcys, Pontus, Thaumas. Apollodorus; *Theogony; Aeneid; Homeric Hymns.*

Galanthis (ga lan' this). Also Galinthias, Galen. Alcmena's maid, who eased the labors of her mistress when Heracles was born. She solicited the aid of Ilithyia (goddess of childbirth). For lying to the goddess Lucina, Galanthis was changed into a weasel. *Met.* ix.

Galatea (gal a tē' a). Also Galathaea. **1.** A daughter of Nereus and Doris. Polyphemus pursued her, but she was in love with Acis, the son of Faunus. The rejected Poly-

phemus killed Acis with a rock. *Aeneid* ix; *Met.* xiii. **2.**
The name of Pygmalion's statue. The celebrated sculptor
Pygmalion saw so much female debauchery on the island
of Cyprus that he came to hate all women and resolved
never to marry. But when he made a lovely ivory statue
beyond compare with living woman, he fell in love with
it and asked Aphrodite to give it life. His request was
granted, and the statue Galatea came to life. Pygmalion
and Galatea became the parents of a daughter, Paphos.
Met. x. The English authors Lang and Morris wrote
poems about Pygmalion and his statue.

Galen (gā′ len). See GALANTHIS.

Ganymeda (gan i mē′ da). Also Hebe; Juventas (Roman).
A daughter of Zeus and Hera; goddess of youth, cupbearer to the gods until succeeded by Ganymede. She
became the wife of Heracles and bore him two sons. *Met.*
ix; Keats; Milton; Spenser.

Ganymede (gan′ i mēd). Also Ganymedes (gan i mē′ dēz).
A beautiful Trojan boy, son of Tros and Callirrhoe;
carried by the eagle of Zeus to Olympus to succeed
Ganymeda (Hebe) as cupbearer to the gods. Homer calls
Ganymede "the most beautiful of mortal men." *Iliad* xx;
Aeneid v; *Met.* x.

Garden of the Hesperides (hes per′ i dēz). In this garden,
owned by Atlas, grew a tree with golden apples, a gift
from Gaea to Hera, and from Hera to Zeus on their
wedding day. Three celebrated nymphs, the Hesperides,
and a fierce dragon named Ladon carefully guarded the
golden apples. The eleventh labor of Heracles was to
obtain some of these apples. He achieved this by tricking
Atlas and slaying Ladon. After Eurystheus had the apples
for a while they were returned to the Garden of the
Hesperides, for they could be preserved in no other place.
Atalanta was defeated by Hippomenes with three of these
apples, and Eris used one at the wedding of Peleus and
Thetis, and Paris used one at the Judgment of Paris.
Met. iv; *Theogony*. See also ATALANTA.

Gargaphia (gar gā′ fi a). Also Gargaphie. A dark and

shaded valley, sacred to Diana, where Actaeon was torn to pieces by twenty-six of his own hounds.

Gasterocheires (gas ter ō kī' rēz). Seven Cyclops who built the walls of Tiryns.

Gate of Horn. The gate through which true dreams come to men from the cave of Hypnos, the god of sleep.

Gate of Ivory. The gate through which deceitful dreams come to men from the cave of Hypnos, the god of sleep.

Gates of Dreams. The two sets of gates in the underworld, the gate of horn and the gate of ivory.

Gates (Pillars) of Heracles. When Heracles was in search of the oxen of Geryon, he reached the frontiers of Libya and Europe; there he raised two mountains—Abyla in Africa and Calpe in Europe—as monuments to his progress. Some accounts say he rent one mountain in two and left half on each side, thus forming the Strait of Gibraltar.

Gelanor (jē lā' nor). A king of Argos deprived of his kingdom by Danaus. Pausanias ii.

Gemini (jem' i nī). Also Dioscuri, the Twins. See CASTOR. The third sign of the zodiac, which the sun enters May 21.

Genius (jē' ni us). Roman divinity who presided over the birth and life of every man, place, or thing, and determined character, conduct, and destiny. See DAEMON.

Genius Loci (lo' sī). The presiding spirit of a place.

Georgics, The (jor' jiks). Four poems by Vergil that contain much mythological material. The fourth contains the earliest account of Orpheus and Eurydice.

Geryon (jē' ri on; ger' i on). A son of Chrysaor and Callirrhoe. A celebrated monster, with three united bodies or three heads, that lived at Gades in Spain, twenty-five miles from the Gates (Pillars) of Heracles. He had many flocks, guarded by the two-headed dog Orthos and by the shepherd Eurythion. The tenth labor of Heracles was to bring these flocks and herds to Eurystheus. *Aeneid* vii; Apollodorus ii; *Theogony*.

Giants (jī′ antz). Also Gigantes (jī′ gan tēz). Sons of Uranus and Gaea. Among the Giants were the Cyclops, the Hecatoncheires (Centimani), Alcyoneus, Aloeus, Antaeus, Clytius, Enceladus, Ephialtes, Otus, Polybotes, Porphyrion, Rhoetus, Tityus, and Polyphemus (some accounts say he was a son of Poseidon). *Aeneid* vi; Apollodorus i; *Met.* i; *Odyssey* vii; Pausanias i.

Gigantomachy (jī gan tom′ a ki). The war between the Olympians and the Giants. Some authorities call this war the Titanomachy.

Girdle of Venus. Also CESTUS, q.v. This "girdle" (scanty drapery) gave any goddess or mortal woman who wore it the power of exciting love.

Glauce (glô′ kē; glô′ sē). 1. Another name for CREUSA, q.v., daughter of Creon, king of Corinth, whom Jason planned to marry. 2. The mother of Telemon; some accounts say she was his wife. 3. One of the Danaides. 4. One of the Nereides.

Glaucus (glô′ kus). Some twenty characters and places in mythology bear this name. 1. A grandson of Bellerophon who assisted Priam at Troy; killed by Greater Ajax. *Aeneid* vi; *Iliad* vi. 2. A fisherman and Argonaut; observing the fact that fish which he caught came back to life when he threw them on the grass, he desired to live in the sea; he was changed into a sea deity by Oceanus and Tethys. *Met.* xiii. 3. A son of Minos and Pasiphae who was smothered in a cask of honey. Apollodorus ii. 4. A son of Antenor killed by Agamemnon. 5. A son of Sisyphus and Merope; he prevented his mares from breeding in the hope that they would become swifter; this offended Aphrodite, who inspired the mares with such fury that they tore him to pieces.

Gnossus (nos′ us). See CNOSSUS.

Gods, The. Today the Greeks speak of twenty supreme gods, of whom only twelve were admitted to the grand council on Olympus. The gods are divided into four classes: (1) The supreme gods. (2) Gods and goddesses whose abode was not in the celestial regions. (3) Demigods and heroes; the demigods were the children of a god or goddess and a mortal; the heroes were mortals who because of their heroic deeds were raised to the rank of gods. (4) Personifications of virtues, vices, blessings, evils, etc. The twenty Greek gods and goddesses of the first class (Roman name in parentheses) were: 1. Uranus (Coleus), representative of heaven. 2. Gaea (Vesta Prisca), representative of the earth. 3. Cronus (Saturn), god of time. 4. Rhea (Cybele), goddess of the earth. 5. Zeus (Jupiter), ruling power of earth and sky, supreme god of the pagan world 6. Hera (Juno), queen of heaven. 7. Poseidon (Neptune), god of the sea. 8. Hades (Pluto), god of the lower regions. 9. Hestia (Vesta), goddess of fire. 10. Demeter (Ceres), goddess of agriculture. 11. Apollo, god of day, music, and poetry. 12. Artemis (Diana), goddess of hunting and chastity. 13. Hermes (Mercury), god of eloquence and messenger of the gods. 14. Athena (Minerva), goddess of wisdom. 15. Ares (Mars), god of war and tumult. 16. Dionysus (Bacchus), god of wine and revelry. 17. Hephaestus (Vulcan), god of fire. 18. Aphrodite (Venus), goddess of love and beauty. 19. Helios (Sol), god of the sun. 20. Selene (Luna), goddess of the moon. Many temples to the gods were erected in Greece; 95 per cent were built in honor of the big four—Apollo, Athena, Poseidon, and Zeus. For Roman gods, see also DII.

Golden Age. The first age of mankind, the age of innocence. There were no bodily infirmities, and nobody had to work. Perfect happiness, truth, and right prevailed. There was perpetual spring. There were no arts, no crafts; the earth brought forth everything needed. There were no wives, no daughters, no women! Only men were on earth during this age of Cronus and the elder gods.

Golden Apples. See GARDEN OF THE HESPERIDES.

Golden Ass, The. Apuleius wrote this clever satire in the form of a romance or supposed autobiography of the author, who is transformed into an ass by the mistake of the servant of an enchantress. The ass passes from master to master, observing the vices and follies of men, and finally recovers human form by the intervention of the goddess Isis. The story includes a number of episodes, of which the best known is the beautiful allegory of Cupid and Psyche.

Golden Bough. For Aeneas, the passport to the underworld. The Sibyl of Cumae tells Aeneas to obtain the Golden Bough sacred to Persephone, for without it Charon would not permit him to cross the Styx. *Aeneid* vi.

Golden Bough, The. A work by Sir James George Frazer (1854–1941), it is a study of cults, myths, rites, with their origins and their importance in the historical development of religions, and a comparative study of the beliefs and institutions of mankind.

Golden Fleece. The pelt of the golden-fleeced winged ram on whose back Phrixus and Helle, children of Athamas and Nephele, fled Boeotia. Helle fell off during the journey and was drowned in what later became known as the Hellespont. Phrixus reached his destination at Colchis, was kindly treated by the king, and married Chalciope, the daughter of Aetes. Phrixus sacrificed the ram, and its fleece of pure gold was hung in a sacred grove in Colchis and guarded by a dragon. With the aid of Medea, another daughter of Aeetes, Jason and the Argonauts were able to recover the Golden Fleece and carry it away.

Golgi (gol′ jī). A city in Cyprus beloved by Aphrodite.

Gordian Knot (gor′dian). A knot tied by Gordius, father of King Midas of Phrygia. The knot was so complicated that it resisted all attempts to untie it; legend said that whoever could untie the knot would rule over all Asia. No one succeeded, but Alexander the Great cut the knot in two with his sword. "Cutting the Gordian knot" is today a figure of speech for solving a problem by direct action.

Gordius (gor′ dius). He tied the GORDIAN KNOT, q. v.

Gorgons (gor′ gonz). Also Gorgones. Three daughters of Ceto and Phorcys; two, Euryale and Stheno, were immortal; the third, Medusa, was mortal. The three were monsters with serpents for hair, brazen claws, and staring eyes whose glance turned men into stone. Their wings were the color of gold, their bodies were covered with impenetrable scales, and their teeth were as long as the tusks of a wild boar. Aeschylus says they had only one tooth and one eye among them. While they were exchanging the eye, Perseus cut off Medusa's head. *Aeneid* vi; *Iliad* v, xi; *Met.* iv; *Theogony*.

Gracchi (grak′ ī). The souls of unborn Roman heroes, seen in Hades by Aeneas and Anchises. *Aeneid* vi.

Graces (grās′ es). See CHARITES.

Gradivus (gra dī′ vus). Name for Ares (Mars) as leader of armies.

Graeae (grē′ ē). Also Graiae. Three hoary witches, daughters of Ceto and Phorcys, with gray hair from birth, and one eye and one tooth among them, which they used in turn. The three, Dino, Enyo, and Pephredo, were surprised by Perseus and gave him the information that led him to the abode of their sisters the Gorgons.

Graiae (grī′ ē). See GRAEAE.

Gratiae (grā′ shi ē). See CHARITES.

Great Bear. See ARCAS.

Great Expeditions of the Greeks. The Trojan War; Seven against Thebes; the Argonauts in Search of the Golden Fleece; the Calydonian boar hunt.

Great Mother. Goddess of birth and fertility, known by the names Rhea (Greek); Ops, Bona Dea (Roman); Cybele (Phrygian); Astarte (Phoenician); Ishtar (Babylonian); Isis (Egyptian).

Great Stories in Mythology. See FORTY OF THE GREATEST STORIES FROM MYTHOLOGY.

Griffins (grif′ inz). The hounds of Zeus; monsters half-eagle, half-lion, that guarded the gold of the north, which the Arismapsi tried to steal. These hounds never barked.

Groups in Mythology. *Twelve:* Titans; Olympians; Labors of Heracles. *Nine:* Muses. *Seven:* hills of earliest Rome; of later Rome; Pleiades; against Thebes; wonders of the ancient world; famous destroyers of monsters. *Five:* rivers of Hades; groups of nymphs; condemned to unusual punishment in Hades. *Four:* winds; Panhellenic Festivals; sons of Ares. *Three:* Graces; Furies; Fates; Gorgons; Graeae; Harpies; judges of the Dead; contestants for the Golden Apple; Hesperides; Cyclopes; Hecatoncheires. *Two:* Gemini; messengers; cupbearers.

Gyas (jī′ as). A companion of Aeneas. At the funeral games for Anchises, his boat came in third. *Aeneid* v.

Gyges (jī′ jēz). One of the three HECATONCHEIRES, q.v.

H

Hades (hā′ dēz). Also Ades, Aides, Aidoneus; Dis, Pluto, Pluton, Orcus (Roman). Son of Cronus and Rhea. One of the great Olympians; ruler of the underworld; husband of Persephone. His abode was called by his name.

Hades, The House of. Hell; underworld; lower world; nether world.

Hades, The Celebrated Dog of. Cerberus.

Hades, The Three Judges of. Aeacus, Minos, Rhadamanthus.

Hades, The Five Rivers of. Acheron, Cocytus, Lethe, Phlegethon, Styx.

Hades, Severe Punishment in. Danaides, Ixion, Sisyphus, Tantalus, Tityus.

Haemon (hē′ mon). Also Haimon. Son of Creon; lover of ANTIGONE, q.v., the daughter of Oedipus; ordered by his father to bury Antigone alive. Sophocles, *Antigone*.

Haemonia (he mō′ ni a). 1. A name for Thessaly; the general name for northern Greece. 2. A town where Morpheus assumed the form of Ceyx and told Halcyone about the shipwreck in which Ceyx was drowned. See also CEYX.

Haemus (hē′ mus). Son of Boreas and Orithyia; husband of Rhodope. Haemus and Rhodope were so happy that they assumed the names of Zeus and Hera, for which they were changed into mountains (the Balkans). *Met.* vi.

Haimon (hī′ mon.) See HAEMON.

Halcyone. Same as ALCYONE, q.v., See also CEYX.

Halirrhothius (hal i rō′ thi us). Son of Poseidon and Euryte. He ravished Alcippe the daughter of Ares and was killed by Ares. Poseidon brought Ares to trial for murder at the Areopagus, but he was acquitted. Apollodorus iii; Pausanias i.

Halitherses (hal i ther′ sēz). Also Halithersus. A man who "excelled his peers in knowledge of birds" and who told Penelope's suitors that Odysseus would return. *Odyssey* ii.

Hamadryads (ham a drī′ adz). Also Hamadryades. Tree nymphs whose lives were bound up with those of the trees in which they lived.

Happy Isles. The free, sunny section of Hades.

Harmonia (har mō′ ni a). Also Hermione, Hermionea. Daughter of Ares and Aphrodite. Wife of Cadmus, king of Thebes; they were the parents of Agave, Autonoe, Ino, Polydorus, and Semele. Harmonia was the owner of a beautiful necklace (some legends say a robe) which inspired her children with wickedness and impiety and figured in the story of the Seven against Thebes and of the Epigoni. Some accounts say a Harmonia was the mother of the Amazons by Ares. See also HERMIONE, wife of Cadmus.

Harpalyce (har pal′ i sē). 1. A daughter of Harpalycus, king of Thrace; a famous and swift huntress who preyed upon peasants and shepherds, she was finally caught in a net and killed. *Aeneid* i. **2.** A daughter of GLYMENUS, q.v. She had an incestuous relationship with her father which resulted in a son whom she killed, cut up, and served to her father as food. Her punishment was to be changed into an owl. Clymenus killed her and then hanged himself.

Harpalycus (har pal′ i kus). **1.** Son of Hermes; king of Thrace; father of Harpalyce. He taught boxing to Heracles. **2.** A companion of Aeneas, killed by Camilla. *Aeneid* xi.

Harpies (har′ piz). Also Harpyiae. Daughters of Poseidon and Gaea; some legends say they were the daughters of Thaumas and Electra. They were fierce, filthy, winged monsters, with the faces of women, bodies of vultures, and sharp claws. They left a loathsome stench, snatched and defiled the food of their victims, carried away the souls of the dead, served as ministers of divine vengeance, and punished criminals. They were sent by Hera to plunder the tables of Phineus, from which they were driven away by Zethes and Calais to the Strophades. They plundered Aeneas on his way to Italy, and predicted many calamities that would overtake him. *Aeneid* iii. Most mythologists name three Harpies, Aello, Celaeno, and Ocypete. Homer names only one and calls her Podarge. Some name two, Aello and Ocypete; Hesiod names these two in his *Theogony*.

Hearth, Goddess of the. See HESTIA.

Heaven. From Mother Earth came the starry vault of heaven. First, Erebus and Night, the children of Chaos, were married; from them sprang Light and Day; then GAEA, q.v., bore Uranus, the personification of Heaven who covered Earth; from Gaea and Uranus came the first race, the Titans. See also ELYSIAN FIELDS.

Hebe (hē′ bē). Also GANYMEDA, q.v. She was dismissed from her office as cupbearer to the gods when she fell down and indecently exposed herself while pouring nectar to the gods at a grand festival. She was succeeded by Ganymede.

Hebrus (hē′ brus). A river in Thrace; its sand was of gold. Into this river the Bacchantes threw the head, dismembered body, and lyre of Orpheus. *Aeneid* iv; *Met.* xi.

Hecabe (hek′ a bē). Also Hecuba. Wife of Priam at the time of the Trojan War. Most unfortunate mother of fifty sons and twelve daughters. Many of her sons were slain, Polyxena was sacrificed, Polydorus drowned, Cassandra was murdered, Hecabe herself changed into a bitch. *Aeneid* iii; *Met.* xi.

Hecale (hek′ a lē). An old woman who was kind to Theseus when he went to capture the Marathonian bull.

Hecate (hek′ a tē). Also Hekate. See also TRIVIA. Daughter of Perses and Asteria. A triple goddess: as moon goddess she is called Luna, as earth goddess Diana, as underworld goddess Hecate or Persephone. *Hecate* is one of the eight names for the moon. *Aeneid* iv; *Met.* vii; *Theogony*.

Hecatomb (hek′ a tōm; –tōōm). In Greek antiquity, the sacrifice to the gods of a hundred oxen or cattle at the same time; or the sacrifice of a large number of victims; or a costly sacrifice.

Hecatoncheires (hek a ton kī′ rēz). Also Centimani. The sons of Uranus and GAEA, q.v. The three hundred-handed Giants, Briareus, Cottus, and Gyges.

Hector (hek′ tor). Son of Priam and Hecabe (Hecuba). Husband of Andromache; father of Astyanax. Hector was the captain of the Trojan forces in the Trojan War and their chief hero. He fought with great valor, engaged the bravest of the Greeks, and killed no fewer than 31 of them, including Patroclus. Hector was killed by Achilles. *Aeneid* i; Hyginus; *Iliad; Met.* xii, xiii; Pausanias i, ix.

Hecuba (hek′ u ba). See HECABE.

Hecuba. A tragedy by Euripides.

Hekate (hek′ a tē). See HECATE.

Helen of Troy (hel′ en). Also Helena. Daughter of Zeus and Leda (wife of Tyndareus). The most beautiful woman of the age. Theseus and Pirithous carried her away when she was nine years old. Twenty-seven princes of Greece sought her hand. She chose Menelaus, king of Sparta; they had one daughter, Hermione. Helen's elopement with Paris was the immediate cause of the Trojan War. Euripides, in his drama, *Helen*, holds that Helen never went to Troy at all; he says that there never was any Helen of Troy; she was confined by Proteus, king of Egypt, during the Trojan War, and Menelaus recovered her from Egypt after the war. Some authorities mention a problem: if Castor and Pollux (her brothers, born when she was born) were only fifteen years old when they went with the Argonauts, Helen was sixty years old when Troy fell; but Homer says she was very beautiful. Apollodorus; Euripides, *Helen;* Hyginus; Herodotus; *Heroides* xvi, xvii; *Iliad; Odyssey;* Pausanias; Yeats, "Leda and the Swan"; Tennyson, "A Dream of Fair Women"; Brooke, "Menelaus and Helen"; Landor, "Menelaus and Helen"; Lang, "Helen of Troy." See also PROTEUS, THEOCLYMENUS.

Helen. A play by Euripides.

Helena (hel′ e na). HELEN OF TROY, q.v.

Helenor (he lē′ nor). A Lydian prince who went with Aeneas to Italy. He was killed by the Rutulians. *Aeneid* ix.

Helenus (hel′ e nus). Son of Priam and Hecuba; twin of Cassandra; the only one of Priam's fifty sons who survived the Trojan War. A celebrated soothsayer, respected by all Trojans, he foretold that Troy could not be taken (1) while the city retained possession of the Palladium; (2) without the arrows of Philoctetes, who had been on the island of Lemnos for nearly ten years; (3) unless Neoptolemus joined the Greek army. After the fall of Troy, Helenus became king of Epirus. He was given Andromache as a slave, married her after the death of Neoptolemus. In Epirus he was visited by Aeneas on his way to Italy. Helenus the prophet told Aeneas that the journey would be long and difficult and that Aeneas would recognize the place of settlement when he found a white sow suckling thirty white pigs. *Aeneid* iii; *Iliad* vi; *Met.* xiii; Pausanias i.

Heliades (hē lī' a dēz). Daughters of Apollo and Clymene; sisters of Phaethon—Aegiale, Aegle, Lampethusa, Lampetie, and Phaethusa. They grieved so at the death of their brother that they were changed by the gods into poplars. *Met.* ii.

Helicon (hel' i kon; –kun). A mountain in Boeotia, sacred to Apollo and the Muses, who had a temple there. The fountain Hippocrene flowed from this mountain. *Aeneid* vii; *Met.* ii; Pausanias ix.

Heliconiades (hel i kō nī' a dēz). Another term for the nine Muses, derived from Helicon, a place where they were worshiped.

Heliopolis (hē li op' o lis). **1.** A city in Egypt where Apollo had a temple and an oracle, to which the Phoenix made regular pilgrimages. **2.** A very ancient city in what is now Syria (modern Baalbek), today famous for the best-preserved Roman ruins in the world, with notable temples of Zeus, Bacchus, and Aphrodite. It was once the center of worship of Baal as a sun god, hence its name.

Helios (hē' li os; –us). Also Helius, Hyperion, Apollo. Son of Hyperion (a Titan) and Thia; brother of Eos and Selene. Sometimes called the Titan sun god. Known by the names Sol (Roman); Mithras (Persian); Baal (Chaldean); Moloch (Canaanite); Osiris (Egyptian); Adonis (Syrian). Homer calls him Helios Hyperion, the sun god. *Odyssey* xii; *Homeric Hymns*.

Hellas (hel' las). Ancient name for Thessaly, generally applied to all of Greece; a name received from Deucalion. Pausanias ii; Strabo.

Helle and **Phrixus** (hel' lē; frik' sus). Daughter and son of Athamas and Nephele; both rode away on a ram with golden fleece, but Helle fell into the body of water that now bears her name (Hellespont), and drowned. See also INO.

Hellen (hel' len). Son of Deucalion and Pyrrha. Gave his name to his subjects, who were called Hellenes; considered the ancestor of the Hellenic race. Pausanias iii.

Hellenes (hel′ lēnz; he lē′ nēz). The inhabitants of ancient Greece, the name given by Hellen. Some accounts say the name was given by Deucalion, in honor of his son Hellen.

Hellespont (hel′ es pont). Narrow strait between Asia and Europe. Named for Helle, who fell here and drowned.

Hemera (hem′ er a). The Day. One of the two beautiful children of Erebus and Nyx. The other was *Aether* (Light). Together they dethroned their parents and seized power.

Henna (hen′ a). See ENNA.

Hephaestia (he fes′ ti a). Festivals held in Athens in honor of Hephaestus.

Hephaestus (he fes′ tus). Also Vulcan (Roman), Halciber. Son of Zeus and Hera, according to Homer. His mother was so disgusted with him that as soon as he was born she threw him into the sea, where he remained for nine years. Some accounts say he broke his leg when Zeus kicked him out of Olympus to the island of Lemnos. Hephaestus wanted Athena for his wife, but she refused him, and Aphrodite is generally considered the wife of this deformed and lame god; he was the father of Eros by Aphrodite. The infidelity of Aphrodite with Ares is proverbial; Alectryon was lookout for the lovers and forgot to wake Ares when Apollo approached, discovered the lovers, and reported them to the other gods. Hephaestus was the god of fire and patron of all artists who worked with iron and metal. His most famous forges were under Mount Aetna. In mythology he is the famous blacksmith; his five most famous creations were (1) the arms of Achilles; (2) the arms of Aeneas; (3) the shield of Heracles; (4) the necklace of Harmonia, a gift which proved fatal to all who wore it; (5) the scepter of Agamemnon. *Aeneid;* Apollodorus; *Homeric Hymns;* Herodotus; *Iliad;* Pausanias; *Theogony;* John Milton makes Hephaestus the architect of Pandemonium.

Hera (hē′ ra; her′ a). Also Here (hē′ rē); Juno (Roman). Daughter of Cronus and Rhea; sister and wife of Zeus. Goddess of women and of childbirth. Queen of the gods and of heaven. The most jealous wife in mythology. She spied much on Zeus' love affairs, persecuted his mistresses, and was most vindictive toward the offspring of his many liaisons, especially Heracles, Semele, and Leto. Apollodorus; *Homeric Hymns;* Apollonius; Homer; Ovid; Pausanias; Vergil; Spenser; Milton; Tennyson; Bridges; and many others tell her story. See also TEMENUS.

Heracles (her′ a klēz); Hercules (her′ kū lēz) (Roman). Son of Zeus and Alcmena. Renowned for feats of strength, particularly of the Twelve Labors. One of the seven great destroyers of monsters and the mightiest and most famous of all the Greek heroes. At the time of his birth Hera, jealous of Alcmena, sent two large serpents to destroy Heracles, but the fearless infant seized one in each hand and squeezed them to death. He had many teachers: Chiron taught him many of the polite arts; Castor, how to fight; Eurytus, how to shoot a bow; Autolycus, how to drive a chariot; Linus, how to play the lyre; Eumolpus, how to sing. The Olympians completely armed him for his Twelve Labors: from Athena he received a coat of arms and a helmet; from Hermes, a sword; from Neptune, a horse; from Zeus, a shield; from Apollo, a bow and arrows; from Hephaestus, a golden cuirass and brazen buskins, with a celebrated club of bronze. The Twelve Labors of Heracles were (the order varies with the several ancient writers): (1) Killing the Nemean lion, which he strangled. (2) Killing the Lernean Hydra. (3) Capturing the Cerynean stag. (4) Capturing the Erymanthian boar. (5) Cleaning the stables of AUGEAS, q.v. (6) Killing the man-eating Stymphalian birds. (7) Capturing the man-eating mares of DIOMEDES, q.v. (8) Capturing the Cretan bull. (9) Procuring the girdle of Hippolyta, queen of the Amazons. (10) Fetching the cattle of Geryon. (11) Obtaining three golden apples from the Garden of the Hesperides. (12) Bringing Cerberus to earth from the lower world, called the most dangerous of his labors. For the so-called thirteenth labor of Heracles, see THESPIUS. There were many lesser labors: (1) Killing a huge lion near Mount Cithaeron. (2) Slaying Cacus, a cattle thief. (3) Crushing Antaeus.

(4) Killing Busiris. (5) Slaying Eryx, a boxer. (6) Accompanying the Argonauts. (7) Assisting the gods in the war against the giants, enabling Zeus to win. (8) Conquering Laomedon and plundering Troy 79 years before the Trojan War. (9) Clearing Queen Omphale's country of Lydia of a huge serpent and robbers. (10) Restoring Tyndareus to the throne of Sparta. (11) Defeating Achelous (by wrestling) for the hand of Deianira. (12) Rescuing Hesione from a sea monster. He had many wives, mistresses, and children. See HERACLIDAE. All of the ancient authors have written about Heracles: Apollodorus, Apollonius Rhodius, Diodorus Siculus, Euripides, Herodotus, Hesiod, Homer, Hyginus, Ovid, Pausanias, Pindar, Plautus, Seneca, Sophocles, Statius, Strabo, and Vergil. Molière and Giraudoux among the French, and Chaucer, Spenser, Shakespeare, Milton, and Dryden have used his story. See also NESSUS.

Heracles. A drama by Euripides.

Heraclidae (her a kli' dē). The descendants of Heracles. Heracles fathered many children. By 49 of the daughters of Thespius he had 51 sons. Some of the wives and some of the children were: (1) by Astydamia: Ctesippus; (2) by Astyoche: Tlepolemus; (3) by Auge: Telephus; (4) by Autonoe: Palemon; (5) by Chalciope: Thessalus; (6) by Deianira: Macaria, Glycisonetes, Gyneus, Hyllus, Odites; (7) by Echidna: Agathyrus, Gelon, Scytha; (8) by Epicaste: Thestalus; (9) by Megara: Deicoon and Therimachus; (10) by Omphale: Agelaus, Lamon; (11) by Parthenope: Eueres. His children by Megara he killed in a fit of madness; some legends say he also killed Megara. Euripedes, *The Heraclidae.*

Heraclidae, The. A drama by Euripides.

Heraeum (hē rē' um). Site of a famous grove and temple, sacred to Hera, near Mycenae in the Peloponnesus.

Hercules. See HERACLES.

Hercules. A tragedy by Seneca.

Hercules Furens (fū' renz). Same as *Heracles,* the play by Euripides.

Hercules Oetaeus (ē tā′ us). A tragedy by Seneca.

Hermaphroditus (her maf rō dī′ tus). Son of Hermes and
Aphrodite. He was loved by the nymph Salmacis, who
wished to be united with him in one person. The union
took place and a hermaphrodite developed—an individual with both male and female sexual characteristics.

Hermes (hur′ mēz). Also Mercury (Roman). Son of Zeus
and Maia. Father of Autolycus by Chione. The messenger of the gods; his attributes are the most complex
and varied of those of any of the major gods. He was
responsible for increase in the animal world; he was a
deity of wealth, god of trade and travelers, of commerce,
manual skill, oratory and eloquence, of thieves, and of
the wind—with whose speed he was able to move; he
was also patron of athletes. Within a few hours after his
birth, he had stolen Apollo's cattle. He invented the lyre
and gave it to Apollo who, in turn, gave him the caduceus,
a golden staff with wings at the top, intertwined with
serpents—symbol of today's medical profession. His son
Autolycus became the champion thief of the world. The
name "Hermes" means hastener, and representations of
him are symbolic of the messenger or of speed and
majesty in flight. Milton; Keats; Shelley. The most interesting stories related are about the things he did on
the first day of his life: (1) stealing the cattle of Apollo;
(2) making the lyre; (3) inventing the winged sandals
which were called *talaria;* (4) making fire by rubbing
sticks together; (5) making, of Apollo's cattle which he
stole, killed, and butchered, the first flesh offering to the
gods. All this in the first 24 hours of his life! Zeus gave him
a winged cap called *petasus.* His duties as messenger involved many acts: (1) conducting the souls of the dead
to Hades; (2) taking the three goddesses to the Judgment of Paris; (3) accompanying Zeus on his visit to
Baucis and Philemon; (4) killing the hundred-eyed
Argos; (5) delivering Ares from his long confinement;
(6) purifying the Danaides (7) tying Ixion to the
wheel; (8) warning Aeneas to hasten to Italy; (9) com-
manding Calypso to send Odysseus away on a raft; (10)

selling Heracles to Omphale—and these are only a few of many. The story of this great Olympian with the caduceus, petasus, and talaria is told by many, among them Apollodorus; Homer; Apollonius; *Homeric Hymns;* Ovid; Pausanias; and Vergil.

Hermione (hur mī′ o nē). Also Harmonia. 1. Wife of CADMUS, q.v. 2. Daughter of Menelaus and Helen. She was promised in marriage to Orestes, but Menelaus, ignorant of this, gave her to Pyrrhus, son of Achilles, for the services Pyrrhus rendered in the Trojan War. *Heroides* viii; *Odyssey* iv; Euripides, *Andromache, Orestes.*

Hero and **Leander** (hē′ rō; le an′ der). Hero was a beautiful priestess of Aphrodite at Sestos. At a festival there, Leander saw and fell in love with her. Thereafter, guided by a torch that Hero placed in a tower, Leander swam from his home at Abydos, on the opposite side of the Hellespont, to be with Hero. One stormy night he was drowned, and the next day his body was washed ashore at Sestos. Hero discovered the dead body, and in grief drowned herself. *Heroides* xviii, xix; Marlowe, *Hero and Leander.* Shakespeare; Bryon; Keats; Tennyson; D. G. Rossetti; Cowley; Hood; Nash and others have used this story.

Herodotus (hē rod′ ō tus). 484–424 B. C. A great Greek historian who has been called the "Father of History." His *History,* a work in nine books named after the nine Muses, contains much mythological material.

Heroic Age. One of the five ages of mankind, according to Hesiod. He placed this age after the Bronze Age and before the Iron Age. In *Works and Days* he calls this age the "wonderful generation of heromen," and lists such glorious exploits as the Trojan War and the Seven against Thebes.

Heroides, The (hē rō′ i dēz). Ovid's collection of twenty-one letters written by heroes and heroines of mythology to their lovers. Among the letters were those written by Penelope to Odysseus, Phaedra to Hippolytus, Oenone to

Paris, Dido to Aeneas, Paris to Helen, Helen to Paris, Leander to Hero, Hero to Leander.

Herse (hur′ sē). Daughter of Cecrops, king of Athens; she was loved by Hermes. *Met*. ii.

Hesiod (hē′ si od; hes′ i od). A Greek poet of the eighth century B.C., called the "Father of Greek Didactic Poetry." His *Theogony*, an account of the gods, is the earliest source material available on Greek mythology. His *Works and Days* and *The Shield of Heracles* also provide much mythological information.

Hesione (hē sī′ o nē). Daughter of Laomedon, king of Troy. She was rescued from a sea monster by Heracles (the Jonah of mythology—who spent three days in the belly of the monster and tore the creature to pieces). Laomedon refused to pay Heracles for his work, and in revenge the mighty warrior attacked Troy, killed Laomedon and his sons (except Priam). Heracles then gave Hesione to Telamon, his assistant in the war. Telamon took her to Greece. Priam sent Paris to Greece to reclaim his sister, but he fell in love with Helen, wife of Menelaus, and carried her away to Troy, thus causing the Trojan War. Her story is told by Apollodorus, Diodorus, Homer, Ovid, and others.

Hespera (hes′ per a). A name for EOS, q.v., daughter of Erebus and Nyx, originally goddess of the dawn. Later she accompanied the sun and became Evening. Some accounts say she is one of the Hesperides.

Hespere (hes′ per ē). One of the Hesperides.

Hesperia (hes pē′ ri a). An ancient name which means the land of the evening, given by Aeneas to Italy.

Hesperides (hes per′ i dēz). Daughters of Atlas and Hesperis. See GARDEN OF THE HESPERIDES, ERYTHEIS.

Hesperis (hes′ pe ris). Daughter of Hesperus; wife of Atlas; mother of the Hesperides.

Hesperus (hes′ per us). Also Hesper, Vesper. Son of Iapetus; brother of Atlas; father of Hesperis. He went to Italy, and some accounts say Italy was named after him.

The name is also used for the planet Venus, when the planet appears after the setting of the sun. In English poetry Hesperus is the evening star. Spenser; Jonson; Donne; Milton.

Hestia (hes′ ti a); also Vesta (Roman). The firstborn child of Cronus and Rhea; goddess of the hearth and symbol of the home. The virgin goddess, the oldest and most sacred of the 12 great Olympians. (The other two virgin goddesses were Artemis and Athena.) At Rome, a famous temple of Hestia was kept by six priestesses called Vestal Virgins. Since a chaste protectress of the household is not to be gossiped about, the Greeks and Romans told no stories about her. Apollodorus; *Theogony; Homeric Hymns;* Pausanias; *Aeneid.* She is seldom mentioned in English literature.

Hicetaon (hi se tā′ on). Also Hiketaon. A son of Laomedon and brother of Priam. Too old to fight in the Trojan War, he was a wise counselor who advised the restoration of Helen to Menelaus. *Odyssey* iii.

Hilara (hi lā′ ra). Also Hilaira (hil a ī′ ra). Sometimes called Talaira. Daughter of Leucippus and Philodice; sister of Phoebe. Hilara and Phoebe were on their way to marry Lynceus and Idas when they were intercepted and carried away by Castor and Pollux; the twins married the sisters. In the resulting fight over the sisters, Castor killed Lynceus, Idas killed Castor, and Pollux killed Idas. Apollodorus iii; Pausanias ii.

Himeros (hī′ mer os). Also Himerus, Longing. God of desire; personification of the longing of love; an attendant of Eros.

Hippocoon (hip ō′ kō on). 1. A friend of Aeneas; distinguished himself at the funeral games for Anchises. *Aeneid* v. 2. A participant in the Calydonian boar hunt. *Met.* viii. 3. An ally of Rhesus, king of Thrace; he aroused the Trojan camp when Diomedes and Odysseus were killing Rhesus and stealing the marvelous horses. *Iliad* x.

Hippocrene (hip′ ō krēn; –krē nē). Celebrated fountain in Boeotia, on Mount Helicon, sacred to the nine Muses.

It first rose from the ground when struck by the horse Pegasus. Hippocrene is called the source of poetic inspiration. *Met.* v.

Hippodamia (hip ō da mī′ a). **1.** Daughter of Oenomaus, king of Pisa; wife of Pelops; mother of Atreus and Thyestes. She bribed Myrtilus, her father's charioteer, to remove a spoke from the royal chariot wheels so that Pelops could win her. Oenomaus had already defeated and killed 13 other suitors whom he had challenged to chariot races. After killing Oenomaus, Pelops murdered Myrtilus. These murders were primal sins, all paid for later by the many troubles of the house of Atreus. *Heroides* viii, xvii. **2.** A daughter of Adrastus, king of Argos. Wife of Pirithous, king of the Lapithae. *Met.* xii.

Hippolyta (hi pol′ i ta; –tē). Also Hippolyte. Sometimes called Antiope. **1.** Queen of the Amazons. Some accounts say Heracles killed her and took her girdle; others say she willingly gave the girdle to him; still others say Heracles gave her to Theseus as his wife, and by Theseus she became the mother of Hippolytus. Some accounts say she is the same as ANTIOPE, q.v.; other accounts name Antiope as her sister. **2.** The wife of Acastus. She fell in love with Peleus, who was in exile at her husband's court; he refused her love and she falsely accused him of molesting her; Chiron prevented Peleus from being killed by Acastus; some accounts say Peleus later killed Acastus.

Hippolytus (hi pol′ i tus). Son of Theseus and Hippolyta. After the death of Hippolyta, Theseus married Phaedra, daughter of King Minos and sister of Ariadne. Phaedra fell in love with Hippolytus, and when he refused her advances, she falsely accused him to Theseus. Theseus readily believed Phaedra's charges; he asked Poseidon to punish his son. As Hippolytus fled from his father, his horses were frightened by the sea-calves of Poseidon; the chariot overturned and Hippolytus was killed. *Aeneid* vii; *Met.* xv. Chaucer, *The Legend of Good Women;* Racine, *Phèdre;* Edmund Smith, *Phaedra and Hippolytus.*

Hippolytus. A tragedy by Euripides; a play by Seneca.

Hippomedon (hi pom' e don). One of the Seven against Thebes. Father of Polydorus, one of the Epigoni.

Hippomenes (hi pom' e nēz). Also Melanion, Milanion. Winner of the race with ATALANTA, q.v. *Met.* x.

Hippona (hi pō' na). Roman goddess of horses.

Hipponous (hi pon' o us). 1. The father of Periboea and Capaneus. 2. A son of Priam. 3. The first name of BELLEROPHON, q.v. 4. In literature later than the *Iliad,* Hipponous is a Trojan killed by Achilles just before the great warrior expired.

Hippotades (hi pot' a dēz). Another name for Aeolus, god of the winds.

Hippotas (hip' ō tas). Also Hippotes (hip' ō tēz). The father of Aeolus, from whose name the god of the winds is called Hippotades.

Hippothous (hi pō' thō us). Also Hippothoos. A Trojan ally, leader of the Pelasgians, killed by Telamonian Ajax when he tried to take the body of Patroclus to the Trojan camp. *Iliad* ii, xvii.

History. A work by Herodotus.

Homer (hō' mer). Various dates from 850–1200 B. C. have been assigned to the greatest of all Greek poets. According to ancient tradition, he is the author of the *Iliad* and the *Odyssey.* He is often called "the father of poetry." His power of sheer storytelling is undisputed. Seven cities claimed to be his birthplace—Athens, Argos, Chios, Colophon, Rhodes, Salamis, Smyrna.

Hope. 1. An ancient deity. 2. The good spirit left in Pandora's fabled box.

Hora (hō' ra). Roman goddess of beauty; married Romulus. *Met.* xiv.

Horace (hor' is; –as). 65–8 B.C. Roman lyric poet. His *Odes* and *Epodes* provide information about Greek and Roman mythology.

Horae (hō' rē). Also Hours, Seasons. Goddesses of the seasons. See DICE.

Horn of Plenty. See CORNUCOPIA.

Horses of Diomedes. See DIOMEDES.

Hours. Also HORAE, q.v. See also DICE.

Hundred-handed Giants. Sons of Uranus and Gaea. See BRIAREUS, HECATONCHEIRES.

Hyacinthus (hī a sin' thus). A youth loved by both Apollo and Zephyrus; killed by Zephyrus with a discus. Apollo changed Hyacinthus into the flower that bears his name, and placed his body among the constellations. *Met.* x.

Hyades (hī' a dēz). Also Dodonides. The five (some accounts say seven) daughters of Atlas and Aethra. They grieved deeply for the death of their brother Hyas, a great hunter who was killed by a wild boar. For their inconsolable grief and as a reward for their faithful nursing of the infant Bacchus, Zeus placed them among the stars.

Hyas (hī' as). Brother of the HYADES, q.v.

Hydra, The Lernaean (hī' dra; ler nē' an). A huge serpent with nine heads (some accounts say seven; others say fifty) ; killed by Heracles as his second labor. As soon as one head was cut off, two more grew, until Heracles commanded his friend Iolaus to cauterize the wound with a hot iron. Heracles dipped his arrows in the venom of the Hydra and whoever was wounded with one of these arrows was doomed to die. One of these arrows wounded Chiron; Philoctetes stepped on one of them; the death of Nessus by one of these poisoned arrows indirectly caused the death of Heracles himself. *Aeneid* vi; *Met.* ix; *Theogony;* Pausanias v.

Hygea, Hygeia (hī jē' a). Also Salus (Roman). The daughter of Aesculapius; sister of Machaon, Panacea, and Podalirius. The goddess of health; her brothers were highly skilled in medicine and healing.

Hyginus (hi ji' nus). Latin writer of the first century B.C., the author of a collection of mythological legends. This mythological history, which Hyginus called *Fables*, has been lost.

Hylas (hī' las). A beautiful youth taken to Colchis by

Heracles on the *Argo*. On the way to Colchis, Hylas was drowned (some accounts say nymphs carried him away). Heracles sought him in the woods and mountains, and at last abandoned the Argonautic expedition to continue the search. *Argonautica* i.

Hyllus (hil′ lus). Son of Heracles and Deianira. Like his father, he was persecuted by Eurystheus, and he finally killed him. To his grandmother Alcmena, he sent the head of Eurystheus. He married Iole. *Met*. ix.

Hylonome (hi lon′ ō mē). The most beautiful of the female centaurs. CYLLARUS, q.v., was murdered by the Lapithae, and Hylonome, passionately fond of him, killed herself. *Met*. xii.

Hymen (hī′ men). Also Hymenaeus (hī me nē′ us). Son of Dionysus and Aphrodite, according to some accounts; other accounts say he was the son of Apollo and one of the nine Muses. He is the god of marriage, the personification of the wedding feast, and the leader of the nuptial chorus.

Hymettus (hī met′ is). A mountain elevation of 3,365 feet, two miles from Athens. After Tithonus was changed into a grasshopper, Eos fell in love with Cephalus, a young hunter whom she often visited on this mountain. The ancients erected a statue to Zeus here.

Hymns, The Homeric (hō mer′ ik). Thirty-three Greek poems addressed to twenty-one different gods and goddesses. Three each are to Aphrodite, Apollo, and Dionysus. Artemis, Athena, Demeter, Hermes, and Hastia are addressed twice. These poems, whose authorship is unknown, were originally attributed to Homer and first mentioned as a collection by Diodorus Siculus. The poems contain attributes of and legends concerning the gods and goddesses.

Hyperbius (hī per′ bi us). A son of Aegyptus, he helped Eteocles defend Thebes.

Hyperboreans (hī per bō′ rē anz). A fabulous people who lived in perpetual springtime north of the great river

Oceanus. They lived to an incredible age, even to a thousand years, and enjoyed all possible happiness. Vergil places them under the North Pole. The word "hyperboreans" is applied in general to all who inhabit a cold climate.

Hyperenor (hĭ pe rē' nor). 1. One of the SPARTAE, q.v., 2. In the *Iliad* xiv, a Trojan, the brother of Euphorbus and Polydamas, killed by Menelaus.

Hyperion (hĭ pēr' i on). Son of Uranus and Gaea; one of the Titans; husband of Thea; father of the sun and moon. Hyperion often refers to the sun itself.

Hypermnestra (hĭ perm nes' tra). One of the fifty daughters of Danaus (see DANAIDES). She married Lynceus, son of Aegyptus, and was the only one of the Danaides who did not murder her husband on their wedding night. Apollodorus ii; *Heroides* xiv; Pausanias ii.

Hypnos (hip' nos; –nus). Also Hypnus; Somnus (Roman). God of sleep; father of Morpheus, god of dreams. *Aeneid* vi; *Iliad* xiv; *Met.* xi; *Theogony.*

Hypsipyle (hip sip' i lē). Queen of Lemnos. The women of Lemnos put to death all other males, but Hypsipyle saved the life of her father Thoas, king of Lemnos. When the Argonauts landed at Lemnos, all the women of Lemnos became pregnant. By Jason, Hypsipyle became the mother of twins. Jason forgot his vows of fidelity to Hypsipyle, abandoned her, and the women of Lemnos banished the queen to Nemea. *Heroides* vi; Chaucer, *The Legend of Good Women.*

I

Iacchus (ĭ' a kus). 1. A name for BACCHUS (Dionysus), q.v., associated with the festivals of Bacchus at Athens. 2. A minor deity connected with the Eleusinian Mysteries.

Ianthe (ī an' thē). A girl of Crete, who was in love with a girl named IPHIS, q.v. Iphis was changed into a man, and Ianthe married him. *Met.* ix.

Iapetus (ī ap′ e tus). One of the Titans; husband of Themis; father of Atlas, Epimetheus, Menoetius, and Prometheus. The Greeks looked on him as the father of all mankind. *Met.* iv; *Theogony.*

Iapis (ī ā′ pis). A Trojan favorite of Apollo. He received from Apollo the knowledge of the power of medicinal herbs. *Aeneid* xii.

Iarbas (i ar′ bas). A son of Zeus; rejected suitor of Dido who bought from him the land on which to build Carthage. When Aeneas came to Carthage and interfered with his suit, Iarbas prayed to Zeus to send his rival away. Some accounts say Dido killed herself rather than marry Iarbas. *Aeneid* iv.

Iasion (ī ā′ zi on). Also Iasius. A son of Zeus and Electra; husband of the goddess Rhea. By Demeter, he was the father of Plutus. He was interested in agriculture. He was killed by a thunderbolt of Zeus. The inhabitants of Arcadia ranked him among the gods. *Aeneid* iii; *Theogony.*

Iaso (ī ā′ sō). A daughter of Aesculapius; goddess of healing; sister of Machaon, Podalirius, Hygeia, Panacea, and Aigle.

Iason (ē ā′ son). Same as JASON, q.v.

Iasus (ī′ a sus). Father of Atalanta.

Icaria (ī kā′ ri a). A small island in the Aegean Sea, where the body of Icarus was washed ashore and was buried by Heracles. Some accounts say Daedalus brought the body of his son there and buried him.

Icarian Sea (ī kar′ i an). The body of water into which Icarus fell when he tried to fly with the wings invented by his father for their escape from the labyrinth of Minos in Crete.

Icarius (ī ka′ ri us). Father of Penelope. *Odyssey* xvi.

Icarus (ik′ a rus; ī′ ka rus). Son of DAEDALUS, q.v. *Met.* viii.

Icelus (īs′ e lus; is′ e lus). Also Icelos. A son of Somnus who had the power to change himself into all sorts of animals. *Met.* xi.

Ida (ī′ da). **1.** A Phrygian nymph for whom Mount Ida was named. **2.** Celebrated mountain in Phrygia, noted for the abundance of its waters and as a source of many rivers, among them the Simois, Scamander, Aesepus, and Granicus. **3.** A nymph of Crete who helped care for the infant Zeus. **4.** Celebrated mountain in Crete where Zeus was educated. To this mountain Zeus sent Hera, Aphrodite, and Athena for the famous Judgment of Paris.

Idaea (ī dē′ a). **1.** A name for Rhea, because she was worshiped on Mount Ida. **2.** Second wife of Phineus, the blind king of Thrace, a man troubled by the Harpies. His brothers-in-law Zetes and Calais delivered him from the Harpies. Aided by the Argonauts, he recovered his sight.

Idaean Dactyls (ī dē′ an dak′ tilz). Workers of magic and priests of Rhea who lived on Mount Ida, Phrygia, near Troy.

Idaean Mother. Name for Rhea because she was worshiped on Mount Ida.

Idalium (ī dā′ li um). A mountain and a city, both in Cyprus, both sacred to Aphrodite.

Idas and Lynceus (ī′ das; lin′ sūs). Sons of Poseidon (some say Aphareus) and Arene. Idas was famous for his valor and military glory. Both brothers participated in the Calydonian boar hunt and went with Jason to Colchis. The brothers planned to marry their cousins Phoebe and Hilara (called Leucippides, daughters of Leucippus), but the sisters were carried away by Castor and Pollux. Then Idas married Marpessa, but Apollo too loved her and carried her away. Idas pursued the god with bows and arrows (one of the few mortals who dared to challenge a god). Zeus allowed Marpessa to choose between Apollo and Idas, and she chose Idas; Zeus compelled Apollo to restore her to her husband. According to another legend, Idas and Lynceus and Castor and Pollux raided some cattle which were to be equally divided among the four. In revenge for the loss of the Leucippides, Idas and Lynceus refused to give Castor and Pollux their share. In the fight that ensued, Idas, Lynceus, and Castor were killed. Apollodorus i, iii; *Iliad* ix; Pausanias ii, v.

Idmon (id' mon). 1. A son of Apollo and Asteria (some accounts say Cyrene); a prophet who accompanied the Argonauts. He foretold that the quest for the Golden Fleece would be successful and that he would not return with them; he was killed by a wild boar. 2. The father of Arachne. 3. A son of Aegyptus, killed on his wedding night by one of the DANAIDES, q.v.

Idomeneus (ī dom' ē nūs; ī do me nē' us). Husband of Meda. The son of Deucalion, he succeeded his father as king of Crete. Went to the Trojan War, was renowned for his valor, slaughtered many of the enemy. On his way home from Troy to Crete, he rashly promised Poseidon that if he escaped a dangerous tempest he would upon arrival in Crete sacrifice what he first saw. His own son was the first to appear to congratulate his father. Some accounts say Idomeneus kept the vow and sacrificed his son to Poseidon; others that a pestilence interrupted the sacrifice. Homer; Hyginus; Ovid; Pausanias; Vergil.

Idothea (ī dō' thē a). Also Eidothea. A daughter of the sea god Proteus. She told Menelaus how to catch Proteus and to persuade him to tell what angry god had prevented Menelaus from arriving safely home.

Idya (ī dī' ya). Also Idyia. A daughter of Oceanus and Tethys. She married Aeetes and became the mother of Medea and Absyrtus. *Theogony.*

Ilia (i' li a). Also Rhea, Rhea Silva. A daughter of Numitor, dedicated to the service of Vesta in order that she might not become a mother and deprive her uncle Amulius of his usurped crown. But Ilia was raped by Mars, and became the mother of Romulus and Remus. The two sons killed Amulius and restored the crown to their grandfather Numitor. *Aeneid* i, vi.

Iliad, The (il' i ad). The great epic poem by Homer about the Trojan War. The poem actually covers about fifty days in the ninth year of the war; some accounts say the events covered took place early in the tenth year. The wrath of Achilles is the main story, but the calamities that befell the Greeks are also delineated. The poem ends with the death of Hector, whom Achilles had sacrificed to the shade of his friend Patroclus. Many of the later events of the Trojan War are not covered in *The Iliad,* among them the death of Thersites, the contest between Odysseus and Greater Ajax for the armor of Achilles, the killing of Achilles by Paris, the great wooden horse built by Epeus, the coming of Philoctetes; the stealing of the Palladium, and other events, which are related in *The Odyssey* and in other works by writers later than Homer.

Ilion (il′ i on). Also Ilios (il′ i os), Ilium (il′ i um). Names of the citadel of Troy, founded by ILUS, q.v.

Ilione (il ī′ ō nē; il i ō′ nē). Also Iliona. Oldest daughter of Priam and Hecuba. *Aeneid* i.

Ilioneus (il ī ō′ nē us; il ī′ ō nūs). A Trojan who accompanied Aeneas to Italy; he told Dido that they were not pirates but Trojans on their way to Italy. *Aeneid* i.

Ilios. See ILION.

Ilissus (i lis′ sus). 1. A river near Athens where Boreas abducted Orithyia. 2. Statue of a reclining god from the Parthenon, now among the Elgin Marbles in the British Museum.

Ilithyia (il i thī′ ya). Also EILEITHYIA, q.v.

Ilium. See ILION.

Illyria (i lir′ i a). A country of western Greece to which Cadmus, king of Thebes, fled. Later he became king of Illyria.

Illyrius (i lir′ i us). Son of Cadmus born in Illyria.

Ilus (ī′ lus). 1. Fourth king of Troy, for whom the city was named Ilion. After adding much to the building of the city, Ilus named it Troy for Tros, his father, who gave his name to the Trojans. 2. At Troy, the son of Aeneas and Creusa was called ASCANIUS, q.v.; in Italy he was called Ilus or Iulus. *Aeneid* i.

Inachus (in′ a kus). 1. Son of Oceanus and Tethys; father of Io. The first king of Argos; he reigned sixty years. **2.** Rivers in Argos and in Epirus. **3.** When Poseidon contended with Hera for control of Argolis, Zeus asked the river god Inachus and others to settle the quarrel. When they awarded Argolis to Hera, Poseidon was so angry that he caused all the rivers to be dry in summer.

Indigetes (in dij′ i tēz). Also Indiges. **1.** The name given to deities worshiped in particular places. **2.** Name for the heroic men who were made gods, such as Heracles, Aeneas, and Romulus. See DII. *Met.* xiv.

Infernal Regions. Same as Hades, Lower World, Underworld.

Ino (ī′ nō). A daughter of Cadmus and Harmonia; sister of Agave, Autonoe, Polydorus, and Semele. After Athamas left Nephele, the mother of Helle and Phrixus, he married Ino. Ino became the mother of Learchus and Melicertes. Ino hated Nephele's children and planned to destroy them so her own children might ascend the throne. Helle and Phrixus escaped on the golden-fleeced ram. Athamas later killed Learchus, but Ino and Melicertes escaped, and both were changed into sea deities; Ino became Leucothoe and Melicertes became Palaemon. Apollodorus ii; *Met.* iv; *Odyssey* v; Pausanias i, ii.

Io (ī′ ō). A daughter of Inachus loved by Zeus. To avoid Hera's suspicion of his love affair, Zeus changed Io into a heifer. Hera ordered the hundred-eyed Argus to guard the heifer. Zeus sent Hermes to kill Argus. Io, tormented by a gadfly (some accounts say one of the Furies), wandered over many parts of the world. She finally returned to Egypt, where she was transformed by Zeus from a heifer to a woman, and bore Zeus a son named Epaphus. *Met.* i.

Iobates (i ob′ a tēz). King of Lycia; father of Stheneboea and Philonoe. Stheneboea became the wife of Proetus, king of Tiryns. Bellerophon succeeded Iobates as king and married Philonoe.

Iocaste (i ō kas′ tē). See JOCASTA.

Iolaus (i ō lā′ us). Also Iolas. A son of Iphicles, king of Thessaly. Iolaus assisted Heracles in conquering the Lernean Hydra by cauterizing the place where the head had been cut off. At the request of Heracles, Iolaus restored Hebe to youth. *Met.* ix.

Iolcus (i ol′ kus). A town in Thessaly where Aeson, father of Jason, was born and became king. From this town the Argonauts sailed in search of the Golden Fleece.

Iole (ī′ ō lē). Her father promised her in marriage to Heracles, and when he refused to keep the promise, Heracles carried her away. To extinguish the love of Heracles for Iole, Deianira sent Heracles the poisoned tunic which caused his death. Iole then married Hyllus, the son of Heracles. *Met.* ix.

Ion (ī′ on). Son of Apollo and Creusa, the daughter of King Erechtheus of Athens; grandson of Hellen. Ion was abandoned by his mother, but Apollo rescued him and sent him to Delphi. Creusa married Xuthus, but they had no children. The oracle at Delphi gave Ion to Xuthus as a son, thus reuniting the son with his mother. Ion became the ancestor of the Ionians.

Ion. A play by Euripides.

Ionia (ī ō′ ni a). A country in Asia Minor, named for ION, q.v.

Ionian Sea (ī ō′ ni an). Some legends say this sea was named for Io, who swam across it after she was changed into a heifer.

Iphicles (if′ i klēz). Also Iphiclus. Twin brother of Heracles; son of Amphitryon and Alcmena. At the same birth, Heracles, the son of Zeus, was born. Hera, jealous of Alcmena, sent two large serpents to destroy Heracles. Though not yet a year old, Heracles squeezed the serpents to death. Iphicles was the father of Iolaus, who helped Heracles conquer the Lernean Hydra. A companion of Heracles in several adventures, he was killed in the war Heracles fought against Augeas.

Iphigenia (if i jē nī′ a). Daughter of Agamemnon and

Clytemnestra; sister of Orestes and Electra. The Greeks, detained at Aulis by contrary winds and unable to sail for Troy, were informed by a soothsayer that Iphigenia must be sacrificed to appease the gods, for Agamemnon had provoked Artemis by killing her favorite stag. As Agamemnon was about to strike the fatal blow, a large and beautiful stag appeared in Iphigenia's place. The winds became favorable and the Greeks sailed for Troy. In *Iliad* ix, Iphigenia is called Chrysothemis. *Aeneid* ii; *Met.* xii; Aeschylus, *Agamemnon;* Pausanias ii.

Iphigenia in Aulis. A play by Euripides.

Iphigenia in Tauris. A play by Euripides.

Iphimedia (if i me dī′ a). Also Iphimedeia. Wife of the giant ALOEUS, q.v. She left her husband, and by Poseidon she had two sons, Ephialtes and Otus, the two Giants who fought against the gods. *Odyssey* xi.

Iphinoe (i fin′ ō ē). **1.** A daughter of Proetus and Anteia. She was driven mad for offending Bacchus or Hera, and the physician Melampus was unable to cure her. **2.** One of the chief women of Lemnos, who served as messenger for Queen Hypsipyle to invite the Argonauts to land on the island.

Iphis (ī′ fis). **1.** Iphis was the daughter of Telethusa of Crete. She was reared as a boy, for the father Ligdus had ordered the mother to kill the child if it was a girl. Telethusa kept the secret from Ligdus. Ianthe, a lovely girl, fell in love with Iphis, and when the mother implored the goddess Isis she changed Iphis into a man so he could marry Ianthe. *Met.* ix. **2.** A king of Argos who advised Polynices to bribe Eriphyle with the necklace of Harmonia, so that she would persuade her husband Amphiaraus to join the expedition against Thebes. Eriphyle knew all would be killed except Adrastus. **3.** A youth of Salamis who was spurned by Anaxerete. He hanged himself on the door of her house; she saw him hanging, but showed no emotion or pity; the gods changed her into a stone. *Met.* xiv.

Iphitus (if′ i tus; ī′ fi tus). **1.** A brother of Iole. He tried to persuade his father to give Iole to Heracles, and gave Heracles a famous bow and arrows. Homer says Iphitus gave the bow and arrows to Odysseus, who used them to slay the suitors of Penelope. In a fit of madness Heracles killed Iphitus by throwing him from the walls of Tiryns. *Odyssey* xxi. **2.** A Trojan who accompanied Aeneas to Italy. *Aeneid* ii. **3.** A king of Elis who re-established the Olympic games.

Iphthime (if' thi mē; if thī' mē). A sister of Penelope, whose form was assumed by Athena to persuade Penelope to cease her weeping and lamentation. *Odyssey* iv.

Irene (ī rē' nē). Also Eirene; Pax (Roman). Daughter of Zeus and Themis. Goddess of peace.

Iris (ī' ris). Goddess of the rainbow; messenger of the gods. *Iliad* ii, viii.

Iron Age. The fourth age of mankind; the hardest and the worst. Much crime; modesty, truth, and honor fled; an age filled with fraud, violence, war, slaughter. Mankind degenerated. ASTRAEA, q.v., the last of the goddesses on earth, was driven to heaven by the impiety of mankind.

Irus (ī' rus). A beggar of Ithaca, the messenger of Penelope's suitors. His name was Arnaeus, but all called him Irus (after Iris, messenger of the gods) because he ran errands. When Odysseus returned home, disguised as a beggar, Irus would have driven Odysseus out of his own house. He challenged Odysseus to a fight, was knocked down with one blow and dragged out of the house. *Odyssey* xviii.

Ishtar (ish' tar). Chief goddess of the Mesopotamian pantheon. The Earth Mother, goddess of love and of the reproductive forces of nature. The principal goddess of the Assyrians and Babylonians; their goddess of love, fertility, sex, and war.

Isis (ī' sis). Principal Egyptian goddess; sister-wife of Osiris; goddess of fertility.

Isles of the Blest. See ELYSIAN FIELDS.

Ismarus (is' ma rus). **1.** The city of the Cicones, sacked by

Odysseus. In the battle, Odysseus lost six men from each ship. From this city Odysseus obtained the wine that made Polyphemus drunk before he was blinded. *Odyssey* ix. **2.** A Theban who killed Hippomedon in the war of the Seven against Thebes. **3.** A Lydian who fought with Aeneas against the Rutulians. *Aeneid* x.

Ismene (is mē′ nē). Daughter of Oedipus and Jocasta; sister of Antigone, Eteocles, and Polynices. When her sister Antigone was condemned by Creon to be entombed alive for giving burial to their brother Polynices, Ismene declared herself as guilty as her sister and demanded to be punished equally, but Antigone did not want Ismene to be involved in her calamities. Sophocles, *Antigone, Oedipus at Colonus, Oedipus Tyrannus.*

Ismenos (is mē′ nos). Oldest of Niobe's seven sons. Killed with his six brothers by the arrows of Apollo, because Niobe with fourteen children preferred herself to Leto, who only had two children, Apollo and Artemis. *Met.* vi.

Ismenus (is mē′ nus). See ISMENOS.

Isthmian Games (is′ mi an; isth′ mi an). One of the four great Panhellenic festivals, begun in 776 B.C. One of them is now called the Olympic Games, revived in 1896 in Athens. The other three were called Isthmian (582 B.C.), Pythian (582 to 586 B.C.), Nemean (573 B.C.).

Ithaca (ith′ a ka). A celebrated island in the Ionian Sea west of the Greek mainland, part of the kingdom and the legendary home of Odysseus. *Iliad* ii; *Odyssey* i.

Itylus (it′ i lus; ī′ ti lus). Also Itys. Son of Tereus, king of Thrace, by Procne, daughter of King Pandion of Athens. He was killed by his mother when he was about six years old; his body was cut up, cooked, and served to Tereus in revenge for ravishing Philomela (sister of Procne) and cutting out her tongue. Itylus was changed into a sandpiper or a pheasant, Tereus into a hoopoe (some accounts say an owl or hawk), Philomela into a nightingale, and Procne into a swallow. *Met.* vi. Apollodorus; Hyginus; Ovid; Pausanias; Strabo; Vergil. In English literature, Philomela has become the poetic name for the nightingale. Chaucer; Milton; Thomson; Swinburne; Arnold; Wilde.

Itys (ĭ′ tus; ĭt′ us). See ITYLUS.

Iulus (ī ū′ lus). See ILUS.

Ixion (ik′ sĭ on; ik′ si on). A king of Thessaly; a celebrated sinner, cited by Aeschylus as the first murderer. After he murdered his father-in-law, he planned to seduce Hera. He was prevented by Zeus, who created a cloud in the shape of Hera. Ixion made love to the cloud and fathered the monstrous race of centaurs. Zeus struck him with a thunderbolt and ordered Hermes to tie him to a wheel in hell, ceaselessly revolving and lashed with serpents. He is one of those who suffer extremely severe punishment in Hades; others particularly punished are the Danaides, Sisyphus, Tantalus, and Tityus. *Aeneid* vi; *Met.* xii; *Odyssey* xi.

J

Jana (jä′ na). The wife of Janus.

Janiculum (ja nik′ ū lum). The highest hill in Rome (about three hundred feet), which served as a citadel to protect the city. The hill was on the opposite side of the Tiber from Rome, joined to it by a wooden bridge. This was the first bridge ever built across the Tiber, and some accounts say it was the first bridge in Italy.

Janus (jä′ nus). Also Janus Bifrons. 1. The most ancient king who reigned in Italy. 2. The god of beginnings, openings, entrances, doorways, and endings. His place in Roman mythology is second only to that of Zeus (Jupiter). The month January is named for Janus. *Aeneid* vii. Janus is not signally popular in English poetry, but he has provided many allusions in the works of Shakespeare, Milton, Swift, Spenser, and others.

Jason (jä′ sun). Son of Aeson. Educated by Chiron, the wisest of the centaurs. Leader of the Argonauts in the quest for the Golden Fleece. Many of the famous heroes of Greece accompanied Jason on the ARGO, q.v., when he sailed for Colchis—among them Admetus, Augeas, Butes, Calais, Castor, Heracles, Hylas, Idmon, Meleager, Orpheus, Peleus, Polydeuces (Pollux), and Zetes. Jason's love affairs with Hypsipyle, Medea, and Glauce (Creusa) are famous. *Argonautica; Met.* vii; Euripides, *Medea;* Pindar; Seneca, *Medea;* Chaucer, *The Legend of Good Women;* Corneille; William Morris, *The Life and Death of Jason;* Graves, *Hercules My Shipmate;* Anouilh; Robinson Jeffers.

Jocasta (jo kas′ ta). Also Epicaste, Iocasta. Wife of Laius, king of Thebes; mother of OEDIPUS, q.v. After Laius was killed, Jocasta unwittingly married her own son Oedipus, who became king of Thebes. Jocasta had four children by Oedipus: Eteocles, Polynices, Antigone, and Ismene. When Jocasta learned that her husband was her own son, she killed herself. *Odyssey* xi; Seneca, *Oedipus;* Sophocles, *Oedipus Rex, Oedipus Tyrannus.*

Jove (jōv). A Roman name for Zeus. Also called Jupiter (Roman).

Judgment of Paris. The judgment took place on Mount Ida, in Phrygia, near Troy. Zeus had appointed Paris to judge the contest for the golden apple marked "For the Fairest." It was this golden apple which Eris (Discordia) had rolled across the floor at the wedding of Peleus and Thetis. The apple was claimed by Aphrodite, Athena, and Hera; Hera offered Paris power and all the kingdoms of Asia if she were awarded the apple; Athena offered Paris victory in battle, beauty, and wisdom if he awarded the apple to her; Aphrodite offered Paris the most beautiful woman in the world for his wife if he would give her the prize. Paris awarded the apple to Aphrodite, goddess of love. This won for Paris the eternal hatred of Hera and Athena, who helped the Greeks in the Trojan War—caused by Paris' abduction of Helen, "the most beautiful woman in the world." Many ancient writers used the story; among modern writers are Tennyson in "Oenone" and Blackie in "Judgment of Paris."

Juno (jōō′ nō). See HERA.

Jupiter (jōō′ pi ter). See ZEUS.

Justice (jus′ tis). Themis, the second wife of Zeus, has been called the goddess of justice; Dice, daughter of Themis by Zeus, is also known as goddess of justice.

Juturna (jōō′ tur na). The sister and charioteer of Turnus, king of the Rutulians. Aeneas in Italy fought against Turnus. By the Romans she was called the goddess of springs, and in the Roman forum there was a fountain sacred to her. *Aeneid* xii.

Juventas (jōō′ ven tas). Also Juventus. The goddess of youth. See GANYMEDA, HEBE.

K

Kakia (kā′ ki a). Goddess of vice. Promising Heracles ease, love, and riches, she tried to mislead him while he was a student of Chiron and of Arete, goddess of virtue.

Keres (kē′ rēz). A Greek name for evil spirits (sometimes thought to be the same as the Furies) associated with death.

Knights, The. A comedy by Aristophanes.

Knossos (nos′ us). See CNOSSUS.

Kore (kō′ rē). See CORA.

Korinthos (ko′ rēn thos). See CORINTH.

Kronos (krō′ nus). See CRONUS.

L

Labdacus (lab′ da kus). King of Thebes; father of Laius, who was the father of Oedipus.

Labors of Heracles. See HERACLES.

Labyrinth (lab′ i rinth). A building of numerous passages, perplexing windings, intricate mazes; built by Daedalus at Cnossus on Crete for King Minos' confinement of the Minotaur. *Aeneid* v; Herodotus ii.

Lacedaemon (las e dē′ mon). Son of Zeus and Taygeta, he gave his name to a country (Lacedaemon) and his wife's name Sparta to a city in southern Greece. He introduced the worship of the Graces and built them a temple.

Lachesis (lak′ e sis). One of the three Fates. See ATROPOS.

Laconia (la kō′ ni a). Also Laconica. A country in the Peloponnesus in southern Greece to which Lacedaemon gave his name.

Ladon (lā′ don). 1. The dragon that guarded the Apples of the Hesperides. 2. One of the followers of Aeneas into Italy. 3. A river in Arcadia. 4. A dog of ACTAEON, q.v. *Aeneid* x; *Met.* iii.

Laelaps (lē′ laps). A marvelous dog given to Procris by Artemis. It never failed to catch the animal it was ordered to catch. The faithful dog saw Procris die when Cephalus accidentally killed her. *Met.* vii.

Laertes (lā ur′ tēz). Father of Odysseus; husband of Anticlea, the daughter of Autolycus. Homer says Laertes was the father of Odysseus, but later writers hint that it was Sisyphus. *Met.* xiii; *Odyssey* xi, xiv, xxiii, xxiv.

Laestrygones (les trig′ ō nēz). Also Laestrygonians (les tri gō′ ni anz). The most ancient inhabitants of Sicily. Antiphates was their king. They were cannibal giants who fed on human flesh and were fiercer than the Cyclopes. When Odysseus came by their land, they sank eleven of his twelve ships and ate the men. *Met.* xiv; *Odyssey* ix, x.

Laius (lā′ yus; lā′ us; li′ us). Son of Labdacus. Father of Oedipus. Driven from the throne of Thebes by Amphion and Zethus but afterward restored. Married Jocasta, daughter of Creon. When an oracle informed Laius that his newborn son Oedipus would later kill him, Laius ordered a herdsman to destroy the child. The herdsman took pity on the infant and, instead of killing it, pierced its feet and left it exposed to the elements on a mountain. There a shepherd found the child, rescued it, and took it to Corinth. Years later, in an unfortunate meeting along a road, Laius and Oedipus became involved in an argument, and Oedipus killed his father without knowing who he was. Apollodorus iii; Pausanias ix; Sophocles, *Oedipus Rex*.

Lamia (lā′ mi a). 1. A daughter of Poseidon. 2. A Cretan deity whose worship was the same as at Eleusis. 3. A daughter of Belus loved by Zeus. Some accounts say that Hera, out of jealousy, deformed Lamia and killed all her children but one. Lamia had the face and breasts of a woman and the body of a serpent. Because she could not avenge herself on Hera, Lamia lured strangers so that she might devour them. Keats, "Lamia." 4. In Latin, a witch who sucks children's blood; a man-devouring monster; a sorceress.

Lampetia (lam pē′ shi a). 1. Daughter of Apollo and Neaera; sister of Phaetusa, with whom she guarded her father's sacred cattle on the island of Thrinacia, where Odysseus and his men arrived. Although warned by Odysseus to keep their hands off the sacred cattle of Apollo, the men carried away and killed some of the sacred beasts. (The hides of the oxen walked about, the flesh roasting in the fire began to bellow, and nothing was heard but dreadful noises and loud lowings.) Lampetia informed her father of the sacrilege; Apollo requested that Zeus punish the offenders; as the men sailed away from Thrinacia, a terrible storm rose and all of the Greeks perished—except Odysseus, who held on to a piece of broken mast and saved himself from the shipwreck. *Odyssey* xii. 2. One of the HELIADES, q.v., who, with her sisters, was changed into a poplar tree at the death of her brother Phaethon. *Met*. ii.

Laocoon (lā ok′ ō on). Son of Priam and Hecuba. A priest of Apollo; he distrusted the Wooden Horse. Athena sent a huge serpent (some accounts say two) that crushed Laocoon and his two sons to death. *Aeneid* ii.

Laodamia (lā od a mī′ a). Daughter of Acastus; wife of

Protesilaus. When she learned that her husband had been killed by Hector, she committed suicide. *Aeneid* vi; *Iliad* ii; *Met.* xii; *Heroides* xiii; Wordsworth, "Laodamia."

Laodice (lā od′ i sē). A daughter of Priam and Hecuba. Homer calls her "fairest favoured of Priam's daughters; fairest of his daughters to look on." She fell in love with Acamas, son of Theseus and Phaedra, when he and Diomedes came from the Greeks to demand the restoration of Helen. *Iliad* iii, vi. (In *Iliad* ix, Laodice is Homer's name for Electra, the daughter of Agamemnon.)

Laomedon (lā om′ e don). The son of Ilus and Eurydice; king of Troy; father of Priam and HESIONE, q.v. Zeus punished Apollo and Poseidon by sending them to Laomedon to build the walls of Troy; Laomedon refused to pay the two gods, and a sea monster was sent to ravage Troy. Heracles killed Laomedon and all his sons except Priam. *Aeneid* ii, ix; *Iliad* xxi; *Met.* xi.

Lapithae (lap′ i thē). Also Lapiths (lap′ iths). A people of Thessaly ruled by Pirithous, the great friend of Theseus. The Lapithae continually fought the centaurs; at the wedding of Pirithous and Hippodamia, they threatened Hippodamia, and in the ensuing battle many centaurs were killed. *Aeneid* vi; *Met.* xii.

Lar (singular), **Lares** (lā′ rēz; plural). Among the Romans, minor household deities that presided over house and family. See also PENATES.

Lara (lar′ a). Wife of Hermes; mother of two Lares.

Lares. See LAR.

Larissa (la ris′ a). 1. The acropolis at Argos. 2. The home of Achilles. 3. The city in Thessaly where Perseus inadvertently killed his grandfather Acrisius. 4. The city between Egypt and Palestine where Pompey was murdered.

Larvae (lar′ vē). Also Lemures. Among the Romans, wicked spirits and apparitions which came from their graves at night to terrify the world; they especially frightened children and correspond to the modern idea of ghosts.

Lasthenes (las' the nēz). He helped Eteocles defend Thebes.

Latinus (la tī' nus). A son of Odysseus and Circe. King of Latium; husband of Amata; father of Lavinia. Amata was anxious that Lavinia marry Turnus, but an oracle advised Latinus that Lavinia must become the wife of a foreign prince. Aeneas married Lavinia, and after the death of Latinus succeeded him as king of Latium. *Aeneid* ix; *Met.* xiii.

Latium (lā' shī um). The region of Italy conquered by Aeneas. *Aeneid* vii.

Latmos (lat' mos). Also Latmus. The mountain in Caria in Asia Minor where Endymion sleeps immortally, visited each night by Artemis.

Latona (la tō' na). Also Leto (Greek). Daughter of the Titans Coeus and Phoebe. Mother of Apollo and Artemis. See also LYCIA. Herodotus ii; *Iliad* xxi; *Met.* vi; Pausanias ii, iii; *Theogony.*

Laurel (lo' rel; lor' el). The tree sacred to Apollo. Daphne, the first girl Apollo loved, was changed by her father Peneus into a laurel tree when Apollo pursued her.

Laurentium (lo ren' shi um). Also Laurentum (lo' ren tum). The capital of Latium in the time of Latinus and Aeneas. *Aeneid* vii.

Lausus (lo' sus). 1. The son of Mezentius, the "scorner of the gods." Lausus fought with Turnus against Aeneas who killed him. Aeneid vii, x. 2. A son of Numitor; brother of ILIA, q.v.; put to death by his uncle AMULIUS, q.v., who had usurped Numitor's throne. Ovid.

Laverna (la ver' na). Roman goddess of thieves and impostors.

Lavinia (la vin' i a). Daughter of LATINUS, q.v., and Amata, second wife of Aeneas. *Aeneid* vi, vii; *Met.* xiv.

Lavinium (la vin' i um). City founded by Aeneas, named for his wife Lavinia.

Leander (lē an' der). See HERO.

Leda (lē' da). Daughter of Thespius (or Thestius according to some accounts) ; wife of Tyndareus, king of Sparta. In the form of a swan, Zeus seduced her, and she bore quadruplets: Pollux and Helen by Zeus; Castor and Clytemnestra by Tyndareus. Apollodorus; Hesiod; Hyginus; *Met.* vi; *Odyssey* xi; Euripides, *Helen;* Aldous Huxley, "Leda"; Yeats, "Leda and the Swan."

Leiodes (lē ī' ō dēz). The only one of the suitors of Penelope who was righteous at heart. He was the priest or soothsayer among the 108 wooers, but Odysseus nevertheless did not spare him. *Odyssey* xvi, xxii.

Lelaps (lē' laps). See LAELAPS.

Lemnes (lem' nēz). Also Lemnians (lem' ni anz). The women on the island of Lemnos who murdered their husbands. HYPSIPYLE, q.v., was their queen. The Argonauts stopped on the island, and all the women became pregnant; Jason had twin sons by the queen. *Aeneid* viii; Herodotus vi; *Iliad* i.

Lemnos (lem' nos). An island in the Aegean Sea noted for: (1) The fact that the Lemnian women murdered their husbands; (2) they murdered all the children their men had fathered by Athenian women; (3) the visit of the Argonauts to the island, and Hypsipyle's love affair with Jason; (4) it was here that Hephaestus landed when Zeus kicked him out of heaven. Although the islanders took care of him and nursed him back to health, he remained forever lame. Lemnos became sacred to Hephaestus and most of the inhabitants were blacksmiths; (5) On this island the Greeks abandoned Philoctetes. *Argonautica* i–iv.

Lemprière's Classical Dictionary (lem' pri er). A book on mythology and the ancients by an English classical scholar, John Lemprière (1765–1824) ; first published in 1788. John Keats knew this book almost by heart.

Lemures (lem' ū rēz). See LARVAE.

Lenaeus (lē nē' us). Another name for Bacchus.

Leo (lē′ ō). The constellation represented by a lion; the fifth sign of the zodiac, which the sun enters about July 23.

Lerna (lur′ na). 1. A section of Argolis; into a lake in this region the Danaides threw the heads of their murdered husbands. 2. In this district Heracles killed the Lernaean Hydra. *Aeneid* vi; Apollodorus ii; *Met.* i.

Lernaean Hydra (lur nē′ an). See HYDRA.

Lesbos (les′ bos; lez′ bos). 1. An island in the Aegean Sea whose inhabitants were skilled in music, whose women were noted for their beauty but whose characters became debauched and dissipated; hence the word "Lesbian" is often used to signify debauchery, extravagance, and sensuality. 2. On this island Phaon received from Aphrodite an ointment possessing the magical qualities of youth and beauty and became one of the most beautiful men of the age. The women of Lesbos went wild with love for him, none more so than the poetess Sappho; she wrote to him a very warm and rare love song. 3. On this island Sappho (also the poet Alcaeus) was born about 600 B.C. She was noted for her beauty, poetical talents, and amorous disposition. She is often called the tenth Muse of poetry.

Lestrygonians. See LAESTRYGONES.

Lethe (lē′ thē). River of forgetfulness (oblivion) in Hades.

Leto (lē′ to). See LATONA.

Leucippides (lōō sip′ i dēz). The two daughters (HILARA, q.v., and Phoebe) of Leucippus. The daughters were to marry IDAS, q.v., and Lynceus, their cousins; but Castor and Pollux abducted the sisters, married them, and had sons by them.

Leucippus (lōō sip′ us). 1. Father of the LEUCIPPIDES, q.v. 2. A son of Oenomaus; he loved Daphne and disguised himself as a woman in order to be her attendant and bathe with her; his sex was discovered by Apollo, who also loved Daphne; with Apollo's darts Daphne and her attendants killed Leucippus.

Leucosia (lu kō′ si a). One of the three SIRENS, q.v.; the other two were Ligeia and Parthenope. They were the daughters of Achelous, the river god and the Muse Calliope. They lived on a rocky coast, sang sweet songs, and lured sailors to disaster and death. Odysseus, returning home from Troy, had heard of the Sirens' lure; he stuffed the ears of his companions with wax so that none would hear their seductive songs. When the Sirens failed to lure Odysseus and his men, they threw themselves into the sea and perished. *Met.* v; *Odyssey* xii.

Leucothea (lu koth′ ē a). Also Leucothoe (lu koth′ ō ē). 1. INO, q.v., was changed into a sea goddess of this name; she presided over brooks and fountains. 2. A daughter of King Orchamus and Euryonome. When her love affair with Apollo was revealed to Orchamus by the jealous Clytie, Leucothea was buried alive by her father. She was changed into the sweet-scented shrub that bears frankincense. *Met.* iv.

Leucothoe. See LEUCOTHEA.

Leucus (lū′ kūs). 1. A companion of Odysseus killed at Troy by Antiphus, a son of Priam. *Iliad* iv. 2. The paramour of Meda, wife of Idomeneus, while Idomeneus was engaged in the Trojan War. Leucus murdered Meda and her children to usurp the throne of Crete.

Libation (lī bā′ shun). A liquid, such as wine, poured on the ground or on a victim in sacrifice, in honor of a deity.

Liber (lī′ ber). Another name for BACCHUS, q.v.

Libera (lī′ ber a; lib′ e ra). Another name for PERSEPHONE, q.v.

Libitina (lib i tī′ na). Roman goddess of death.

Libra (lī′ bra). Seventh sign of the zodiac (the Scales), which the sun enters about September 23.

Library. See BIBLIOTHECA.

Libya (lib′ i a). The name of the ancients for Africa. Dido, Carthage, and the pillars of Heracles are some of the mythological associations with Libya. *Aeneid* iv.

Lichas (lī′ kas). The servant of Heracles. Deianira sent Lichas to deliver to Heracles the poisoned tunic of Nessus, which caused the death of Heracles; the garment stuck to his flesh, and when he tried to wrench it off, large pieces of his body were torn away. In his agony, Heracles blamed Lichas, hurled him high into the air, where he turned into stone and fell into the sea. *Met.* ix.

Ligeia (li jī′ a). One of the three SIRENS, q.v. See also LEUCOSIA.

Limnades (lim′ na dēz). Dangerous nymphs of lakes, marshes, and swamps; they lured travelers to destruction by their songs and false screams for help.

Limoniades (lī mō nī′ a dēz; lim ō nī′ a dēz). Nymphs of meadows and flowers.

Linus (lī′ nus). A name of several mythical persons. 1. A son of Apollo and Psamanthe who was torn to pieces by dogs. 2. A son of the Muse Urania and Amphimarus. 3. A son of Ismenius; he taught Heracles music. In a fit of anger, Heracles struck Linus on the head with his lyre and killed him. 4. A son of Calliope; brother of Orpheus. Like Hyacinthus, some of these mythological characters died in youth under the excessive love of some deity; this symbolizes the sudden withering of herbs, flowers, and animal life under the fierce shafts of summer. A lament or dirge for a dead hero, taken from the refrain "woe is me," is called a linus song.

Lips. The southeast wind.

Liriope (lir ī′ o pē). An Oceanid; wife of Cephisus; mother of Narcissus. *Met.* iii.

Litae (lī′ tē). Daughters of Zeus; they placed before him the prayers of those who invoked his assistance. They were sweet-natured goddesses who helped persons whom Ate had reduced to distress. "Litae" means prayers of the penitent. *Iliad* ix.

Litai (lī′ tī; lit′ ī). See LITAE.

Little Bear. The constellation into which ARCAS, q.v., was changed.

Lityerses (lit i er' sēz). 1. An illegitimate son of Midas; a king of Phrygia who cut off the heads of guests he defeated in reaping contests. Heracles overcame and killed him. 2. A harvest song.

Locrians (lō' kri anz). Peoples who inhabited the central part of ancient Greece.

Locris (lō' kris; lok' ris). A country in the central part of ancient Greece.

Lotis (lō' tis). A beautiful nymph, daughter of Poseidon. Pursued by Priapus, she fled from his lust and prayed to the gods to help her; she was changed into a tree called the lotus. *Met.* ix.

Lotophagi (lō tof' a jī). The people of coastal Africa. They received the name "Lotophagi"—lotos-eaters—from a honey-sweet fruit that made those who ate it lose all desire to return home. Odysseus visited these people on his journey home from the Trojan War. *Odyssey* ix; Tennyson, "The Lotos-Eaters."

Lotos (lō' tos). The fruit that produced dreamy contentment, languor, and forgetfulness.

Lotos-eaters. See LOTOPHAGI.

Lotus (lō' tus). See LOTIS, LOTOS.

Lower World. See HADES.

Lucifer (lū' si fer). 1. Venus as the morning star. 2. The son of Zeus and Eos, according to some mythologists.

Lucina (lū sī' na). Same as EILEITHYIA (Greek), q.v. The Roman goddess of the travails of women and of childbirth. See also ARTEMIS.

Lucretia (lū krē' sha). Also Lucrece, Lucresse. The wife of Tarquinius, a king of Rome; she was ravished by a nobleman. She told her husband of the deed, then stabbed herself with a dagger. Shakespeare, "The Rape of Lucrece."

Luna (lū' na). Goddess of the moon. See ARTEMIS.

Luperca, Lupercus (lū per' ka; –kus). Roman gods, protectors of flocks; also deities of fertility.

Lupercal (lū′ per kal). A cave or den at the foot of Mount Aventine, sacred to Pan; the Lupercalia were celebrated there annually. Some writers say that the Lupercal is where the she-wolf nursed Romulus and Remus. *Aeneid* viii.

Lupercalia (lū per kā′ li a). Festivals in honor of Pan, held in Rome on February 15. Two goats and a dog were sacrificed—the goat because Pan was supposed to have the feet of a goat, the dog representing the guardian of the sheep.

Luperci (lū pur′ sī). The priests who assisted in the celebration of the LUPERCALIA, q.v.

Lupercus. See LUPERCA.

Lutinus (lū tī′ nus). Roman name for PRIAPUS, q.v.; god of fertility in man, cattle, and crops.

Lyaeus (lī ē′ us). See BACCHUS. "Lyaeus" means liberator, because wine, over which Bacchus presides, gives freedom to the mind and delivers it from all cares and melancholy.

Lycabettus (lī ka bet′ us). A hill about 1,000 feet high in the city of Athens. Legend has it that Athena was carrying a large rock to fortify the Acropolis when she heard about the death of Agraulos and her daughters, who had jumped from the Acropolis; Athena dropped the rock, which formed a huge hill like a mountain, and it was named Mount Lycabettus.

Lycaeus (lī sē′ us). The mountain in Arcadia on which Zeus was born to Rhea.

Lycaon (lī kā′ on). 1. A king of Arcadia who had many wives, fifty sons, and a daughter named Callisto. Apollodorus iii; Pausanias. 2. Another king of Arcadia, noted for his cruelties and changed into a wolf by Zeus; to test the divinity of Zeus, who had disguised himself as a mortal, Lycaon had killed his own son, cut up and cooked the body, and offered the flesh as food to the god. *Met.* i. 3. A son of Priam and Hecuba. He was captured by Achilles, who sold him as a slave to the king of Lemnos; Achilles received a silver mixing bowl as slave price.

Lycaon escaped from Lemnos, returned to the Trojan War, and was killed by Achilles. *Iliad* xxi. 4. The father of Pandarus.

Lycia (lish' i a). A country in Asia Minor, ruled by Iobates, who sent Bellerophon to slay the Chimera. The country received its name from Lycus, a son of Pandion. The people were expert in the use of the bow. The ancient writers tell that when Leto (Latona) fled to escape the wrath of Hera, she and her two children came to Lycia and were refused water to drink. Leto asked the gods to change the people into frogs so that they might live in water forever.

Lycidas (lis' i das). 1. A shepherd in the ninth *Eclogue* of Vergil. 2. A centaur killed by the Lapithae at the nuptials of Pirithous. 3. A beautiful youth who was the admiration of Rome in the age of Horace. Milton, "Lycidas."

Lycius (lis' i us). A name for Apollo as the killer of many wolves; "Lycius" means wolf-god. Apollo had once cleared Athens of wolves. A famous temple of Apollo stood at Patra in Lycia from which name "Lycius" was derived. *Aeneid* iv.

Lycomedes (li kō mē' dēz). Son of Apollo and Parthenope. King of Scyros; to him Thetis entrusted the care of Achilles, dressed as a woman to escape fighting in the Trojan War (Thetis knew Achilles would be killed at Troy). Later Lycomedes became infamous for throwing Theseus from a cliff and killing him. Apollodorus iii; Pausanias i.

Lycurgus (li kur' gus). 1. A king of Nemea, raised from the dead by Asclepius. 2. A giant, killed by Osiris in Thrace. 3. The son of Dryas; a cruel and impious king of Thrace. He offered violence to Dionysus, opposed his worship, drove the god out of Thrace, and in turn was driven mad by the gods. Some accounts say he killed his son with an ax, thinking that the boy was a tree; and finally, in his fury, he cut off his own legs, thinking they were the branches of a tree. *Aeneid* iii; *Iliad* vi; *Met.* iv. 4. A king of Arcadia. *Iliad*. 5. A son of Heracles by

Praxithea, one of the fifty daughters of THESPIUS, q.v., all of whom became mothers by Heracles. 6. A celebrated lawgiver of Sparta in the ninth century B.C.; a friend of the gods, he reformed many abuses of the state and abolished all social distinctions. His laws remained in force for seven hundred years. 7. A famous Athenian orator in the age of Demosthenes.

Lycus (lī′ kus). Many mythological persons were named Lycus, among them 1. A son of Pandion; brother of Aegeus, Nisus, and Pallas. 2. A king whom Heracles assisted in the war against the Bebryces. 3. A king of Thebes; husband of DIRCE, q.v.; killed by Amphion and Zethus because he had mistreated their mother Antiope. 4. A son of Lycus and Dirce; he killed Creon, father of Megara, the first wife of Heracles, and he threatened to kill Megara and her children; he was killed by Heracles. 5. A king of Boeotia. 6. A king of Libya. 7. A son of Poseidon. 8. A son of Ares. 9. A son of Aegyptus. 10. One of the companions of Aeneas in Italy. 11. A son of Priam. 12. A centaur.

Lyde (lī′ dē). A girl loved by a satyr with whom Echo was in love.

Lydia (lid′ i a). A country in Asia Minor whose early inhabitants were called Phrygians. About the time of the Trojan War, the Heraclidae reigned there; the last king was Candules. The fabled Croesus was once king there.

Lykabettos. See LYCABETTUS.

Lynceus (lin′ sūs). 1. A son of Aegyptus, who married Hypermnestra, the daughter of Danaus, the only one of the fifty Danaïdes who did not murder her husband on their wedding night. Apollodorus ii; *Heroides* xiv; Pausanias ii. 2. A companion of Aeneas, killed by Turnus. *Aeneid* ix. 3. A son of Aphareus (some say Poseidon). An Argonaut and a member of the Calydonian boar hunt. Fabled for his keen sight, he could see through the trunk of a tree and could distinguish objects nine miles away. With his brother IDAS, q.v., he stole some oxen, and both were killed by Castor and Pollux. Apollodorus i, iii; *Argonautica; Met.* iii; Pausanias iv.

Lyra (li′ ra). See LYRE.

Lyre (lir). Also Harp. Invented by Hermes by stretching strings across a tortoise shell. Hermes presented the lyre to Apollo.

Lysippe (li sip′ ē). 1. One of the fifty daughters of THESPIUS, q.v. 2. A daughter of Proetus and Anteia, she was driven mad; according to some accounts, she was cured by Melampus, whom she married.

Lysistrata (li sis′ tra ta). A comedy by Aristophanes.

Lytyerses (lit i er′ sēz). Same as LITYERSES, q.v. The illegitimate and wicked son of King Midas.

M

Macareus (ma ka′ rē us; mak′ a rōōs). A son of Aeolus; he committed incest with his sister CANACE, q.v. *Heroides* xi.

Macaria (ma kar′ i a). The only daughter of Heracles and Deianira; she sacrificed herself to insure victory for Heracles and the Athenians over Eurystheus and the Peloponnesians in a battle near Marathon. The Athenians paid great honor to her patriotism, and a fountain at Marathon bears her name. Pausanias i.

Machaon (ma kā′ on). A famous physician; son of Asclepius; brother of Hygeia, Panacea, and Podalirius. With thirty ships, Machaon and Podalirius accompanied the Greeks to the Trojan War, where both healed many Greeks, including Philoctetes (legends credit both brothers with curing him). Machaon was one of those concealed in the Wooden Horse and was killed in the war; Nestor returned his body to Greece, where a temple of healing was built in his honor. *Aeneid* ii; *Iliad* ii.

Macris (mak′ ris). 1. A daughter of Aristaeus and Autonoe; sister of Actaeon. Nursed the infant Dionysus in a cave near Mount Nysa, where Dionysus invented wine. 2. A small island near Corcyra and a small cave on that island where Jason and Medea, on their way home from Colchis, were married.

Mad Heracles; The Madness of Heracles. Same as *Heracles*, a play by Euripides.

Maeander (mē an' der). 1. Son of Oceanus and Tethys. 2. A winding river in Asia Minor about six hundred miles long, origin of the word "meander." It was noted for its fine swans, and some myths say that all swans, when they felt the approach of death, returned to the Maeander to sing their dying song. Herodotus ii; *Met.* viii; *Iliad* ii. Pope, "The Rape of the Lock": "Thus on Maeander's flowery margin lies/Th' expiring swan, and as he sings he dies."

Maenads (mē' nadz). Same as Bacchae, Bacchantes. Also Thyiades. Female followers and priestesses of Bacchus.

Maenalus (men' e las; mē' na lus). 1. A mountain in Arcadia sacred to Pan; often frequented by shepherds; greatly celebrated by the ancient poets. 2. The father of Atalanta. 3. The oldest son of Lycaon (who served human flesh to Zeus as food). *Met.* i; Pausanias; *Eclogues* viii, *Georgics* i.

Maeonia (mē ō' ni a). 1. A country in Asia Minor, one of the seven that claims to be the birthplace of Homer. 2. Heracles, after he murdered Iphitus, went to Maeonia to serve as a slave to its queen Omphale.

Maeonides (mē on' i dēz). One name for the nine Muses, because Homer, their greatest and most worthy favorite, was supposed to be a native of MAEONIA, q.v.

Maera (mē' ra). The faithful dog of Icarius that led Erigone to the spot where her father had been murdered and buried by peasants. Maera was changed into the Lesser Dog Star.

Magic Girdle of Venus. See CESTUS.

Magna Mater (mag' na mā' ter). Same as Cybele, Rhea. The Roman mother of the gods.

Magnes (mag' nēz). A young man who found himself immobilized by the iron nails in the soles of his shoes as he walked over a stone mine. This was the magnet; hence the word "magnet." Some accounts say Medea changed a slave into a magnet.

Maia (mā' ya; mā' a; mī' a). The oldest and loveliest of the Pleiades, daughters of Atlas and Pleione. She was the mother of Hermes by Zeus. *Aeneid* i; Apollodorus iii.

Maidens of Trachis. Same as *The Women of Trachis*, a play by Sophocles.

Majestas (ma jes' tas). Roman goddess of honor and reverence.

Mallophora (mal lō fō' ra). A temple of Demeter at Megara, where she taught the utility of wool and the tending of sheep. One of the oldest temples in the ancient world. In Pausanias i (written in the second century A.D.) there is a reference to the temple, then falling into decay.

Manes (mā' nēz). The Roman name for the good spirits of the dead in Hades. *Aeneid* iii.

Mania (mā' ni a; mān' ya). Roman goddess of the dead, often called the mother or grandmother of ghosts; the mother of the Lares, and of the Manes.

Manto (man' tō). Daughter of Teiresias. She was endowed with the gift of prophecy, made prisoner by the Argives when they invaded Thebes, and given to Apollo at the oracle of Delphi. *Aeneid* i; *Met.* vi; Apollodorus iii.

Marathon (mar' a thon). A famous plain near the sea, about eighteen miles from Athens. It is celebrated for the great victory gained there over the Persians on September 28, 490 B.C., by the 10,000 Athenians and the 1,000 Plataeans under the command of Miltiades; the Persian army consisted of 100,000 infantry and 10,000 cavalry (some accounts say 300,000 to 600,000 Persians). Herodotus says the Greeks lost 192 men and the Persians 6,300. A large mound covers the single grave of the Greek heroes. Legend has it that a fully armed figure of Theseus led the attack. Herodotus vi; Byron, *Don Juan.*

Marathonian Bull (mar a thō′ ni an). Same as CRETAN BULL, q.v. After Heracles captured this bull in his seventh labor, he rode it from Crete to Greece, then turned it loose to roam the countryside. The bull roamed on the plains of Marathon and was ravaging all the neighboring territory when Aegeus, king of Athens, sent Androgeus on a mission to kill it; but the bull killed Androgeus. Androgeus had been in Athens, taking part in the Panathenean games, all of which he had won, for which reason Aegeus, to get rid of him, had sent him on the mission. To avenge the death of Androgeus, his father King Minos of Crete imposed upon the Athenians an annual tribute of seven youths and seven maidens to be sent from Athens to Crete to feed the Minotaur. Theseus later killed the Marathonian bull.

Marpessa (mar pes′ a). Homer calls her the "fair-ankled daughter of Euenos (Evenus)." She married IDAS, q.v., by whom she had Cleopatra, who became the wife of Meleager. Idas loved Marpessa; when Apollo tried to abduct her, Idas pursued him, resolved on revenge. Zeus gave Marpessa her choice, and she elected to remain with Idas instead of Apollo. *Iliad* ix; *Met.* viii.

Mars (marz). See ARES.

Marsyas (mar′ si as). A skillful player of the flute (some accounts say he invented it). Loved Cybele and traveled with her to Nysa, where he challenged Apollo to a music contest, the loser to be flayed alive and killed. The Muses judged the contest; Marsyas lost. The Fauns, Dryads, and satyrs universally lamented his death. *Met.* vi.

Martius Campus (mar′ shi us). See CAMPUS MARTIUS.

Mater Matuta (mā′ ter ma tū′ ta). Roman goddess of sea travel.

Mater Turrita (tū rē′ ta). A Roman name for CYBELE, q.v.

Matronalia (mat rō nā′ li a). Festivals in Rome in honor of Mars and Hera, celebrated by married women in commemoration of the rape of the Sabines.

Matuta (ma tū′ ta). Same as MATER MATUTA, q.v.

Mechaneus (mē kā′ nŭs). Another name for Zeus as the manager and contriver.

Mechanitis (mek a nī′ tus). Another name for Athena as the patroness of undertakings.

Meda (mē′ da). Wife of Idomeneus, king of Crete; murdered by Leucus while her husband was at the Trojan War. Leucus usurped the throne, but was banished when Idomeneus returned. Apollodorus ii.

Medea (mē dē′ a). A daughter of Aeetes, king of Colchis; niece of Circe. Medea was a powerful enchantress; she aided Jason in obtaining the Golden Fleece; she restored Aeson, Jason's aged father, to the vigor of youth; she caused the death of Glauce. When Jason abandoned her, she killed their two children, Mermerus and Pheres, and fled to Athens. There she married Aegeus, king of Athens, became jealous of his son Theseus, and finally left him and returned to Colchis. *Met.* vii; *Heroides* xii; Euripides, *Medea;* Seneca, *Medea.*

Medea. 1. A great tragedy by Euripides. **2.** A play by Seneca.

Mediterranean Sea (med it te rā′ nē an). The name never occurs in the classics, and in the Bible it is called the Great Sea. Greece, Italy, and the Holy Land are on its shores.

Meditrina (med i trī′ na). Roman goddess of medicine.

Medon (mē′ don). Many characters in mythology have this name, among them: **1.** A centaur. **2.** One of Penelope's reluctant suitors (he favored Odysseus); he was a herald and served as messenger and unwilling singer for the suitors; he and Phemios the minstrel were spared when Odysseus killed the suitors. **3.** The last king of Athens.

Medusa (mē dū′ sa). One of the three GORGONS, q.v., the daughters of Phorcys and Ceto. Medusa was mortal; the other two, Euryale and Stheno, were immortal. The eyes of the three Gorgons had the power of killing or turning onlookers into stone. Perseus killed Medusa, cut off her head, and placed it on the shield of Athena, where it had the same petrifying power as when Medusa was alive.

Megaera (me jē′ ra). See ERINYES.

Meganira (meg a nī′ ra). Also Metanira. Wife of Celeus, king of Eleusis; mother of Abas and Triptolemus, to whom Demeter taught agriculture.

Megapenthes (meg a pen′ thēz). 1. An illegitimate son of Menelaus by a slave girl. 2. The son and successor of Proetus, king of Tiryns. *Odyssey* iv.

Megara (meg′ a ra). 1. Daughter of Creon, king of Thebes. The first wife of Heracles; Heracles killed Lycus for insulting Megara; in a fit of madness, Heracles murdered Megara and her three children, thinking them wild beasts. 2. A city of Achaia, built on two rocks; the people of the city furnished twenty ships for the battle at Salamis.

Megareus (meg′ a rus; me gar′ ē us). 1. A son of Apollo. 2. The father of Hippomenes. 3. A man who helped Eteocles defend Thebes.

Melampus (mē lam′ pus). 1. Brother of Bias. Melampus was a celebrated soothsayer and physician of Argos; he could foretell the future and understand the speech of all creatures. *Aeneid* x; *Odyssey* xi. 2. A son of Priam. 3. The name of one of the dogs of ACTAEON, q.v.

Melanion (mē lan′ yōn). See HIPPOMENES, ATALANTA.

Melanippe (mel a nip′ ē). 1. A daughter of Aeolus; she had two children by Poseidon; their eyes were put out by Aeolus, but their eyesight was restored by Poseidon. 2. A daughter of Ares; she was a queen of the Amazons and sister of Hippolyta. Heracles captured her, but Hippolyta ransomed her with the famous girdle she gave to Heracles.

Melanippus (mel a nip′ us). 1. A priest of Apollo. 2. A son of Ares. 3. A son of Priam. 4. A son of Theseus. 5. The name of three Trojans. 6. A man who helped Eteocles defend Thebes in the war of the Seven against Thebes.

Melanthius (mē lan' thi us). The unfaithful goatherd of Odysseus; killed by Telemachus after Odysseus returned home from Troy. *Odyssey* xxii.

Melantho (mē lan' thō). A daughter of Dolius; sister of Melanthius. Melantho was a servant to Penelope, who treated her with great kindness; like her brother, Melantho proved unfaithful and was among the unfaithful servants killed by Odysseus. *Odyssey* xviii.

Meleager (mel ē ā' jer). An Argonaut and the main hero of the CALYDONIAN BOAR HUNT, q.v.

Melian Nymphs (mē' li an). Nurses of Zeus in his infancy.

Melicerta (mel i ser' ta). See MELICERTES.

Melicertes (mel i ser' tēz). Also Melicerta, Melicertus. Son of Athamas and Ino; saved by his mother from the fury of his father. Mother and son jumped into the sea, and Poseidon changed them into sea deities; Ino became Leucothea and Melicertes became Palaemon.

Melissa (me lis' a). A daughter of Melissus, king of Crete; sister of Amalthea. The two sisters fed the infant Zeus the milk of goats. Melissa learned how to collect honey and was changed into a bee. "Melissa" in Greek means bee.

Melpomene (mel pom' e nē). The Muse of tragedy. Her symbol is the tragic mask and buskin (*cothurnus*), a thick-soled high boot worn by actors in tragic drama in ancient times.

Memnon (mem' non). Son of Tithonus and Eos; king of Ethiopia. He took 10,000 men to Troy to assist his uncle Priam in the Trojan War; he behaved with great valor, and killed Antilochus, Nestor's son. Nestor challenged Memnon to single combat, but Memnon refused because of Nestor's venerable age. Achilles took up the challenge for Nestor; Memnon accepted and was killed in the combat. *Met.* xiii.

Memory. Same as Mnemosyne. A daughter of Uranus and Gaea; mother by Zeus of the nine Muses. The word "mnemosyne" means memory; the poets call Memory the Mother of the Muses. *Met.* vi; *Theogony.*

Mena (mē' na). Roman goddess who presided over the monthly menstrual period of women. "Menses," "menstrual," and "menstruate" are words derived from the name of this goddess.

Menalippe (men a lip' ē). 1. Same as MELANIPPE, q.v., sister of Hippolyte; queen of the Amazons. 2. A daughter of the centaur Chiron; ravished by Aeolus, she was changed into a mare and called OCYRRHOE, q.v. *Met.* ii.

Menelaus (men e lā' us). Son of Atreus and Aerope; Hesiod and Apollodorus say Menelaus was the son of Aerope and Plisthenes. Brother of Agamemnon. Husband of Helen; after the Trojan War, he took Helen back to Sparta, where he was king; according to Euripides, he went to Egypt after the war to obtain Helen, who had been detained there. *Aeneid;* Apollodorus; Hesiod; *Iliad;* Pausanias; Euripides, *Helen;* Sophocles.

Menephron (men' e fron). A man who criminally attacked his own mother. *Met.* vii.

Menestheus (mē nes' the us; me nes' thūs). Ruler of Athens during the absence of Theseus. As a former suitor of Helen, he took fifty ships to the Trojan War. *Iliad* ii.

Menetius (me nē' shi us). Also Menoetius. One of the four sons of Iapetus and Clymene. Brother of Atlas, Epimetheus, and Prometheus.

Menoeceus (mē nē' sūs). 1. A descendant of one of the Spartae, the men who sprang from the dragon's teeth sown by Cadmus. The father of Creon and Jocasta. When Teiresias foretold that the plague in Thebes would not be checked until a descendant of the Spartae offered his life for the city, Menoeceus jumped from the walls of the city to his death. 2. A son of Creon. Like his grandfather, when Teiresias said the Thebans could not win in the war of the Seven against Thebes unless a descendant of the Spartae sacrificed his life, he killed himself at the gates of Thebes and victory came to the Thebans.

Menoetius (me nē' shi us). See MENETIUS.

Mentes (men' tēz). A king of the Taphians; his name and form were assumed by Athena when she first visited Telemachus. *Odyssey* i.

Mentha (men' tha). Also Minthe. A daughter of Cocytus, loved by Pluto; the amour was discovered by Persephone, who changed Pluto's mistress into an herb called "mint." *Met.* x.

Mentor (men' tor). 1. A loyal friend and adviser of Odysseus and the guardian and teacher of Telemachus. *Odyssey* xvii. 2. A steward whose name and form Athena assumed when she acted as a guide to Telemachus. *Odyssey* iii. 3. A son of Heracles.

Mera (mē' ra). Same as Maera. 1. The dog whose cries revealed the burial place of Erigone's murdered father. The dog belonged to Icarius and when he died of grief for his mistress, he was changed into the constellation Canis (the Lesser Dog Star). 2. A priest of Aphrodite. *Met.* vii.

Mercury (mur' kū ri). See HERMES.

Meriones (mē rī' ō nēz). A friend and charioteer of Idomeneus, the king of Crete. Fought with valor at Troy; wounded Deiphobus, son of Priam. *Iliad* ii.

Mermaids (mur' mādz). Fabled marine creatures with the body of a woman and the tail of a fish. The Nereids and the Oceanids were Mermaids.

Mermerus (mer' me rus). A son of Jason and Medea, who with his brother Pheres was killed at Corinth. Pausanias thought they were stoned to death by the Corinthians; according to Euripides and Apollodorus, Medea killed the children to revenge the infidelity of Jason with Glauce.

Merope (mer' ō pē). 1. One of the Atlantides, offspring of Atlas; one of the seven Pleiades. Wife of Sisyphus, king of Corinth. According to legend, either because of her shame when Sisyphus was sent to Hades for severe punnishment or because she was the only one of the Pleiades who had married a mortal, Merope left her six sisters in the heavens and is no longer visible. She is called "the lost Pleiad." Some accounts say Electra is the lost Pleiad, for she withdrew from the Pleiades group so that she would not have to witness the fall of Troy. **2.** A girl loved by Orion, who insulted her; as punishment Dionysus blinded him. **3.** The wife of Cresphontes, king of Messenia; mother of Aepytus. **4.** A daughter of Erechtheus; mother of Daedalus. **5.** The wife of Polybus, king of Corinth; the reputed mother of Oedipus; she reared him and led him to believe he was her own son. Some accounts call her ERIBOEA, q.v., or Periboea. Apollodorus, Diodorus, Pausanias, Alfieri, Arnold, and Voltaire have accounts of Merope.

Merops (mē' rops; mer' ops). **1.** A celebrated soothsayer in the Trojan War. *Iliad* ii. **2.** A companion of Aeneas, killed by Turnus. *Aeneid* ix. **3.** A king of Cos, husband of Clymene; he was changed into an eagle and placed among the constellations. *Met.* i.

Messene (me sē' nē). Daughter of Triopas, king of Argos. Wife of Polycaon; he conquered a province in the Peloponnesus and named it Messenia, after his wife.

Messenia (me sē' ni a). A part of the Peloponnesus near the sea; a land of fertile valleys and a mild climate, enviously eyed and eventually conquered by the Lacedaemonians under the leadership of Polycaon.

Metabus (met' a bus). A haughty tyrant, father of Camilla. *Aeneid* xi.

Metamorphoses (met a mor fō' sēz). A work in fifteen books by Ovid. About two hundred and fifty stories, in poetic form, from Greek and Roman mythology tell of miraculous transformations from the time of creation to the time of Julius Caesar. The work, translated by scholars and by many English poets—Adison, Congreve, Dryden, Eusden, Gay, Pope, Rowe, Tate—has provided material for many literary allusions; it has been called "the major treasury of classical mythology." See also GOLDEN ASS.

Metanira (met a nī′ ra). See MEGANIRA.

Meteorological Gods and Goddesses. Also Sidereal Gods and Goddesses; Sky Deities. They relate to the constellations, and to sky divinities; among them are Apollo, Artemis, Diana, Eos, Helios, Hyperion, Orion, Phoebe, Phoebus Apollo, Selene, Sol, Theia, Uranus, Zeus.

Metis (mē′ tis). An Oceanid, one of the three thousand daughters of Oceanus and Tethys; the first wife of Zeus. Zeus swallowed Metis when he learned she was pregnant, and Athena was born from Zeus' head, which was split open with an ax by Hephaestus. Apollodorus; Hyginus; *Theogony.*

Metra (mē′ tra). Daughter of Erisichthon. She was loved by Poseidon and received from him the power to change herself into any animal she chose. Her father, afflicted by Demeter with a continual hunger, sold Metra again and again to gratify his hunger. *Met.* viii.

Metus (mē′ tus). A son of Ares, and one of his attendants.

Mezentius (mē zen′ shi us; –shus). Father of Lausus; an extremely cruel king of the Tyrrhenians. He killed his subjects by slow tortures; he would tie a live man face to face with a corpse and let him die a lingering death. Finally expelled by his subjects, he fled to Turnus and fought against Aeneas, who killed him. Vergil calls him "scorner of the gods." *Aeneid* vii.

Midas (mī′ das). A king of Phrygia. There are two stories about Midas: (1) He requested of the gods that everything he touched might be turned into gold, but he soon regretted the request; everything he touched, including his food, drink, and even his daughter turned to gold. He begged to be rid of his gift. He was told to wash himself in the river Pactolus; he did so, and ever since the river has had golden sands. (2) Midas was at the music contest between Apollo and Pan. Tmolus, the judge, said Apollo was the better player and singer, but Midas foolishly maintained that Pan was the superior. Such rashness offended Apollo, and he at once changed Midas' ears into those of a donkey. *Met.* xi.

Milanion. See HIPPOMENES, ATALANTA.

Miletus (mī lē' tus). The son of Apollo and Deione. Father of Biblis and Caunus. Miletus fled from Crete when King Minos suspected him of trying to usurp the throne; he went to Ionia in Asia Minor, where he founded the capital city and named it Miletus after himself.

Miltiades (mil tī' a dēz). See MARATHON.

Minerva (mi nur' va). See ATHENA.

Minervalia (min er vā' li a). Festival in honor of Minerva held annually in Rome in March and June.

Minoid (mi nō' id). Patronymic of Ariadne, daughter of King Minos of Crete.

Minos (mī' nos). 1. Son of Zeus and Europa. Brother of Rhadamanthus and Sarpedon. Famous lawgiver whose laws remained in force nearly 1,000 years, with his justice, wise legislation, and moderation approved by all the Greeks and all the gods. He was the father of Minos II. When he died he was made one of the three judges of the dead (the other two were Aeacus and Rhadamanthus). 2. Minos II was king of Crete; husband of Pasiphae; father of Ariadne, ANDROGEUS, q.v., Deucalion, Glaucus, and many other children. For him, Daedalus built the labyrinth to house the Minotaur. King Minos died about thirty-five years before the Trojan War.

Minotaur (min' ō tor). A celebrated monster born of Pasiphae (wife of Minos II) and a magnificent white bull called the Cretan or Marathonian bull; it had the body of a man and the head of a bull. It was housed in the labyrinth built by Daedalus, where it was fed human flesh—seven boys and seven girls—an annual tribute from Athens. It was killed by Theseus. *Aeneid* vi; *Met.* viii.

Minthe (min' thē). See MENTHA.

Misenus (mī sē' nus). A son of Aeolus; the piper of Hector in the Trojan War. He followed Aeneas to Italy, where he challenged the gods to a musical contest and was drowned by a Triton. *Aeneid* iii.

Mnemosyne (nē mos' i nē). See MEMORY.

Mnesthus (nes' thē us; nes' thūs). A Trojan who went to Italy with Aeneas, and distinguished himself at the funeral games of Anchises by competing in both the sailing contest and the archery contest. *Aeneid* v.

Moerae (mē' rē). Another Greek name for the three Fates. See ATROPOS.

Moeragetes (mē raj' e tēz). Names for Apollo and Zeus as leaders or guides of the three Fates.

Molorchus (mō lor' kus; mol or' kos). An old Nemean shepherd whose son was killed by a lion. Heracles, who visited him, was treated with great hospitality and promised to repay the kindness by killing the Nemean lion, his first labor. The Nemean games were established on this occasion and held in a grove planted by Molorchus.

Molossus (mō los' sus). In Euripides' *Andromache*, the son of Andromache and Neoptolemus (same as Pyrrhus). He became king of Epirus, where, at Dodona, is situated the famous temple of Zeus; Molossus is the name for Zeus in Epirus. (Pausanias i.)

Moly (mō' li; mō' lē). The magic herb, a plant with a black root and white flower, given by Hermes to Odysseus; it saved Odysseus from enchantment by CIRCE, q.v., on her island Aeaea, where he was detained for one year. *Odyssey* x; Spenser, *Faerie Queene;* Milton, *Comus;* Peacock, *Grill Grange;* Arnold, *The Strayed Reveller;* D. G. Rossetti, *The Wine of Circe*.

Momus (mō' mus). The faultfinder of Olympus. Hesiod's *Theogony* lists him as the son of Nyx (Night). God of adverse criticism, faultfinding, mockery, and pleasantry. He blamed, censured, ridiculed, and satirized Zeus, Poseidon, Hephaestus, Athena, and Aphrodite. Finally the gods banished him from Olympus. George Meredith's "Ode to the Comic Spirit" is based on this story of Momus and reminds that healthy criticism is necessary for reason and sense.

Monoecus (mō nē' kus). Another name for Heracles, who

had a temple in the Ligurian port of Monoecus, today called Monaco.

Monsters. There are many monsters in mythology; a few of the best known are the Calydonian boar, the Cyclopes, the Chimera, the Hecatoncheires, the Lernean Hydra, the Minotaur, the Nemean lion, Polyphemus, and the Sphinx. See also DESTROYERS OF MONSTERS.

Mopsus (mop' sus). 1. Two celebrated soothsayers bore this name. 2. An Argonaut who also participated in the Calydonian boar hunt and in the battle between the centaurs and the Lapithae. Hyginus. 3. A son of Manto, the daughter of the famous prophet Teiresias. Pausanias vii.

Morpheus (mor' fūs; mor' fē us). The god of dreams; also called the god of sleep.

Mors (morz). Also Thanatos. The god of death.

Mother Goddesses. Earth (Ge, Gaea, Tellus, Terra) the great mother of all. Two of Gaea's daughters, Rhea and Themis, have mother-goddess attributes.

Mulciber (mul' si ber). Same as HEPHAESTUS, VULCAN, q.v. In Milton's *Paradise Lost* he is the architect of Satan's "high capital" Pandemonium.

Musae (mū' zē). The nine Muses, daughters of Zeus and Mnemosyne. Other names for them are Camenae (Roman); Pierides (from their birthplace, Pieria); and Aganippides, Castalides, Heliconiades, and Maeonides (from places sacred to them and where they were worshiped). See CALLIOPE, CLIO, ERATO, EUTERPE, MELPOMENE, POLYHYMNIA, TERPSICHORE, THALIA, URANIA. Hesiod, Homer, *Homeric Hymns,* and Vergil among the ancients have noteworthy invocations to the Muses; in English literature there are famous invocations to the Muses by Blake, Byron, Milton, Pope, Spenser, and others. Famous accounts of the Muses are in Apollodorus i; *Theogony;* Pausanias ix; *Met.* v; *Homeric Hymns.*

Musaeus (mu zē' us). 1. Ancient Greek poet, 1400 B.C., highly regarded by Vergil. 2. A poet, fifth century A.D., who wrote the famous poem about Hero and Leander. *Aeneid* vi.

Musagetes (mū saj′ a tēz). Apollo's name when he led the choir of the Muses, or as the patron of the Muses.

Muses. See MUSAE.

Musicians. Among mythology's musicians are Apollo, Hermes, Pan, Orpheus, Linus, Marsyas, Thamyris, and Amphion.

Muta (mū′ ta). Roman goddess of silence.

Mycenae (mī sē′ nē). Ancient town in Argolis in the Peloponnesus, built by Perseus, son of Danae. Among the mythological characters associated with Mycenae are Atreus, Thyestes, Agamemnon, Aegisthus, Clytemnestra, Orestes. Heinrich Schliemann made some epochal archeological discoveries in Mycenae in 1876.

Myrmidons (mur′ mi donz). Originally ants, they were turned into soldiers and accompanied Achilles to the Trojan War. *Met.* vii; *Iliad* ii.

Myrrha (mir′ a). See CINYRAS.

Myrtilus (mir′ ti lus). A son of Hermes; arm-bearer and charioteer of Oenomaus, king of Pisa, whose death he caused in a chariot race so that Pelops could win both the race and HIPPODAMIA, q.v. When Myrtilus claimed his reward, Pelops killed him. Apollodorus ii.

N

Naenia (nē nī′ a). Roman goddess of funerals.

Naiades (nā′ a dēz). Also Naiads. Water nymphs that lived in, presided over, and gave perpetuity to lakes, rivers, springs, and fountains. *Met.* xiv; *Odyssey* xiii; *Eclogues.*

Napaeae (nā pē′ ē). Ancient divinities that presided over dells, hills, and woods.

Narcissus (nar sis′ us). Son of Cephisus and Liriope. There are two stories about Narcissus. The most popular is that of the beautiful youth who fell in love with his own reflection in a pool; he was so enamored of himself that he scorned the love of Echo and all others. Some legends say that Nemesis (others say Artemis) punished his arrogance and pride by causing him to fall in love with his own reflection. When he began to pine away with his longing, he was changed into the flower that bears his name. *Met.* iii. A less familiar story is told by Pausanias. Narcissus had a twin sister with whom he fell in love, and when she died, he went to a pool, saw his reflection, and imagined that he saw not his own image but that of his sister. Pausanias ix. Many English poets, among them Chaucer, Spenser, Marlowe, Milton, Shelley, and Keats, have used the story. In current psychoanalysis the word "narcissism" is used to mean excessive self-love.

Nauplia (no′ pli a). A famous naval station of the Argives; the first capital of Greece after independence in 1822.

Nauplius (no′ pli us). 1. Father of OEAX, q.v., and of the celebrated PALAMEDES, q.v., unjustly sacrificed by the Greeks during the Trojan War to appease the resentment of Odysseus toward Nauplius and his son. 2. An Argonaut; a man remarkable for his knowledge of sea affairs and of astronomy; builder of the town of Nauplia.

Nausicaa (no sik′ ā a). Daughter of Alcinous, king of the Phaeacians; she befriended the shipwrecked Odysseus and persuaded her father to be kind to the visitor. Some accounts say Nausicaa later married Telemachus, Odysseus' son. *Odyssey* vi.

Nausithous (no sith′ ō us). Son of Poseidon; father of Alcinous. *Odyssey* vi; *Theogony*.

Nautes (nō′ tēz). A Trojan soothsayer who accompanied Aeneas to Italy. When the old Trojan women set fire to Aeneas' ships during funeral games for Anchises in Sicily, Nautes advised Aeneas to leave the old and fainthearted women behind with Acestes and sail on to Italy. *Aeneid* v.

Naxos (nak′ sos). Island in the Aegean Sea, the largest and most fertile of the Cyclades (a group of 220 islands). Dionysus was the chief deity, and Theseus once visited here. The smallest island is Delos, where Apollo and Artemis were born. Theseus abandoned Ariadne on Naxos and Dionysus married her. *Aeneid* iii; *Met.* iii; Pausanias vi.

Neaera (nē ē′ ra). 1. The mother of Aegle. 2. Mother of Lampetia and Phaethusa by Helios. 3. Wife of Autolycus, the famous thief. 4. A daughter of Amphion and Niobe.

Necessitas (nē ses′ i tas). The goddess who presided over the destinies of mankind; mother of the three Fates (see ATROPOS). Pausanias ii.

Nectar. The drink of the gods. Cupbearers were Ganymeda (Hebe) and Ganymede.

Neda (nē′ da). A nymph who helped care for the infant Zeus.

Nekyia (nek′ wi a). "The Book of the Dead"; *Odyssey* xi has been called by this name.

Neleus (nē′ lūs). Son of Poseidon and Tyro. Twin brother of PELIAS, q.v. The brothers seized Iolchos, kingdom of Aeson, but Pelias finally expelled Neleus. Neleus went to build Pylos, married Chloris, and had a daughter and twelve sons by her—all of whom, except Nestor, were killed by Heracles. Apollodorus i; *Met.* vi; Pausanias iv.

Nemea (nē mē′ a). A town in Argolis, Greece, where Heracles at the age of sixteen, as his first labor, killed the Nemean lion.

Nemean Games. One of the four Panhellenic festivals, established 573 B.C.

Nemean Lion. Born of the hundred-headed Typhon. Heracles found the skin of the animal impenetrable; his arrows and club useless against the animal, Heracles seized it in his arms and squeezed it to death. When he frightened King Eurystheus with the carcass, the king made a brazen vessel in which to hide and used it when Heracles brought him the Erymanthian boar.

Nemesis (nem′ e sis). Goddess of vengeance. Daughter of Erebus and Nyx.

Neoptolemus (nē op tol′ e mus). Also called Pyrrhus. Son of Achilles and DEIDAMIA, q.v. He went to the Trojan War after the death of his father. Helenus, the Trojan seer, had foretold that Troy could not be taken without the aid of Neoptolemus, and Odysseus and Diomedes were sent to fetch him. No Greek exceeded him in valor; he was the first to enter the Wooden Horse. He was as cruel as his father; he killed Priam, and hurled Astyanax from the walls of Troy, took Andromache captive and made her his concubine, wielded the knife when Polyxena was sacrificed, and married Hermione (who had been promised to Orestes). *Aeneid* ii, iii; *Iliad* xix; *Met.* xiii; *Odyssey* xiii.

Nepenthe (nē pen′ thē). A magic drink that banished sorrow, pain, suffering, and grief; given to Helen of Troy by Polydama, queen of Egypt; given by Helen to Telemachus when he visited Sparta in search of information about his father. *Odyssey* iv.

Nephele (nef′ e lē). Wife of Athamas, king of Thebes; mother of Phrixus and Helle.

Neptune (nep′ tūn). See POSEIDON.

Nereides (nē rē′ i dēz). Also Nereids. The fifty daughters of Nereus and Doris, of whom Amphitrite, Galatea, Thetis, Glauce, and Clymene were famous. Attendants of Poseidon. *Iliad* xviii; *Met.* xi; *Theogony*.

Nereus (nē′ rūs; nē′ rē us). Son of Oceanus and Gaea; father of the Nereides. *Iliad* xviii; *Theogony*.

Nessus (nes′ us). Son of Ixion and the Cloud; a celebrated centaur who attempted to make love to Deianeira, the wife of Heracles, and was killed by Heracles with one of the arrows poisoned with the blood of the Lernean Hydra. The poisoned blood stained Nessus′ tunic (shirt), and before he died he gave it to Deianeira, telling her it had magical power to reclaim a husband from unlawful loves; Deianeira later sent the tunic to Heracles and it caused his death. Apollodorus ii; *Met.* ix; Pausanias iii.

Nestor (nes′ tor; nes′ ter). Son of Neleus and Chloris, the only one of twelve brothers not killed by Heracles. He was present at the wedding of Peirithous and Hippodamia, when a bloody battle was fought between the Centaurs and Lapiths. He engaged in the Trojan War, where he distinguished himself by his eloquence, justice, prudence of mind, and wisdom. The most perfect of all of the heroes of Homer, he lived three generations. *Iliad* i; *Met.* xii; *Odyssey* iii.

Nice (nēs). Also Nike; Victoria (Roman). The goddess of victory; highly honored by the Greeks, especially at Athens.

Nicippe (Nī sip′ ē). Daughter of Pelops and Hippodamia. Wife of Sthenelos, king of Mycenae; mother of Eurystheus, whose birth Hera hastened so that he would be born before Alcmena bore Heracles, and thus be able to command the labors of Heracles.

Nicostrata (nī kos′ tra ta). Also CARMENTA, q.v. Mother of Evander by Hermes. Accompanied Evander to Italy and chose the location of Pallanteum on the Tiber. The Romans called her *Carmenta* because she was a seer.

Night. Also Nox, Nyx. Daughter of Chaos. A prime element of nature, from which sprang Light. By her brother Erebus she had many children: the three Fates, Thanatos, Sleep, Dreams, Momus, Care, the Hesperides, Nemesis, Discord, Fraud, Eris, and others. *Aeneid* vi; *Theogony*.

Nike (nī′ kē). See NICE.

Nimrod (nim′ rod). He built the tower for the use of the Giants (Titans) in their attack against the gods on Olympus; similar to the tower of Babel in the Bible.

Ninus (nī′ nus). Son of Belus; a king of ancient Babylon, whose tomb was the trysting place of Pyramus and Thisbe. Known as the Assyrian Zeus and as the Chaldean Heracles.

Niobe (nī′ ō bē). Daughter of Tantalus and Dione; sister of Pelops. Hesiod says she married Amphion and had ten sons and ten daughters; others claim that she had seven sons and seven daughters, and some say six sons and six daughters. She taunted Leto (Latona) for having only two children, and the outraged mother appealed to the gods for revenge. As a result, all Niobe's children were killed except Chloris, wife of Neleus and mother of Nestor; and Niobe was turned into stone. Apollodorus iii; *Iliad* xxiv; *Met.* vi; *Theogony*. See also SIPYLUS.

Niobid (nī′ o bid). Also Niobide (nī′ o bīd). A child of Niobe.

Nisa (nī′ sa). 1. The name of the ancients for Megara, Greece. 2. A plain near the Caspian Sea, celebrated for its horses.

Nisus (nī′ sus). 1. Friend of EURYALUS, q.v. *Aeneid* ix. 2. A king who had a shining purple lock of hair, which he must keep or lose his kingdom. His daughter SCYLLA (the monster), q.v., fell in love with Minos, king of Crete. Scylla cut off her father's fatal lock of hair to win Minos, but he refused the infamous monster, and she leaped into the sea and was changed into a bird. *Met.* viii.

Noemon (nē′ mon). Also Noman. The name Odysseus assumed in his conversation with Polyphemus to mislead him. *Odyssey* ix.

Noman (nō′ man). See NOEMON.

Nomios (nō′ mi os). Also Nomius. Apollo as herdsman of the flocks of King Admetus of Thessaly. By order of Zeus, Apollo also served as herdsman in Arcadia, Laconia, and on Mount Ida for King Laomedon. Lowell, "Shepherd of King Admetus."

Nomius (nō′ mi us). See NOMIOS.

North Wind. Also Boreas; Aquilo (Roman).

Notus (nō′ tus). Also Auster. The south wind; some accounts say southwest.

Nox. See NIGHT.

Numa Pompilius (nu′ ma pom pil′ i us). Second king of Rome. Husband of Tatia, daughter of Tatius, king of the

Sabines. Legend says he was a celebrated philosopher born on the day Rome was founded by Romulus; he succeeded Romulus as king, and ruled for forty-three years. He founded the Vestal Virgins, and built temples to Janus and to Vesta. When Tatia died, he received legal advice from EGERIA, q.v., and she became his wife. *Aeneid* vi; *Met.*

Numanus (nū mā′ nus). Brother-in-law of Turnus, who taunted Aeneas and the Trojans for remaining in their stronghold, and contrasted the austere life of the Rutulians with the luxurious ways of Aeneas and the Trojans; this made Ilus so furious that he shot Numanus through the head. *Aeneid* ix.

Numina (nū′ mi na). The name for Pomona, and Vertumnus as protective spirits of the household, fields, individuals, gardens, and spring. Others also called Numina were: Pales, Silvanus, and Terminus.

Numitor (nū′ mitor). Father of Rhea Silvia; grandfather of Romulus and Remus. He was dispossessed of his crown by his brother Amulius. The grandsons killed Amulius and restored the crown to Numitor. *Aeneid* vi.

Nycteus (nik′ tūs). Father of Nyctimene and Antiope. Nyctimene committed incest with her father without his knowing who she was; when he learned it was his daughter, he attempted to kill her, but Athena changed Nyctimene into an owl. By Zeus Antiope became the mother of Amphion and Zethus.

Nyctimene (nik tim′ e nē). Daughter of NYCTEUS, q.v.

Nymphs (nimfs). Lesser divinities in the form of lovely girls, closely akin to the gods whose children or wives they often were. The word "nymph" came from the Greek word for bride, which has become generalized to mean maiden. The nymphs were eternally young. Many were attendants of the higher gods—Apollo, Artemis, Bacchus, Hermes, Pan, Poseidon. Among the groups of nymphs were the Dryades, Hamadryads, Limoniades, Naiades, Napaeae, Nereides, Oceanides, Nyseides, and Oreades. Two of the Nereides were very famous—Thetis, the mother of Achilles, and Amphitrite, the wife of Poseidon. Other famous nymphs include Echo, who talked too much; Arethusa, who was turned into a fountain; Oenone, who was deserted by Paris; Dryope, Panope, Sabrina, and Calypso, who were involved in interesting affairs. Some nymphs possessed the gift of prophecy.

Nysa (nī′ sa). A mountain in Thrace where nymphs cared for Bacchus.

Nyseides (nī sē′ i dēz). Also Nysiades. The nymphs who cared for Bacchus on Mount Nysa and were rewarded by Zeus by being placed among the group of stars now called HYADES, q.v.

Nysiades (ni sī′ a dēz). See NYSEIDES.

Nyx (niks). See NIGHT.

O

Oceanides (ō sē an′ i dēz). Also Oceanids. The three thousand daughters of Oceanus and Tethys, nymphs of the great river Oceanus. *Theogony.*

Oceanus (ō sē′ a nus). 1. According to the ancients, the great stream of water that encircled the world. Later it was called the Outer Sea (the Atlantic Ocean). 2. One of the twelve Titans, son of Uranus and Gaea; husband of Tethys. He was the oldest of the Titans, the first race. Apollodorus; *Iliad; Theogony.*

Ocrisia (ō kris′ i a; ok ri′ shi a). A Roman slave; by Hephaestus she became the mother of Tullius, the sixth king of Rome.

Ocypete (ō sip′ e tē). One of the three HARPIES, q.v. The other two were Aello and Celaeno.)

Ocyrrhoe (ō sir′ ō ē). A daughter of Chiron and Chariclo. The gods, angry because she could foretell the future, changed her into a mare. *Met.* ii. See also MENALIPPE.

Odes, The. A work by Pindar.

Odes and Epodes, The. A work by Horace.

Odysseus (ō dis′ ūs; ō dis′ ē us). Also Ulysses (Roman). Son of Laertes and Anticlea (some say of Sisyphus and Anticlea). One of the suitors of Helen. Married Penelope, daughter of Icarius. Father of Telemachus. Superior prudence, sagacity, activity, and valor characterized him in the Trojan War, where he was a leading Greek hero. *The Iliad* and *The Odyssey*, two of the greatest books of the Western world, contain the interesting account of his accomplishments and misfortunes. In addition to these two great epics, Odysseus is prominent in the works of Apollodorus, Hyginus, Ovid, Pausanias, Sophocles, and Vergil among the ancients; and there are many references to him in English literature, including Tennyson's "Ulysses" and Spenser's *The Faerie Queene,* which treats Penelope as the symbol of a faithful wife. See also PENELOPE, TELEMACHUS.

Odyssey, The (od′ i si). The great epic poem, in twenty-four books, about the wanderings of ODYSSEUS, q.v. The first twelve books recount adventures on the sea, the last twelve incidents on land; the companion poem to *The Iliad,* and both are attributed to Homer. *The Odyssey* has been called "the greatest tale of all time"; "the first novel"; "the best story ever written"; "the first expression of the Western mind in literary form."

Oeager (ē āj′ er). Also Oeagrus. A king of Thrace; by Calliope, the mortal father of Orpheus.

Oeax (ē′ aks). Son of Nauplius, king of Euboea, and Clymene; brother of the famous PALAMEDES, q.v. When Palamedes was unjustly killed to satisfy the resentment of Odysseus (Homer, to whom Odysseus was a great hero, is strangely silent about the fate of Palamedes), Oeax told his father, and both became bitter enemies of Agamemnon, because he had consented to the death of Palamedes. This enmity brought about a plan for revenge on the part of both Nauplius and Oeax. The father lighted fires near dangerous rocks on the coasts of Euboea so that the Greek ships returning from the Trojan War might be shipwrecked. The son told Clytemnestra that Agamemnon was bringing home Cassandra, the most beautiful of Priam's fifty daughters, and thus encouraged Clytemnestra to murder her husband. Apollodorus ii; Hyginus.

Oedipus (ed' i pus; ē' di pus). Son of LAIUS, q.v., king of Thebes, and Jocasta. He murdered his father and unwittingly married his own mother, Jocasta, after he had destroyed the Sphinx and ascended the throne of Thebes. By Jocasta, Oedipus was the father of Eteocles, Polynices, ANTIGONE, q.v., and Ismene. When his crimes were revealed, he put out his eyes, banished himself from Thebes, and, led by his daughter Antigone, retired to Colonus near Athens, where the earth opened and Oedipus disappeared. Apollodorus; *Theogony; Odyssey* xi; Pausanias; Euripides, *The Phoenician Women;* Seneca; Sophocles. The story of Thebes, with particular reference to Oedipus, has been told by Dryden; Voltaire; Corneille; Gide; Cocteau. See also ANTIGONE.

Oedipus. A work by Seneca.

Oedipus at Colonus. A tragedy by Sophocles that deals, with the fate of Oedipus.

Oedipus the King. Same as *Oedipus Rex, Oedipus Tyrannus.* A tragedy by Sophocles that deals with the curse on the houses of Labdacus, Laius, and Oedipus.

Oedipus Complex. A complex arising in early childhood which involves a primary attachment by the son to the mother, with hostility to the father. See also ELECTRA COMPLEX.

Oeneus (ē' nūs). King of Calydon; father of Meleager and Deianeira by Althaea, of Tydeus by Periboea. He forgot to make proper sacrifice to Artemis, who sent the savage boar to ravage his kingdom. The boar was killed by his son Meleager, in the Calydonian boar hunt, in which many of the heroes of the age participated. *Iliad* ix; *Met.* viii.

Oenomaus (ē nō mā′ us). Son of Ares and Sterope; king of Pisa; father of Hippodamia, who married PELOPS, q.v., after Pelops bribed Myrtilus, Oenomaus' charioteer. Oenomaus was killed in the race with Pelops. Apollodorus; Ovid; Pausanias.

Oenone (ē nō′ nē). A nymph of Mount Ida in Phrygia; wife of Paris. She foretold that her husband would desert her, abduct Helen, and bring ruin to Troy. *Heroides* v; Tennyson, "Oenone."

Oenopion (ē nō′ pi on). Son of Ariadne by Theseus (some accounts say Bacchus); father of Merope, who was loved by the Giant ORION, q.v., whose eyes Oenopion put out to avenge an insult to his daughter.

Oeta (ē′ ta). A mountain in Thessaly near Thermopylae with its pass and stream. Here Hercules, wearing the poisoned tunic of NESSUS, q.v., hurled himself into the waters for relief. On Mount Oeta he prepared his own funeral pyre and was cremated. *Met.* ii.

Ogyges (oj′ i jēz; ō ji′ jēz). A son of Gaea. Some accounts say he was a son of Poseidon, and married Thebe, a daughter of Zeus. He is said to have been the most ancient monarch in Greece, about 1764 B.C., and during his reign there was a deluge, antedating the flood in the days of Deucalion. Pausanias ix.

Ogygia (ō jij′ i a). The island where Calypso detained Odysseus for seven years as prisoner and husband. Zeus sent Hermes to Ogygia to have Calypso send Odysseus on his way to Ithaca. *Odyssey* iv, v, xii.

Oicles (ō′ i klēz; ō ik′ lēz). Also Oicleus. Son of Antiphates; married Hypermnestra, the daughter of Thestius (not of Danaus); father of Amphiaraus. Killed by Laomedon while he defended the ships Heracles used in his war against Troy. *Odyssey* xv.

Oileus (ō wī′ lus; ō i′ lūs). Father of the Lesser Ajax. King of the Locrians and an Argonaut. *Aeneid* i; *Iliad* xiii, xv.

Old Man of the Sea. A name the Greeks gave to NEREUS, q.v., and to Phorcys.

Olenus (ō' lē nus). Son of Hephaestus; husband of Lethaea, a very beautiful woman who preferred herself to the goddesses. Olenus and Lethaea were changed into stones by the deities. *Met.* x.

Olive. The tree sacred to Athena, which she planted, and for which she was awarded Athens in her contest with Poseidon.

Olympia (ō lim' pi a). A town in the northwestern part of the Peloponnesus where Zeus had a famous temple with a celebrated statue by Phidias; the statue was reckoned one of the Seven Wonders of the Ancient World. At Olympia the Olympic games originated in 776 B.C.

Olympiad (ō lim' pi ad). Also Olympic Games, so called for Olympia, where they were observed, or for Zeus Olympius, to whom they were dedicated. The only award a winner obtained was a crown of olive.

Olympians, The Twelve Great (ō lim' pi anz). (Some accounts list thirteen.) The Greek name is listed first, with the Roman name in parentheses. 1. Zeus (Jupiter). 2. Hera (Juno). 3. Poseidon (Neptune). 4. Demeter (Ceres). 5. Apollo (Apollo). 6. Artemis (Diana). 7. Hephaestus (Vulcan). 8. Pallas Athena (Minerva). 9. Ares (Mars). 10. Aphrodite (Venus). 11. Hermes (Mercury). 12. Hestia (Vesta). [13. Pluto or Hades (Orcus or Dis).]

Olympian Zeus. A name for Zeus, and the name of the famous statue by Phidias in the temple at Olympia, one of the Seven Wonders of the ancient world.

Olympic Games. See OLYMPIAD.

Olympus (ō lim' pus). 1. A Phrygian flute-player, taught by Marsyas; he also learned from Pan how to play the syrinx. 2. A mountain, the highest in Greece (elevation 9,794 feet), located in Macedonia in northern Greece; home of the gods and goddesses. Heaven and The Sky are other names for Mount Olympus. *Aeneid* ii, vi; *Iliad* i.

Omphale (om' fa lē). A queen of Lydia who had a desire

to see Heracles. Omphale bought Heracles as a slave, and he spent three years in her service. She became his mistress, had several children by him, and after the three years released Heracles to return to Tiryns. Apollodorus i; Diodorus Siculus iv.

Omphalus (om′ fa lus). Also Omphalos. **1.** A sacred stone, the stone that Cronus swallowed; when Cronus disgorged the stone it was placed in the temple of Apollo at Delphi. **2.** Omphalus (or Omphalos) is the name of a place in Crete sacred to Zeus. It received its name from the umbilical cord of Zeus, which fell there soon after his birth.

Oneicopompus (ō nē cō pom′ pus). The name for Hermes as a conductor of dreams.

Opheltes (ō fel′ tēz). A son of Lycurgus, king of Thrace. Opheltes was killed by a serpent; the Seven against Thebes gave him a splendid funeral because he had assisted them. Apollodorus ii, iii; Pausanias viii.

Ophion (ō fi′ on). One of the Titans; husband of Eurynome. Some accounts say this pair ruled heaven before the age of Cronus. Some legends say Ophion was a great serpent.

Opis (ō′ pis). An attendant of Diana. *Aeneid* xi.

Oppius (op′ i us). One of the seven hills of earliest Rome.

Ops (ops). Roman goddess of the harvest. Same as Rhea (Greek). She was the wife of Saturn (Greek Cronus).

Oracle at Delphi. The future was made known to all who consulted this famous oracle of Apollo at Delphi; this oracle, along with that of Zeus at Dodona, attracted many people. The sacred stone which Rhea compelled Cronus to swallow is at Delphi.

Oracles. Zeus' oracle was the oldest in Greece, Apollo's the most renowned. Some writers believe the oracles ceased at the birth of Christ. There were twenty-five oracles in Boeotia and the same number in the Peloponnesus, where deities answered human inquiries. The ancients wrote much about oracles; and in English literature, the oracles and prophets of mythology represent divine inspiration, as in the works of Milton, Byron, Tennyson, Housman, and others.

Oraculum (ō rak' u lum). The answer of the gods to the questions of men, or the place where these answers were given.

Orchamus (or kā' mus). A descendant of Belus; king of Persia. Husband of Eurynome; father of LEUCOTHEA, q.v.

Orcus (or' kus). The Roman name for Pluto, Hades.

Oreades (ō rē' a dēz). Also Oreads. The nymphs of mountains and grottoes, attendants of Artemis in her hunting.

Orestea (ō res tē' a). Also Oresteia. The dramatic trilogy by Aeschylus consisting of *Agamemnon, The Choephoroe,* and *The Eumenides.*

Orestes (ō res' tēz). Son of Agamemnon and Clytemnestra. Brother of Electra, Iphigenia, and Chrysothemis (some accounts say Homer gave the name Chrysothemis to Iphigenia). Orestes was educated by his uncle Strophius, king of Phocis who had married a sister of Agamemnon. Pylades, a son of Strophius, became a great friend of Orestes. When they grew to manhood, they went to Mycenae and with the aid of Electra murdered Clytemnestra and her lover Aegisthus, and avenged the murder of Agamemnon. See also ERIGONE. Orestes won the approbation of the gods, ascended the throne of Argos; then, after killing Neoptolemus (Pyrrhus), he married Hermione, the daughter of Menelaus and Helen, and lived in peace and security to the age of ninety. Pylades married Electra. Apollodorus; Homer; Herodotus; Ovid; Pausanias; Vergil; Aeschylus, *Agamemnon, The Choephoroe, The Eumenides;* Euripides, *Andromache, Iphigenia in Tauris;* Sophocles, *Electra;* Alfieri; Goethe; Hofmannsthal; Giraudoux; Sartre.

Orestes. 1. A tragedy by Euripides. 2. A work by Baron de Tabley.

Orgia (or' ji a). Festivals in honor of BACCHUS, q.v.

Orion (ō rī' on). There are many stories about the parentage of this celebrated hunter of gigantic stature. Some accounts say he was the son of Poseidon and Euryale; others say he sprang from the urine of Zeus, Poseidon, and Hermes. He loved Merope, the daughter of Oenopion, king of Chios, who had promised Merope to Orion if he would clear the kingdom of wild beasts; but Oenopion failed to keep his promise, and blinded Orion while he slept. His sight was restored when he turned his face toward the rising sun. Eos fell in love with him and carried him to the island of Delos, where Artemis became jealous of Orion and killed him with her arrows. There are also other stories about the nature of his death; Ovid says the bite of a scorpion killed him. Artemis placed him in the heavens as the constellation which still bears his name. Orion met and desired the Pleiades; the ladies ran and Orion pursued, so Zeus turned them into stars. No wonder Zeus decided to help these ladies; three of them had been his mistresses: Maia the mother of Hermes; Electra the mother of Dardanus; Taygeta the mother of Lacedaemon. Orion still pursues the Pleiades across the heavens. Homer; Ovid; Vergil; Spenser; Milton; Keats; Tennyson; Housman.

Orion's Dog. According to some accounts, Orion's dog was also placed in the skies and became the dog star Sirius, following at his master's heels. The brightest of the stars has been called Orion's Dog and also Canis Major, the brightest star in heaven.

Orithyia (or i thī′ ya). Daughter of Erechtheus. Carried away by Boreas as she rested unattended on a riverbank; mother of the winged twins Zetes and Calais and of Chione and Cleopatra. *Met.* vi.

Oropus (ō rō′ pus). A town of Boeotia, near the borders of Attica, the frequent cause of quarrels between the Boeotians and the Athenians. Amphiaraus had a temple there.

Orpheus (or′ fūs; or′ fē us). Son of Apollo and Calliope. Husband of EURYDICE, q.v. A masterful player on the lyre which Apollo (some say Hermes) gave him. Rivers ceased to flow, beasts forgot their wildness, mountains moved from place to place to listen; all nature was charmed and animated when Orpheus played. His married happiness with Eurydice was brief; Aristaeus became enamored of her, and as she fled from him, a serpent bit her foot; she died of the poisonous wound. With lyre in hand, Orpheus went to the infernal regions, where Pluto and Persephone agreed to restore Eurydice, provided he did not look back, but Orpheus forgot his promise. Stories of his last days and his end vary. His lyre was translated into the constellation Lyra. Orpheus is the most famous musician and poet in Greek mythology. Apollodorus; Ovid; Pausanias; Vergil; in English literature there are many references to Orpheus in the works of Shakespeare; Milton; Shelley; Browning; Morris; Giles Fletcher; operas, and plays by French writers Anouilh and Cocteau all have told his story.

Orphic (or' fik). Characteristic of, or pertaining to, Orpheus; such as music ascribed to, or religion centered about the life of Orpheus.

Orthos (or' thōs). Also Orthrus. The two-headed monster (dog), son of Typhon and Echidna; brother to Cerberus. From Orthos and the CHIMERA, q.v., sprang the Nemean lion and the Sphinx. Orthos guarded the cattle of Geryon, and was killed by Heracles when for his tenth labor the hero came to capture the cattle of Geryon. Apollodorus ii; *Theogony.*

Orthrus (orth' rus). See ORTHOS.

Ortygia (or tij' i a). 1. A famous grove near Ephesus. 2. A small island in Sicily on which the waters of Arethusa and Alpheus were joined. 3. An ancient name for Delos, where Artemis was born. *Aeneid* iii.

Osiris (ō sī' ris). Also Serapis. One of the great Egyptian deities; son of Zeus and Niobe; husband of Isis; murdered by his brother Typhon. He is the Egyptian god of the underworld and the judge of the dead. Milton, *Aeropagitica.*

Ossa (os' a). A high mountain in Thessaly (6,400 feet) which the Titans in their futile attack on the gods piled on Mount Pelion (5,300 feet), then both mountains on

Mount Olympus (9,794 feet). The centaurs once lived on this mountain. *Met.* i.

Othryadas (oth rī' a das). See ALCENOR.

Othrys (oth' ris). Mountain stronghold of the Titans in Thessaly. The centaurs once lived there. *Aeneid* vii.

Otionia (ō shi ō' ni a). Daughter of Erechtheus; she sacrificed herself to give the Athenians victory over the Eleusinians.

Otus (ō' tus). One of the Giants, who with his brother Ephialtes attacked the gods. *Aeneid* vi; *Iliad* v; *Odyssey* xi; Pausanias ix.

Oukalegon (u kal' e gon); also Ucalegon. 1. A Trojan councelor of Priam. *Iliad* iii. 2. A friend of Anchises. *Aeneid* ii.

Ouranos. See URANUS; COELUS.

Ovid (ov' id). 43 B. C.–A. D. 17. Full Latin name Publius Ovidius Naso (pub' li us o vid' i us nā' sō). Roman narrative poet whose *Metamorphoses* has been called "the major treasury of classical mythology." His *Heroides* is a series of twenty-one imaginary letters of mythological characters to their lovers; the *Fasti* is a mythological poem that describes the ceremonies of Roman festivals. Ovid's works have exerted tremendous influence on both Roman and English literature. He seems to have been read more than any other ancient poet, even Vergil. The great story-teller who predicted in Book xv of the *Metamorphoses* "I shall be read, and through all centuries . . . I shall be living, always," particularly influenced the greatest English poets: Chaucer, Spenser, Shakespeare, and Milton.

P

Pactolus (pak tō' lus). The sands of this river were turned to gold when MIDAS, q.v., bathed in it. *Aeneid* x; *Met.* xi.

Paean (pē' an). Also Paeon. 1. The term *paean* means healer. It is a name for Apollo as healer, and also for Aesculapius as the god of healing. 2. A son of Apollo (in *Met.* xv, the name is *Paeeon* or *Paieon*).

Paeans (pe' anz). Also Paeons. Solemn songs, hymns of praise or triumph addressed to Apollo.

Paedagogus (ped a gō' jus). In Sophocles' *Electra,* an old servant who had cared for Orestes when he was a boy.

Paeon (pe' on). See also PAEAN. 1. A celebrated physician who cured the wounds the gods and goddesses (Ares, Hades, Hera) had received during the Trojan War. *Iliad* v. 2. A son of Endymion. Pausanias v.

Pagasae (pag' a sē). A seaport in Thessaly where the *Argo* was built, from which it sailed to Colchis, and to which it returned. *Argonautica* i.

Palaemon (pa lē' mon). Also Portumnus, Portunus (Roman). A sea divinity into which MELICERTES, q.v., was changed when his mother INO, q.v., leaped into the sea with him.

Palamedes (pal a mē' dēz). Son of Nauplius and Clymene; brother of OEAX, q.v. Palamedes was sent to fetch Odysseus (who was pretending insanity) to serve in the Trojan War. Because Palamedes perceived the deceit of Odysseus, an enmity grew up between the two. At Troy, Odysseus falsely accused Palamedes, and the Greeks stoned him to death.

Palatine (pal' a tīn). The largest of the seven hills of Rome. Romulus built the original city on this hill. For names of all seven, see AVENTINE.

Palatium (pa lā' shum; –shi' um). One of the seven hills of earliest Rome. For names of all seven, see CERMALUS.

Pales (pā' lēz). Also NUMINA, q.v. Roman goddess of cattle and pastures; strengthener of cattle.

Palici (pa lī' sī). Also Palisci. Two deities, twin sons of Zeus and Thalia, they were born out of the bowels of the earth. They were highly revered by the Sicilians and their shrine was the place of justice and a sanctuary of refuge for slaves. *Aeneid* ix.

Palinurus (pal i nū' rus). Pilot of one of Aeneas' ships. He fell asleep at his post, tumbled into the sea, swam for four days, reached the shore of Italy and was murdered by "barbarous people" and left unburied. Aeneas saw him in the Underworld, wandering about, unable to cross the Styx because he had not been properly buried. *Aeneid* iii, v, vi.

Palisci (pa li' sī). See PALICI.

Palladium (pa lā' di um). A celebrated statue of Athena, especially the famous one in Troy, on the preservation of which was supposed to depend the safety of the city. Odysseus and Diomedes carried it away. *Aeneid* ii; *Iliad* x; *Met.* xiii.

Pallanteum (pa lan tē' um). The town in Italy, founded by EVANDER, q.v., on the Palatine hill and named for Pallas, the name both of an ancestor and of his son. *Aeneid* viii. Other accounts say the name was derived from Pallantium, a town in Arcadia from which Evander had migrated to Italy.

Pallantides (pal an tī' dēz). Fifty sons of Pallas (son of Pandion; brother of Aegeus) were killed by Theseus (son of Aegeus), whom they had opposed when he came to take possession of his father's kingdom. Pausanias i.

Pallantium (pa lan' shi um). A town in Arcadia, Greece, founded by Pallas, ancestor of Evander; from here Evander had migrated to Italy. See also PALLANTEUM.

Pallas (pal' as). Common name in mythology. 1. Another name for Athena. 2. A beautiful daughter of Triton and associate of Athena; accidentally killed by the goddess; in grief for her friend, Athena took the name Pallas and placed it before her own. 3. A giant slain by Athena in the Gigantomachy, the war between the Olympians and the Giants. 4. One of the Giants, son of Uranus and Gaea. 5. A forefather of Evander. 6. A son of Evander who fought with Aeneas in Italy and slaughtered many of the Rutuli; he was killed by Turnus, king of the

Rutulians. *Aeneid* viii–x. **7.** A brother of Aegeus, king of Athens; uncle of Theseus; he tried to usurp his brother's kingdom. **8.** A Titan, son of Crius and Eurybea; husband of STYX, q.v.

Pallas Athena. ATHENA, q.v.; Minerva (Roman).

Pallor (pal' er). Same as Terror. Son and attendant of Ares.

Pan (pan). Faunus (Roman). Son of Hermes and Dryope. Greek god of flocks and shepherds, forests and wild life, and·fertility; patron of shepherds and hunters. Part man, part goat, with ears, horns, tail, and hind legs of a goat— playful, lascivious, unpredictable, always lecherous. He invented the flute with seven reeds which he called syrinx after the nymph Syrinx who had been transformed into the reed he cut for his first Pan-pipe. Shepherds loved his reed pipe, and Pan's musical contest with Apollo is famous. He loved and pursued many nymphs, among them Echo, Syrinx, and Pithys. *Aeneid* viii; Herodotus ii; *Met.* i; *The Homeric Hymns;* Pausanias viii. In English literature, poems about Pan are more numerous than distinguished; references to him are made by Spenser; Milton; Marvell; Cowley; Wordsworth; Shelley; Keats; Swinburne; Forster.

Panacea (pan a sē' a). Roman goddess of health, daughter of Aesculapius; sister of Machaon, Podalirius, and Hygeia.

Panathenaea (pan ath e nē' a). Annual festivals in Athens in honor of Athena.

Pandareus (pan dār' ē us). Also Pandarus. A son of Merops who stole the golden dog made by Hephaestus to guard the infant Zeus; for the theft Zeus later killed him.

Pandarus (pan' da rus). **1.** A son of Lycaon. He helped the Trojans in the Trojan War; a brave warrior, he wounded Diomedes and Menelaus, but was killed by Diomedes. *Aeneid* v; *Iliad* ii, v. **2.** The great go-between in the love affair of Troilus and Criseyde in the works of Boccaccio, Chaucer, and Shakespeare. **3.** See also PANDAREUS.

Pandion (pan dī' on; pan' di on). Son of Erichthon and

Pasithea; father of Erechtheus, Butes, Philomela, and Procne. King of Athens; he reigned forty years and died of sorrow following the transformation of his daughters into birds.

Pandora (pan dō′ ra). The "Eve" of mythology. Hesiod says she was the first mortal female who lived. She was made with clay by Hephaestus at the request of Zeus, who desired to punish Prometheus for stealing fire from heaven by giving him a wife. All the gods and goddesses of Olympus vied in giving her gifts: Aphrodite gave her beauty and the art of pleasing; the three Graces gave the power of captivating; Apollo gave the talent of singing; Hermes gave her eloquence and deceit; Athena gave rich ornaments and skill in woman's work; others gave lovely clothes, beautiful flowers, and a crown of gold; Zeus gave her a beautiful box. But Prometheus, sensible to the deceit of Zeus, refused to accept Pandora; his brother Epimetheus (Afterthought) did not possess the same sagacity and prudence, and he married her. They became the parents of Pyrrha, the future wife of Deucalion. Pandora opened the box (some say it was Epimetheus). When the box was opened, a host of plagues escaped to harass hapless man; only Hope remained in the box. John Milton pictures the great beauty of Eve: ". . . in naked beauty more adorn'd/More lovely than Pandora, whom the Gods/Endow'd with all their gifts. . . ." Apollodorus, Hesiod, Hyginus, Pausanias, Milton, Rossetti, and Longfellow told her story.

Pandrosos (pan′ drō sos). A daughter of Cecrops and Agraulos; priestess of Athena in the temple on the Acropolis where grew the olive tree given to Athens by Athena; sister to Herse and Aglauros (Agraulos). Pandrosos and Herse leaped from the Acropolis and were killed. *Met*. ii.

Panhellenic Festivals (pan hel len′ ik). See ISTHMIAN GAMES.

Panhellenius (pan he lē′ ni us). A name for Zeus as god of all the Greeks.

Panic (pan′ ik). Son of Ares; brother of Eris (Discord), Trembling, Phobos (Alarm), Metus (Fear), Demios (Dread), and Pallor (Terror).

Panope (pan′ o pē). Also Panopea. Greatest of the Nereids, she was invoked by sailors in storms. The name *Panope* means giving every assistance or seeing everything. *Aeneid* v; *Theogony*.

Panopeus (pan′ ō pūs). Father of Epeus who built the famous Wooden Horse at Troy. He was a twin of Crisus, with whom he fought in his mother's womb, a hatred that continued through their lives. Apollodorus ii; Pausanias ii.

Pantheon (pan thē′ on). The circular temple in Rome to all of the gods. It was built by Agrippa in 27 B.C. during the reign of Augustus. Later it was partially destroyed by lightning, then rebuilt by Hadrian, and converted into a Christian temple.

Panthia (pan′ thi a). Also Panthea. The mother of Eumaeus, the faithful servant of Odysseus. *Odyssey* xiii–xvii, xxi.

Panthous (pan′ thō us). A counselor of Priam and the father of Euphorbus, Hyperenor, and Polydamus, all of whom were killed in the Trojan War. *Iliad* iii, xiii, xvi, xvii.

Paphia (pā′ fi a). A name for Aphrodite; she was worshiped at Paphos.

Paphian Goddess (pā′ fi an). A name for Aphrodite as the goddess of sexual love. The word "Paphian" means erotic, illicit love; also a term for prostitute.

Paphos, Paphus (pā′ fos; pā′ fus). 1. The daughter of Pygmalion and Galatea. *Met.* x. 2. The island of Paphos. 3. A famous city on the island of Cyprus, near which Aphrodite rose from the sea and where she was specially worshiped.

Parcae (par′ sē). The three Fates. See ATROPOS.

Paris (par′ is). Also called Alexander. Son of Priam and Hecuba, destined before his birth to become the ruin of his country Troy. Married OENONE, q.v., a nymph of Mount Ida. Presided at the JUDGMENT OF PARIS, q.v.; awarded the golden apple to Aphrodite, abducted Helen of Sparta, caused the Trojan War, fought with little courage, and died of a wound from one of the poisoned arrows of Philoctetes. *Iliad* iii; Apollodorus; Ovid; Pausanias; Euripides; Vergil; *Heroides* xvi, xvii.

Paris, Judgment of. See JUDGMENT OF PARIS.

Parnassus (par nas' us). A mountain in Phocis, elevation 8,070 feet; one of the highest in Greece; named for Parnassus, a son of Poseidon. The mountain was sacred to the Muses, to Apollo, and to Dionysus. Delphi is located on one of its slopes. Deucalion and Pyrrha landed there after the deluge. *Met.* i, ii, v; Pausanias x.

Parthenia (par thē' ni a). Another name for Athena as the chief of the three virgin goddesses Athena, Artemis, and Hestia. (Some accounts say Parthenia is another name for Hera.)

Parthenium (par thē' ni um). The mountain on which Atalanta was exposed.

Parthenius (par thē ni us). 1. A brother of Pandion; blinded by Phineus. 2. A river in which Artemis loved to bathe. 3. A mountain in Arcadia, noted for tortoises, where Telephus the son of Heracles and Auge was born. Apollodorus; Herodotus; Pausanias.

Parthenon (par' thē non). The Doric temple of Athena on the Acropolis in Athens; built in the fifth century B.C., the age of Pericles. It is the highest achievement of Greek architecture. The sculpture, some of the finest in the world, is attributed to Phidias, and was built under his supervision; the gold-and-ivory statue of Athena was executed by Phidias himself. The face, throat, arms, and feet of the statue were ivory; the clothing and armor were gold, and the complete statue was forty-two feet high.

Parthenopaeus (par thē nō pē' us). Son of Hippomenes and Atalanta; some accounts say of Meleager and Atalanta.

Parthenope (par then′ ō pē). One of the three SIRENS, q.v.; the other two were Leucosia and Ligeia; the three were the daughters of Achelous by Calliope (some accounts say by Melpomene, others by Terpsichore). The Sirens threw themselves into the sea after their songs failed to lure Odysseus into a shipwreck. *Odyssey* xii.

Parthenos (par′ thē nos). Another name for Athena as one of the three virgin goddesses (the other two, Artemis and Hestia). The word "Parthenos" means virgin.

Pasiphae (pa sif′ a ē). A daughter of Helios and Persa; sister of Aeetes and Circe; wife of Minos II; mother of Ariadne, Androgeus, Phaedra, and the Minotaur.

Pasithea (pa sith′ ē a). 1. A Nereid. 2. The mother of Pandion. 3. Also called Aglaia; said to be one of the three Graces, daughters of Zeus and Eurynome: Pasithea personified "Brilliance"; Euphrosyne, "Joy"; Thalia, "Bloom of Life." See CHARITES.

Patroclus (pa trō′ klus). In the Trojan War, the beloved friend and constant companion of Achilles. Achilles permitted Patroclus to wear his armor; he routed the Trojans. With Apollo's intervention, Patroclus was killed by Hector. Achilles, grieved at the loss of his friend, forgot his anger and resentment against all the Greeks, re-entered the war to avenge the death of Patroclus; his anger was gratified by the slaughter of Hector. *Iliad* ix, xi, xvi, xvii, xviii; *Met.* xiii.

Pausanias (po sā′ ni as). Second century A. D. traveler and geographer. His *Periegesis* or *Description of Greece,* is a valuable source of information about the art, mythology, history, and religious customs of Greece.

Pavor (pā′ vor). Roman name for Phobos (Alarm), a son and attendant of Ares.

Pax (paks). Also Concordia. Roman goddess of peace.

Peace. A comedy by Aristophanes.

Peacock. Bird sacred to Hera. She set the hundred eyes of Argus in the peacock's tail.

Pegasus (peg' a sus). The fabulous winged horse which sprang from the blood of Medusa when Perseus cut off her head. Soon after Pegasus was born, he flew to Mount Helicon, struck the earth with his foot, and raised the fountain called Hippocrene. He became the favorite of the nine Muses and the symbol of poetic inspiration. Later he was given to Bellerophon, to conquer the Chimera; after the victory he flew to heaven and was made a constellation. Some accounts say Mohammed rode him to heaven from the temple area in Jerusalem. Hyginus; *Iliad* vi; *Met.* iv; Pausanias; *Theogony*.

Peirene (pī rē' nē). Also PIRENE, q.v. A fountain behind Aphrodite's temple on Acrocorinth. Some accounts say it gushed forth when Pegasus struck the ground with his hoof; others that the river god Asopus created it to supply water for the city of Corinth. At this fountain Pegasus was bridled by Bellerophon when he prepared to conquer the Chimera. The fountain was also sacred to the nine Muses. Pausanias ii.

Peirithous (pī rith' ō us). Also Pirithous. King of the LAPITHAE, q.v.; intimate friend of Theseus. Invited the heroes of the age to his wedding with Hippodamia, where a quarrel and battle between Lapiths and centaurs ensued; Heracles, Peirithous, Theseus, and the Lapiths triumphed, but many were slain. Apollodorus i; *Aeneid* vii; *Iliad* ii; *Met.* xii; Pausanias v.

Peisenor (pī sē' nor). Also Pisenor. One of the ancestors of Eurycleia, the nurse of Odysseus. *Odyssey* i, ii.

Peisistratus (pī sis' tra tus). Also Pisistratus. A son of Nestor; he befriended Telemachus on his way to Pylos for further information about Odysseus. *Odyssey* iii.

Peitho (pī' thō). Also Pitho, Suada, Suadela. A daughter of Hermes and Aphrodite. Goddess of persuasion among the Greeks and Romans, she was an attendant of Eros.

Pelagia (pē lā' ji a). A name for Aphrodite.

Pelasgi (pe laz' jī). Also Pelasgians. One of the earliest groups of people mentioned by the classical writers as primitive inhabitants of Greece and the islands of the eastern Mediterranean. Two thousand years before Christ they were in Argolis, Crete, and Lesbos. All Greeks were indiscriminately called Pelasgians and their country was called Pelasgia, from Pelasgus, their first king. Herodotus; Ovid; Pausanias; Strabo; Vergil.

Pelasgia (pe laz′ ji a). Ancient name for that part of Arcadia and Argolis in the Peloponnesus, which was the home of the PELASGI, q.v.

Pelasgians (pe laz′ ji anz). See PELASGI.

Pelasgus (pe laz′ gus). Founder of the Pelasgians; some accounts say he was a son of Gaea and "the first man."

Peleus (pē′ lūs; pē′ lē us). Son of Aeacus and Endeis. King of the Myrmidons in Thessaly. Father, by Thetis, of Achilles (the only instance where a goddess married a mortal; Aphrodite and Anchises were the parents of Aeneas, but they never married). Peleus was an Argonaut and participated in the Calydonian boar hunt; he helped Heracles conquer Troy when it was ruled by Laomedon, the father of Priam. At his famous wedding to Thetis, attended by all of the gods, Eris rolled in the golden apple for which Athena, Aphrodite, and Hera contended. Peleus was too old to take part in the Trojan War, but he gave his golden armor to his son Achilles. Peleus lived to a very old age, outliving both his son and his grandson Neoptolemus. Apollodorus iii; *Iliad* ix; *Met.* xi; Pausanias ii; Euripides, *Andromache*.

Pelias (pē′ li as). A son of Poseidon by Tyro. Twin brother of Neleus. Father, by Anaxibia, of Acastus, Alcestis, and several other daughters; uncle of Jason. Pelias unjustly seized the throne of his brother Neleus, the king of Iolcus. He promised Jason the crown if he would go to Colchis to avenge the murder of Phrixus, who had been killed by Aeetes. When Jason returned from Colchis with Medea, she tricked Alcestis, Hippothoe, Pelopea, and Pisidice, the four daughters of Pelias, into murdering their father, and refused to use her magic to restore him to life. Apollodorus i; *Met.* vii; Pausanias viii.

Pelides (pē lī′ dēz). Also Peliades. 1. A name for the daughters of PELIAS, q.v. 2. A name for Achilles, as son of Peleus.

Pelion (pē′ li on). Also Pelios. A celebrated mountain in Thessaly, elevation 5,305 feet. The giants in the war against the gods, piled Mount OSSA, q.v., on Pelion better to scale the heavens. Achilles' spear Pelios had been cut from one of the giant pine trees on Pelion and given to Achilles by Chiron; Chiron and the centaurs lived on Mount Pelion. *Met.* i.

Pelopea (pe lō pē′ a). Also Pelopia. 1. A daughter of Pelias. 2. A daughter of THYESTES, q.v.; by her own father she became the mother of Aegisthus, who was adopted and reared by Atreus, Thyestes' brother. Pelopea later married her uncle Atreus, who was finally murdered by Aegisthus, his wife's illegitimate child.

Pelopia (pe lō pī′ a). See PELOPEA.

Pelopidae (pe lop′ i dē). Descendants of Pelops; the name is usually applied to Atreus, Thyestes, Agamemnon, Menelaus, and Orestes.

Peloponnesus (pel ō po nē′ sus). Also called Morea (mo ré′ a). A peninsula of southern Greece; named for Pelops.

Pelops (pē′ lops). 1. Grandson of Zeus; son of Tantalus, king of Phrygia; brother of Niobe; father of Atreus and Thyestes; husband of Hippodamia, whom he won from Oenomaus in a rigged chariot race; grandfather of Agamemnon and Menelaus. His father Tantalus, in contempt of the gods, killed Pelops, roasted his body, and served it as food to the gods and goddesses; all refused to eat, except Demeter, who ate one of the shoulders; Zeus restored Pelops to life and gave him a shoulder of ivory. *Met.* vi; Apollodorus ii; Pausanias v. 2. The name of a son of Agamemnon and Cassandra. See TELEDAMUS.

Pelorus (pe lō′ rus). One of the SPARTAE, q.v.

Penates (pē nā′ tēz). Household and domestic gods of the Romans. See also LAR.

Penelope (pē nel' ō pē). A celebrated princess of Greece, daughter of Icarius and Periboea. Wife of Odysseus and mother of Telemachus. During the absence of her husband, she was beset with 108 suitors whom she treated with coldness and disdain. The three most persistent were Amphinomus, Antinous, and Eurymachus, but she was relieved of their unwelcome attentions when Odysseus returned home after an absence of twenty years. With the aid of Athena, Telemachus, Eumaeus, and Philoetius, Odysseus killed his rivals. Homer describes Penelope as a model of feminine virtue and chastity. *Odyssey* xvi, xxii; Apollodorus iii; *Iliad; Heroides* i; Pausanias iii.

Peneus (pē nē' us). A river god; father of Daphne, whom he changed into a laurel tree when Apollo pursued her. *Met.* i.

Penthesilea (pen the si lē' a). A queen of the Amazons; ally of Troy in the Trojan War. She was slain by Achilles; he was so struck by her beauty when he stripped her of her armor that he wept for having killed her in anger. When Thersites laughed at the weeping Achilles, Achilles killed him. *Aeneid* i; *Met.* xii; *Aethiopia,* a very old Greek epic poem, a continuation of the *Iliad,* fragments of which remain and probably date to about 775 B.C.; the poem tells of the arrival of Penthesilea and the Amazons at the Trojan War, the deaths of Penthesilea, Thersites, and Achilles.

Pentheus (pen' thūs). Son of Echion and Agave; king of Thebes. He refused to acknowledge the divinity of Dionysus. He was torn to pieces while watching the wild ceremonies of the Bacchae, who in their frenzy mistook him for a wild boar. His mother Agave was the first to attack him, followed by her two sisters, Ino and Autonoe. *Met.* iii; Apollodorus iii; *Aeneid* iv; Pausanias ii; Euripides, *The Bacchae.*

Pephredo (pē frē' dō). One of the GRAEAE, q.v. (The other two were Dino and Enyo.)

Perdix (pur' diks). Also Talos, Talus. Son of the sister of Daedalus. He invented the saw; because he gave promise of being a greater inventor than his uncle, Daedalus killed him. He was transformed into a partridge. Apollodorus iv; *Met.* viii.

Pergamos (pur' ga mos). Also Pergamus, Pergamum. The citadel of Troy. The word *Pergamos* is sometimes used for Troy. *Aeneid* i; *Iliad* iv.

Pergamus (pur' ga mus). A son of Neoptolemus and Andromache. See also PERGAMOS.

Periander (per i an' der). One of the seven sages (wise men) of Greece. Greek statesman; tyrant of Corinth 625–585 B.C.; conquered Epidaurus; patron of men of letters. Committed incest with his mother; murdered his wife; banished his son; murdered the richest and most powerful citizens of Corinth.

Periboea (per i bē' a). Same as ERIBOEA, q.v. See also MEROPE.

Periclymenus (per i klī' me nus). Son of Neleus and Chloris. Received from Poseidon the power to assume any form. Changed himself into a lion, a serpent, a bee, and an eagle; tried to peck out the eyes of Heracles, who killed him. *Met.* xii.

Periegesis (per i ē jē' sis) or *Description of Greece.* The work in ten books by Pausanias.

Perigone (per i gō' nē). Also Perigune (per i gū' nē). A daughter of Sinis, the Pine Bender killed by Theseus. She bore Theseus a son named Melanippus. Pausanias x.

Perimedes (per i mē' dēz). A follower of Odysseus who accompanied Odysseus on his descent into Hades. *Odyssey* xi.

Periphetes (per i fē' tēz). Also Periphates. **1.** A son of Hephaestus and Anticleia. He was a brigand of Epidaurus who killed travelers with an iron club—in fact Apollodorus calls him the "club man" (Apollodorus iii). He was killed by Theseus. Some mythologists say Daedalus was the father of Periphetes; one legend cites Poseidon as the father. **2.** A son of Copreus of Mysenae, killed by Hector. *Iliad* xv.

Pero (pē′ ro). Also Perone. The daughter of Neleus and Chloris whose beauty attracted many admirers. She married BIAS, q.v. *Odyssey* xi.

Persa (per′ sa). Also Perse, Perseis. One of the Oceanids, the three thousand daughters of Oceanus and Tethys. Wife of Apollo and by him the mother of Aeetes, Circe, Pasiphae, and Perses. Apollodorus iii; *Theogony.*

Persae (per′ sē). Same as *The Persians,* a tragedy by Aeschylus.

Perseis (per sē′ is). See PERSA.

Persephone (per sef′ ō nē). Also CORA, q.v., Core, Kore; Libera, Proserpina, Proserpine (Roman). The Greek word "Persephone" means maiden. The daughter of Zeus and Demeter; wife of Pluto; queen of Hades. Pluto abducted her while she was gathering flowers on the plain of Enna in Sicily. Demeter sought her everywhere, and threatened destruction for all mankind by withdrawing fertility from the earth if she could not find her. Zeus promised to restore Persephone to her mother provided Persephone had eaten nothing in Hades; but she had eaten some pomegranate seeds and was compelled to spend six months each year with Pluto but allowed six months with her mother. Apollodorus i; *Aeneid* iv, vi; *Met.* v; *Odyssey* xi; Pausanias viii, ix; *Theogony; Homeric Hymns.* Browning, Meredith, Swinburne, and Tennyson have told her story.

Perses (per′ sēz). 1. A son of Perseus and Andromeda. The Persians received their name from Perses, and the Persian kings claimed descent from him. Herodotus vii. 2. A son of Crius and Eurybia (two of the twelve Titans). He was the father of Hecate by Asteria. 3. A brother of Aeetes, Circe, and Pasiphae.

Perseus (pur′ sūs; pur′ sē us). Son of Zeus and DANAE, q.v., to whom Zeus appeared in a shower of gold. Husband of Andromeda, to whom he was always faithful, a rare occurrence in mythology. The story of Perseus has been called a model for the career of a hero; he was one of the best-known and pleasantest heroes in Greek mythology; Homer calls him the "most renowned of all men." His killing of MEDUSA, q.v., with the assistance of Athena and Hermes; his punishment of Atlas by turning him into a mountain; the rescue of a beautiful maiden (ANDROMEDA, q.v.) from a rock and winning her as his wife; the rescue of his mother from the evil intentions of POLYDECTES, q.v., whom he turned into stone, and whose throne he gave to the kind fisherman Dictys as a reward for caring for Danae and himself after Dictys had rescued them from the sea; the accidental killing of his grandfather Acrisius; his kingship of Argos and Tiryns; his founding of Mycenae; his worship as a hero in Athens and Seriphus are part of his great story, told by many of the ancients, among them Apollodorus, Herodotus, Hesiod, Homer, Ovid, and Pausanias. In English literature, Andromeda has been more popular than Perseus, and her story has been recounted by Spenser, Chapman, Morris, Tennyson, Browning, Kingsley, Hopkins, Auden, and others.

Persians, The. Same as *Persae*. A tragedy by Aeschylus. The only one of the thirty-three surviving tragedies by Aeschylus, Sophocles, and Euripides that is not based on mythology.

Petasus (pet′ a sus). Also Petasos. The winged cap of Hermes.

Peteus (pē′ te us). A monster, half-man and half-beast; a grandson of Erechtheus, a son of Orneus, father of Menestheus, and a king of Athens. Apollodorus iii; Pausanias x.

Phaea (fē′ a). Some legends say she was the owner of the wild sow of Crommyon (Cromyon), some that Phaea was the name of the wild sow killed by Theseus, some that she was a prostitute who murdered and plundered, and still others that the sow was the mother of the Calydonian boar. See CROMMYONIAN SOW. Apollodorus iii.

Phaeacia (fē ā′ shi a). An island in the Ionian Sea near the coast of Epirus. On this island Odysseus was shipwrecked, and treated kindly by King Alcinous and his daughter

Nausicaa. The gardens on this island are highly praised in *Odyssey* vii. *Met.* xiii.

Phaeacians (fē ā' shanz). The inhabitants of Phaeacia, who befriended Odysseus. The men were valiant seamen; the women were noted weavers. *Odyssey* vi, vii, vii.

Phaeax (fē' aks). Son of Poseidon and Corcyra; ancestor of the Phaeacians.

Phaedra (fē' dra). Daughter of Minos and Pasiphae; sister of Ariadne; wife of Theseus; mother of Acamas and Demophon. Phaedra became infatuated with her stepson Hippolytus and made overtures to him, but was rejected. In anger and humiliation she hanged herself, but left a message accusing Hippolytus of having attacked her. The outraged Theseus, without hearing Hippolytus' side of the story, appealed to Poseidon, god of the sea, for appropriate revenge. Poseidon sent a sea monster which terrified Hippolytus' horses so that they bolted and dragged their master to his death under the wheels of his own chariot. *Aeneid* vi; *Heroides* iv; Pausanias i; Euripides, *Hippolytus;* Seneca, *Hippolytus;* Racine, *Phèdre;* Edmund Smith, *Phaedra and Hippolytus.*

Phaethon (fā' e thon). Also Phaeton. Son of Apollo and Clymene; brother of the Heliades, who grieved so at their brother's death that the gods changed them into poplar trees. Phaethon was a foolish son; he insisted on driving for one day the chariot of the sun. His inability to guide the horses on course threatened heaven and earth with conflagration; Zeus killed him with a thunderbolt. *Aeneid* v; *Met.* ii; *Theogony;* George Meredith, "Phaethon."

Phaethusa (fā thū' sa). A sister of Phaethon; one of the HELIADES, q.v.

Phaeton (fā' e ton). See PHAETHON.

Phantastus (fan tas' tus). Also Phantasus (fan tas' us). The god of dreams of inanimate objects; brother of Hypnos (Sleep) and Thanatos (Death). Morpheus and Icelus were also his brothers, according to some accounts.

Phaon (fā′ on). The boatman of Mytilene in Lesbos, who received from Aphrodite a small box of ointment that made him one of the most beautiful men of the age. Many were captivated by him; Sappho fell in love with him, enjoyed the pleasures of his company, and wrote her rarest and warmest love songs to him. Phaon soon tired of her, and Sappho threw herself into the sea. *Heroides* xv.

Pharos (fā′ ros). A small island in the bay of Alexandria, Egypt, site of the lighthouse of Pharos, called "Phares of Alexandria." The tower, built of white marble by Ptolemy II, could be seen from a distance of a hundred miles away, and was considered one of the Seven Wonders of the ancient world.

Phasis (fā′ sis). 1. A son of Apollo and Ocyrrhoe. 2. A river in Colchis on the banks of which lived many large pheasants. The Argonauts, after their long and perilous voyage, sailed this river; hence perilous voyages are sometimes called "sailing to the Phasis." Apollodorus i.

Phebe (fē′ bē). See PHOEBE.

Phegeus (fē′ jūs; fē′ gē us). Also Phlegeus. 1. A companion of Aeneas in Italy who was killed by Turnus. *Aeneid* ix, xii. 2. A priest of Dionysus, who purified Alcmaeon of his mother's murder. *Met.* ix.

Pheidias (fid′ i as). See PHIDIAS.

Pheme (fē′ mē). Also Fama (Roman). Goddess of fame.

Phemios (fē′ mi os). Also Phemius. A minstrel with a beautiful harp, forced by the suitors of Penelope to serve them; Odysseus spared him and Medon because of their friendly deeds and because a singer was thought to be sacred. *Odyssey* i, xxii.

Phenix (fē′ niks). See PHOENIX.

Pherephatta (fer e fat′ a). Also Pherophatta, Phersephatta. Another name for PERSEPHONE, q.v., associated with her growing of corn.

Pheres (fer′ ēz; fē′ rēz). 1. The father by Clymene of Admetus, according to Euripides. (Admetus and Alcestis made their home in Pherae, a town in Thessaly.) **2.** A brother of Aeson, the father of Jason; Pheres supported Jason in his claim to the throne of Iolcus. **3.** A son of Jason and Medea, and brother of Mermerus; he was stoned to death by the Corinthians, according to Pausanias, because Medea caused the death of Glauce, the daughter of Creon, king of Corinth. Other versions say Medea killed her two children. See MERMERUS.

Phidias (fid' i as). Also Pheidias. One of the greatest of the ancient Greek sculptors (died 432 B.C.) in the age of Pericles. Famous for his statue of Olympian Zeus at Elis, described by Pausanias as forty feet high and regarded as his greatest work; the statue was one of the Seven Wonders of the ancient world. The ivory-and-gold statue of Athena Parthenos in the Parthenon, done by Phidias himself, was also widely celebrated for its remarkable artistry.

Phidippides (fi dip' i dēz). A famous Athenian runner, sent from Athens to Sparta in 490 B.C. to seek assistance against the invading Persians who had landed at Marathon. In two days he ran the distance of 152 miles. Herodotus vi. The modern marathon race, a distance of a little more than 26 miles, commemorates not the feat of Phidippides but the sprint of a Greek from Marathon to Athens to carry the news of the victory of the Athenians over the Persians.

Philammon (fi lā' mon). Famous musician; son of Apollo and Chione. See also CHIONE. *Met.* xi.

Philemon (fi lē' mon; fī lē' mon). See BAUCIS.

Phillo (fil' o). A daughter of Alcimedon, ravished by Heraacles. Pausanias viii.

Philoctetes (fil ok tē' tēz). A friend of Heracles who was present at Heracles' death; because he had erected and set afire the funeral pyre, and promised Heracles never to reveal the burial place, Heracles had given him his bow and the arrows which had been dipped in the poison of the Hydra. Since he was one of the suitors of Helen and had sworn to protect her, he went with seven ships to join the Greek expedition against the Trojans. He was regarded as the greatest archer in Greece. En route to Troy he was bitten by a snake (some say he stepped on one of the poisoned arrows), and the wound did not heal. The stench of the wound was so repulsive and his cries of pain so saddening that the Greeks abandoned him on the island of Lemnos, where he remained in torment and anger until the ninth year of the Trojan War. After the death of Achilles, the Greeks learned from Helenus that Troy could not be taken without the bow and arrows of Heracles. Odysseus and Diomedes (some myths say Neoptolemus) were sent to Lemnos to fetch Philoctetes and bring him to Troy. When Philoctetes saw the Greeks, he considered killing them for deserting him, and refused to go with them. But the spirit of the deified Heracles appeared and told Philoctetes it was his duty to fight at Troy, and that there his wound would be healed. At Troy his wound was cured by Podalirius (some accounts say Aesculapius or Machaon) and he went into battle. He killed Paris and many other Trojans. After the war, he refused to return to Greece because of his shoddy treatment at the hands of the Greeks. He went to Italy where he founded two cities and where he died. *Iliad* ii; *Met.* ix, xiii; Lord De Tabley, *Philoctetes, A Metrical Drama;* Sophocles, *Philoctetes;* Thomas Russell, "Suppos'd to Be Written on Lemnos."

Philoctetes. A drama by Sophocles.

Philodice (fil od' i sē). Mother of Hilara and Phoebe.

Philoetius (fi lē' shus). The faithful herdsman of Odysseus who promised to help destroy the suitors of Penelope. *Odyssey* xx.

Philomela (fil ō mē' la). Also Philomena. Daughter of King Pandion, of Athens; sister of Procne (Progne), who married Tereus, king of Thrace. Tereus attacked Philomela, then cut out her tongue. She wove a tapestry depicting her violation and sent it to Procne. The sisters planned to revenge themselves on Tereus. They killed and cooked the body of Itylus, the five-year-old son of Tereus and Procne, and served him as food to Tereus. During the dinner, Philomela threw the head of Itylus on the table.

The gods changed Tereus into a hoopoe or hawk, Philomela into a nightingale, Procne into a swallow, and Itylus into a sandpiper or pheasant. Apollodorus iii; *Met.* vi; Pausanias i. Philomela has become the poetical word for nightingale. The bird's song expresses eternal passion and pain in its classic sadness. Among the English poets who have used the story are Chaucer; Spenser; Shakespeare; Milton; Sidney; Keats; Arnold; Swinburne; Wilde; Eliot; and others.

Philomena (fil ō mē′ na). See Philomela.

Philonis (fil ō′ nis). Same as CHIONE, q.v.

Philonoe (fil ō nō′ ē). Daughter of Iobates. Wife of Bellerophon.

Philyra (fil′ i ra). The mother of Chiron by Cronus, according to some sources.

Phineus (fī′ nūs; fin′ ē us). 1. Brother of Cepheus, king of Ethiopia; uncle of Andromeda. Phineus lacked the courage to slay the sea monster that threatened Andromeda. After Perseus had killed the monster, Phineus came to claim Andromeda as his betrothed; but Perseus won her and turned Phineus to stone. Apollodorus ii; *Met.* v. 2. A king of Thrace, son of Poseidon. Husband of Cleopatra the daughter of Boreas. He deprived his children of their sight and was himself blinded by the gods. The Harpies stole and spoiled his food until his brothers-in-law Zetes and Calais rescued him. For aiding the Argonauts by telling them how safely to pass the dangerous SYMPLEGADES (clashing rocks), q.v., the gods restored his sight. Apollodorus i; *Argonautica* ii.

Phlegethon (fleg′ e thon). Also Pyriphlegethon. The river of fire; one of the five rivers in Hades. *Met.* xv; *Odyssey* x.

Phlegeus (flej′ jūs). See PHEGEUS.

Phlegra (fleg′ ra). Also Phlegraean Fields or Plain Phelgraeus Campus, Campi Plegrei. The place in Macedonia where the giants attacked the gods and were defeated by Heracles.

Phlegyas (flej′ i as). Son of Ares and Chryse; king of the Lapithae; father of Ixion and Coronis. Coronis was the mother of Aesculapius by Apollo. When Phlegyas learned that Apollo had violated his daughter, he burned the temple at Delphi; for this deed Apollo killed him, placed him in hell, and had a huge stone hung over his head. The stone keeps him in continual alarm by appearing to be about to fall on him at any moment. *Aeneid* vi.

Phobos (fō′ bos). Son of Ares and Aphrodite; god of alarm, fear, dread, and terror.

Phocis (fō′ sis). A country in Greece. Parnassus is its most celebrated mountain; Delphi its best-known town. Orestes, Pylades, and King Strophius lived in Phocis.

Phocus (fō′ kus). 1. A son of Aeacus and Psamathe; half-brother of Peleus and Telamon, killed by them out of jealousy because he was a great favorite of Aeacus. 2. A man who colonized the country around Delphi and from whom Phocis received its name. 3. A man from Corinth who cured Antiope of her insanity (incurred by Dirce's persecution) and married her.

Phoebad (fē′ bad). Also Phoebas. The name of a priestess of Apollo at Delphi. Phoebad is a name for a prophetess, seeress, or any "inspired" woman.

Phoebe (fē′ bē). 1. Another name for ARTEMIS, q.v., as the moon goddess. 2. Some accounts say Phoebe, one of the first twelve Titans, and wife of Coeus, was the first moon goddess, and the grandmother of Artemis. She was also the mother of Asteria and Leto. 3. The daughter of Leucippus; she and her sister HILARA, q.v., were carried away by Castor and Pollux. 4. A daughter of Tyndareus and Leda; sister of Castor and Pollux, and Helen and Clytemnestra. Sometimes called TIMANDRA, q.v. Apollodorus i, ii; Pausanias ii, iii, iv; *Theogony*.

Phoebus (fi′ bus). A name for Apollo as the sun god.

Phoenice (fi nē′ sē). See PHOENICIA.

Phoenicia (fi nish′ i a; fē nē′ sha). Also Phoenice. A province in Asia Minor, at the east end of the Mediterranean;

Phoenicia, Syria, Palestine are names used for this area. Sidon and Tyre were the two most important towns. There are many references to Phoenicia in the writings of Apollodorus, Herodotus, Homer, Ovid, and Vergil.

Phoenician Maidens, The. A drama by Euripides. Also called *The Phoenician Women* and *The Phoenissae.*

Phoenicians (fi nē′ shanz). The inhabitants of Phoenicia. They received their name from Phoenix the son of Agenor, who was one of their kings. The Phoenicians invented the alphabet and founded colonies such as Carthage.

Phoenissae, The. Dramas by Euripides and Seneca.

Phoenix (fē′ niks). Also Phenix. **1.** A mythical Egyptian bird of great beauty that lived for six hundred years in the Arabian desert. It was the only one of its kind; it built its own funeral pyre, lighted the fire by fanning its wings, burned upon the pyre, and arose eternally young from its ashes. **2.** A son of King Amyntor of Argos; the preceptor of Achilles. He lost his sight, but it was restored by Chiron. He fought with the Greeks at Troy. **3.** A son of Agenor and Telephassa; brother of Cadamus, Cilix, and Europa. While on his unsuccessful search for Europa, abducted by Zeus, he settled in Phoenicia, which was named for him. **4.** According to Hesiod, a Phoenix was the father of Adonis.

Pholus (fō′ lus). A famous centaur, half-horse, half-man. He entertained Heracles, and gave him wine, the smell of which attracted and maddened the other centaurs, who began to fight with Heracles. Heracles used his poisoned arrows and killed many of them. As Pholus buried them, he wounded himself in extracting one of the poisoned arrows. Heracles tried to save Pholus, but the poison was too deadly. Heracles buried Pholus on a mountain and named it Pholoe after Pholus. *Aeneid* viii.

Phorbas (for′ bas). **1.** A famous boxer killed by Apollo. **2.** A man who owned many cattle and was a favorite of Hermes. *Iliad.* **3.** A leader of the Phrygians against the Greeks in the Trojan War.

Phorcids (for' sidz). Also Phorcides, Phorcyads, Phorkyads. A name for the offspring of Phorcys and Ceto: the Graeae, the Gorgons, Ladon, Echidna, the Sirens, Scylla, and, according to some accounts, the Hesperides.

Phorcys (for' sis). Also Phorcus, Phorkys. 1. A son of Gaea and Pontus; husband of CETO, q.v.; father of the PHOR-CIDS, q.v. The Greeks called him the "Old Man of the Sea." Apollodorus ii; *Theogony*. 2. A Trojan killed by Telamonian (Greater) Ajax at Troy. *Iliad* xvii. 3. A man whose seven sons assisted Turnus against Aeneas. *Aeneid* x.

Phosphor (fos' for). Also Phosphorus. Son of Eos and Astraeus. The morning star; the planet Venus when it is visible at early dawn.

Phosphorus (fos' fō rus). See PHOSPHOR.

Phrixus (frik' sus). Also Phryxus. Son of Athamas, king of Thebes, and Nephele. Phrixus and his sister Helle rode on the golden-fleeced ram from Thebes to Colchis. He married Chalciope, daughter of King Aeetes of Colchis. Apollodorus i; *Argonautica* ii; Herodotus vii; *Heroides* xviii; *Met.* iv.

Phrontis (fron' tis). 1. A son of Phrixus and Chalciope, and the grandson of Aeetes, king of Colchis. 2. A skillful pilot of a ship of Menelaus. *Odyssey* iii. 3. The wife of Panthous, and the mother of Euphorbus, Hyperenor, and Polydamus. *Iliad* xvii.

Phrygia (frij' i a; frig' i a). A country of Asia Minor. Its most famous town was Troy, whose inhabitants were skilled at all kinds of needlework. The Phrygians (as well as all other peoples) were called barbarians by the Greeks. The Amazons, Baucis and Philemon, Gordius, Midas, and others were associated with Phrygia. It is mentioned in the writings of Herodotus, Homer, Ovid, Pausanias, and Vergil.

Phryxus (frik' sus). See PHRIXUS.

Phthia (thī' a). 1. The name of a town in Thessaly where Achilles was born. 2. A daughter of Niobe, killed by Artemis. **3.** A mistress of Zeus, seduced when he changed himself into a pigeon. **4.** A mistress of Apollo. **5.** A mistress of Phoenix.

Phylacus (fī′ la kus). The owner of fine cattle which Melampus tried to steal for his brother Bias.

Phyleus (fī′ lē us; –lūs). **1.** A son of Augeas. He blamed his father for refusing to pay Heracles for cleaning the Augean Stables; Heracles killed Augeas and placed Phyleus on the throne. He participated in the Calydonian boar hunt. **2.** One of the Greek captains at Troy.

Phyllis (fil′ is). A daughter of Lycurgus, king of Thrace. She fell in love with Demophon, son of Theseus, who stopped in Thrace on his return from the Trojan War; he married her and became king. Shortly thereafter, Demophon went to Athens, and when he failed to return after one month, Phyllis threw herself into the sea. *Heroides* ii; Chaucer, *The Legend of Good Women.*

Picus (pī′ kus). In Roman myth, the son of Saturn; father of Faunus; lover of Pomona; husband of CANENS, q.v. Circe also loved him, and when he remained faithful to Canens and rejected Circe's love, she turned him into a purple woodpecker. *Aeneid* vii; *Met.* xiv.

Pieria (pī ēr′ i a). A spring on the slopes of Mount Olympus. Near this spring the Muses and Orpheus were born; Apollo's cattle pastured there; Hermes stole the cattle from there. The word "Pierian" was applied to the Muses, and to poetical composition.

Pierian Fountain, Pierian Spring. Other names for PIERIA, q.v.

Pierides (pī er′ i dēz). A name for the nine Muses, from their birthplace Pieria.

Pierus (pī er′ us). A rich man in Pella, whose nine daughters challenged the nine Muses to a musical contest; the daughters were defeated, and changed into magpies. *Met.* v.

Pietas (pī′ e tas). A virtue, represented by the Romans as goddess of piety, duty, respect, affection, obligation to the gods, country, and parents.

Pillars of Heracles. See GATES OF HERACLES.

Pindar (pin' der). 522–443 B.C. Greatest of the Greek lyric poets. His forty-four odes that celebrate the winners of the Panhellenic Festivals—Olympian, Pythian, Nemean, and Isthmian—are extant and are a valuable contribution to our knowledge of mythology.

Piplea (pip lē' a). A beautiful maiden loved by DAPHNIS, q.v.

Piraeus (pī rē' us). Seaport of Athens, and the leading port of all Greece. Sanctuaries of Athena, Aphrodite, Bacchus, and Zeus were built at Piraeus.

Pirene (pī rē' nē). Also PEIRENE, q.v. A daughter of Achelous (some accounts say of Asopus). She grieved so much for her son, killed by Artemis, that she was dissolved by her continual weeping into the fountain of the same name on Acrocorinth. Pausanias ii.

Pirithous (pī rith' ō us). See PEIRITHOUS.

Pisander (pī san' der). 1. A Trojan, killed by Agamemnon. *Iliad* xi. 2. A Trojan killed by Menelaus. *Iliad* xiii. 3. A captain of the Myrmidons, excellent at fighting with the spear; sent with Patroclus by Achilles when Patroclus went to fight in the armor of Achilles. *Iliad* xvi. 4. The name of an early epic poet of Greece (seventh century B.C.); author of *Heracleia,* of which only a few lines remain, but which give for the first time the stories of the twelve labors of Heracles, of his club, and of his lion's skin.

Pisces (pis' ēz). The Fish or Fishes; a constellation, the twelfth sign of the zodiac, which the sun enters February 19.

Pisenor (pī sē' nor). See PEISENOR.

Pisistratus (pī sis' tra tus). See PEISISTRATUS.

Pitheus (pī' thūs). See PITTHEUS.

Pitho (pī' thō). See PEITHO.

Pithys (pit' is). Also Pitys. A nymph loved by Pan. She was also loved by Boreas, but fled from him; she fell against a rock and was changed into a pine tree.

Pittacus (pit' a kus). One of the SEVEN WISE MEN of Greece, q.v.

Pittheus (pit' thūs). Also Pitheus. Son of Pelops and Hippodamia. He was king of Troezen in Argolis, a wise and learned teacher, and taught school in Troezen. His daughter Aethra married Aegeus, king of Athens; she became the mother of Theseus. Theseus was educated by Pittheus in Troezen, for had Theseus been in Athens, he would have been killed by the fifty sons of Pallas. Pausanias i, ii.

Pitys (pit' is). See PITHYS.

Pleasure (plezh' er). Also Delight. A daughter of Eros (love) and Psyche (soul), born to them some time after they were taken to Olympus by Hermes.

Pleiades (plē' ya dēz; plē' a dēz; plī' a dēz). The seven daughters of Atlas by Pleione; born on Mount Cyllene in Arcadia: Alcyone, Celaeno, Electra, Maia, Merope, Sterope (Asterope), and Taygeta. After their death, they were placed in the heavens as a constellation. Only six are visible; the lost Pleiad is Merope, ashamed to show her face because she married a mortal. According to some mythologists, it is the Pleiad Electra who hides her face because she was unable to witness the fall of Troy. *Met.* xiii.

Pleione (plī ō' nē; plē ō' nē; plē ī' ō nē). A daughter of Oceanus and Tethys; mother of the PLEIADES, q.v.

Pleisthenes (plīs' the nēz). Also Plisthenes. A son of Atreus, king of Argos and Mycenae. Pleisthenes was reared by Thyestes, the brother of Atreus. To get the throne of Mycenae, Thyestes sent Pleisthenes to kill Atreus; instead, Atreus killed Pleisthenes, not knowing he was his own son. Atreus feigned reconciliation with Thyestes, and invited him to a banquet. Atreus killed three of the sons of Thyestes, cut them up and cooked them as food, and served them to Thyestes. Apollodorus says Atreus was the father of Agamemnon and Menelaus.

Plexippus (pleks ip′ pus; plek si′ pus). **1.** A son of Thestius; brother of Toxeus; their sister was Althaea the mother of Meleager, the hero of the Calydonian boar hunt. Both brothers participated in the hunt; they resented Meleager awarding the prize hide of the boar to Atalanta, contending that it was "too much honor to be paid to a woman." In his anger at their contention, Meleager killed his two uncles, Plexippus and Toxeus. **2.** A son of Phineus and Cleopatra; brother of Pandion, king of Athens.

Plisthenes. See PLEISTHENES.

Pluto (plōō′ tō). **1.** The Greek name for the king of hell, or for hell itself; his other Greek names are Ades, Aides, Aidoneus, Hades, Pluton; Roman names: Dis, Orcus. See also PERSEPHONE. **2.** The name of a nymph (Oceanid) who was the mother, by Zeus, of Tantalus (the father of Niobe and Pelops). Hesiod calls her the "ox-eyed Pluto" (similar to Homer's epithet for Hera—"the ox-eyed Hera"). Pausanias ii; *Theogony*.

Plutus (plōō′ tus). Son of Iasion by Demeter. God of riches, wealth. Origin of the word "plutocrat." *Theogony*.

Plutus. A comedy by Aristophanes.

Pluvius (plōō′ vi us). The Roman name Jupiter Pluvius given to Zeus (Jupiter) as the god of rain.

Podalirius (pō da li′ ri us). Son of Aesculapius and Epione; brother of Machaon, Panacea, and Hygeia. At Troy he stopped a pestilence, and healed Philoctetes of the poisoned arrow wound.

Podarces (pō dar′ sēz). **1.** A commander of the Phthians in the Trojan War. **2.** The original name of Priam. Before the Trojan War, when Troy was ruled by Laomedon, Heracles attacked Troy (because Laomedon had reneged on a promise) and killed Laomedon and all of his sons except Priam. A sister of Priam, Hesione, was captured by Heracles, awarded to Telamon, and later was allowed to ransom prisoners; she redeemed her brother Podarces, thereafter called Priam or Priamus.

Podarge (pō dar' jē; –gē). One of the HARPIES, q.v.; sometimes called Celaeno. The other two were Aello and Ocypete.

Poeas (pē' as). The father of Philoctetes.

Poena (pē' na). Also Poine. In Greek mythology, an attendant of Nemesis. In Roman mythology, the goddess of punishment.

Poenae (pē' nē). A name for the Furies.

Poets of Mythology. *Greek:* Homer, Hesiod, Stesichorus, Alcaeus, Sappho, Arion, Simonides, Pindar, Aeschylus, Sophocles, Euripides, Aristophanes, Apollonius of Rhodes, Theocritus; among the historians Apollodorus, Herodotus, Lucian, Pausanias. *Roman:* Apuleius, Catullus, Horace, Ovid, Propertius, Seneca, Tibullus, Vergil.

Poine. See POENA.

Polites (po li' tēz). 1. One of the fifty sons of Priam, killed by Neoptolemus; the last of Priam's sons to be killed. (His brother, Helenus, was the only one of the fifty sons to survive the Trojan War.) *Aeneid* ii. 2. A son of Polites, also named Polites, was the friend of young Ascanius, the son of Aeneas. *Aeneid* v. 3. One of Odysseus' men, turned into a swine by Circe, later rescued and changed again into a man. *Odyssey* x.

Pollux (pol' uks). The Roman name for the Greek Polydeuces. See CASTOR.

Polybotes (pol i bō' tēz). One of the giants who fought against Zeus. Poseidon killed him by crushing him under part of the island of Cos. Pausanias i.

Polybus (pol' i bus). 1. A king of Egyptian Thebes during the Trojan War. 2. A king of Corinth, who reared Oedipus as his own son. 3. One of the suitors of Penelope. *Odyssey* xx.

Polycaon (pol i kā' on). Husband of MESSENE, q.v.

Polycaste (pol i kas' tē). **1.** The youngest daughter of Nestor; she married Telemachus when he came to Nestor to seek information about Odysseus. *Odyssey* iii. **2.** The sister of Daedalus; mother of Talos. Daedalus killed Talos because he was jealous of the inventive powers of his nephew. Some accounts say that Polycaste was changed into a bird that chattered in derision while Daedalus was burying his own son Icarus.

Polycletus (pol i klē' tus). Also Polycleitus, Polyclitus. Ranked among the ancients as the most skillful sculptor. As an older contemporary, he was the only rival of Phidias. His most famous work was his gold-and-ivory statue of Hera at Argos. There are many Roman copies of his sculpture.

Polycrates (pō lik' ra tēz). A son of Aeacus; tyrant of Samos; famous for his continual good fortune, power, respect, riches. He was killed by a Persian governor who was envious of the continuous prosperity of Polycrates. Herodotus iii; Pausanias viii.

Polydama (pō lid' a ma). Also Polydamna. Wife of Thonis, king of Egypt. She entertained Helen of Troy, and gave her a certain drug which had the wonderful power of banishing care and melancholy. *Odyssey* iv.

Polydamas (pō lid' a mas). Also Polydamus. **1.** The Trojan son of Antenor by Theano, a sister of Hecabe. He married Lycaste, a daughter of Priam. *Iliad*. Stories later than *The Iliad* make both Antenor and Polydamas traitors to the Trojan cause. **2.** A Trojan son of Panthous, born on the same night as Hector; inferior in valor to none save Hector. After he had slaughtered many Greeks, he was killed by Ajax. *Iliad* xii, xiii.

Polydamna. See POLYDAMA.

Polydectes (pol i dek' tēz). A king of Seriphus, who cared for Danae and her son Perseus. He fell in love with Danae, but was rejected. Dictys, a fisherman and the brother of Polydectes, opposed the attempt of Polydectes to ravish Danae. When Perseus returned to Danae with the head of the Medusa, he turned Polydectes to stone, and gave the kingdom to Dictys. *Met.* v.

Polydeuces (pol i dū′ sēz). Same as Pollux; see CASTOR.

Polydora (pol i dō′ ra). 1. The wife of Protesilaus; usually called LAODAMIA, q.v. 2. A daughter of Peleus; half-sister of Achilles. *Iliad* xvi.

Polydorus (pol i dō′ rus). 1. A son of Cadmus and Harmonia; brother of Agave, Autonoe, Ino, and Semele. Married Nycteis (a daughter of Nycteus), by whom he had Labdacus (the father of Laius, and the grandfather of Oedipus). When Cadmus went into exile in Illyria, Polydorus became king of Thebes. Apollodorus iii. 2. The youngest son of Priam and Hecuba. He was too young to fight when the Trojan War began, and his father sent him, with much treasure, to King Polymnestor of Thrace. Polymnestor betrayed the Trojans, stole the treasure, and killed Polydorus. *Aeneid* iii; *Met.* xiii. According to Homer, Polydorus fought at Troy and was killed by Achilles. *Iliad* xx. Other accounts say this was another son of Priam, by the same name of Polydorus. 3. A son of Hippomedon; one of the Epigoni.

Polyhymnia (pol i him′ ni a). Also Polymnia. One of the nine Muses, daughters of Zeus and Mnemosyne. She is the muse of sacred song, oratory, lyric, singing, rhetoric. Her symbol is the veil.

Polyidus (pol i ī′ dus). A wise seer of Corinth; advised Bellerophon to capture Pegasus; restored Glaucus, a son of Minos, to life. Apollodorus iii.

Polymede (pol i mē′ dē). Daughter of Autolycus; wife of Aeson; mother of Jason. Apollodorus i. Other names for the mother of Jason are Perimede, Amphinome, and Alcimede.

Polymnestor (po lim nes′ tor). A king of Thrace; married Ilione, the oldest daughter of Priam; murdered Polydorus. After the Trojan War, Hecuba stopped on the coast of Thrace, found the body of her son Polydorus, blinded Polymnestor, and murdered his two children. *Aeneid* iii; *Met.* xiii; Euripides, *Hecuba*.

Polymnia (pō lim′ ni a). See POLYHYMNIA.

Polyneices (pol i nī′ sēz). See POLYNICES.

Polynices (pol i nī′ sēz). Also Polyneices. A son of Jocasta and Oedipus, king of Thebes. Brother of Eteocles, Antigone, and Ismene. Inherited his father's throne, as did also his brother Eteocles; it was mutually agreed between them that they should reign alternately yearly. Eteocles first took the throne, but refused to relinquish the crown to Polynices. Polynices went to Argos, where he married Argia, daughter of King Adrastus. With the king's help, an army was raised to march against Thebes, in the campaign known as the Seven against Thebes. There, in single combat, Eteocles and Polynices killed each other. Apollodorus iii; Pausanias ii; Aeschylus, *Seven Against Thebes;* Euripides, *The Phoenician Women;* Seneca, *Oedipus, Phoenissae or Thebais.*

Polypemon (pol i pē′ mon). Another name for PROCRUSTES, q.v. Father of Sinis the pine bender. Both Polypemon and Sinis were killed by Theseus. (According to Ovid, Polypemon was the father of Procrustes.) Apollodorus iii; *Heroides* ii; *Met.* vii.

Polyphemus (pol i fē′ mus). 1. A one-eyed giant, son of Poseidon; chief of the Cyclopes; loved Galatea (daughter of Nereus and Doris); he killed Acis whom Galatea loved. The seer Telemus warned Polyphemus that one day Odysseus would come and blind him. On the way home from the Trojan War, Odysseus and his men stopped at the island where Polyphemus lived. They explored the island and entered a huge cave where there was a large store of food. Presently Polyphemus returned, driving in his herd of sheep, and blocking the cave entrance with a huge pile of wood. Odysseus politely asked for hospitality in the name of the gods; in answer, Polyphemus seized two of Odysseus' men and devoured them. Odysseus made Polyphemus drunk with the wine brought as a gift, and when he fell asleep Odysseus took a brand, heated it, and stuck it in the one eye of the giant. Odysseus conceived the idea of tying his remaining companions and himself under the bodies of the sheep to escape the hands of Polyphemus. *Aeneid* iii; *Met.* xiii; *Odyssey* ix; Euripides, *The Cyclops*. 2. A son of Elatus of Arcadia; he fought against the Lapithae; he was one of the Argonauts. *Argonautica*.

Polyphontes (pol i fon' tēz). A Theban general who helped Eteocles defend Thebes. He was killed by Aepytus.

Polypoetes (pol i pē' tēz). 1. A son of Pirithous and Hippodamia. 2. A son of Apollo and Phthia. 3. A son of Odysseus and Callidice. Apollodorus iii.

Polyporthis (pol i por' this). A son of Odysseus and Penelope, born after Odysseus returned from twenty years' absence. Apollodorus iii.

Polyxena (pō lik' sē na). A daughter of Priam and Hecuba; beautiful and accomplished, she was courted by Achilles, but the marriage was opposed by Hector. She accompanied her father when he went to Achilles to claim the body of Hector. When Achilles was killed by Paris, Polyxena sacrificed herself at his tomb. Some accounts say the sacrifice was not voluntary but that the spirit of Achilles appeared to the Greeks and demanded her sacrifce. She is not mentioned by Homer, but her story is in *Aeneid* iii; *Met.* xiii; Euripides, *Hecuba;* Seneca, *Troades.*

Polyxo (pō lik' sō). A priestess of Apollo's temple in Lemnos, and the nurse of Queen Hypsipyle. She advised the Lemnian women to murder their husbands, and suggested to Hypsipyle welcoming the Argonauts so that they would father sons by the Lemnian women, in order that the race would not become extinct. *Argonautica* i.

Pomona (pō mō' na). The Roman goddess of gardens and fruit trees, one of the Numina. She was courted by Pan, Priapus, and Silenus, and by Vertumnus, who finally adopted various disguises and won her as his wife.

Pompilius (pom pil' i us). See NUMA POMPILIUS.

Pontia (pon' sha). A name for Aphrodite (Venus), refers to her having risen from the foam of the sea.

Pontus (pon' tus). Same as Oceanus. An ancient sea deity; the personification of the sea; father, by Gaea, of Ceto,

Phorcys, Eurybia, and Thaumas. Pontus is the Latin name for the sea which the Greeks called first Axine, then Euxine, and which is today called the Black Sea.

Porphyrion (por fir′ i on; por fī′ ri on). A son of Uranus and Gaea; one of the giants who warred against the gods.

Portumnus (por tum′ nus). Also Portunus; Palaemon, Melicerta, MELICERTES, q.v. Melicertus (Greek). A sea deity; the god of harbors and ports.

Portunus (por tu′ nus). See PORTUMNUS.

Porus (pō′ rus). The Roman god of plenty.

Poseidon (pō sī′ don). Also Neptune (Roman). Son of Cronus and Rhea. The god of the sea; one of the twelve great Olympians; brother of Zeus, Hades, Demeter, Hera, and Hestia. He created the horse. Seldom successful in his contests with other gods: Athena defeated him for Athens, Hera for Argos, Apollo for Corinth. He aided the Greeks in the Trojan War. His love affairs were almost as numerous (though not so celebrated) as those of Zeus. He had many sons, some of whom were horses. Apollodorus; Herodotus; *The Homeric Hymns;* Hesiod; Homer; Hyginus; Ovid; Pausanias; Vergil; Spenser; Shakespeare; Milton; Jonson; Beaumont and Fletcher; Yeats; and others.

Postverta (pōst vur′ ta). Also called Carmenta. Roman goddess of the travails of women; guardian of women in childbirth. Some accounts name her as a goddess of prophecy. Poets refer to her as the mother of Evander, whom she accompanied from Arcadia to Latium (Italy).

Postvorta (pōst vor′ ta). Roman goddess of the past. She and her sister Antevorta (goddess of the future) were companions of POSTVERTA, q.v.

Potameides (pō tam′ i dēz). Nymphs who presided over rivers, fountains, springs, lakes.

Pothos (pō′ thos). Same as HIMEROS, q.v.

Potina (pō tī′ na). Roman goddess of children's potions.

Praxidice (praks id′ i kē). Also Praxidicae, Praxidike.

Greek goddess of enterprises, of punishment of evil actions, of justice, and of retribution. Pausanias ix.

Praxiteles (prak sit' e lēz). A noted famous Greek sculptor (fifth century B.C.) of figures from classic myths. His "Aphrodite of Cnidus" (second only to the "Zeus" of Phidias) was the most highly admired statue of antiquity. He made two statues of Aphrodite, one with conventional drapery, the other a nude—said to have been the first time a female figure had been made without drapery. The Athenians bought the conventional figure, the people of Cnidus took the nude.

Praxithea (prak si' thē a). A daughter of Thespius; by Heracles she became the mother of Lycurgus.

Priam (prī' am). Also Priamus. Originally called PODARCES, q.v. Son of Laomedon; husband of Hecuba; father of fifty sons and twelve daughters, according to *Iliad* vi. Besides the sixty-two children mentioned, he had, at least, forty-two other children by concubines, of which he had many. His most famous children were Hector, Paris, Deiphobus, Helenus, Antiphus, Polites, Polydorus, Hipponous, Troilus, Cassandra, Creusa, Laodice, Polyxena. When Heracles killed Laomedon, he placed Priam on the throne; Priam was the last king of Troy. He did much to embellish, fortify, repair, and restore the ruined city left by his father. The story of Priam and the disaster of the Trojan War (1194–1184 B.C.) is told by many of the ancients—Apollodorus; Cretensis; Dares Phrygius; Dictys; Herodotus; Homer; Hyginus; Pausanias; Vergil; Euripides; and others. In English literature, references to Priam are in the writings of: Chaucer; Spenser; Shakespeare; Lydgate; Milton; Dryden; Pope; Marlowe; Byron; Wordsworth; Tennyson; Landor; Keats; Morris; Rossetti; Lang; Meredith; Bridges; Brooke; Masefield.

Priamus (prī ā' mus). See PRIAM, PODARCES.

Priapus (prī ā' pus). Also Lutinus. The god of fertility in nature and in man. Son of Aphrodite by Dionysus (some say by Adonis, or Hermes, or Zeus). There are numerous references to him in the writings of the ancients; he is mentioned in the writings of Chaucer, Shelley, Swinburne, T. S. Eliot, and D. H. Lawrence, "Hymn to Priapus."

Procne (prok' nē). Also Progne. Daughter of Pandion, king of Athens. Wife of Tereus, king of Thrace. Sister of PHILOMELA, q.v.

Procris (prō' kris; prok' ris). Wife of CEPHALUS, q.v.

Procrustes (prō krus' tēz). Same as Polypemon and Damastes. He tied travelers to his bed and made them fit; if their legs were too short, he stretched them; if they were too long, he cut them off. He was killed by Theseus. In literature Procrustes has been used as a symbol of tyranny and enforced order. Apollodorus iii; *Met.* vii; *Heroides* ii.

Proetus (prō ē' tus; prē' tus). Son of Abas; twin brother of Acrisius with whom he fought even in his mother's womb; the dissension increased with their maturing years. Both brothers desired the kingdom of Argos: Acrisius prevailed. The attempts of Proetus to kill Bellerophon are told in *Iliad* vi.

Progne (prog' nē). See PROCNE.

Promachos (prom' a kos). Also Promachus. **1.** One of the Epigoni; son of Parthenopaeus. **2.** A son of Aeson, killed by Pelias. **3.** A name for Athena as guardian and protectress.

Promenaea (prō me nē' a). In Herodotus ii a priestess at Dodona. Two doves had flown from Thebes in Egypt; one came to the temple at Dodona, the other went to the temple at Ammon; both doves gave oracles.

Prometheus (prō mē' thē us; prō mē' thūs). Also Forethought. Son of Iapetus and Clymene; brother of Atlas, Menoetius, and Epimetheus (Afterthought). He ridiculed the gods; surpassed all in cunning and fraud; suspected the trickery of Zeus in offering him Pandora, whom he refused to accept as a wife; stole fire from heaven, for which crime Zeus ordered Hermes to chain Prometheus to a rock on Mount Caucasus where a vulture fed daily on his liver, which grew back daily for thirty years (according to some mythologists for thirty thousand years). He was finally freed by Heracles. Among the contributions of Prometheus to mankind were, according to Apollodorus: making with clay the first man and woman; giving mankind the fire he had stolen from heaven; teaching mankind the use of plants, with their medicinal power; teaching the cultivation of the ground; teaching how to tame horses. After he was freed from Mount Caucasus, he was brought to Olympus, to join the gods he had ridiculed. There are many varying stories about Prometheus, but the myth about him is one of the great stories in mythology. Apollodorus; Hyginus; Pausanias; *Theogony; Works and Days;* Aeschylus, *Prometheus Bound;* in English literature, he is depicted as a champion of mankind, in works such as Shelley's *Prometheus Unbound,* Byron's "Prometheus," and in poems by Rossetti; Coleridge; Mrs. Browning; Bridges.

Prometheus Bound. A famous tragedy by Aeschylus.

Propertius (prō per′ shus). Roman poet, 50–15 B.C. Author of elegiac, amatory, and mythological poetry. Friend of Ovid and Vergil.

Propylea (prop i lē′ a). Also Propylaea. A vestibule, entrance, or gateway of architectural importance before a building or enclosure. This gate or entrance to a temple was usually on the east side; churches were entered from the west side. The most famous propylea in the world is that of the Acropolis at Athens; famous for its beauty and originality, it was completed about 432 B.C.

Proserpina (prō sur′ pi na), **Proserpine** (prō sur′ pi nē). See PERSEPHONE.

Protagenia (prō ta je nī′ a). The only daughter of Deucalion and Pyrrha; sister of Hellen and Amphictyon. She was beloved by Zeus, and became the mother of a son by him.

Protesilaus (prō tes i lā′ us). A king of Thessaly; brother of Alcimede, the mother of Jason. He married Laodamia, the daughter of Acastus. He went to the Trojan War, was the first Greek to set foot on Trojan soil, and the first to be killed. His wife killed herself when she heard of his death. *Heroides* xiii; *Met.* xii; *Odyssey* ii; Wordsworth, "Laodamia."

Proteus (prō′ tūs; prō′ tē us). 1. A sea deity; son of Oceanus and Tethys. Poseidon gave him the gift of prophecy, and the power to assume different shapes. *Met.* viii; *Odyssey* iv. 2. A king of Egypt, the father of Theoclymenus, with whom Helen stayed while an illusionary Helen went with Paris to Troy. Euripides, *Helen*.

Protogenia (prō tō je nī′ a). Also Protogenea. The only daughter of Deucalion and Pyrrha; sister of Hellen and Emphictyon; mother of Opuns by Zeus. Some mythologists say Protagenia was also the mother of Aethlius, who became the father of Endymion.

Psamathe (sam′ a thē). 1. One of the Nereids; the mother, by Aeacus, of Phocus. After the death of Aeacus, she married Proteus, king of Egypt, by whom she had Theoclymenus and Theonoe. *Met.* xi. 2. The mother, by Apollo, of Linus, who was torn to pieces by dogs. When her father condemned her to death for her affair with Apollo, the god sent a monster to ravage Argos, and did not withdraw the monster until a shrine to Apollo had been built between Argos and Delphi. Pausanias i.

Psyche (sī′ kē). The personification of the human soul. She married Cupid (Eros), the god of love, and was made immortal by Zeus. Apuleius, *The Golden Ass, or Metamorphoses*. See also CUPID, EROS.

Psychopompus (sī kō pom′ pus). A name given to Hermes as the conductor of souls to Hades.

Ptah (p ta′). The chief god of ancient Memphis in Egypt, the shaper of the world and creator of gods and men.

Publius Ovidius Naso (pub′ li us ōvid′ i us nā′ sō). Ovid's full Latin name. His great work *Metamorphoses* is the major treasury of classical mythology.

Punishment in Hades, Unusual. Condemned to unusually severe punishment are: 1. The Danaides, murderers of

their husbands; they must forever pour water into a sieve.
2. Ixion, who had outraged the gods by attempting to seduce Hera; he is bound to a continually spinning wheel, and lashed with serpents. **3.** SISYPHUS, q.v., for several crimes, must forever roll a huge stone up a hill, the stone immediately rolling down again. **4.** Tantalus, q.v., for three crimes against the gods; punished with an insatiable thirst while standing in a pool of water up to his neck; each time he stoops to drink, the water recedes from him; at his side is a tree full of delicious fruit which is blown away each time he tries to grasp some; above his head hangs a huge stone which seems at any moment to fall and crush him, keeping him in continual alarm and constant fear. **5.** Tityus, for outraging Latona; punished by vultures continually gnawing at his liver, which (like that of Prometheus) always grows back again.

Pygmalion (pig mā′ li on). **1.** A king of Cyprus, and a celebrated sculptor. Thoroughly disgusted with the debauchery of females, he developed an aversion for women and resolved never to marry. He bestowed his affection upon a beautiful marble statue of a lovely girl, fell in love with the statue, and prayed to Aphrodite to give it life. Aphrodite changed the statue into a woman, Galatea, whom Pygmalion married. They had a daughter, Paphos. *Met.* x; John Marston; William Morris, "Pygmalion and the Image," in *The Earthly Paradise;* Thomas Beddoes; W. S. Gilbert; G. B. Shaw have used this myth in their stories and plays. **2.** A son of Belus; king of Tyre; brother of Dido; murderer of Sichaeus (husband of Dido). Instead of obtaining the treasure for which he had killed Sichaeus, he got nothing, because Dido took the riches and fled from Tyre to Africa, where she founded Carthage. *Aeneid* i; Apollodorus iii.

Pygmies (pig′ mēz). A fabled race of dwarfs in Central Africa; they were attacked by Heracles who gathered them up, wrapped them in his lion's skin, and sent them to Eurystheus. Herodotus.

Pylades (pil′ a dēz). Son of Strophius, king of Phocis, by a sister of Agamemnon. He was educated with his cousin

ORESTES, q.v., whose close friend and companion he became, and whom he assisted in the murders of Aegisthus and Clytemnestra to avenge the murder of Agamemnon, the father of Orestes. Orestes rewarded Pylades by giving him his sister Electra in marriage. The story of the friendship of Orestes and Pylades has become proverbial. Aeschylus; Euripides; Homer; Sophocles; Vergil.

Pylos (pī' los). Also Pylus. Town in Messenia in the Peloponnesus in southern Greece. Nestor's magnificent palace was in Pylos, where he was born. He was the only one of the twelve sons of Neleus to survive when Heracles attacked, captured, and burned Pylos. Nestor had entertained Telemachus at Pylos when he came to seek information about Odysseus. The words "sacred" and "sandy" are attributed to Pylos in the *Iliad* and the *Odyssey*.

Pyramus (pir' a mus). Two lovers in ancient Babylon, during the reign of Queen Semiramis. Their story was not originally a classical myth, but became closely associated with classical mythology when Ovid incorporated it in his *Metamorphoses* (iv). Forbidden by their parents to see each other, though they lived in adjoining houses, they held conversation and confessed their love through a chink in the wall that separated their two houses. They agreed to run away and meet at the tomb of Ninus outside the city walls, under a white mulberry tree. Thisbe arrived first, but was frightened away from the meeting place by a lioness; in her flight Thisbe dropped her veil which the lioness besmeared with blood. When Pyramus arrived, he found the bloody veil and concluded that Thisbe had been torn to pieces by wild beasts; in despair he killed himself with his sword. Thisbe returned, found her lover dead, took his sword and stabbed herself. Their blood soaked the ground under the white mulberry tree, causing the white mulberry to turn purple. Ovid, Chaucer, and Shakespeare use the story.

Pyrene (pī rē' nē). Also Pirene, Peirene. A woman violated by Heracles; she gave birth to a serpent, was killed by beasts.

Pyrgo (pir′ gō). The nurse of Priam's children. She followed Aeneas in his flight from Troy. *Aeneid* v.

Pyriphlegethon (pir i fleg′ e thon). Same as Phlegethon. The river of fire in Hades. *Odyssey* x.

Pyrrha (pir′ a). 1. A daughter of Epimetheus and Pandora. She married Deucalion, a son of Prometheus. Deucalion and Pyrrha were the only survivors of the deluge which Zeus sent to destroy mankind. The couple replaced the loss of mankind by throwing stones behind their backs; those Deucalion threw became men, those Pyrrha threw became women. Hellen was their son. *Met.* i. 2. A daughter of Creon, king of Thebes. Pausanias ix. 3. The name Achilles assumed when, dressed as a girl, he lived at the court of Lycomedes; Thetis, the mother of Achilles, had sent him there to escape fighting in the Trojan War where, as she knew, he would be killed. Hyginus, *Fables*.

Pyrrhus (pir′ us). Another name for NEOPTOLEMUS, q.v.

Pytheus (pith′ i us). Also Pythius. A name given to Apollo in reference to his killing the PYTHON, q.v.

Pythia (pith′ i a). The famous priestess of Apollo at Delphi. She was fifty years old before she assumed the office; she delivered the answers of Apollo to those who came to consult the famous oracle. The oracle could be consulted only one month in the year, and rich presents were required for Apollo; hence the opulence, splendor, and magnificence of the celebrated temple at Delphi. Pythia is another name for Delphi. Euripides, *Ion;* Apollodorus iii.

Pythian Games (pith′ i an). One of the four great Panhellenic festivals of Greece, established 586 or 582 B.C. in honor of Apollo. The games were held near the temple of Delphi, to celebrate Apollo's victory over the serpent Python. The gods themselves were often contestants in the games. Among the famous winners were Pollux (boxing), Castor (horse-racing), Calais (running), Heracles (Pancratium—which involved both boxing and wrestling), Zetes (fighting with armor), and Peleus (quoits and discus).

Pythias (pith′ i as). See DAMON.

Pythius. See PYTHEUS.

Pytho (pī′ thō): The ancient name for Delphi; it is derived from the name Python, the serpent Apollo killed and left there to rot.

Python (pī′ thon). The serpent killed by Apollo. It sprang from the stagnant waters which remained after the Deluge sent by Zeus in the age of Deucalion. Some accounts say this serpent was a son of Gaea, others that he was produced from the earth by Hera to persecute Latona while she was pregnant with Apollo and Artemis, and that as soon as Apollo was born he strangled this serpent. In memory of this killing, the Pythian Games were instituted. *Met.* i; Pausanias ii.

Pythoness (pī′ thō nes). See PYTHIA.

Q

Queens of the Amazons. Antiope, Hippolyta, Penthesilea.

Quinquatria (kwin kwat′ ri a). Festivals in Rome in honor of Minerva.

Quirinal (kwir′ i nal; kwi rī′ nal). The highest of the seven hills of Rome. It became the site of a palace for the kings of Italy when it was taken from the papal government in 1870. Today it is the residence of the president of Italy. See AVENTINE for the names of the seven hills.

Quirinalia (kwir i nā′ li a). Roman festivals in honor of Romulus.

Quirinus (kwi rī′ nus). 1. Among the Romans, a name for Ares. 2. A name given Romulus when he became a minor god of war.

R

Raven. The bird sacred to Apollo. It angered Apollo by bringing news of the unfaithfulness of his love Coronis; for this news, the bird's color, originally white, was changed to black by the god. Chaucer, "The Manciple's Tale."

Rea Silvia. See RHEA SILVIA.

Regilus (rē jil' us). A small lake in Italy where Castor and Pollux aided the Romans in 496 B.C. in a battle that gave the Romans control in Latium.

Remus (rē' mus). A son of Mars by Rhea Silvia; twin brother of Romulus. When the twins were quite young, they were thrown into the Tiber by Amulius, who had usurped the crown of his brother Numitor; but the twins were washed ashore and preserved by a she-wolf who fed them her milk. Later they were found by a shepherd who educated them as his own children. In an argument about building Rome, Romulus killed Remus. *Aeneid* vi; *Met.* xiv.

Rhadamanthus (rad a man' thus). Also Rhadamanthys. A son of Zeus and Europa; brother of Minos and Sarpedon. When he died, Zeus appointed him one of the three judges in Hades; the other two were Aeacus and Minos. *Aeneid* vi; *Iliad* xiv; *Met.* ix.

Rhea (rē' a). A daughter of Uranus and Gaea; sister and wife of Cronus. Mother of Zeus, Poseidon, Hades, Demeter, Hera, and Hestia. She was called the "mother of the gods," or the "great mother goddess." Her Roman names were Bona Dea, Magna Mater, Ops, Opis, Tellus, Terra; her Phrygian name was Cybele.

Rhea Silvia (rē' a sil' vi a). Also ILIA, q.v.; Rea Silvia, Rhea Sylvia. The mother, by Mars, of Romulus and Remus. The twin sons founded Rome in 753 B.C.

Rhesus (rē' sus). A son of the river god Strymon; king of

Thrace. He tried to assist Priam in the Trojan War. He was the owner of "the fairest horses . . . the greatest, whiter than snow, and for speed like the wind." An oracle had decreed that Troy would never be taken if the horses of Rhesus drank the waters of the river Xanthus and ate the grass of the Trojan plains. Therefore, Priam awaited with the greatest impatience the arrival of Rhesus and his horses. Since this oracle was well known to the Greeks, they sent Odysseus and Diomedes to intercept Rhesus, which they did; Rhesus was killed, and the horses were taken to the Greek camp. Apollodorus i; *Aeneid* i; *Iliad* x; *Met.* xiii.

Rhesus. A drama attributed to Euripides.

Rhexenor (reks ē' nor). Son of Nausithous, a king of the Phaeacians. Brother of Alcinous, the king of the Phaeacians who befriended Odysseus. Father of Arete, who married Alcinous. Apollo killed him with his silver bow. *Odyssey* vii.

Rhode (rō' dē). A daughter of Poseidon, born on the island of Rhodes. Mother, by Helios, of seven sons and one daughter. Some mythologists name her as the mother of Phaethon.

Rhodes (rōdz). Island in the Aegean Sea. Named by Apollo after Rhode, with whom the god fell in love. Many figures from myths are associated with the island of Rhodes, among them Danaus, Cadmus, Helen, Polyxo, Helios.

Rhodes, Colossus of. One of the Seven Wonders of the ancient world; the large statue of the sun god Helios was erected on the island of Rhodes about 280 B.C. It was 120 feet high, and known as the most famous colossus in antiquity. It was destroyed by an earthquake in 224 B.C.

Rhodius, Apollonius (rō' di us   ap o lō' ni us). See APOLLONIUS RHODIUS.

Rhodope (rod' ō pē). 1. An attendant of Artemis. She thought herself more beautiful than Hera, and the goddess changed her into the high mountain in Thrace that bears her name. 2. Another Rhodope was changed by the gods into a fountain. *Met.* vi.

Rhoecus (rē′ kus). 1. A young man who propped up a falling oak tree and saved the life of the dryad who lived in it. For reward, he asked for her love; she said she would send him a bee to tell him when to meet her. But when her messenger arrived, Rhoecus had already forgotten the tryst, and he waved the bee away impatiently and wounded it. The dryad, insulted by his indifference, avenged herself by blinding him. 2. A giant killed by Dionysus in the war against the gods. 3. A centaur killed by Dionysus at the wedding of Pirithous and Hippodamia. *Met.* xii.

Rhoetus (rē′ tus). A giant who warred against the gods.

Ripheus (rif′ ūs). 1. A Trojan who joined Aeneas on the night Troy fell. He was killed by the Greeks after he had slain many. *Aeneid* ii. 2. A centaur taller than trees. He was killed by Theseus at the wedding of Pirithous and Hippodamia. *Met.* xii. Dante made him the symbol of the love of equity and of justice.

River gods. Achelous, Alpheus, Cephissus, Peneus, and Simois. See entries under each.

Rivers of Hades. Acheron, Cocytus, Lethe, Phlegethon, Styx.

Robigo (rō bī′ gō). Roman goddess of corn and other grain.

Robigus (rō bī′ gus). Roman god of corn and other grain.

Roma (rō′ ma). A daughter of Evander; he named the city of Rome for her.

Rome (rōm). The city on the river Tiber in Italy; according to mythology, founded by Romulus on April 21, 753 B.C. The city, founded by Ascanius, son of Aeneas, was called Alba Longa at the time Romulus and Remus decided to found a city of their own. Macaulay, *Lays of Ancient Rome.*

Romula (rom′ ū la). The name given to the fig tree under which Romulus and Remus were found by a shepherd.

Romulus (rom′ ū lus). A son of Mars by Rhea Silvia; twin brother of REMUS, q.v. Founder of Rome; reigned thirty-nine years; died 714 B.C. The Romans ranked Romulus as a god, gave him the name Quirinus, and built temples in his honor. *Aeneid* ii; *Met.* xiv.

Rumina (rōō′ mi na). Roman goddess of suckling infants, human and animal. She had a shrine near the fig tree where the infants Romulus and Remus were suckled by a she-wolf.

Rumor (rōō′ mer). The last daughter of Gaea. She was swift-footed, feathered, ominous, a sinister monster, "obstinate in perverseness and forgery no less than messenger of truth." She was quick to tattle to Iarbas, the lover of Dido, the story of Dido and Aeneas, and then just as quick to tell Dido that Aeneas was preparing to leave her. In *Iliad* ii, she is "Rumor, messenger of Zeus"; and in *Aeneid* iv, "Rumor, than whom none other is more swift to mischief."

Rutuli (rōō tū′ lī). See RUTULIANS.

Rutulians (rōō tū′ li anz). The name of a people in Italy. Their king was Turnus, rival of Aeneas for Lavinia; he fought against Aeneas and the Trojans when they came to Italy. *Aeneid* vii, x, xi, xii.

S

Sabines (sā′ bīnz). Ancient people of Italy; famous in history as the first to fight the Romans, to avenge the rape of their women. *Met.* xiv. See also TARPEIA.

Sabrina (sa brī′ na). 1. A river nymph invented by Milton in his *Comus*. 2. The name of the Severn River in England.

Saces (sā′ sēz). A friend of Turnus. He warned Turnus against meeting Aeneas in the single combat wherein Turnus was killed. *Aeneid* xii.

Sages, Seven. See SEVEN WISE MEN OF GREECE.

Sagittarius (saj i tā′ ri us). A constellation depicting a centaur shooting an arrow; the ninth sign of the zodiac, into which the sun enters about November 22.

Salacia (sa lā′ shi a; –sha). Roman name for Amphitrite.

Salamis (sal′ a mis). A daughter of Asopus and Metope. She was carried away by Poseidon to an island in the Aegean Sea, about three miles off the coast of Attica; the island was named for her. Teucer and Aias the Greater were natives of Salamis. On October 20, 480 B.C., a naval battle was fought in the harbor of the island between the Greeks and the Persians under Xerxes; the Persians lost two hundred large ships and many others were captured with all of their ammunition, while the Greeks, under the command of Themistocles, lost only forty ships.

Salii (sā′ li ī; sal′ i ī). Roman priests of Mars, appointed by Numa, to care for the Ancile, the sacred shields of Mars.

Salius (sā′ li us). A contestant in a foot race held at the funeral games on the anniversary of the death of Anchises. Two close friends, Euryalus and Nisus, contended in the race; they were so dear to each other that each would rather see the other win. Nisus was ahead, followed by Salius, with Euryalus well behind. Nisus flung himself purposely in front of Salius, tripped him, and Euryalus won the race. Vergil seems to admire Nisus for this trick, but another viewpoint would regard Nisus as totally deficient in the first elements of sportsmanship. *Aeneid* v.

Salmacis (sal′ ma sis). A fountain in Caria, near Halicarnassus, which rendered effeminate all who drank its water. At this fountain Hermaphroditus changed his sex. The nymph Salmacis united with Hermaphroditus, making him the first hermaphrodite, an individual with both male and female reproductive organs. *Met.* iv.

Salmoneus (sal mō′ nē us; –nūs). A son of Aeolus and Enarete; brother of Sisyphus; husband of Alcidice; father of Tyro; king of Elis. Later married SIDERO, q.v., who mistreated Tyro. Arrogant and insolent, he wanted to be considered a god, and had his subjects call him Zeus. Zeus soon tired of such comedy and impiety; he killed Salmoneus with a thunderbolt, and placed him in Hades near his wicked brother Sisyphus. *Aeneid* vi; *Odyssey* xi; Apollodorus i.

Salus (sā′ lus). Same as HYGEIA (Greek), q.v. Roman goddess of health.

Samos (sā′ mos). An island in the Aegean Sea, famous for its religious mysteries. Daedalus and Icarus flew over Samos. Pythagoras was born there. Some mythologists say that Hera was born on Samos (Pausanias says he saw the willow tree under which she was born). Zeus and Hera spent their wedding night (it lasted three hundred years) on the island. It was a chief place for the worship of Hera, and most of her temples were there.

Samothrace (sam′ ō thrās). An island of the Aegean Sea, famed for religious mysteries. The CABIRI, q.v., were sometimes called Samothracian gods because of the celebration of their secret mysteries, so secret that nothing is known of them on the island. In 1863 a French expedition explored the ancient ruins of the island and recovered a famous statue which is called the "Victory of Samothrace," now in the Louvre in Paris.

Sandals of Hermes. Also called TALARIA, q.v.

Sangarius (sang gar′ i us). Sometimes called Sangaris. The name of a river in Phrygia and of its god; his daughter of the same name became pregnant merely from eating an almond that grew on the banks of the river. Some mythologists say Sangarius was the mother of Hecuba, wife of Priam. Pausanias vii.

Sappho (saf′ ō). Lyric poetess, born about 600 B.C. at Mytilene on the island of Lesbos. Along with her contemporary Alcaeus, also born at Mytilene, she was supreme as a lyric poetess. Little is known of her life history; of her lyrics only one ode to Aphrodite and some fragments remain. Among the ancients, she was ranked with Homer. Plato in *Phaedras* refers to her as the tenth Muse: "Some say there are nine muses. So few then?/ Sappho of Lesbos makes their number ten." The story that she threw herself into the sea because of her unrequited love for PHAON, q.v., a boatman of Mytilene, is probably legendary. *Heroides* xv; Herodotus ii.

Sarpedon (sar pē' don). A son of Zeus and Europa; brother of Minos and Rhadamanthus. When his older brother Minos became king of Crete, Sarpedon, who had coveted the throne, went into exile. He allied himself with Priam against the Greeks; with his close friend Glaucus he commanded the Lycians in defense of Troy, fought valiantly and killed many Greeks. He was finally slain by Patroclus. *Iliad* xvi; Apollodorus iii. Homer says Sarpedon was the son of Zeus and Laodamia (daughter of Bellerophon), but she lived about a hundred years after Europa. Other accounts say that Sarpedon was the son of Poseidon, and that he was killed by Heracles for his barbarian treatment of strangers. Herodotus i.

Saturn (sat' ern). Also Saturnus (Roman); CRONUS, q.v. (Greek).

Saturnalia (sat er nā' li a). Harvest festivals held in Rome in honor of Saturn as the god of agriculture. During these festivals unusual liberty prevailed; slaves were permitted to ridicule their masters; friends exchanged presents; all quarrels ceased; no criminals were executed; schools were closed; war was never declared; all was mirth, riot, and debauchery.

Saturnia (sa tur' ni a). A name given to Italy because Saturn reigned there during the Golden Age. Sometimes this name was given to Juno as being the daughter of Saturn.

Saturnus (sa tur' nus). See CRONUS.

Satyrs (sā' terz; sat' erz). Also Satyri. Sylvan deities that represented the luxuriant forces of nature; attendants of Dionysus. They were known for their orgies and lasciviousness. They looked like men, but had the legs and feet of goats, with short horns on their heads, and their entire bodies covered with hair. Some Satyrs were gods of the woods, and followers of Pan.

Scaean Gate (sē' an). The chief northwest entry to the city of Troy. The tomb of Laomedon was near the Scaean

Gate. When the gate was opened, it signified war. *Iliad* iii.

Scamander (ska man' der). Also Skamandros. A river of Troy that rose from two springs near Mount Ida. One spring flowed with warm water; the other spring, even in summer, was icy cold. *Iliad* xxii. The waters of the river gave a beautiful color to human hair and to the wool of animals. Hera, Athena, and Aphrodite bathed in it before appearing at the Judgment of Paris. Homer says that this river was called Xanthos by the gods, and Skamandros by men. *Iliad* xx.

Scheria (skē' ri a). The island of the Phaeacians where Odysseus was befriended. *Odyssey* vi.

Schoeneus (skē' ni us). Also Schoenius. The father of Atalanta of Boeotia.

Scinis (skī' nis). See SINIS.

Sciron (sī' ron). A celebrated thief in Attica, who plundered the country and threw people from the highest rocks into the sea where a great turtle ate them. Theseus attacked him, threw him into the sea, and Sciron himself became food for the turtle. *Met.* vii; Pausanias i; Apollodorus iii.

Scorpio (skor' pi ō). The Scorpion, the eighth sign of the zodiac, into which the sun enters October 24.

Scylaceus (sil a sē' us). Companion of Sarpedon and Glaucus, all allies of the Trojans. He was wounded by the Lesser Ajax, and returned to his home in Lycia. When he told the Lycian women that their husbands and sons had all been killed at Troy, they stoned him to death for bringing the evil tidings. After his death, Apollo commanded that the Lycians worship him as a god. A tomb was made for him near Bellerophon's tomb of the stones which had killed him.

Scylla (sil' a). 1. A sea nymph. Stories of her parentage vary: daughter of Typhon; of Triton; of Echidna; of Phorcys; of Zeus. Glaucus, a sea deity, fell in love with her, but she scorned his attentions. Glaucus appealed to

Circe for help; instead of helping him, Circe fell in love
with him and tried to make him forget Scylla. To punish
her rival, Circe poured the juices of poisonous herbs into
the waters in which Scylla bathed. Scylla was changed
into a frightful monster, the upper part of her body and
her head remaining a beautiful maiden, the lower part
of her body encircled with the necks and heads of six
hideous barking dogs who, whenever a ship passed,
reached out to grab six seamen (as they did when the
ship of Odysseus passed) and devour them. Scylla threw
herself into the sea that separates Italy and Sicily, and
was changed into rocks that continued to bear her name
and to be dangerous to sailors. The rocks, opposite the
whirlpool CHARYBDIS, q.v., are still a navigation hazard.
Met. xiii, xiv; Pausanias ii. 2. A daughter of Nisus, king
of Megara. She fell in love with King Minos of Crete,
and promised to deliver her father's kingdom into his
hands if he would marry her. Her father had a purple
lock of hair upon which depended his fate and the safety
of his kingdom. While her father slept, Scylla cut off the
lock of hair. When she delivered it to Minos he accepted
the lock of hair in order to capture the kingdom of
Megara, but he shrank from her with revulsion and contempt at her infamy, and refused to marry her. She
killed herself, was changed into a lark; her father was
changed into a hawk. *Met.* viii.

Scyros (sī′ ros). Also Scyrus, Skyros. A famous island in
the Aegean Sea. To this island Theseus returned after all
his adventures; Lycomedes, the king of Scyros, pushed
Theseus over a cliff and killed him. Achilles was hidden
by his mother at the court of Scyros to avoid fighting
in the Trojan War. Neoptolemus, the son of Achilles, was
born on the island. *Met.* vii, xiii.

Sea Gods, Goddesses, Deities, Divinities. *Males:* Oceanus,
Pontus, Nereus, Poseidon, Thaumas, Phorcys, Proteus,
Glaucus, Melicertes. *Females:* Amphitrite, Doris, Leu-
cothea, Thetis.

Seasons. Also Horae. See DICE.

Selena (se lē′ na). Also Selene. Another name for the moon. See ARTEMIS.

Selli (sel′ ī). Ancient people of Dodona in Epirus; priests of Zeus in his sacred grove. Perseus sought their advice when he wanted to find Medusa.

Semele (sem′ e lē). A daughter of Cadmus and Harmonia. Sister of Agave, Autonoe, Ino, and Polydorus. Mother, by Zeus, of Dionysus. *Iliad* xiv; *Met.* iii; Pausanias iii; *Theogony;* Euripides, *The Bacchae.*

Semiramis (sē mir′ a mis). Mythical Assyrian queen, wife of Ninus, founder of Nineveh, whom she succeeded as ruler. Famed for her beauty, wisdom, and voluptuousness. She is said to have built Babylon with its hanging gardens, and many other cities; conquered Egypt and much of Asia and Ethiopia, and unsuccessfully attacked India. She was queen of Babylon during the days of Pyramus and Thisbe. Herodotus i; *Met.* iv.

Semnae (sem′ nē). Same as ERINYES, q.v.

Semones (sem ō′ nēz). Roman deities not numbered among the twelve great gods (Greek Olympians). Among them were Faunus, the Satyrs, Priapus, Vertumnus, Pan, Janus, Silenus, and all the illustrious heroes who had been deified after death.

Seneca (sen′ e ka). 4 B.C.–A.D. 65. Lucius Annaeus Seneca, also called Seneca the Younger, Roman tragedian. His *Hercules Furens, Troades, Medea, Hippolytus, Oedipus, Agamemnon, Thyestes, Hercules Oetaeus,* and *Phoenissae* are all based on Greek mythology.

Serapis (sē rā′ pis). Same as Osiris, Egyptian god and judge of the dead.

Serestus (ser es′ tus). In *Aeneid* iv and v, a sailor and companion of Mnestheus and Sergestus.

Sergestus (ser jes′ tus). One of the three Trojans with Aeneas in Carthage (the other two were Mnestheus and Serestus) ; ordered by Aeneas to "silently equip the fleet, gather their crews . . . , prepare the armament, keeping the cause of the commotion hid" for a quick departure, for a message from Hermes had urged him to leave Dido and to proceed to Italy. Sergestus finished last in the boat race at the funeral games of Anchises, and later founded the Sergii (Sergian) family at Rome. *Aeneid* iv, v.

Seriphos (se rī' fos). Also Seriphus. An island in the Aegean Sea. From its coast, Acrisius put Danae and her son Perseus into a large wooden cask and set them adrift. A fisherman of the island, Dictys, the brother of Polydectes the king of the island, found the mother and child, and took them to his home and cared for them for several years. Polydectes fell in love with Danae, but she spurned him. When Perseus returned to the island, he turned Polydectes to stone. *Met.* v.

Servius Tullius (ser' vi us tul' li us). The sixth king of Rome; great legislator and warrior. Much loved by his people for beautifying and adorning Rome by adding the Esquiline, Quirinal, and Viminal hills to the city, and by building temples to the goddesses of fortune and of the moon (Fortuna and Diana).

Sestos (ses' tos). Also Sestus. A town in Thrace on the shores of the Hellespont, opposite Abydos. The home of Hero. From Sestos Xerxes built a bridge across the Hellespont when he invaded Europe. The men of Sestos and Abydos aided the Trojans in the Trojan War. *Iliad* ii.

Seven against Thebes, The. Adrastus, Amphiaraus, Capaneus, Hippomedon, Parthenopaeus, Polynices, and Tydeus.

Seven Against Thebes. A tragedy by Aeschylus.

Seven Hills of Rome. 1. Of earliest Rome: Cermalus, Cispius, Fagutal, Oppius, Palatium, Sucusa, and Velia. 2. Of later Rome; Aventine, Caelian, Capitoline, Esquiline, Palatine, Quirinal, and Viminal.

Seven Wise Men (Sages) of Greece. The list differs among ancient authorities as to names and number, but the list below is most generally accepted. 1. Bias (bī' as). Sixth century B.C. 2. Chilon (kī' lon). Sixth century B.C. 3. Cleobulus (klē o bū' lus; klē ob' ū lus). Sixth century B.C.

4. Periander (per i an' der). Sixth and seventh century B.C. **5.** Pittacus (pit' ta kus). Seventh century B.C. **6.** Solon (sō' lon). Seventh century B.C. **7.** Thales (thā' lēz). Seventh century B.C. There is a story of a golden tripod, dropped by Helen on her way home from Troy, found by the inhabitants of Cos, and taken to the priestess of Apollo at Delphi; the Coans were told to give it to the wisest man of Greece. It was given to Thales, who sent it to Bias, and so on until all seven had received it and refused to keep it, for each was wise enough to know that he was not the wisest man. It was finally dedicated to Apollo.

Seven Wonders of the World. **1.** The Pyramids of Egypt. **2.** The Phares (Pharos, or Lighthouse) at Alexandria. **3.** The Walls and Hanging Gardens of Babylon. **4.** The Temple of Diana (Artemis) at Ephesus. **5.** The Statue of Zeus by Phidias, at Olympia. **6.** The Mausoleum erected by Artemisia, at Halicarnassus. **7.** The Colossus of Rhodes.

Shield of Mars. ANCILE, q.v.

Shirt of Nessus. The celebrated centaur Nessus, having been wounded in the heart by one of the poisoned arrows of Heracles, gave his shirt (tunic) to Deianeira, and told her it had the power to call a husband away from his unlawful loves. When Heracles wore the poisoned shirt, it caused his death.

Sibyl of Cumae. See CUMAEAN SIBYL.

Sibyllae (si bil' ē). Also Sibyls (sib' ilz). Certain women, young and old, inspired by heaven and endowed with prophetic powers, who interceded with the gods on behalf of men. Their number is unknown. Plato speaks of only one; others of two; Pliny of four; Varro says there were ten—the number that is usually accepted. These ten generally resided in Persia, Libya, Delphi, Cumae, Samos, Cimmeria, Erythrae, Tibur, Marpessa on the Hellespont, and Phrygia. The most famous of the sibyls was that of Cumae in Italy, a woman of wisdom and vision.

Sibylline Books (sib' i lĭn). Also called Sibylline Verses, or *Sibylline Leaves,* the latter also the title of a volume of poems by Samuel Taylor Coleridge published in 1817. It was usual for the Sibyl to write her prophecies on leaves, place them at the entrance of her cave to be taken away before they were scattered by the wind, for then they became incomprehensible. One of the Sibyls went to Tarquin II with nine vólumes, which she offered to sell for a very high price, but when the king refused to buy them, she disappeared, returned with six (she had burned three) for the same price, and when again she was refused, disappeared, burned three more, returned again, asking the same price for three volumes. The king was so astonished that he purchased the three remaining volumes, and the Sibyl vanished, never to reappear. These books were preserved with great care in a college of priests, and deposited in the Capitol, where they were destroyed by fire in the time of Sulla. The Romans sent commissioners to different parts of Greece to search for more Sibylline verses, and it is said they found eight books, all spurious, for they speak of later events, such as Jesus, his suffering, and his death.

Sichaeus (si kē′ us). Also Sychaeus; sometimes called Acerbas. A priest of Heracles; he married Dido. He was murdered by his brother-in-law Pygmalion, who wanted his riches. Sichaeus appeared to Dido in a dream, revealed her brother's treachery, where his wealth was hidden, and advised her to flee Tyre. She left Phoenicia and founded Carthage. *Aeneid* i.

Sicily (sis′ i li). Largest and best-known island in the Mediterranean. Its mythological associations include the forges of Hephaestus and the Cyclopes; the Plains of Enna, from which Pluto abducted Persephone, the straits between Italy and Sicily; Scylla and Charybdis; Mount Aetna, under which Enceladus was buried; Trinacria (Thrinacia), where Helios Hyperion pastured his sacred cattle, *Odyssey* xii; the favorite home of Demeter, where she gave grain to the world; Drepanum, where Anchises was buried and where his funeral games were held a year later. *Aeneid* iii, v.

Sicyon (sish′ i on; sis′ i on). An ancient city in the Peloponnesus near Corinth, the most ancient kingdom of Greece. Ruled by Aegaleus, Agamemnon, and the Heraclidae. Apollodorus iii; Pausanias ii.

Side (sī′ dē). The first wife of Orion; thrown by Hera into Hades for boasting that she was more beautiful than the goddess.

Sidereal Gods and Goddesses (sī dēr′ ē al). Also called Sky Deities, or Meteorological Gods and Goddesses. Among them are Uranus, Zeus, Phoebe, Hyperion, Artemis, Apollo, Helios, Sol, Selene, Luna, Diana, Delia, Cynthia, and Eos.

Sidero (sī dē′ rō). Second wife of Salmoneus; stepmother of Tyro. She was called "the iron one." Salmoneus' daughter Tyro had by Poseidon become pregnant of twins (Pelias and Neleus). Salmoneus was induced by Sidero to punish his daughter for the love affair, for Sidero refused to believe that the love affair had been with a god; she forced Salmoneus to imprison Tyro. Sidero exposed the twins, but they were preserved, suckled by a horse and a dog, rescued, and reared by shepherds. When Pelias and Neleus reached maturity and learned their parentage, they rescued Tyro from captivity and killed Sidero. Apollodorus i.

Sileni (sī lē′ nī). A name for the wood gods that were followers of Bacchus and Pan.

Silenus (sī lē′ nus). Stories about his parentage vary. He has been named the son of Pan, of Gaea, and of Hermes. One account calls Silenus the brother of Pan. He became the nurse, teacher, and follower of Bacchus. Silenus is usually represented as a fat and jolly old man, riding a donkey, crowned with flowers, and always intoxicated. The Fauns and Satyrs were often called Sileni. He is sometimes pictured with ears and legs of a goat, at others with ears and legs of a horse. Pausanias i, ii, iii, vi; *Met.* iv, xi; Apollodorus ii.

Silvanus (sil vā′ nus). Also Sylvanus. One of the Numina; a rural deity; a wood god, half-man, half-goat. He is often confused with Silenus and the Fauns and Satyrs, for his worship prevailed only in Italy as god of boundaries, gardens, and woods.

Silver Age. Second Age of Mankind; followed the Golden Age. Not a bad age, but less glorious than the first. Women had arrived. Man ignored the gods, was less devout, fought other men, and did not live as long as in the Golden Age.

Silvia (sil′ vi a). Also Sylvia, Rhea Silvia, or Ilia. The mother of Romulus and Remus.

Silvius (sil′ vi us). Also called Aeneas Silvia, Aeneas Silvius, Silvius Aeneas. Anchises, when Aeneas visited the underworld, tells his son that Silvius would be his last child, born to him and Lavinia when they were both old, and that Silvius would be nurtured in woodland surroundings. Anchises further tells Aeneas that Silvius would be a king and father of kings of Alba Longa. *Aeneid* vi.

Simois (sim′ ō is). A river god of the river of Troy. The river rises on Mount Ida and flows into the Xanthus (Scamander). In the neighborhood of this river, most of the battles of the Trojan War were fought. *Aeneid* iii; *Iliad* v; *Met.* xiii.

Simonides (sī mon′ i dēz). 1. Simonides of Amorgos (a mor′ gos), Greek poet born on the island of Samos, sixth century B.C. A fierce misogynist, much of his poetry compares different kinds of women, mostly unfavorably and unpleasantly, to animals: a fat, lazy woman to a pig; an obstinate woman to a donkey; an ugly woman to a monkey. 2. Simonides of Ceos (sē′ os). Sixth century B.C. The most prolific of the early poets of Greece, he wrote lyric verse, odes, elegies, dirges, epigrams, and hymns to the gods. His elegy on the fallen at Marathon was preferred to that of Aeschylus; his epigrams for the Spartan heroes of Thermopylae were called by John Ruskin the noblest group of words ever uttered by man: "Go tell the Spartans, thou that passeth by,/That here, obedient to their laws, we lie." (The translations of this epitaph from the Greek vary, as: "Go, stranger, and to Lacedaemon tell/That here, obeying her behests, we fell.") Of his lyrics, there is a lovely description of Danae and her baby son Perseus, in the chest on the dark sea, highly praised by the ancients. Simonides wrote: "Poetry is vocal painting, as painting in silent poetry."

Sinis (sī′ nis; sin′ is). Also Scinis. Called the Pine Bender. A notorious bandit on the Isthmus of Corinth, he induced travelers to help him bend down a great pine tree and then unexpectedly released it so that the helpful travelers were catapulted into the air and killed. Theseus came along, was asked to help bend down a tall pine tree, released his grasp first, and Sinis was thrown into the air and killed. Apollodorus iii.

Sinon (sī′ non). A son of Sisyphus. He accompanied the Greeks to the Trojan War, and was distinguished for his cunning, fraud, and intimacy with Odysseus. When the Greeks built the Wooden Horse, put out their campfires, and sailed their ships behind the island of Tenedos to hide them from view of the Trojans and to make them believe they had left Asia and returned to Greece, Sinon went to Troy with his hands bound behind his back, allowed himself to be captured, and told Priam the Greeks had left Asia. He advised Priam to bring into Troy the Wooden Horse which the Greeks had left behind, and to consecrate it to Athena. The horse was brought into Troy; in the night, Sinon opened the side of the Horse, from which emerged many Greeks, who surprised the Trojans and pillaged the city. *Aeneid* ii; *Odyssey* viii, xi.

Sipylus (sip′ i lus). 1. In *Met.* vi, the name of one of the seven sons of Niobe. Apollo's arrows killed him and his six brothers: Ismenus, Phaedimus, Tantalus, Alphenor, Damasichthon, and Ilineus. There were also seven sisters. See NIOBE. In *Iliad* xxiv, Homer says there were only twelve children. 2. The name of the mountain in Lydia on which stood the statue of Niobe, with tears flowing down her marble cheeks for her great loss of her children.

Sirens (sī′ renz). According to most mythologists, three sea nymphs, daughters of Achelous by Calliope, Melpomene, or Terpsichore. Their names were Leucosia, Ligeia, and Parthenope (some accounts give different names). They were part bird, part woman, who by seductive singing lured sailors to death on rocky coasts. Some sailors were so charmed by their melodious voices that they forgot their work, listened with rapt attention, and at last died for want of food. Odysseus was informed by Circe of their power; as his ship was about to pass the rocky coasts, he stuffed wax into the ears of his companions, and ordered himself tied to the mast of his ship. When the Sirens failed to lure Odysseus, they threw themselves into the sea and perished. They once were defeated by the Muses in a singing contest. *Aeneid* v; *Met.* v; *Odyssey* xii.

Sirius (sir′ i us). The dog star, Orion's faithful hound, placed in the heavens as the constellation Canis Major. It has been called the brightest star in the heavens, and the ancients believed it always caused great heat on earth, and scorched the fields into barrenness. *Aeneid* iii.

Sisyphus (sis′ i fus). A son of Aeolus; brother of Athamas and Salmoneus; husband of Merope, the daughter of Atlas; father of Glaucus (the father of Bellerophon), Ornytion, and Sinon. Ravished Anticlea (daughter of Autolycus), who bore Odysseus. (Since Anticlea was the wife of Laertes, Odysseus was reared as the son of Laertes; many authorities claim Odysseus was in fact the son of Laertes.) Violated Tyro, daughter of his brother Salmoneus; but Tyro killed all her children by Sisyphus. After his death, he was condemned to unusually severe punishment in Hades—to roll a large stone to the top of a hill; the stone immediately rolled down again. The punishment was assessed by Zeus, for stealing, plundering, killing, and for insulting Pluto, and accusing Zeus of abducting Aegina, daughter of Asopus. Zeus was guilty of the abduction, but he punished Sisyphus for tattling to Asopus. Homer calls Sisyphus "the craftiest of men." *Aeneid* vi; *Met.* iv; *Odyssey* xi.

Skamandros (ska man′ dros). See SCAMANDER.

Sky Deities. Also Sky Divinities; see SIDEREAL GODS AND GODDESSES.

Skyros (skī' ros). See SCYROS.

Sleep. Greek: Hypnos; Roman: Somnus. The god of sleep.

Smilax (smī' laks). A shepherdess who loved Crocus; both were changed into the flowers that bear their names. Some accounts say that Smilax was changed into a yew tree. *Met.* iv.

Smyrna (smer' na). Another name for Myrrha, the daughter of Cinyras; she committed incest with her father. See CINYRAS.

Sol (sol). Roman sun god. *Greek:* Apollo, Helios, Hyperion; *Persian:* Mithras (mith' ras); *Chaldean:* Baal; *Syrian:* Adonis; *Canaanite:* Moloch; *Egyptian:* Osiris. The sun was the object of great veneration among the ancients.

Solon (sō' lon). One of the Seven Wise Men (Sages) of Greece. A man who grew old "ever learning new things." One of the most cultivated and wisest lawgivers of all time. From his name we call lawgivers solons.

Solymi (sol' i mē). 1. A race of mighty warriors who fought against Bellerophon. When Proetus wanted to get rid of Bellerophon, he sent him to battle the Solymi, but to his amazement Bellerophon conquered them. 2. A town in Lycia. 3. Solyma (Solymae) was the ancient name for Jerusalem. *Iliad* vi.

Somnus (som' nus). Roman god of sleep. Greek: Hypnos.

Soothsayers, The Seven Great. Amphiaraus, Calchas, Cassandra, Helenus, Melampus, Mopsus, and Teiresias.

Sophocles (sof' ō klēz). 496–406 B.C. Ranked with Aeschylus and Euripides as one of the greatest of Greek tragedians. Only seven of his one hundred twenty plays are extant; all seven are based on mythology: *Oedipus at Colonus, Oedipus Tyrannus* or *Oedipus Rex* (*Oedipus the King*), *Ajax, Antigone, Electra, Philoctetes,* and *The Women of Trachis* (*Maidens of Trachis*).

Soteira (so tī' ra). Another name for Athena.

Soter (sō' ter). 1. Another name for Zeus. The word

"Soter" means savior. 2. The name for the several Greek gods that deliver from danger.

Soteria (sō tē′ ri a). Days of sacrifice and thanksgiving for deliverance from peril.

Sounion. See SUNIUM.

South Wind. Called Notus (nō′ tus), or Auster (os′ ter).

Sparta (spar′ ta). A celebrated city of the Peloponnesus. It received its name from Sparta, the daughter of Eurotas; she married Lacedaemon, son of Zeus and Taygete (the city was also called Lacedaemon). The city of Sparta is important in mythology; many persons and events are associated with it, among them Menelaus and Helen; one of the favorite cities of Hera; the grave of Orestes; Odysseus who ran a race to win Penelope; Tyndareus, Leda, and Zeus; Lycurgus, the great lawgiver; the famous Leonidas and his three hundred at Thermopylae.

Spartae (spar′ tē). Also Sparti (spar′ tĭ). The word "Spartae" means sown men, the sons of the dragon's teeth (see CADMUS). After Cadmus slew the dragon that had killed his warriors, Athena commanded him to sow its teeth in the ground. As soon as he had done so, a company of armed men, the Spartae, arose from the ground. Athena directed Cadmus to cast a stone into their midst. In the resulting melee, all were killed with the exception of five—Chthlonius, Echion, Hyperenor, Pelorus, and Udaeus. These men joined forces with Cadmus, helped him in the building of Thebes, and became the founders of some of its most noble families.

Spheres, The Nine. Moon, Mercury, Venus, Sun, Mars, Jupiter, Saturn, Fixed Stars, Crystalline Sphere. Milton, *Arcades.*

Sphinx (sfingks). A terrible monster with the head and breasts of a woman, body of a dog, tail of a serpent, wings of a bird, paws of a lion, and a human voice. Accounts of her parentage vary: Orthos and the Chimera; Typhon and Echidna; Orthos (Orthrus) and Echidna. Hera sent the Sphinx to the vicinity of Thebes to punish the family of Cadmus. Perched on a rock near Thebes, the Sphinx proposed the following riddle: "What creature walks on four legs in the morning, two at noon, and three in the evening?" Those who could not answer were dashed against rocks or devoured by the monster. The Thebans were told the Sphinx would destroy herself when the riddle was explained. Creon, king of Thebes, promised the crown of Thebes and his sister Jocasta in marriage to him who could deliver Thebes from the monster. Oedipus solved the riddle with this answer: "Man walked on his hands and feet when he was young, at noon in middle life he walked erect, and in the afternoon of life he walked with the aid of a walking stick." With the riddle solved the Sphinx killed herself. Apollodorus iii; Sophocles, *Oedipus the King; Theogony.*

Spindle of Fate. The spindle the three Fates—Atropos, Clotho, and Lachesis—touch from time to time to keep it turning. See ATROPOS.

Statius (stā' shus). A.D. 45–96. Roman poet, author of an epic *Thebaid* or *Thebais* (twelve books) about the struggles of Oedipus to control Thebes. Chaucer summarized the *Thebaid* in his *Troilus and Criseyde* (v, 1485–1510). Statius is also the author of an unfinished epic, called *Achilleid* or *Achilleis,* of which only fragments are extant.

Stentor (sten' tor). One of the Greeks who went to the Trojan War, who had a "voice of bronze, whose cry was loud as the cry of fifty other men." Our word stentorian meaning extremely loud, is derived from his name. But the voice of Stentor was a mere whisper compared with the voice of Ares when the spear of Diomedes pierced his "nethermost belly" and the god "bellowed loud as nine thousand warriors or ten thousand cry in battle as they join in strife and fray." *Iliad* v.

Sterope (ster' ō pē). Also Asterope. One of the PLEIADES, q.v.

Steropes (ster' ō pēz). Son of Uranus and Gaea. One of the three Cyclopes; the other two: Arges and Brontes.

Stesichorus (stē sik' ō rus). A Greek lyric poet of the sixth century B.C. who wrote much about the myths of Thebes and Troy, of whose work only fragments are extant.

Stheneboea (sthen e bē′ a). Also Sthenoboea. She is also called Antaea, Anteia, or Antia. Daughter of Iobates, king of Lycia. She married Proetus, king of Argos. She fell in love with Bellerophon, falsely accused him of attacking her; and when he rejected her approaches, she killed herself. *Iliad* vi.

Sthenelos (sthen′ e los). Also Sthenelus. 1. A son of Actor; comrade of Heracles in his war against the Amazons. 2. A son of Capaneus; one of the Epigoni; one of the suitors of Helen; went to the Trojan War; one of those who emerged from the Wooden Horse; companion and charioteer of Diomedes. *Aeneid* ii, x; *Iliad* ii, v. 3. A son of Perseus and Andromeda; king of Mycenae; husband of Nicippe the daughter of Pelops; father of two daughters and a famous son, Eurystheus, whose birth Hera hastened so that he would be born before Heracles (Eurystheus commanded Heracles to perform the Twelve Labors). *Iliad* xix. 4. A son of Androgeus, the son of Minos; made king of Thrace by Heracles. *Apollodorus* ii.

Stheno (sthē′ nō; sthen′ ō). Also Sthenno. One of the three Gorgons; the other two: Euryale and Medusa.

Sthenoboea. See STHENEBOEA.

Strabo (strā′ bō). 63 B.C.–A.D. 24. Greek Stoic who wrote a geography of seventeen books which describes Europe, Asia, Egypt, and Libya. A valuable source for accounts of countries, people, customs, manners, history, geography, religion, governments, prejudices, and mythology.

Strenua (stren′ ū a). Roman goddess who gave vigor and energy to the weak and indolent.

Strife. A son of Eris. Eris (Roman: Discordia) is also called Strife, or the goddess of discord and strife.

Strophades (strof′ a dēz). Two small islands in the Ionian Sea west of the Peloponnesus. Home of the Harpies. Here they were pursued by Calais and Zetes, driven from the tables of Phineus. Later, when Aeneas stopped here on his way from Troy to Italy, the Harpies harassed him and his men, and predicted a hard journey to Latium. *Aeneid* iii; *Met.* xiii.

Strophius (strō′ fi us). 1. A king of Phocis. Married a sister of Agamemnon; father of Pylades, great friend of Orestes. After Orestes and Pylades murdered Aegisthus and Clytemnestra, Strophius disowned his son. Hyginus i; Pausanias ii. 2. The name of the son of Pylades and Electra.

Strymon (strī′ mon). The name of a river of Thrace, named after the river god Strymon, the father of Rhesus. Apollodorus i; *Met.* ii; *Aeneid* x.

Stymphalian Birds (stim fā′ li an). Also Stymphalides (stim fā′ li dēz). These were long-legged birds like storks or cranes, but were brazen-clawed, cruel-beaked, voracious, and man-eating. They were destroyed near Lake Stymphalus by Heracles as one of his labors, with the assistance of Athena. Pausanias v, viii.

Stymphalus (stim fā′ lus). 1. A king of Arcadia, killed by Pelops. 2. A district and a lake (some accounts say a river or fountain) were named for King Stymphalus. Near the lake, Heracles killed the Stymphalian Birds. Pausanias viii.

Styx (stiks). A daughter of Oceanus and Tethys. Mother, by Pallas, of three daughters—Nike (Victory), Strength, and Valor. Styx was the first to go to the aid of Zeus when the Titans attacked. Zeus rewarded her by taking her and her children to Clympus, and making her the goddess by whom all swore the most inviolable oaths. Some accounts say these oaths were sworn by the river of Hades named Styx, which flows around Hades nine times, and is the river across which Charon ferries the dead. If an oath taken by the Styx was broken, banishment for nine years from the councils of the gods resulted, and violators were deprived of ambrosia and nectar. Some accounts say Zeus made them drink of the waters of the Styx, which lulled them for a year into insensibility before exile from the councils. Some mythologists say Styx (the daughter) for whom Styx (the river) was named was also the mother of Persephone by Zeus, but the more common accounts list Persephone as the daughter of Demeter by Zeus. *Aeneid* vi; Apollodorus i; *Met.* iii; *Odyssey* x; Pausanias viii; *Theogony.*

Suada (swā' da). Also called Suadela (swā dē' la) by the Romans; Greek: Peitho, Pitho. The goddess of persuasion.

Sucusa (su kū' sa). One of the seven hills of earliest Rome. See CERMALUS for the list of seven.

Summanus (su mā' nus). Roman god of thunderstorms.

Sun, Sun gods. Apollo, Hyperion, Helios Hyperion, Helios, Helius, Phoebus, Sol. There are many names for the sun or sun gods.

Sun, Cattle of the. On the island of Thrinacia, Helios Hyperion pastured his sacred flocks and herds, some of which, to the horror of Odysseus, were slaughtered and roasted by his men. In punishment, as they sailed away from the island, a mighty storm arose, shattered the last of the twelve ships, and all perished except Odysseus. *Odyssey* xii.

Sun Chariot. The chariot of Apollo the sun god, in which his son Phaethon was killed when he insisted on driving it for one day. Apollo had sworn by the Styx that he would grant any request of his son, and could not take back the promise.

Sun Gods. See SUN.

Sunium (sū' ni um). Also Sounion. The famous cape of southeastern Attica, on which is located a magnificent temple of dazzling white marble dedicated to Poseidon.

Suppliant Maidens, The. A tragedy by Aeschylus, about the Danaides.

Suppliant Women, The. A tragedy by Euripides, about the request of the Argives to recover for burial those who had fallen in the war of the Seven against Thebes.

Sychaeus. See SICHAEUS.

Sylvani (sil vā' nī). Also Sylvans. Wood gods that followed Pan.

Sylvanus. See SILVANUS.

Sylvia (sil' vi a). Also Silvia, Rhea Silvia, Ilia. The mother of Romulus and Remus.

Symplegades (sim pleg' a dēz). Also called Clashing Cliffs, Clashing Islands, Cyaneae, or Planetae. Two dangerous rocks at the entrance to the Euxine (Black) Sea. Phineus told the Argonauts how they might pass the Symplegades, for the ancients believed they came together and crushed any vessel that tried to pass between them. A dove flew between the rocks, lost only its tail feathers, and at the favorable moment as the rocks rebounded, the Argonauts sailed through. The *Argo* lost only the rudder, and after this failure, say some ancients, the Symplegades united into one rock. In return for the help of Phineus, Calais and Zetes rid the tables of Phineus of the Harpies. *Argonautica* ii; Herodotus.

Syrinx (sir' ingks). A nymph loved by Pan, transformed into a reed from which Pan fashioned his pipe (flute), which was called syrinx. *Met.* i.

Syrtes (sur' tēz). The singular form is Syrtis (sur' tis). Quicksands off the northern coast of Africa, considered dangerous to ships. The word Syrtes means any part of the sea that is perilous to navigation, either from storms or hidden rocks and quicksands. *Aeneid* iv.

T

Taenarum (tē' nar um). Also Taenarus (tē' na rus). A promontory of Laconia, southernmost point in Europe, where Poseidon had a temple. Near here was a deep cave from which emanated such foul odors that birds could not fly across, and ancient writers imagined it as one of the entrances to Hades. This place has also been called the back entrance or back door to Hades, where Hermes as conductor of the dead and Charon as ferryman of the dead who charged a fee were evaded. Heracles brought Cerberus out this way, and Theseus descended here to get

Persephone. Apollodorus ii; *Met.* x; Pausanias iii; Strabo viii. See LAKE AVERNUS.

Tages (tā′ jēz). A son of Genius, and grandson of Zeus. He taught prophecy to the twelve nations of the Etrurians. *Met.* xv.

Tagus (tā′ gus). 1. A river in Spain, whose sands were covered with gold. *Met.* ii. 2. A Rutulian, killed by Nisus. *Aeneid* ix.

Talaira (ta lā i′ ra). Also called Hilaira (hil ā i′ ra), or Hilara (hi la′ ra). She and her sister Phoebe were carried away by Castor and Pollux as they were preparing to marry their cousins, Idas and Lynceus. Apollodorus iii; Pausanias ii.

Talaria (ta lā′ ri a). The winged sandals of Hermes. Winged sandals were also worn by Iris, Eos, Eros, the Furies, and the Harpies.

Talos (tā′ los). Also Talus. Some accounts call him Perdix. Perdix or Talos was a son of Polycaste, the sister of Daedalus. He invented the saw and the compass, gave great promise in inventive genius, and made Daedalus extremely jealous. Daedalus pushed him off a tower and killed him. Talos was changed into a partridge. The story of Perdix is in *Met.* viii.

Talthybios (tal thī′ bi os). Also Talthibius (tal thib′ i us). The chief herald of Agamemnon. He performed many unpleasant missions: brought Iphigenia to be sacrificed at Aulis; abducted Briseis from the tent of Achilles and took her to Agamemnon; told Hecuba that Astyanax must die, and that Polyxena must be sacrificed; told Hecuba that she would be a slave of Odysseus; advised Cassandra that she would go with Agamemnon to his home in Mycenae after the Trojan War; and told Andromache that she would be a slave of Neoptolemus. Later accounts say that when Agamemnon was murdered, this herald of unpleasant missions took care of Orestes and hid him from Clytemnestra and Aegisthus. *Iliad* i; Pausanias vii.

Talus. See TALOS.

Tantalus (tan' ta lus). Son of Zeus by an Oceanid named Pluto. The earliest ancestor of the tragic house of Atreus. Father of Pelops and Niobe. He is the victim of unusually severe punishment in Hades: he is within reach of water he cannot drink, food he cannot eat; and a huge stone hangs over his head, ever ready to fall. His crimes: stealing a favorite golden dog of Zeus; taking ambrosia and nectar and giving it to mortals; and killing his son Pelops and serving him to the gods for food. *Odyssey* xi.

Tarpeia (tar pē' ya; tar pē' a). Daughter of Tarpeius, the governor of Rome. Bribed by Tatius, king of the Sabines, to open the gates of the fortress of the citadel, in return for the gold bracelets the Sabines wore on their left arms. To punish her treachery, Tatius threw not only the captured bracelet at her but also his shield, knocking her to the ground. His fellow warriors followed his example, and she was crushed to death. She was buried in the Capitol, which has been called the Tarpeian rock, from which Roman malefactors were later thrown. *Met.* xiv.

Tarpeian Rock (tar pē' an). Named so in memory of the treason of TARPEIA, q.v.

Tarquinius (tar kwin' i us). The husband of LUCRETIA, q.v.

Tartarus (tar' ta rus). The lowest region of Hell, where the most wicked of mankind were punished; the rebellious Titans were also confined there by Zeus. Some accounts say this region was surrounded by a brazen wall and was three times as dark as the darkest night. Hesiod states it was a separate prison; Vergil has it surrounded by three impenetrable walls and by Phlegethon, the river of fire, where punishment was meted out to those who hated their brethren, were disobedient to their parents, struck their parents, were adulterers, traitors, or faithless ministers, who had betrayed their friends for the sake of money, or had waged cruel and unjust wars. There is a long list in *Aeneid* vi, wherein is also the account of the visit of Aeneas to the Underworld. In *Met.* iv, Ovid gives a vivid account of the Danaides, Ixion, Sisyphus, Tantalus, and Tityus. In *Odyssey* xi the descent of Odysseus into hell is described. In *Theogony* Hesiod not only describes Tartarus, the gloomy region of the Underworld, but also lists a Titan named Tartaros as the father by Gaea of Typhon (or Typhoeus), who had a hundred heads like those of a serpent or a dragon.

Tatia (tā′ sha). Daughter of Tatius, king of the Sabines; wife of Numa Pompilius.

Tatius (tā′ shus). Also Titus Tatius. The king of the Sabines, who warred against Rome after the rape of the Sabine women, and to whom Tarpeia betrayed the citadel.

Tauri (to′ rī). Also Taurians (to′ ri anz). A barbarous and warlike people of European Sarmatia (now the Crimea), who sacrificed all strangers to Artemis. The stranger was hit on the head with a club, his head was then cut off and nailed to a cross, and the body was thrown into the sea. The Tauri believed that their statue of Artemis had fallen from heaven, and later was carried away to Sparta by Iphigenia and Orestes. Herodotus iv; Pausanias iii; Euripides, *Iphigenia in Tauris*.

Taurica (to′ ri ka). Ancient name for the Crimean peninsula.

Tauris (to′ ris). Name of a city in the country of the ancient Taurians.

Taurus (to′ rus). 1. The second sign of the zodiac, the Bull, into which the sun enters about April 20. 2. The name of a great mountain range in Asia Minor (also called Caucasus or Amaranta). Prometheus was chained in this mountain range.

Taygeta (tā ij′ e ta). Also Taygete (tā ge′ tē). One of the seven daughters of Atlas and Pleione; mother of Lacedaemon, by Zeus; one of the Pleiades. Hesiod, *Works and Days*.

Tecmessa (tek mes′ sa). The wife of the Greater Ajax. Some accounts say she became the wife of Telamonian (Greater) Ajax after he had killed her father, king of Thrace, in a war. When in rage after he lost the contest for Achilles' armor to Odysseus, Ajax wished to stab himself, she moved him to pity by her tears. Sophocles, *Ajax*. See also AIAS.

Teiresias (ti rē′ si as). Also Tiresias. Son of Evereus and Chariclo. The greatest of all mythological prophets. He was descended from the Spartae. He lived to a great age, said to span seven generations. His life covered the reigns of the Theban kings Polydorus, son of Cadmus and Harmonia; Labdacus; Laius; Oedipus; and the sons of Oedipus. Teiresias is a very important figure in many of the stories of Thebes, one of the most famous in ancient myth. There are several stories about his blindness. One is that he saw two snakes mating, killed the female, and immediately became a woman. Seven years later he again saw two snakes mating, killed the male, and became a man again. An argument arose between Zeus and Hera. Zeus maintained that women derived more pleasure from sex than men; Hera argued the opposite, and added that this was the reason Zeus was so often unfaithful to her. They consulted Teiresias, who could speak from experience, for he had been both a man and a woman, and had married during his seven years as a woman. Teiresias said a woman received more pleasure from the physical aspects of love than did the man, and Hera, infuriated, blinded Teiresias. Some accounts say he was blinded by Athena for watching her and his mother Chariclo (an attendant of Athena) bathe in the fountain of Hippocrene (as Actaeon had surprised Artemis). To compensate Teiresias for his blindness, Zeus bestowed on him the gift of prophecy and promised him an extremely long life; others say Athena conferred these gifts. His prophecies were numerous: the greatness of Heracles; the death of Pentheus; the defeat of the Seven against Thebes; the victory of the Epigoni; in Hades (*Odyssey* xi) he still retained his prophetic power, and told Odysseus of the dangers which would threaten him en route home to Ithaca. Among the ancients, many tell the story of Teiresias: Homer, Aeschylus, Apollodorus, Diodorus, Hyginus, Pausanias, Pindar, Sophocles, Statius. In English literature, Tennyson's "Tiresias," Swinburne's "Tiresias,"

T. S. Eliot's *The Waste Land,* Arnold's "The Strayed Reveller" are examples. According to myth Teiresias' death was finally caused by drinking of the icy waters of the fountain of Telphusa.

Telamon (tel′ a mon). Son of Aeacus and Endeis; father of Ajax (called Telamonian, after his father, also Greater Ajax) and Teucer. He married Glauce, daughter of King Cychreus of Salamis, and succeeded him as king of the island; after her death, he married Periboea, daughter of king Alcathous of Megara, who became the mother of Ajax. Teucer was a bastard son of Telamon by Hesione, a daughter of Laomedon, king of Troy, and a sister of Priam. Hesione was given to Telamon by Heracles, as a reward for his aid to the hero in the conquest of Troy during a war that took place before the Trojan War. Ajax and Teucer fought bravely side by side in the Trojan War. Ajax committed suicide, Teucer buried him in the sands of Troy, and when he returned home to Salamis with this news and without the bones of Ajax, Telamon banished him as he had been banished by his own father when years before with his brother Peleus he had murdered his half-brother Phocus. Telamon participated in the Calydonian boar hunt and also sailed the *Argo* to Colchis in search of the Golden Fleece. Apollodorus i, ii; *Met.* xiii; Pausanias i, ii, viii; Sophocles, *Ajax.*

Telamus (tel′ a mus). See TELEMUS.

Telchines (tel kī′ nēz). The nine children of Pontus and THALASSA, q.v. Pausanias ix.

Teledamas (tē led′ a mas). According to the ancients, Teledamas and Pelops were the names of the twin sons of Agamemnon and Cassandra. The two boys were murdered in their infancy by Aegisthus and buried near their mother's tomb at Mycenae. Pausanias ii. Hesiod has Teladamas as a name for Telegonus.

Telegonus (tē leg′ ō nus). Son of Odysseus and Circe, according to post-Homeric legend; born on the island of Aeaea, educated there, and sent by Circe to his father in Ithaca. Shipwrecked on the coast of Ithaca, he plundered some of the inhabitants, but Odysseus and Telemachus came to their defense; Telegonus killed his father without knowing who he was. Accompanied by Penelope and Telemachus, Telegonus returned to Aeaea, carrying with him his father's body, and buried it there. Upon orders of Athena, Telegonus married Penelope, and they had a son named Italus, after whom Italy was named. This post-Homeric story is in the works of Diodorus, Hyginus, Ovid, and Plutarch. Hesiod calls Telegonus Teladamas, and makes him a son of Calypso.

Telemachus (tē lem′ a kus). Son of Odysseus and Penelope. After twenty years of his father's absence, Telemachus was advised by Athena to seek information about his whereabouts, which he did at the courts of Menelaus and Nestor. When he returned to Ithaca, he learned that Penelope's many suitors had planned to murder him, but he avoided the trap, and with the help of Athena learned that Odysseus had arrived home two days before and was staying in the house of the faithful swineherd Eumaeus. With the help of his father and others, he slew his mother's suitors. After the death of his father, he went to the island of Aeaea, married Circe (some accounts say he married Cassiphone, the daughter of Circe), by whom he had a son named Latinus. Some time later he killed Circe and fled to Italy. In this post-Homeric story by Hyginus and Ovid is also an account that he married Nausicaa. The chief story of Telemachus is in several books of the *Odyssey,* especially in books i–iv, xv–xvii, xix, xxii, xxiv.

Telemus (tel′ e mus; tē′ le mus). Also Telamus. A Cyclops endowed with the power of prophecy, who told Polyphemus "That single eye in the middle of your forehead Odysseus will take away!" Polyphemus mocked him and called him stupid, but recalled the prophecy after he had been blinded. *Met.* xiii.

Telephassa (tel e fas′ a). Also called Argiope. Apollodorus names her as the wife of Agenor, king of Phoenicia, and as the mother of Cadmus, Cilix, Europa, Phineus, Phoenix, and Thasus.

Telephus (tel′ e fus). Son of Heracles and Auge. Exposed on Mount Parthenius, nursed by a goat (some accounts say a doe), and nurtured by kindly shepherds. An oracle had declared that Troy could not be taken without the aid of a son of Heracles. Telephus had married a daughter of Priam, but was so grateful to the Greeks for healing a severe wound that he fought with Greeks against his father-in-law. Apollodorus ii; Pausanias i, iii, viii, ix.

Telesphorus (te les' fo rus). The god whose strength sustained the convalescent. An attendant of Aesculapius, god of medicine.

Telethusa (tel e thū' sa). The wife of Ligdus, and mother of IPHIS, q.v. *Met.* ix.

Tellus (tel' us). Also Terra. Roman goddess of the earth. Greek: Ge, Gaea.

Telphusa (tel fū' sa). Also Thelpusa. A nymph of Arcadia (some accounts say of Boeotia), daughter of the river god Ladon (not the many-headed dragon named Ladon that guarded the Apples of the Hesperides), who gave her name to a town and a fountain in Arcadia. The waters of the fountain Telphusa were so cold that Teiresias died when he drank them. Pausanias ix; Apollodorus iii. Some accounts say she asked Apollo not to build an oracle at her fountain, but to go to Delphi. She was a prophetess and knew that Apollo would have to kill the Python.

Temenus (tem' e nus). 1. The name for the first of the Heraclidae. 2. The name of a son of Pelasgus, who cared for Hera in her infancy in Arcadia. At Stymphalus in Arcadia, Temenus erected three shrines in honor of Hera: she was worshiped as a child, as a bride, and as a widow, for she finally left philandering Zeus on Olympus, and went to live at Stymphalus.

Tempe, Vale of (tem' pē). A beautiful valley between Mount Olympus and Mount Ossa in Thessaly, in olden days regarded as the chief seat sacred to Apollo. Through this valley the Peneus River flows into the Aegean. The ancient poets described it as the most delightful spot on earth, with cool shades, verdant walks, singing birds, a place so lovely that the gods often honored it with their presence. The Vale of Tempe is about five miles long, and in some places only a few hundred yards wide. Because valleys are mild and pleasant, many valleys are called Tempe by the ancient poets. Daphne, an early love of Apollo, lived in this valley, and was changed into a laurel tree. *Met.* i; Vergil, Diodorus, and Strabo describe this pleasant place.

Tempestates (tem pes tā′ tēz). Roman goddess of winds and storms.

Tenedos (ten′ e dos). A small, fertile island in the Aegean Sea, opposite Troy, named after Tenes, son of Apollo, who was killed by the Greeks. The island was sacred to Apollo. It became famous during the Trojan War, for it was behind this island that the Greeks withdrew their ships when they left the Wooden Horse in Troy and were trying to persuade the Trojans that they had left Asia. *Aeneid* ii; *Odyssey* iii; Strabo xiii.

Tenes (ten′ ēz). A son of Apollo (some accounts say of Cycnus and Proclea). The island of Tenedos was named for him and he became king. He was killed by Achilles, who forgot his mother's warning that if he killed a son of Apollo he would be killed by Apollo, who guided the arrow of Paris to the vulnerable heel. Pausanias x; Strabo xiii.

Tenth Muse. SAPPHO, q.v.

Tereus (tē′ rŭs; tē′ rē us). King of Thrace, who married Procne, daughter of King Pandion of Athens, with whom he allied himself in a war against Megara. He violated his sister-in-law Philomela, with most disastrous results. See PHILOMELA.

Terminalia (tur mi nā′ li a). Annual festivals in Rome in honor of Terminus, god of boundaries, landmarks, and limits.

Terminalis (tur mi nā′ lis). A name for Zeus when he presided over boundaries of land.

Terminus (tur′ mi nus). Roman god of boundaries, landmarks, and limits. See also NUMINA.

Terpander (tur pan′ der). The father of Greek classical music and of lyric poetry, born on the island of Lesbos about 675 B.C. Strabo tells that he invented the seven-stringed lyre by adding three strings to the four-stringed lyre which had been used up to that time. Although a historical person, not much is known about him, and some of the stories associated with him are probably myths, such as that of his quelling a tumult at Sparta by the sweetness of the music from his lyre, when he was sent there for that purpose by the oracle at Delphi.

Terpsichore (turp sik′ ō rē). One of the nine Muses, daughter of Zeus and Mnemosyne. Some accounts say she was the mother of the Sirens. She presided over dancing, which she invented, and with which she entertained her eight sisters. She wore a crown of laurel, and carried a musical instrument in her hand (the lyre or the cymbal).

Terra (ter′ a; ter′ ra). Roman goddess of the earth. Also called Tellus, Earth, or Mother Earth. Greek: Ge, Gaea.

Terra Mater (ter′ a   mā′ ter). Same as Terra. Also the Roman name for Rhea, the mother of the gods and goddesses.

Terror (ter′ er). Also called Pallor. Son of Ares. Attendant of Ares and Bellona. Brother of Panic, Fear, Trembling, Eris, Phobos, and Demios.

Tethys (tē′ this). One of the first twelve Titans. Wife of Oceanus. This sea deity was the mother of three thousand Oceanids and of all the rivers; known as the "lovely queen of the sea."

Teucer (tū′ ser). 1. A king of Phrygia. Some accounts say he was the first king of Troy; hence, the Trojans are called Teucrians. He introduced the worship of Rhea and the dances of the Corybantes among his subjects. In *Aeneid* iii, Vergil calls him "our forefather." 2. Son of Telamon and Hesione; half-brother of Greater Ajax. The best archer among the Greeks at Troy. His father never forgave him for leaving the death of Ajax unavenged. See also TELAMON. *Aeneid* i; *Iliad* viii.

Teucri (tū' kri). Also Teucrians. Another name for the Trojans, from their first king, Teucer.

Teucria (tū' kri a). Another name for Troy, from Teucer.

Teucrians (tū' kri anz). See TEUCRI.

Teutanius (tū tān' i us). King of Larissa; close friend of Acrisius, the father of Danae and the grandfather of Perseus.

Teuthras (tū' thras). King of Phrygia. Father of Tecmessa. He was killed by Telamonian Ajax, and his daughter became the property of Ajax.

Thalassa (tha las' a). Also Thalatta. A Greek personification of the sea. She has been called the mother of Aphrodite by Zeus. Some accounts say she was the wife of Pontus and the mother of the nine Telchines, who have been called fish children because they had flippers for hands and the heads of dogs.

Thalatta (tha lat' a). See THALASSA.

Thales (thā' lēz). 1. One of the Seven Wise Men (Sages) of Greece, who flourished in the sixth century B.C. He was the first to understand that myths no longer satisfied man's curiosity about the origin of the world. 2. A Greek lyric poet and musician of the seventh century B.C.

Thalia (tha li' a). 1. One of the nine Muses, daughter of Zeus and Mnemosyne, and generally regarded as the Muse of comedy. She carried a shepherd's staff, the comic mask, and wore the "sock," the light, thin-soled shoe of the comic actor. 2. One of the three Graces. 3. One of the Nereides.

Thamyris (tham' i ris). A celebrated musician and minstrel of Thrace, who challenged the Muses to a musical contest, was defeated, blinded, deprived of his melodious voice, and had his lyre destroyed. Apollodorus; *Iliad* ii; Pausanias.

Thanatos (than' a tos). Greek god of death. Roman: Mors.

Thasus (thā' sus). Son of Agenor and Telephassa; brother of Cadmus, Cilix, Europa, Phineus, and Phoenix.

Thaumas (tho' mas). Son of Pontus (some accounts say of Poseidon) and Gaea. One of the sea gods. Husband of Electra, daughter of Oceanus, by whom he had the Harpies and Iris, one of the messengers of the gods.

Thea (thē' a). Also Theia, Thia, Titaea, TETHYS, q.v. Rhea. 1. Daughter of Uranus and Gaea. One of the Titans. Married her brother Hyperion. Her attribute was light, and she was the mother of Helios (the sun), Selene (the moon), and Eos (the dawn). 2. A daughter of Chiron the centaur; a companion of Artemis. She was ravished by Aeolus, and feared her father should he know that she was pregnant; she was changed by Poseidon into a mare named Euippe, and gave birth to a foal named Melanippe. Euippe became a constellation named the Horse; the foal was changed into a girl.

Theano (thē ā' nō). 1. In *Iliad* v, the wife of Antenor; she nursed a bastard son of Antenor named Podaios. 2. In *Iliad* vi, she is named as a daughter of Kisseus (Cisseus) a king of Thrace, as the wife of Antenor, and as a priestess of Athena in Troy. A later account says she gave the Palladium to Odysseus and Diomedes, and on this account Theano and her husband were spared after the fall of Troy, went to Italy and founded Patavium (modern Padua).

Thebae (thē' bē). See THEBES.

Thebaid, The (thē' bā id). Also Thebais. Epic poem in twelve books, by Statius, that deals chiefly with the story of the Seven against Thebes.

Thebais, The (thē' bā is). See THEBAID.

Thebe (thē' bē). According to Apollodorus and Pausanias, a daughter of the river god Asopus and Metope, a nymph of Stymphalus, herself daughter of the river god Ladon. With her twin sister Aegina, she was carried away by Zeus. Later she married Zethus, who rebuilt Cadmea, the ancient name of the citadel or acropolis of Thebes. The name Cadmea, so called after Cadmus, the founder of Thebes, was changed to Thebes in honor of Thebe. Apollodorus iii; Pausanias ii.

Thebes (thēbz). The story of Thebes, the capital of Boeotia, founded by Cadmus, destroyed by Amphion and Zethus, is one of the great stories of mythology. Its kings—Laius, Oedipus, Eteocles—are celebrated for their misfortunes. Two wars, the Seven against Thebes and the war of the Epigoni, are famous stories. When Alexander invaded Greece, Thebes was totally destroyed, except the birthplace of Pindar. Among the mythological characters associated with Thebes are Cadmus, Amphion, Zethus, Agenor, Telephassa, Harmonia, Phoenix, Cilix, Europa, Thasus, Polydorus, Ino, Athamas, Autonoe, Aristaeus, Agave, Echion, Semele, Labdacus, Laius, Jocasta, Oedipus, Eteocles, Polynices, Antigone, Ismene, Haemon, Melicertes, Pentheus, Menoeceus, Creon, Niobe, Antiope, Dirce, Adrastus, Amphiaraus, Capaneus, Hippomedon, Parthenopaeus, Tydeus, Teiresias, the seven Epigoni. Along with the stories of the Argonauts, the Calydonian boar hunt, and the Fall of Troy, the story of Thebes is one of the great incidents and heroic rallying points of Greek mythology. [The four great incidents are usually ranked as follows: (1) The Fall of Troy. (2) War at Thebes. (3) The Argonauts. (4) Calydonian boar hunt.] Apollodorus i; *Met.* iii; Pausanias ii; Strabo ix; Aeschylus, *Seven Against Thebes;* Sophocles, *Oedipus the King, Antigone, Oedipus at Colonus;* Seneca, *Thebais, Oedipus;* Statius, *The Thebaid,* or *The Thebais.* The story of Thebes has been used by later writers such as Corneille, Voltaire, Cocteau, Gide, and Anouilh; Alfieri has a famous Antigone play. In English literature, aspects of the people associated with Thebes have been used by Dryden, Nathaniel Lee, Shelley, E. M. Forster, Tennyson, T. S. Eliot, Milton, Matthew Arnold, and John Lydgate.

Thelpusa (thel pū′ sa). See TELPHUSA.

Themis (thē′ mis). 1. Daughter of Uranus and Gaea. A Titaness; wife of the Titan Iapetus. Later, she became the wife of Zeus. By Iapetus, Themis was the mother of Prometheus, according to some accounts; most mythologists say that Clymene was the mother of Prometheus. By Zeus, Themis was the mother of the three Horae

(Hours, Seasons) and the three Fates. Themis had the power of prophecy, warned Prometheus of all the troubles that lay ahead for him, told Zeus that Thetis would bear a son greater than his father, and advised Deucalion and Pyrrha how to repopulate the earth after the deluge of Zeus. She was the first goddess to whom temples were built on earth. As a mother-goddess, she had an oracle at Delphi before the famous oracle of Apollo. 2. Themis, a daughter of Ilus, the fourth king of Troy, was the mother of Anchises by Capys, a son of Assaracus. Apollodorus i.

Themisto (thē mis′ tō). The third wife of Athamas, king of Thebes. In a fit of jealousy, she tried to kill the two children of Ino (Athamas' second wife, whom he had thought dead). Ino had merely gone on a revel with the Maenads, and when she learned she had been supplanted she was enraged. She disguised Themisto's children and dressed them in mourning garments. Thus Themisto killed her own children by mistake. This drove Athamas mad, and the remorseful Themisto killed herself. Apollodorus i; Pausanias ix.

Theoclymenus (thē ō klī′ mē nus). 1. A soothsayer of Argolis, descended from Melampus. He met Telemachus at the court of Nestor in Pylus, and prophesied that Telemachus' father Odysseus would return from Troy. Theoclymenus also told the suitors of Penelope that they would come to an untimely end, but they laughed at his prophecy. *Odyssey* xv. 2. In Euripides' *Helen*, Theoclymenus is a king of Egypt, determined to marry Helen of Sparta. Helen is held in Egypt, not in Troy, according to Euripides' play. Theoclymenus is about to kill his sister Theonoe for not telling him that Menelaus has landed in Egypt, but Castor and Pollux, the Dioscuri, advise him to spare his sister since it is the will of the gods that Helen return with Menelaus to Sparta.

Theogony (thē og′ ō ni). A Greek poem of 1,022 lines by Hesiod, an account of the gods, beginning with Uranos and Gaea, and telling much about the origin and nature of the gods.

Theonoe (thē on' ō ē). 1. A daughter of Thestor; sister of Calchas and Leucippe. She was carried away by pirates and sold to Icarus, king of Caria, but was later reunited with her father and sister Leucippe. 2. A daughter of Proteus, she fell in love with a pilot of a Trojan ship. 3. A daughter of Proteus, the king of Egypt, and Psamathe; sister of Theoclymenus, who had fallen in love with Helen. Theonoe did not tell her brother of the arrival of Menelaus in Egypt, for Proteus was protecting Helen until Menelaus could come to claim her. Euripides, *Helen*.

Theophane (thē of' a nē). A daughter of Bisaltus, and the cousin of Phrixus and Helle. Poseidon changed himself into a ram and Theophane into a ewe, and by her had the ram with the golden fleece that carried Phrixus to Colchis. Hyginus, *Fables*.

Therapne (thē rap' nē). An ancient town near Sparta in Laconia (also called Laconica, or Lacedaemon) in the Peloponnesus, where Menelaus and Helen, and the Dioscuri (Castor and Pollux) are buried.

Thermodon (thur' mō don). A famous river in Cappadocia, which flows into the Euxine (Black) Sea. The home of the Amazons was near the mouth of this river. *Aeneid* xi; *Met.* ii; Herodotus ix.

Thermopylae (thur mop' i lē). The famous pass where Leonidas and three hundred Spartans made their historic stand against the Persians in 480 B.C. The pass is in Thessaly, and leads into Locris and Phocis. The name means "hot gates." In places, its width is only twenty-five feet. Near here, Heracles donned the poisoned shirt of Nessus, and the heat on his flesh became so extreme that he jumped into waters nearby and from the heat of his body caused the waters to steam, hence the name "hot gates" or "hot springs."

Thersander (ther san' der). Also Thersandros. 1. A son of Polynices, and one of the Epigoni. Like his father, he used bribery to attain his ends. He gave the celebrated robe of Harmonia to Eriphyle (mother of Alcmaeon) to persuade her husband Amphiaraüs to fight in the Trojan War. After the Epigoni captured Thebes, Thersander became king. According to legend, he and the noted warrior Diomedes assembled forty ships and sailed to the Trojan War. Some mythologies state that Thersander never arrived in Troy, but was killed on the island of Mysia, whose people were allies of the Trojans. However, Vergil in *Aeneid* ii indicated that he fought at Troy and was one of those who entered the Wooden Horse. **2.** A son of Sisyphus, king of Corinth.

Thersilochus (ther sil' ō kus). In *Iliad* xxi, a Trojan killed by Achilles; he was seen by Aeneas when he went to the Underworld. *Aeneid* vi.

Thersites (ther sī' tēz). In *Iliad* ii, a deformed, foul-mouthed troublemaker among the Greeks at Troy. Homer calls him "ill-favored beyond all men that came to Ilios. Bandy-legged was he, and lame of one foot . . . head was warped. . . . Hateful was he to Achilles above all and to Odysseus, for them he was wont to revile," along with Agamemnon. In post-Homeric story (Apollodorus), Achilles killed him with one blow of his fist, hitting him so hard that all his teeth fell out; Thersites had laughed at Achilles for mourning the death of Penthesilea, queen of the Amazons, who arrived late in the war to assist the Trojans. Apollodorus "Epitome," v.

Theseum (thē sē' um). A beautiful temple in Athens, near the Acropolis, that contained the bones of Theseus. On its walls are famous paintings, and later authorities say this marble structure is actually the Hephaisteum; it is not dedicated to Theseus, but to Hephaestus, or to Hephaestus and Athena. However, it has been called the Theseum since the Middle Ages because of the many sculptures that represent the exploits of Theseus, such as slaying the Minotaur, carrying away Ariadne, taking part in the Calydonian boar hunt, espousing Phaedra, and others. This beautiful Doric temple is older than the Parthenon by about three years (erected around 450 B.C.). It owes its fame today to its state of preservation; it is today the most intact of all known Greek temples. When the Turks in 1660 ("stupid Turks" is a favorite expression of the Greeks to this day) wanted to demolish the Theseum, the sultan prevented the destruction. Christians have used the structure as a church, and at the beginning of the nineteenth century, English Protestants used the Theseum as a burial place.

Theseus (thē′ sē us; thē′ sūs). The chief Attic hero. The great hero of the Athenians, and one of their early kings. He was the son of Aegeus and Aethra, and became one of the most celebrated heroes of antiquity. His contests and exploits are fabulous. On the way from Troezen to Athens, he engaged in six formidable contests and destroyed (1) Cercyon, (2) Periphetes, (3) Phaea, (4) Procrustes, (5) Sciron, (6) Sinis. Apollodorus iii. Other exploits include the killing of the Minotaur, overcoming the Marathonian Bull, participating in the Calydonian boar hunt, joining in the expedition of the Argonauts, warring with Hercules against the Amazons. He attempted to kidnap Persephone, and some legends say he kidnaped Helen. He aided the Lapithae in their war against the Centaurs, recovered the corpses of those who fell in the war of the Seven against Thebes, and eventually went to the island of Scyrus where King Lycomedes pushed him to his death from a cliff. Cimon, an Athenian general, returned his remains to Athens for burial. There is also the interesting legend that at the Battle of Marathon an image of Theseus, fully armed, arose with the Athenians and rushed forward against the Persians. Another long story is Theseus' proverbial friendship with Pirithous, king of the Lapithae, at whose wedding he battled the drunken Centaurs who attacked Hippodamia, the bride of Pirithous. Among the women in his life were Perigone, daughter of Sinis, who bore him Melanippus; Ariadne, whom he deserted at Naxos; and Antiope. (Some legends claim that she and Hippolyte, mother of Hippolytus, were identical or possibly they were sisters.) Another of his loves was PHAEDRA, q.v., the mother of Acamas and Demophon, who fought in the Trojan War. Among the ancients who tell his story are Apollodorus, Herodotus, Homer, Hyginus, Ovid, Pausanias, Statius, and

Vergil. The involvement of Phaedra with Hippolytus is told in tragedies, such as Euripides, *Hippolytus;* Seneca, *Phaedra* or *Hippolytus;* Racine, *Phèdre;* Smith, *Phaedra and Hippolytus.* In English literature, Ariadne's desertion is a favorite theme, as in works by Auden, T. S. Eliot, and Christina Rossetti. Shakespeare used the story of Theseus in *A Midsummer-Night's Dream,* and Ariadne's story in *The Two Gentlemen of Verona.* Chaucer's *Legend of Good Women* contains the story of Ariadne. Two fine recent novels, *The King Must Die* (1958) about the youth of Theseus; and *The Bull from the Sea* (1962) about the exploits of Theseus the king, both by Mary Renault, have appeared.

Thesmophoriazusae, The (thes mō fō ri a zōō' sē). A very famous comedy by Aristophanes in which the women of Athens rebel against the tragedies of Euripides for "making women so unpleasant."

Thespiades (thes' pi a dēz). The fifty daughters of THES-PIUS, q.v.

Thespiae (thes' pi ē). Also Thespia. A town at the foot of Mount Helicon in Boeotia, which received its name from Thespius. The town was sacred to the nine Muses. The most sacred shrine of Eros was located there. Pausanias ix.

Thespian Lion. A lion in the forests of Cithaeron that ravaged the flocks of Amphitryon, the foster father of Heracles. Heracles, as a young man and before the Twelve Labors, killed this lion and wore its skin as a cloak.

Thespian Maids. One of the names given the nine Muses because they lived at Thespia and their games were played there.

Thespius (thes' pi us). A famous king of Thespia in Boeotia, who desired that his fifty daughters should have children by Heracles. Heracles enjoyed the company of forty-nine of these daughters in one night. One refused and was doomed to lifelong virginity and forced to serve as a priestess in a temple of Heracles. Fifty-one sons were born to the forty-nine daughters; there were two sets of twins. Forty of the fifty-one sons colonized the island of Sardinia. This one-night accomplishment is called by the Greeks, to this day, the thirteenth and most arduous of the labors of Heracles. These daughters are sometimes called Thespiades. Pausanias ix; Apollodorus ii.

Thessalus (thes′ a lus). 1. A son of Heracles by Chalciope; he became king of Thessaly; his two sons took a fleet of thirty ships to the Trojan War. 2. A son of Jason and Medea; he also was king of Thessaly, and named the country and people Thessaly and Thessalians, after himself. The earlier name of the country was Iolcus.

Thessaly (thes′ a li). Also Thessalia. A province in northern Greece, with which many events and characters of mythology are associated. The deluge of Zeus in the age of Deucalion took place in Thessaly; Mounts Olympus, Pelion, Ossa, Larissa, and Othrys are there; the Peneus River and the Vale of Tempe are there; it was the original home of the Achaeans who migrated from Crete; from Thessaly came many of the Argonauts; and from there a large expedition took part in the Trojan War. It was the birthplace of Aeson, Jason, and others.

Thestius (thes′ ti us). 1. One of the kings of Thespia. 2. A king in Aetolia, the father of Plexippus, Toxeus, and Althaea. Althaea became the mother of Meleager, who killed his two uncles at the Calydonian boar hunt.

Thestor (thes′ tor). A son of Apollo (or of Idmon, an Argonaut and a son of Apollo). He was the father of Calchas, called by Homer in *Iliad* i the "most excellent by far of augurs, who knew both things that were and that should be and that had been before."

Thetis (thē′ tis). A sea deity, the daughter of Nereus and Doris. She was courted by both Zeus and Poseidon, but they deserted her when they learned that her son would be greater than his father. She married Peleus, king of the Myrmidons in Thessaly, and became the mother of Achilles. At her wedding, Eris threw the golden apple marked "For the Fairest" which led to the Judgment of

Paris, and to the Trojan War. Thetis rendered her son Achilles invulnerable by plunging him into the waters of the Styx—all except that part of the heel by which she held him. (Into this vulnerable heel, Paris shot his arrow and killed Achilles.) Later she concealed her son, dressed in girl's clothes, at the court of Lycomedes to prevent his going to the Trojan War where she knew he would be killed. She persuaded Hephaestus to make the famous suit of armor for her son, to replace the suit he had loaned to Patroclus, which had been captured by Hector. When Achilles was killed by Paris, Thetis, emerging from the sea with her fifty attending Nereids to mourn his death, collected his ashes in a golden urn, raised a monument to his memory, and instituted festivals in his honor. Apollodorus i, ix; Hyginus; *Iliad* i; *Met.* xi; *Odyssey* xxiv; Pausanias v; *Theogony*.

Thia (thī′ a). Also Thea, Theia. See THEA.

Thisbe (thiz′ be). See PYRAMUS.

Thoas (thō′ as). 1. A Taurian king in the days of Orestes and Pylades. He would have sacrificed both these young men on the altar of Artemis, according to a barbarous custom of Tauria, had they not been rescued by Iphigenia. Euripides, *Iphigenia in Tauris*. 2. A king of Lemnos, son of Dionysus and Ariadne. He was still alive when the Lemnian women conspired to kill all the males on the island, but was saved by his daughter Hypsipyle, in whose favor he resigned his crown and fled to Chios. Apollodorus i; *Argonautica*. 3. A son of Jason and Hypsipyle, the queen of Lemnos. 4. A friend of Aeneas, killed in Italy. *Aeneid* x. 5. A son of Uranus and Gaea. One of the Giants. 6. A son of Andraemon and Gorge; king of Aetolia. As a former suitor of Helen, he took forty ships to the Trojan War. *Iliad* ii.

Thonis (thō′ nis). King of Egypt; husband of Polydama.

Thoon (thō′ on). 1. A Trojan killed by Diomedes. *Iliad* v. 2. A Trojan killed by Odysseus. *Iliad* xi. 3. A Trojan killed by Antilochus. *Iliad* xiii.

Thoth (thōth; tōt). In Egyptian mythology, the scribe of the gods, measurer of time, and inventor of numbers; hence, the god of wisdom and magic. In the judgment hall of Osiris he records the result of the weighing of the heart. He was originally a moon. The Greeks identified him with Hermes, messenger of the gods.

Thrace (thrās). Also Thracia. A large country of Europe, north of the Aegean Sea and east of Macedonia, today a part of European Turkey. The Thracians were warlike, barbarous people, thought brave. They drank heavily, and made cruel sacrifices of their enemies on the altars of their gods. Since the climate was severe and the people fierce, Thrace was called the home of Boreas and Ares. Orpheus, Linus, Musaeus, and Rhesus with his famous white horses came from Thrace.

Thracia (thrā′ sha). See THRACE.

Thrasymedes (thras i mē′ dēz). In *Iliad* ix, a son of Nestor. He was the shepherd of the sentinels (chief of the sentries). After the Trojan War, he returned to Pylus with his father, and Telemachus met him in Pylus when he went in search of information about Odysseus. *Odyssey* iii.

Three Hundred-Handed Giants. Called Centimani, Hecatoncheires. Briareus, Cottus, and Gyges; children of Uranus and Gaea.

Thrinacia (thri nā′ shia). Also Trinacria (tri nā′ kri a), Thrinacria (thri nāk′ ri a). The name for Sicily which means "three points" or "three promontories" triangular in shape. In *Odyssey* xii, this was the island on which Helios Hyperion pastured the cattle of the sun. Vergil makes reference to the Trinacrian waves which must be passed on the way from Troy to Italy. *Aeneid* iii.

Thule (thū′ lē; thū′ le). An island in the northernmost part of the North Sea, to which the ancients gave the name Ultima. Its location has never been accurately ascertained. Some writers have thought it to be Iceland, Greenland, or the Shetland Islands. To the ancients, it was the northern limit of the habitable world.

Thunderbolt of Zeus. A single discharge of lightning with accompanying thunder, so called from the idea that it was caused by a bolt thrown by a god.

Thyestes (thī′ es tēz). Grandson of Tantalus; son of Pelops and Hippodamia; brother of Atreus. He debauched Aerope, the wife of his brother Atreus, in revenge for which Atreus invited him to a banquet, expressing the wish to be reconciled, and served Thyestes the flesh of his own children as food. Thyestes committed incest with his own daughter Pelopea, without knowing who she was, and she became the mother of Aegisthus. When Atreus died, Thyestes ascended the throne of Mycenae, from which he was soon dethroned by Menelaus and Agamemnon, the sons of Atreus. Agamemnon became king of Mycenae. The story of the doomed and tragic family, violent and accursed, is told by many writers, among them the three great Greek tragedians, Apollodorus, Homer, Hyginus, Ovid, Pausanias, Seneca, and Vergil.

Thyia (thī′ a). 1. A daughter of Deucalion; sister of Hellen, the fabled ancestor of the Hellenic race. 2. A daughter of the river god Cephissus; mother by Apollo of Delphus. Some accounts say Delphus gave his name to Delphi.

Thyiads (thī′ yads; thī′ ads). Also Thyiades (thī′ ya dēz). A group of women (maenads, bacchantes) devoted to orgiastic worship of Dionysus on Mount Parnassus. These orgiastic revels were instituted by Thyia; hence, the name Thyiades.

Thymbris (thim′ bris). According to Apollodorus, the mother of Pan by Zeus.

Thyrsus (thir′ sus; thur′ sus). A staff or spear tipped with pine cone, and sometimes wreathed with ivy or vine branches, carried by Dionysus and his votaries. Sometimes leaves with grapes or berries were used as the wreath. The Thyrsus was the symbol or wand of Dionysus and of those practicing his rites.

Tiber (tī′ ber). The river of Rome; mentioned frequently in Roman mythology.

Tiberinus (tī ber ī′ nus). The name of a king in Italy who drowned in the river Albula, which was renamed Tiber. He was later identified with the god of the river. Some accounts say the river gods Tiberinus and Volturnus were merged into one god. There is a story that the river god Tiberinus appeared to Aeneas on the eve of his great battle with Turnus, assured him all would be well, and advised him to look under some oak trees on the banks of the Tiber for a white sow with thirty pigs. That would be the place to found the new city. Tiberinus also advised Aeneas to obtain the help of Evander. However, in *Aeneid* iii Vergil says that when Aeneas stopped over on his way from Troy to Italy to visit Helenus in Epirus, it was Helenus who told him that the site of the city would be at the place where he found a white sow and thirty pigs.

Tibullus (ti bul' us). 54–18 B.C. Roman elegiac poet.

Timandra (tī man' dra). Daughter of Tyndareus and Leda; sister of Helen and Clytemnestra. One story has it that Tyndareus forgot to make proper sacrifices to Aphrodite, and the goddess made all of the daughters of Tyndareus notorious adulteresses. Timandra, like her two more famous sisters, married Echemus, but deserted him for another man (Phyleus).

Timolus (ti mō' lus). See TMOLUS.

Tiphys (tī' fis). In the *Argonautica,* the pilot of the *Argo.*

Tiresias (tī rē' si as). See TEIRESIAS.

Tiryns (tī' rinz). Also Tyrins. A town in Argolis in the Peloponnesus, founded by Tirynx, a son of Argus. Tiryns has many associations with Greek mythology. It was first ruled by the Pelasgians. Danaus, Acrisius, Proetus, Perseus, and Atreus were among its kings. Its tremendous walls, said to have been built by the Cyclopes, were excavated by Schliemann in 1885. Pausanias ii. Heracles lived there; some accounts say he was born there. Vergil in *Aeneid* vii names Heracles the Tirynthian Conqueror, for from this place Heracles went forth to accomplish the Twelve Labors.

Tisamenus (ti sam' e nus). 1. A son of Orestes and Hermione (daughter of Menelaus and Helen). Succeeded to the throne of Argos and Lacedaemon, but the Heraclidae entered his kingdom and forced him to retire to Achaia. Apollodorus ii; Pausanias iii. **2.** A king of Thebes; grandson of Polynices, and the son of Thersander. Pausanias iii. **3.** In Pausanias iii, a native of Elis, and winner of four Olympic contests. With his brother, according to Herodotus, he was the only man not born in Sparta to be admitted to Spartan citizenship in order to aid them in their war against Persia.

Tisander (ti san' der). A son of Jason and Medea; killed by Medea when Jason proposed to marry Glauce of Corinth. Some mythologists point out that Tisander with his brothers and sisters (children of Medea) were stoned to death by the Corinthians because Medea was responsible for the death of King Creon and his daughter Glauce.

Tisiphone (ti sif' ō nē). One of the three Furies. (The other two: Alecto and Megaera.) Euripides' *Alkmeon at Corinth* (a play not now extant, but of which fragments were available when the very early life of the dramatist was written) lists a Tisiphone, the daughter of Alcmaeon and Manto (Manto was a daughter of Teiresias); she was a very beautiful girl, reared by King Creon of Corinth, who on account of his wife's jealousy had to sell Tisiphone as a slave. The purchaser, her own father, Alcmaeon who, at first, did not recognize her as his own daughter.

Titaea (ti tē' a). A name for Gaea, Rhea, Thea, Thia, and Terra.

Titan (tī' tan). The ancient mythologists, such as Apollodorus, Hesiod, and Hyginus (in *The Library, Theogony,* and *Fables,* respectively) mention Titans, who were sons and daughters of Uranus and Gaea. Reference is also made to later races of giant deities who warred against the gods.

Titanids (tī' tan ids). Apollodorus' name for the daughters of Uranus and Gaea.

Titanomachy (tī tan om′ a chi). See GIGANTOMACHY.

Titans, The Twelve (tī′ tanz). Also Titanes, Titani, Titanides. In different accounts, the number of Titans varies, but a theory has gradually developed that there were twelve of them, as there were twelve great Olympian gods and goddesses. The Titans were the first race, the children of Uranus and Gaea.

MALE	FEMALE	ATTRIBUTE
Oceanus	Tethys	sea
Hyperion	Thia	sun
Crius	Eurybia (Mnemosyne)	memory
Coeus	Phoebe	moon
Cronus	Rhea	harvests
Iapetus	Themis	justice; planets

Except Crius and Eurybia, the brothers and sisters married one another as paired above, according to some mythologists. Some accounts say that all married each other. Briareus, Cottus, Gyges, Enceladus, Porphyrion, Rhoetus are called Titans by some writers, but most mythologists call them Giants. Some accounts call Atlas and Prometheus Titans. In English poetry, the sun god Hyperion is best known, as in Keats' "Hyperion" and "The Fall of Hyperion."

Tithonus (tī thō′ nus). Son of Laomedon, king of Troy, by Strymno, daughter of the Scamander River, which was worshiped by the Trojans as a god. Brother of Priam. He was so beautiful that Aurora (Eos), goddess of the dawn, fell in love with him, carried him away, granted him immortality; but he forgot to ask for vigor, youth, and beauty to continue, and he soon grew old, decrepit, and infirm, and as life became insupportable, he begged Aurora to remove him from the world; but since he had been made immortal and could not die, the goddess changed him into a grasshopper. (The Cumean Sibyl also forgot to ask for continuing youth.) *Aeneid* iv, viii; Apollodorus iii; *Theogony;* Tennyson's "Tithonus" is a fine treatment of this legend.

Titus Tatius. See TATIUS.

Tityus (tit' i us). Giant son of Gaea. He insulted Leto, was killed by Leto's children, Apollo and Artemis, and placed in Tartarus, the lowest region of hell, where vultures continually gnaw his liver, which grows again as soon as it is devoured. Homer and Vergil portray his body stretched out over nine acres. *Aeneid* vi; *Odyssey* xi; Apollodorus, Apollonius, and Ovid also tell his story.

Tlepolemus (tle pol' e mus). 1. A son of Heracles; he went to Troy with nine ships; at Troy he was killed by Sarpedon. *Iliad* ii, v. 2. The name of a Lycian killed by Patroclus. *Iliad* xvi.

Tmolus (tē mō' lus). Also Timolus. Husband of Omphale, and king of Lydia. He was killed by Artemis for ravishing one of her attendants. He was the judge of the famous music contest between Pan and Apollo. *Met.* xi.

Toxeus (toks' ē us; –sūs). According to Apollodorus, Toxeus was the son of Oeneus and Althaea; brother of Plexippus, Thyreus, Clymenus, Gorge, Deianeira, and Meleager. Oeneus killed Toxeus for leaping over a ditch which had been dug for defense of Calydon—as Romulus killed Remus for leaping over the wall of Rome. Apollodorus i. Ovid says Toxeus and Plexippus were killed by Meleager when they objected to the giving of spoils to Atalanta at the Calydonian boar hunt, and contends that Toxeus and Plexippus were the brothers, not sons, of Althaea. *Met.* viii.

Trachiniae (tra kin' i ē). Same as *The Women of Trachis, The Maidens of Trachis*. A tragedy by Sophocles that deals with Heracles' life and death.

Trachis (trā' kis). The capital of Trachinia (tra kin' i a). Trachinia is a small country near Mount Oeta where Heracles prepared his own funeral pyre and was cremated. Sophocles, *The Women of Trachis; Met.* xi.

Trembling. Son of Ares. Brother of Terror (Pallor), Panic, Fear, Eris (Discord), Phobos (Alarm), and Demios (Dread).

Triads in Mythology (tri' adz). A union of closely related persons or beings in mythology. It is noticeable that many women are depicted in groups of three or "triads," while the gods are more apt to appear as strong individual personalities, each with his own distinct characteristics. Note the *three* Fates, Furies, Gorgons, Graces, Graeae, Harpies, Sirens, etc.

Trident of Poseidon (**Neptune**). The three-pronged spear which was the god's symbol.

Trinacria (tri nā′ kri a). See THRINACIA.

Triptolemus (trip tol′ e mus). A son of Celeus, king of Attica, by Meganira, although some legends say he was a son of Uranus and Gaea; born at Eleusis, where he established the Eleusinian mysteries and festivals in honor of Demeter. After his death he was made a god. He was a priest of Demeter at Eleusis, gave grain and culture to mankind, taught the use of the plow, and traveled in a chariot drawn by two dragons (a gift from Demeter). He traveled all over the world, teaching mankind the art of growing wheat and corn. He is called an Attic culture hero. In his youth, Demeter cured him of a very severe illness by feeding him with her own milk. In Scythia, this favorite of Demeter nearly lost his life when King Lyncus planned to kill him, but the king was changed into a lynx before he could commit the murder. Apollodorus i; *Met.* v; Pausanias ii.

Tritogeneia (trī tō jē nī′ a). Another name for Athena; the word means "thrice-born," "born on the third day" or "third child."

Triton (trī′ ton). A gigantic sea deity, son of Poseidon and Amphitrite. The messenger and trumpeter of Poseidon. He was half-man, half-fish; above the waist like a man, below like a dolphin. He had the power to calm the ocean at his pleasure. When the Argonauts on the way home from Colchis were driven from the sea by a great storm into the desert of Libya, Triton helped the *Argo* back to the sea. In later mythology, many minor sea deities were also called Triton. *Aeneid* i; Apollodorus i; *Met.* i; Pausanias ix; *Theogony*.

Tritonia (trī tō′ ni a). Another name for Athena. Athens is called Tritonia because the city is dedicated to Athena; it is also called Tritonis (trī tō' nis). *Aeneid* ii.

Tritons (trī' tonz). Name for the descendants of Triton.

Trivia (triv' ia). Also called Hecate or Diana of the Crossways. It was a name given to Diana because she presided over all places where three roads meet. Hecate is sometimes identified with Diana, sometimes with Proserpina. Diana represents the moonlight splendor of the night; Hecate represents the darkness and terror of the night. She haunted crossroads, graveyards, and was the goddess of sorcery and witchcraft, wandered about at night, and was seen only by the barking dogs who told of her approach. *Aeneid* vi; *Met.* ii.

Troad (trō' ad). Also Troas (tros). The region in Asia Minor of which ancient Troy was the capital.

Troades (trō' a dēz). A tragedy by Seneca.

Troezen (trē' zen). Also Troezene. An ancient city in Argolis in the Peloponnesus, about forty miles from Athens. It is also called Theseis, because Theseus was born there, and Posidonia, because Poseidon was worshiped there. It received its name from Troezen, a son of Pelops. King Pittheus of Troezen gave his daughter Aethra to King Aegeus; these were the parents of Theseus, who was educated in Troezen by his grandfather and sent to Athens when he reached maturity. It was on the way from Troezen to Athens that Theseus slew Cercyon, Periphetes, Phaea, Procrustes, Sciron, and Sinis. Hippolytus, son of Theseus, was sent to Troezen to live, and it was there that Phaedra fell in love with him. In the Trojan War, Diomedes led the people from Troezen. *Met.* xv; Pausanias ii.

Troia (trō' ya). Another name for Troy.

Troilus (trō' i lus; troi' lus). A son of Priam and Hecuba; killed by Achilles during the Trojan War. The story of his love for Cressida, a daughter of Calchas, has been told many times, but has no basis in classical antiquity. Among those who have told the story are Dictys Cretensis, Dares Phrygius, Benoit de Sainte-Maure, Guido delle

Colonne, Giovanni Boccaccio, Chaucer, *Troilus and Criseyde;* Henryson, *The Testament of Cresseid;* Shakespeare, *Troilus and Cressida;* Dryden, *Troilus and Cressida.*

Trojans (trō′ janz). Inhabitants of ancient Troy. The word "Trojan" has come to mean pluck, endurance, determined energy. Hence the expression, "He works like a Trojan." Among the famous Trojans, all from Homer's *Iliad,* are: Andromache, Aeneas, Antenor, Briseis, Cassandra, Chryseis, Deiphobus, Dolon, Glaucus, Hecabe (Hecuba), Hector, Helenus, Idaeus, Pandarus, Paris, Polydamas, Priam, and Sarpedon (not a Trojan, but an ally). There were other allies of the Trojans besides Sarpedon, among them Penthesilea and the Amazons, Rhesus and his white horses from Thrace, Memnon and his ten thousand Ethiopians, the men from Sestos and Abydos, the Carians, and others mentioned in *Iliad* ii.

Trojan Horse. See WOODEN HORSE.

Trojan War. Traditional date 1194–1184 B.C. The number-one story in importance of the great incidents and rallying points in Greek mythology. The latest in time and the most familiar of all the great events in Greek lore. Whether history or legend, of all the great stories of the Greeks, none is richer than that of the Trojan War. The consequences of the Trojan War provided the source material for the three great classical epics *Iliad, Odyssey,* and *Aeneid;* for some of the great tragedies of Aeschylus, Sophocles, and Euripides; for many tales, poems, and dramas in both Greek and Latin. Literature on the Trojan War, both ancient and modern, is abundant. In English literature, there are the famous versions of Chaucer and Shakespeare; famous poems or tales by Wordsworth, Tennyson, Meredith, Lord de Tabley, William Morris, D. G. Rossetti, Masefield, and others, to say nothing of hundreds of allusions in both English and American literature, especially in the works of Spenser, Yeats, Marlowe, Landor, Pope, Byron, Rupert Brooke, Geoffrey of Monmouth, Layamon, *Brut;* Arnold, Blackie, Bridges, Daniel, Donne, Drayton, Drummond, Dryden, T. S. Eliot, Graves,

Jeffers, Joyce, Keats, Lang, Lydgate, Lytton, Milton, Peele, Poe, Shelley, Swinburne, to name only a few. Among the famous Greeks who participated in the Trojan War were Achilles, Agamemnon, the two Ajaxes, Antilochus, Automedon, Calchas, Diomedes, Eurypylus, Helen, Idomeneus, Machaon, Menelaus, Menestheus, Meriones, Nestor, Odysseus, Patroclus, Phoenix, Sthenelus, Talthybius, Teucer, Thersites, Tlepolemus, to name the chief characters. Even the great Olympian gods and goddesses took part in the affairs of the Trojan War. Five favored the Greeks: Hera, Athena, Poseidon, Hermes, and Hephaestus; four took the side of the Trojans: Aphrodite, Apollo, Ares, and Artemis; four were neutral: Demeter, Hades, Hestia, and Zeus—though Zeus at times seemed to waver. Many of the events are recorded in *The Iliad*, which covers about fifty days of the action in the ninth (some say tenth) year, but since *The Iliad* closes with the account of the funeral of Hector, many great stories about Troy and the Trojan War are post-*Iliad*, among them the arrival of reinforcements for Troy (Penthesilea and Memnon), the killing of Achilles by Paris, the contest for the armor of Achilles, the stealing of the Palladium, the building of the Wooden Horse, the fall of Troy, and the return home of the Greeks. Only two prominent Trojans escaped the sack of Troy, Aeneas and Antenor, but others were carried away by the Greeks. The prophecies of Helenus are post-*Iliad*. The sacrifice of Polyxena, the slavery of Andromache and Cassandra, and the death of Thersites are other stories not related in *The Iliad*. The two most famous Greeks who returned home were Agamemnon and Odysseus, but there were other famous Greeks who survived the war, among them Nestor, Idomeneus, Diomedes, Philoctetes, Neoptolemus, and Menelaus—who took Helen back to Sparta.

Trojan Women, The. A tragedy by Euripides. It deals with a denunciation of war for both vanquished and victor. The Trojan men have been killed or have fled; the women and children are captives. Poseidon, Athena, Hecuba, Talthybius, Andromache, Cassandra, Menelaus, and Helen are the chief characters in the action, which takes place in a space before the ruined city.

Trophonius (trō fō' ni us). 1. A brother of Agamedes, son of Apollo. The brothers were famous builders of the temples at Delphi and elsewhere. Apollo said he would reward them with the greatest gift within his power; they died peacefully in their sleep. 2. A very ancient earth god. Pausanias ix.

Tros (trōs). Mythical founder of Troy; the Troad and the Trojans received their names from him. He was the grandson of Dardanus; son of Erichthonius; husband of Callirrhoe by whom he had Assaracus, Cleopatra, Ganymede, and Ilus. Apollodorus iii; *Iliad* xx.

Troy (troi). Also called Ilion, Ilios, Ilium, Troia, Troja. An ancient city in northwestern Asia Minor. The city was founded by Teucer, who came there from Crete, and the Trojans are sometimes called Teucrians. The chief event associated with Troy is the Trojan War; for the famous mythological characters associated with Troy see TROJANS and TROJAN WAR. Of all the wars carried on among the ancients, that of Troy is the most famous. The city was celebrated by the great epics of Homer and Vergil, and there are many poems and tales about it, and allusions to it by ancient and modern writers.

Tullius (tul' i us). A son of Hephaestus and Ocrisia; sixth king of Rome.

Turnus (tur' nus). His story is in the *Aeneid,* and Ovid writes about him in *Met.* xiii, xiv. He was the king of the Rutulians (Rutuli) when Aeneas arrived in Italy; was a rival of Aeneas for the hand of Lavinia (daughter of Latinus), who married Aeneas. Turnus fought Aeneas, and was killed by him in single combat. He was a man of uncommon strength, a fearless warrior. Hera and Juturna (sister of Turnus) tried to save him, but he refused to declare a truce with Aeneas. He killed Pallas, beloved son of Evander, and many others.

Tyche (tī' kē). Also Fortuna (Roman). The goddess of fortune and personification of luck. A daughter of Tethys (she was one of the three thousand Oceanids), according to Hesiod. *Theogony*.

Tydeus (tĭ′ dūs; tĭd′ ē us). One of the Seven against Thebes. Son of Periboea and Oeneus, king of Calydon. After he had accidentally killed one of his friends, he fled from his country to Argos and the court of King Adrastus, whose daughter Diephyle he married. They had a son, Diomedes, one of the bravest Greeks in the Trojan War. In the battle of the Seven against Thebes Tydeus, although mortally wounded by Melanippus, managed to sever his enemy's head and eat his brains. This deed was so revolting to Athena that she refused to administer an Olympian drug that would have cured and immortalized Tydeus, and he died. *Aeneid* vi; Apollodorus i; *Iliad* iv; Euripides, *The Suppliant Women*.

Tydides (ti dī′ dēz). A name for Diomedes as the son of Tydeus. *Aeneid* i.

Tyndareus (tin dā′ rē us). Also Tyndarius, Tyndares, Tyndaris, Tyndarus. King of Lacedaemon; husband of Leda who had quadruplets (Pollux and Helen by Zeus; Castor and Clytemnestra by Tyndareus). In some accounts Tyndareus passed as the father of all four children.

Tyndaridae (tin dar′ i dē). A name for Castor and Pollux as the children of Tyndareus.

Tyndaris (tin′ da ris). A name applied to a daughter of Tyndareus—Clytemnestra, Helen, or Timandra.

Typhon (tĭ′ fon). Also Typhoeus (ti fē′ us), Typhaon (ti-fā′ on). Youngest son of Gaea, and the most monstrous of the Giants, born after the Titans were defeated by Zeus. He attacked Zeus, cut the sinews of his hands and feet, and imprisoned him in a cave where a dragon guarded him until he was rescued by Hermes and Pan. Typhon had a hundred dragon heads and his body was covered with serpents. He was taller than the tallest mountain. Flames of fire darted from his mouths, and his horrible shrieks and yells so frightened the gods that they assumed different shapes as they fled when he attacked them on Mount Olympus. Zeus became a ram, Hermes an ibis, Apollo a crow, Hera a cow, Dionysus a goat, and Aphrodite a fish. Zeus was wounded, but he was healed by Pan and Hermes. The father of the gods then conquered Typhon with his thunderbolts and buried him under Mount Aetna. Typhon was the father by Echidna of many monsters, among them Ladon, Orthrus, Cerberus, the Nemean Lion, the Sphinx, the Chimera, and the Lernéan Hydra. *Aeneid* ix; Apollodorus i, ii; Herodotus; Hyginus; *Met.* v; *Theogony.*

Tyrins (tī′ rinz). See TIRYNS.

Tyro (tī′ rō). Beautiful daughter of Salmoneus and Alcidice. She was treated cruelly by her stepmother SIDERO, q.v., who had her imprisoned. After she was released from prison by her sons Neleus and Pelias, Tyro married Cretheus, the founder of Iolcus, and became the mother of Aeson (father of Jason), Amythaon, and Pheres. Apollodorus i; *Odyssey* xi.

Tyrrhenian Sea (ti rē′ ni an). One of the lesser branches of the Mediterranean Sea; lies between the west coast of Italy and the island of Sardinia. The Aegean Sea, with its many islands called the Cyclades, lies between Greece and Asia Minor. Many of these islands have mythological associations.

Tyrrheus (tī′ rūs; tir′ rhē us). The father of Silvia; master of the royal herds of King Latinus. He had a beautiful pet stag that was killed by Ascanius who did not know it was a pet. The Rutulians were very angry with the Trojans about this incident, and furious fighting ensued. *Aeneid* vii.

U

Ucalegon (ū kal′ e gon). See OUKALEGON.

Udeaus (ū dē′ us). One of the SPARTAE, q.v.

Ulysses (ū lis′ ēz). The Roman name for ODYSSEUS, q.v.

Under World. Also called Underworld, Infernal Regions, Tartarus, Hades, Lower World.

Urania (u rā′ ni a). Daughter of Zeus and Mnemosyne. One of the nine Muses; the muse of astronomy. Her symbol is a globe and a pair of compasses. By Apollo, she was the mother of Linus; by Dionysus, she was the mother of Hymenaeus; stories of the parentage vary with Apollodorus, Hesiod, and Hyginus. John Milton and some of the poets of the Renaissance often called Urania the muse of poetry.

Uranus (ū′ ra nus; ū rā′ nus). Also Ouranos, Overhanging Heavens; Coelus (Roman). The most ancient of all the gods. The Sky; Father Sky; The Heavens. The father, by Gaea, of the first race—the twelve Titans. *Theogony*.

Ursa Major (er′ sa mā′ jor). Also Big Dipper. The Great Bear; Callisto was changed into this constellation. See ARCAS.

Ursa Minor (mī′ nor). Also Arcturus, Little Dipper. The Little Bear. Arcas, son of Callisto by Zeus, was changed into this constellation. See ARCAS.

V

Vacuna (va kū′ na). Roman (Sabine) goddess of leisure and repose. Earlier, she was a goddess of agriculture, and later the Romans identified her with several goddesses—Bellona, Venus, and Victoria.

Vale of Tempe. See TEMPE, VALE OF.

Velia (vē′ li a). One of the seven hills of earliest Rome. See CERMALUS.

Venelia (ve nē′ li a). Also Venilia. In *Aeneid* x, the sister of Amata, and the mother of Turnus.

Venti (ven′ ti). Sacrifices by the Athenians to the winds (Aeolus, Boreas, Eurus, Notus, Zephyrus, etc.; see WINDS) as deities, for the ancients believed the winds were intent upon destroying mankind by causing storms, tempests, and earthquakes.

Venulus (ven' ū lus). An elder sent by Turnus to seek the aid of Diomedes against the Trojans; but Diomedes had had enough of fighting Trojans at Troy, and refused to join Turnus against Aeneas. *Aeneid* viii.

Venus (vē' nus). The Roman name for APHRODITE, q.v.

Venus de Milo (mī' lō). A Greek statue now in the Louvre in Paris, regarded as one of the great works of antiquity, found on the island of Melos in 1829 and therefore sometimes called the Venus of Melos.

Vergil. Also Virgil. Full name: Publius Vergilius Maro (pub' li us vur gil' i us mā' rō), 70–19 B.C. Roman poet. Studied in Rome. Close friend of Horace. Chief works: *Eclogues* or *Bucolics* pastoral poems; *Georgics* didactic poems that glorified peasant life and its duties; *The Aeneid,* an epic, considered with those of Homer among the world's great epics; an account of the wanderings of Aeneas after the fall of Troy and his final settling in Latium, now Italy. *The Aeneid* has been called the first and greatest propaganda poem, for it centers upon the national glories of Rome and was intended to influence the thoughts and actions of its original readers. It has also been called the principal secular book of the Western world and praised for its lofty civic and moral ideals, patriotic spirit, taste, and style. At least one printed edition has been published annually for five hundred years. In *The Aeneid* the reader meets some of the greatest characters of mythology—Aeneas, Anchises, Ascanius, Camilla, Dido, Evander, Lavinia, Romulus, and Turnus, to say nothing of the Roman gods Apollo, Cupid, Juno, Jupiter, Mars, Mercury, Minerva, Neptune, Venus, and Vulcan, who appear again and again. In English literature, Chaucer in *The House of Fame* gives us the first summary of *The Aeneid* in English; Milton derived much from Vergil's epic—it was one of his four favorites (the others were by Homer, Hesiod, Ovid); Tennyson has a magnificent poem "To Vergil"; Robert Bridges, Samuel Daniel, John Dryden, Phineas Fletcher,

Marlowe, William Morris, Shelley, and Spenser are other English poets who have derived much inspiration from *The Aeneid* and the other works of Vergil.

Vergiliae (vur jil' i ē). Another name for the Pleiades. When these stars set, the ancients planted their corn.

Veritas (ver' i tas). The word means "truth." It was personified by the ancients as a deity, and called the daughter of Cronus (Saturn), and the mother of Virtue. Democritus, a great philosopher, used to say that Veritas hides herself at the bottom of a well; she is so difficult to find.

Verplaca (vur plā' ka). Also Virplaca. Roman goddess of family harmony.

Vertumnus (vur tum' nus). Also Virtumnus, Vortumnus; Numina. The Roman god of change, changing seasons, burgeoning vegetation, gardens and orchards, commerce; capable of changing himself into any form or shape. He fell in love with Pomona, and adopted various disguises, including those of a common laborer and an old crone, to win her as his wife. The story of Pomona and Vertumnus is in *Met.* xiv. Milton portrays the innocence of Eve in these words: "Likeliest she seemed Pomona when she fled Vertumnus."

Vesper (ves' per). Also Vesperus; Hesperus (Greek). The name is applied to the planet Venus when it is the evening star. In English literature, Spenser, Milton, Donne, and Jonson, among others, use Hesperus as the evening star.

Vesta (ves' ta). The Roman name for HESTIA, q.v. The goddess of the hearth and the symbol of the home.

Vestales (ves' tā lēz; ves tā' lez). Vestal, Vestalis (singular). Also Vestals, Vestal Virgins. Roman priestesses consecrated to the service of Vesta in the oldest temple in Rome, built by Numa Pompilius, the second Roman king. The office of Vestales was very ancient. Rhea Silvia, the mother of Romulus and Remus, was one of the Vestals. Aeneas is supposed to have chosen the first Vestales. The candidate had to be between six and ten years of age, of Italian birth, and near perfection in mind and body.

Her training took ten years; then she spent ten years carrying out her sacred duties watching the sacred fire on the altar of Vesta, kept perpetually burning; bringing water daily from the fountain Egeria; serving as custodian of the sacred Palladium from Troy, which was kept in Vesta's temple, located in the very center of the Roman Forum; she spent another ten years instructing novices. After her service of thirty years, she was free to retire, and could even marry although at her initiation she had pledged herself to celibacy. If she still preferred celibacy, she was allowed to serve the other Vestales. At public games and festivals, a Vestal was given the place of honor; in a court of law, it was not necessary for the Vestal to swear to speak the truth—her simple word was sufficient; if she met a criminal on the way to execution, she could pardon him then and there. The cult of the Vestal Virgins, one of the oldest in Rome, was observed until the advent of Christianity, when, in the year A.D. 380, the sacred fire was quenched and the Vestals dispersed by Emperor Theodosius the Great. To insult a Vestal was a capital crime; the violator was beaten to death. If a Vestal died in office, she was buried within the walls of Rome, an honor granted few Romans. If a Vestal violated her vow, Numa ordered her to be stoned, and Tarquin the Elder ordered her placed in an underground vault. A bed, bread, wine, water, oil, and a lighted lamp were placed in the cave. The Vestal was stripped of her sacred dress, forced into the cavern which was then sealed, and she was left to die. Few Vestals were guilty of incontinence; the Romans claimed that during the thousand years the Vestal office existed, only eighteen girls were punished for violation of their vows.

Vestalia (ves tā′ li a). Festivals in honor of Vesta, observed in Rome June 9; one of the most beautiful and popular festivals; banquets, processions, and offerings to the gods were features.

Vestals (ves′ talz). See VESTALES.

Vestal Virgins. See VESTALES.

Victor (vik' ter). A name applied by the Romans to such gods as Mars, Hercules, Jupiter, and others.

Victoria (vik tō' ri a). Also Nike, Nice (Greek). The goddess of victory. Daughter of the Giant Pallas (or of Titan and Styx). Sister of Strength and Valor. One of the attendants of Zeus. Highly honored by the Greeks, especially at Athens, where Athena was called Athena Nike. In the temple of Jupiter on the Capitoline Hill in Rome was a famous gold statue of Victoria, presented to the Romans by King Hiero of Syracuse.

Victory of Samothrace (sam' ō thrās). Also Nike of Samothrace, Winged Victory. One of the greatest sculptures of the ancients. Like the Venus of Milos, this statue is also in the Louvre in Paris. It was found on the island of Samothrace by the French in 1863.

Viminal (vim' i nal). One of the seven hills of Rome. Jupiter had a famous temple on this hill. See AVENTINE.

Virgil. See VERGIL.

Virgo (vur' gō). The Virgin, a constellation, the sixth sign of the zodiac, which the sun enters about August 23; represented by a robed woman holding in her left hand a sheaf of grain.

Virplaca (vur plā' ka). See VERPLACA.

Virtumnus (vir tum' nus). See VERTUMNUS.

Virtus (vur' tus). The ancient Romans made deities of all the major virtues and built temples to virtue and to honor. The statues of the most important virtues—temperance, honesty, modesty, and liberty—were characterized by their dress. Among the Romans, virtues came to include many of the manly virtues—manliness, courage, integrity, strength, and fortitude.

Volscens (vol' senz). A Rutulian commander of cavalry, who discovered Euryalus and Nisus as they were passing the enemy lines at night by noticing the light reflected from the helmet of Euryalus. He attacked the two friends, killed Euryalus, and was killed by Nisus, who, mortally wounded, then fell dead on Euryalus' body. *Aeneid* ix.

Volsci (vol′ sī). Also Volci, Volscians. People of Latium, who aided Turnus in his war against Aeneas. Their queen was CAMILLA, q.v. *Aeneid* ix, xi.

Volturnus (vol tur′ nus). The god of the river Tiber, later identified with TIBERINUS, q.v. The two gods, Tiberinus and Volturnus, became one god when Tiberinus, a legendary king, was drowned in the Tiber.

Voluptas (vō lup′ tas). The Roman goddess of sensual pleasure.

Vortumnus (vor tum′ nus). See VERTUMNUS.

Vulcan (vul′ kan). The Roman name for the god of fire and metalworking. He established a great forge in the heart of Mount Aetna, in partnership with the Cyclopes. See HEPHAESTUS.

Vulcanalia (vul ka nā′ li a). Festivals observed in Rome on August 23, in honor of Vulcan.

Vulture (vul′ tur). Vultures of Mars; the bird that was sacred to Mars. Vultures and dogs of prey accompanied Mars as he reveled in battle and slaughter, attended by his sons Fear, Panic, Terror, and Trembling, and other offspring of war. Mars (Ares) had four symbols: vultures, dogs, shield, and sword.

W

Wasps, The. A comedy by Aristophanes.

Water Gods and Goddesses. Oceanus, Tethys, Pontus, Nereus, Doris, Nereids, Poseidon, Amphitrite, Thetis, Galatea, Panope, Triton, Proteus, Scylla, Sirens, Glaucus, Phorcys, Ceto, Leucothea.

Water Nymphs. Among others, the three thousand daughters of Oceanus and Tethys.

West Wind. Called Caurus, Favonius, and Zephyrus.

Winds, Gods or Deities of the. God of the Winds: Aeolus, Hippotades. East Wind: Argestes, Eurus. South Wind:

Auster, Notus. West Wind: Caurus, Favonius, Zephyrus. North Wind: Aquilo, Boreas, Thrascias. Southeast Wind: Apeliotes, Auster, Lips. Southwest Wind: Afer, Africus. Northeast Wind: Calcias. Northwest Wind: Corus. Destructive Wind: Typhon. According to Hesiod's *Theogony*, Astraeus, a son of the Titans Crius and Eurybia, and Eos, the goddess of the Dawn were the parents of the Winds. In English poetry, Boreas and Zephyrus are the most celebrated.

Winged Victory. See VICTORY OF SAMOTHRACE.

Wingless Victory, Temple of. A small marble temple on the Acropolis, dedicated to Athena as the goddess of victory, and called the Temple of Athena Nike.

Women of Trachis, The. See TRACHINIAE.

Wooden Horse. Also called Trojan Horse. The building of a large Wooden Horse, inside which many Greeks were to be hidden, was advised by Odysseus and built by Epeus. To persuade the Trojans to allow the horse inside the walls of Troy, Sinon, a Greek who had let himself be captured for that purpose, told the Trojans that it was an offering to Athena. In spite of the warning of Cassandra and Laocoön, who said (*Aeneid* ii), "I fear the Greeks even when they bring gifts," King Priam was deceived by Sinon and allowed the horse to be brought inside Troy. At night, the Greeks hidden within the horse were let out by Sinon, the gates of Troy were opened, and all of the Greeks hidden behind the island of Tenedos returned, entered the city, and sacked it. *Aeneid* ii; Apollodorus ii; *Odyssey* viii.

Works and Days, The. A poem by Hesiod, 826 lines, which deals with the need for justice in a tyrannical age and with the need for work on the part of the farmer. The Five Ages of Mankind, Zeus, the nine Muses, and the story of Pandora, Prometheus, Pleiades, Demeter, Leto, Apollo are some of the mythological stories told in this poem, but the *Theogony* is a more important source for a knowledge of mythology.

X

Xanthus (zan' thus). Also Xanthos. 1. In *Iliad* xvi and xix, Xanthus and Balius, twin foals, horses swift as the wind, offspring of the Harpy Podarge and Zephyrus the west wind. Hera gave Xanthus the power of speech, and the horse told Achilles (the horses had been gifts from Poseidon to Peleus, the father of Achilles) that he would return safely from a particular battle at Troy, but that the day of his death was near. In *Iliad* xvii, these horses wept when Patroclus was killed by Hector. 2. In *Iliad* v, Xanthus is the name of a Trojan killed by Diomedes. 3. In *Iliad* vi, Xanthus is the name of a river so called by the gods, but called Scamander by men. *Iliad* xx. 4. Xanthus was also the name of the god of the river that flooded its banks to check the great slaughter of Trojans by Achilles. Hera requested Hephaestus to set the river afire as it raged after Achilles, and the fierce-blazing fire caused the waters to recede to the banks and protected Hera's protégé Achilles. *Iliad* xxi.

Xuthus (zū' thus). Grandson of Deucalion and Pyrrha. Son of Hellen, the ancestor of the Hellenes (Greeks). Xuthus was banished from Thessaly by his brothers Aeolus and Dorus. He fled to Athens, where he married Creusa, daughter of King Erechtheus, by whom he had Achaeus and Ion. Some legends say that Ion was a son of Creusa by Apollo, and that Ion became a priest of Apollo at Delphi. Xuthus had gone to Delphi to inquire of Apollo why Creusa and he were childless, and was told that the first person he met would be his son. He met Ion and claimed him. Creusa learned that this was the son she had borne to Apollo, but she was told by the Oracle that this must never be revealed to Xuthus. From the sons of Xuthus (Achaeus and Ion), the Achaeans and Ionians derived their names. Apollodorus i; Pausanias i, ii; Euripides, *Ion*.

Z

Zeleia (ze li′ a). The name of a city at the foot of Mount Ida in Phrygia that was the home of the great Trojan archer Pandarus, to whom Apollo himself gave a famous bow. *Iliad* ii.

Zephyrus (zef′ er us). Also Caurus, Favonius. The west wind.

Zetes (zē′ tēz). Also Zethes. Son of Boreas, king of Thrace, and Orithyia (daughter of Erechtheus, king of Athens). Brother of Calais, his winged twin, and of Chione and Cleopatra. The winged twins took part in the Argonaut expedition. In Bithynia, the brothers freed Phineus from the continuous persecution of the Harpies. Apollodorus i; *Argonautica;* Hyginus.

Zethus (zē′ thus). Also Zetus. Son of Zeus and Antiope. Brother of Amphion. The brothers avenged the injuries their mother had received from Lycus, king of Thebes, and his wife Dirce, by killing Lycus, and by tying Dirce to the tail of a wild bull that dragged her to death. The brothers then seized the crown of Thebes which Lycus had usurped after murdering King Creon. Zethus, a man of great physical strength, dragged huge stones to build a strong wall around Thebes, while his brother Amphion, skilled in the use of the lyre which Hermes had given him, charmed the large stones into place. Zethus married Thebe, and in her honor changed the name of the city from Cadmea to Thebes. Amphion married Niobe, daughter of Tantalus, and she became the mother of fourteen children. Apollodorus iii; Hyginus; Pausanias ii.

Zetus (zē′ tus). See ZETHUS.

Zeus (zūs; zōōs). Also Jove, Jupiter (Roman). Son of Cronus and Rhea. The most powerful of all the ancient Greek gods; ruler of heaven and earth, of all gods and all men. He married seven times, in the following order:

Metis, Themis, Eurynome, Demeter, Mnemosyne, Leto, and Hera. His extramarital affairs and children were numerous indeed. He changed himself into many forms to gratify his passions: shower of gold—Danae; satyr—Antiope; swan—Leda; white bull—Europa; flame of fire—Aegina. Among his other amours were Alcmene, Anaxithea, Callisto, Carme, Cassiopeia, Dia, Dione, Elara, Electra, Hesione, Io, Maia, Mera, Neaera, Niobe, the Oceanid Pluto, Protogenia, Semele, Styx, Taygete, Thalia, Thya, and Thymbris. It is small wonder that Hera has been called the most jealous wife in mythology. Zeus' struggles with the Titans, the Cyclopes, the Hecatoncheires, and Prometheus are famous. His oracle at Dodona is the oldest in Greece. The story of Baucis and Philemon reveals Zeus at his best. The Greeks understood his lasciviousness, but they also respected his power and justice. The philandering Zeus is blamed by Plato on Homer, but Homer's successors, both ancient and modern, have continued to tell the story of his numerous flirtations. Much about Zeus has been written by Aeschylus, Apollodorus, Apollonius Rhodius, Euripides, Hesiod, Homer, Ovid, Pausanias, Sophocles, and Vergil. In English literature, Dryden, Milton, Spenser, and Tennyson have used parts of the story of Zeus.

Zodiac (zō′ di ak). The word means "a circle of animals." The ancients used the signs of the zodiac to tell time, and the four greatest English poets—Chaucer, Spenser, Shakespeare, and Milton—along with many other English writers, have used the signs of the zodiac from various stories in Greek myth to add beauty, truth, and vitality to their poetry. Chaucer used all twelve signs in *A Treatise on the Astrolabe;* Spenser listed all twelve in the "Two Cantos of Mutabilitie" to describe the law of change in nature; Shakespeare, with his numerous mythological allusions from Achilles, Agamemnon, and Ajax through Ulysses, Venus, and Vulcan, strangely enough, mentions only one sign of the zodiac, when in *Twelfth Night* Taurus is named; Milton in the tenth book of *Paradise Lost* catalogues seven of the twelve signs as he writes about physical changes in the universe after the fall of man. The chart below includes in the following order the name of the sign, its symbol, its mythological origin, and the approximate date the sun enters the sign.

1	Aries	Ram	Golden-fleeced ram	March 21
2	Taurus	Bull	Europa's mount	April 20
3	Gemini	Twins	Castor and Pollux	May 21
4	Cancer	Crab	Heracles' tormentor	June 22
5	Leo	Lion	Nemean Lion	July 23
6	Virgo	Virgin	Astraea	August 23
7	Libra	Balances	Astraea's scales	September 23
8	Scorpio	Scorpion	Orion's torturer	October 24
9	Sagittarius	Archer	Chiron	November 22
10	Capricornus	Goat	Amalthea	December 22
11	Aquarius	Water Bearer	Ganymede	January 20
12	Pisces	Fish	Disguises of Aphrodite and Eros	February 19

SUGGESTIONS FOR FURTHER READING

𐃌𐃌𐃌𐃌𐃌𐃌𐃌𐃌𐃌𐃌𐃌𐃌𐃌𐃌𐃌𐃌𐃌𐃌𐃌𐃌𐃌𐃌𐃌𐃌𐃌𐃌𐃌𐃌𐃌

Sources

The richest sources of Greek and Roman mythology among the ancient writers are the following:

AESCHYLUS. 525–456 B.C. A Greek tragic dramatist who wrote approximately ninety plays. Only seven have survived. Six of these, *The Suppliant Maidens, Seven against Thebes, Prometheus Bound, Agamemnon, Choephoroe,* and *Eumenides,* are based on mythology. *The Persians* is based on history.

APOLLODORUS. Flourished in Athens in the second century B.C. His *Bibliotheca (Library)* is an important work about the gods.

APOLLONIUS RHODIUS (Apollonius of Rhodes). Greek epic poet of the late third and early second century B.C. His *Argonautica,* an epic poem in four books, tells the story of Jason and the Argonauts in search of the Golden Fleece.

APULEIUS. Roman philosopher and writer of the second century A.D. In his *Metamorphosis* or *The Golden Ass,* the hero is changed into an ass and has many amusing adventures. The book also tells the story of Cupid and Psyche.

ARISTOPHANES. About 448–388 B.C. Only eleven of his Greek comedies have come to us, though the number he wrote is estimated at forty or more. He has been called the greatest comic dramatist in world literature. Lemprière said of him: "By his side Molière seems dull and Shakespeare clownish." The extant plays are *The Acharnians, The Knights, The Clouds, The Wasps, The Peace, The Birds, Lysistrata, The Thesmophoriazusae, The Frogs, The Ecclesiazusae,* and *Plutus.*

DIODORUS SICULUS. Greek historian of the first century

B.C. Of the forty volumes of his *Library of History* only fifteen have survived.

EURIPIDES. 480–406 B.C. A Greek tragic dramatist who wrote approximately ninety plays of which eighteen are extant. A nineteenth, *Rhesus*, is of doubtful authorship. Those surviving are *Alcestis, Medea, Hippolytus, Hecuba, Andromache, The Heracleidae, The Suppliants, The Trojan Women, Heracles, Iphigenia in Tauris, Ion, Helen, Electra, Orestes, The Phoenissae (The Phoenician Women), The Bacchae, Iphigenia in Aulis,* and *The Cyclops.*

HERODOTUS. 484–424 B.C. Herodotus is often called the Father of History. His great work, *History*, is in nine books, named for the nine Muses. It contains much mythological material.

HESIOD. A Greek poet of the eighth century B.C. He was the father of Greek didactic poetry, and his *Works and Days* and *Theogony* are both famous. The first contains accounts of myths and fables along with experiences of daily life. *Theogony* is an account of the beginning of the world and of the gods.

HOMER. Various dates have been assigned to this traditional Greek epic poet—from about 850 B.C. to as early as 1200 B.C. *The Iliad* and *The Odyssey* are the oldest books of the Western world and two of the greatest epics of world literature. They tell the stories respectively of the Trojan War and the wanderings of Odysseus or Ulysses. The poems known as *The Homeric Hymns* were formerly thought to be by Homer but are now believed to be by later anonymous Greek rhapsodists.

HORACE. 65–8 B.C. A Roman lyric poet whose *Odes* abound in Greek and Roman myth.

OVID. 43 B.C.–A.D. 17. A Roman poet whose *Metamorphoses* has been called the major treasury of classical mythology. His *Heroides* is a series of letters by mythological characters to their lovers. The *Fasti,* a poetical Roman calendar, explains ceremonies connected with Roman festivals.

PAUSANIAS. A Greek traveler and geographer of the second

century A.D. His *Description of Greece* is a valuable source of information about mythology, religious customs, art, and history of Greece.

PINDAR. 522?–443 B.C. Greek lyric poet. The *Odes* are full of mythological stories. These are forty-four odes which celebrate the winners of the Panhellenic Festivals—the Olympian, Isthmian, Nemean, and Pythian games.

SOPHOCLES. 496?–406 B.C. Sophocles ranks with Aeschylus and Euripides as the greatest among Greek tragic playwrights. He wrote approximately one hundred twenty plays. Seven survive, all based on mythological subjects: *Oedipus Tyrannus* or *Oedipus Rex* (*Oedipus the King*), *Oedipus at Colonus, Antigone, Electra, Ajax, The Women of Trachis,* and *Philoctetes.*

STATIUS. Roman poet of the first century A.D. Author of two epics, *Thebaid* or *Thebais* in twelve books, and *Achilleid* or *Achilleis,* of which only fragments survive. He also left much lyric verse.

VERGIL. 70–19 B.C. Roman poet, author of *The Aeneid,* an epic of the wanderings of Aeneas after the Trojan War and his settling in what is now Italy. At least one printed edition has been published annually for five hundred years since the invention of printing. Vergil is also noted for his *Eclogues* or *Bucolics,* pastoral poems, and his *Georgics,* poems about peasant life.

Other Greek writers who have contributed to our knowledge of mythology include Alcaeus, Anacreon, Arion, Ibycus, Sappho, Simonides of Ceos, and Stesichorus. Only fragments of the works of these Greek lyric poets have come to us.

Among other Roman writers who are important for their contribution to mythology are: Catullus (84?–54 B.C.), certainly one of the greatest Roman lyric poets; Propertius and Tibullus, elegiac poets; and Seneca the Younger, Roman tragic playwright. Seneca's nine tragedies are based on Greek mythological themes. They are: *Herculus Furens, Troades, Medea, Hippolytus* (*Phaedra*), *Oedipus, Agamemnon, Thyestes, Hercules Oetaeus,* and *Phoenissae.*

A Few Recommended Translations
of the Classics

The Complete Greek Drama, edited by W. J. Oates and
Eugene O'Neill, Jr. Two volumes. Random House.

The Complete Greek Tragedies, edited by David Grene and
Richmond Lattimore. Four volumes. University of Chicago Press.

Greek Tragedies, edited by David Grene and Richmond
Lattimore. Three volumes. University of Chicago Press.

Seven Famous Greek Plays, edited by W. J. Oates and
Eugene O'Neill, Jr. Modern Library.

An Anthology of Greek Drama, edited by Charles A. Robinson. Two volumes. Holt, Rinehart and Winston.

Ten Greek Plays in Contemporary Translation, edited by
L. R. Lind. Houghton Mifflin.

Oedipus Plays of Sophocles, edited by Paul Roche. New
American Library.

Three Great Plays of Euripides: Medea, Hippolytus, Helen,
edited by Rex Warner. New American Library.

The Iliad. Editions by:
  Richmond Lattimore; University of Chicago Press.
  Lang, Leaf and Meyers; Modern Library.
  E. V. Rieu; Penguin Classics.
  W. H. D. Rouse; New American Library, Mentor
    Classics.
  Loeb Classical Library; Harvard University Press.

The Odyssey. Editions by:
  R. Fitzgerald; Doubleday.
  T. E. Shaw; Oxford University Press.
  Butcher and Lang; Modern Library.
  E. V. Rieu; Penguin Classics.
  W. H. D. Rouse; New American Library, Mentor
    Classics.
  The Loeb Classical Library; Harvard University Press.

The Aeneid. Editions by:
  J. W. Mackail; Modern Library.
  P. Dickinson; New American Library, Mentor Classics.

W. F. J. Knight; Penguin Classics.

C. Day Lewis; Doubleday.

K. Guinagh; Holt, Rinehart and Winston.

The Loeb Classical Library; Harvard University Press.

Metamorphoses (Ovid). Editions by:

R. Humphries; University of Indiana Press.

H. Gregory; New American Library, Mentor Classics.

The Loeb Classical Library; Harvard University Press.

HESIOD's works. Editions by:

R. Lattimore; University of Michigan Press.

The Loeb Classical Library; Harvard University Press.

The Loeb Classical Library, Harvard University Press, gives access to almost all that is important in Greek and Latin literature in convenient and well-printed volumes. An up-to-date text in Greek or Latin and a good English translation face each other page by page. The edition is excellent for the Greek plays and for the work of Apollodorus, Apollonius Rhodius, Diodorus Siculus, Herodotus, Horace, *The Heroides* of Ovid, *The Homeric Hymns,* Pausanias, Pindar, Seneca, and Statius.

Other Books On Mythology

Among more recent writers, some but not all contemporary, whose works in the field of mythology are especially helpful, the following are recommended. The titles starred have been found particularly useful.

*AVERY, CATHERINE B. (ed.). *The New Century Classical Handbook.* Appleton-Century-Crofts, Inc.

BULFINCH, THOMAS. *Bulfinch's Mythology.* Modern Library.

BUSH, DOUGLAS. *Mythology and the Renaissance Tradition in English Poetry.* Oxford University Press.

———. *Mythology and the Romantic Tradition in English Poetry.* Oxford University Press.

CARY, M., and others (eds.). *The Oxford Classical Dictionary.* Oxford University Press.

COLUM, PADRAIC. *Myths of the World.* Grosset & Dunlap.

FRAZER, JAMES GEORGE. *The Golden Bough.* Macmillan.

*GAYLEY, CHARLES MILLS. *The Classic Myths in English Literature and in Art*. Ginn & Company.

*GRANT, MICHAEL. *Myths of the Greeks and Romans*. The World Publishing Company.

*GRAVES, ROBERT. *The Greek Myths*. George Braziller, Inc.; Penguin Books, 2 vols., paperback.

*GUERBER, H. A. *The Myths of Greece and Rome*. British Book Centre.

*HAMILTON, EDITH. *Mythology*. Little, Brown & Co.; New American Library, paperback.

HARVEY, PAUL. *The Oxford Companion to Classical Literature*. Oxford University Press.

HERZBERG, MAX J. *Myths and Their Meaning*. Allyn and Bacon, Inc.

HIGHET, GILBERT. *The Classical Tradition*. Oxford University Press.

KERENYI, C. *The Gods of the Greeks*. Vanguard Press; Grove Press, Evergreen paperback.

———. *The Heroes of the Greeks*. Grove Press, Evergreen paperback.

Larousse Encyclopedia of Mythology. Prometheus Press.

*LEMPRIÈRE, J. *Lemprière's Classical Dictionary*. E. P. Dutton & Co., Inc.

*MURRAY, ALEXANDER S. *Manual of Mythology*. Tudor Publishing Co.

*NORTON, DAN S., and RUSHTON, PETERS. *Classical Myths in English Literature*. Holt, Rinehart & Winston, Inc.

*ROSE, H. J. *A Handbook of Greek Mythology*. E. P. Dutton & Co., Inc.

SELTMAN, CHARLES. *The Twelve Olympians and Their Guests*. Apollo Editions, Inc.

SEYFFERT, OSKAR. *Dictionary of Classical Antiquities*. Meridian.

WARNER, REX. *Men and Gods*. Random House.

WARRINGTON, JOHN (ed.). *Everyman's Classical Dictionary*. E. P. Dutton & Co., Inc.